237

THE MYTH OF THE NORTH AMERICAN CITY

THE MYTH OF
THE NORTH AMERICAN CITY

CONTINENTALISM CHALLENGED

MICHAEL A. GOLDBERG
and
JOHN MERCER

University of British Columbia Press
Vancouver
1986

ISBN 0-7748-0238-3

Canadian Cataloguing in Publication Data

Goldberg, Michael A., 1941-
The myth of the North American city

Bibliography: p.
Includes index.
ISBN 0-7748-0238-3

1. Cities and towns – Canada.
2. Cities and towns – United States.
I. Mercer, John, 1942- II. Title.

HT127.G64 1985   307.7′6′0971   C86-091001-6

This book has been published with the help of a grant from the Social Science Federation of Canada, using funds provided by the Social Sciences and Humanities Research Council of Canada.

UBC Press
University of British Columbioa
6344 Memorial Rd.
Vancouver, BC V6T 1Z2
(604) 822-3259
Fax: (604) 822-6083

This book is dedicated affectionately to
Andrea, Betsy, Elizabeth, Helena, Jennifer and Rhoda

Contents

Tables

Charts

Maps

PREFACE

Nearly two decades ago, American humorist Richard Armour suggested that the information explosion was clearly out of control and that resort to mere book burning would prove fruitless to stem the tide. Instead, he advocated burning authors to cut the problem off at its root. While as authors we find the approach too draconian, before proceeding with our addition to the explosion, we provide the reader with some background and justification for worsening this global book crisis.

This volume is clearly an intellectual undertaking. Thus, it follows certain conventions, seeking logical consistency and being rooted in observable and reproducible facts. As with many cerebral projects, the work has a strong visceral origin, growing out of our emotional dissatisfaction as much as our intellectual concerns with constructs that blithely lump Canada and the United States into the same analytical laundry basket without proper appreciation of the diversity of the wardrobe to be laundered.

In the event, our distress arose from the indiscriminate application of American-based ideas about cities and urban policy to a Canadian setting, especially during the 1950s and 1960s. We were both struck by the inappropriateness of the American urban crisis model in Canada. Additionally, we felt a sense of outrage at the imposition of American policies on the Canadian urban framework when these policies and their unintended consequences (most notably freeways and urban renewal) were of dubious value in the United States. In Canada, where an American-style urban dilemma has still to be demonstrated, such a borrowing of inappropriate and enormously costly policies seemed to us singularly unintelligent.

Urban transportation planning in Canada contrasts so sharply with that in the United States that it can serve to place the issue in perspective. The 1950s and 1960s were the heyday of freeway building. The urban transportation problem was defined, in American terms, as one of traffic congestion and insufficient road capacity to meet the demands of the private automobile. The *U.S. National Defense Interstate Highway Acts* of 1956 and 1962 set in motion a massive freeway building program, only now coming to a close. During this period, Canada too was experiencing suburbanization of its population and resulting traffic congestion. The freeway solution was speedily proposed. However, conditions in Canada were very different from those in the United States. Financing arrangements, for example, did not include any significant Canadian federal funding, in contrast to the U.S. where 90 per cent of construction and planning costs were federally funded. Canadian cities had also maintained high quality transit services and much tighter controls on urban growth than had U.S. cities. In short, alternatives to the private automobile were available. Thus, to this day, the City of Vancouver in Canada's third largest metropolitan area does not contain any freeway despite repeated attempts during the 1960s to construct a freeway network. At the onset of the freeway building binge, Toronto, then Canada's second largest urban area, opened in 1954 the first new subway system in North America after the Great Depression. It also improved its streetcar and bus system and combined this public transit investment with a provincially assisted freeway building program. Midway through the latter's development, massive public resistance was encountered. The freeway network was truncated to avoid dissecting viable central city neighborhoods as had happened in numerous U.S. jurisdictions. Obviously, something very different was taking place with respect to metropolitan transportation planning and investment in Canada, warranting a deeper look to distinguish them from the apparently similar U.S. situation. American problems and solutions did not travel well to the Canadian urban environment.

Our concerns date back to the 1960s. The Americanization of Canadian urban issues was rampant when both of us arrived in Canada from New York (Goldberg) and Glasgow (Mercer). To us as outsiders, the fashion of the time for Canadian urban policy analysts, of which there were painfully few back then, to think of Canadian cities and urban issues in American terms appeared ludicrous. Our initial travels around Canada and its cities failed to reveal urban dilemmas on any scale whatsoever that would begin to approximate the urban problems each of us had just left. Over the intervening two decades, our extended observations of cities in North America increased our dissatisfaction with the notion that Canadian cities were essentially American cities with all their attendant problems, only lagging by one or two decades. As a result of these experiences and joint discussions, we decided to delve more deeply into the matter to see if we could in fact discern deep-seated and fundamental differences between Canadian and American cities, differences that would obviate the ill-conceived and unquestioning transfer of urban research and policy and mind-sets from one setting to the other. Usually, the transfer has been from the United States to Canada, but in recent years in reverse as well, with equal inappropriateness. The result is a completely joint effort on our part.

We each bring to our work the experience of living in and studying cities in the United States and Canada as well as frequent travel around the North American continent. As a result, we possess a built-in comparative ability, viewing both the countries and their cities as outsiders and insiders at different periods over the past two decades (an experience akin to that of the late distinguished sociologist John Porter, who saw Canada more sharply upon his return from years of residence in Britain). We also bring two very different, though complementary, disciplinary perspectives, that of the geographer (Mercer) and the economist (Goldberg). Thus, we believe we have gleaned insights that are both interesting and of intellectual and practical importance. They transcend the cities of the two nations which are our immediate focus and apply to the societies that fostered the cities.

As we probed the issues, we were struck by a number of paradoxes. Why, for example, does the United States, with its strong ideological ties to private enterprise and minimal government intervention in the marketplace, demonstrate massive federal involvement in urban affairs and housing markets and also have many more governments at the local level than does Canada where government intervention is quite readily accepted? Additionally, why does the United States, dedicated to equality of opportunity and the rights of the individual, exhibit such strong discriminatory practices toward blacks and Hispanics and continue to have little success at ameliorating income disparities, while a more unabashedly elitist Canada develops more effective means to redistribute income (universal medical care, for instance) and promote ethnic identity? These and other paradoxes led us towards the societal context for urban development.

For expository purposes, the present book has a logical linear structure. We begin (Chapter 1) by setting out the problem, namely the need to place Canadian and American cities in the proper contexts and to analyze the differences in contexts as well as the differences in the cities that flow from them. We then move on to examine these contexts at the national level (Chapters 2 through 5) covering, in order, differences in value and social systems and differences in economic and political institutions and settings. The implications of these national differences for American and Canadian cities are then discussed (Chapter 6) before we move on to explore in detail empirical differences between these sets of cities (Chapters 7 through 9) and the policy and intellectual consequences of the observed differences (Chapter 10).

Our actual exploration followed a somewhat more convoluted and tortuous path. As noted, it is rooted in our travels, research, and living experiences in a number of Canadian and American cities. Then, in a series of initial papers done both separately and together, we documented a range of differences between Canadian and American cities. The results demonstrated forcefully the limitation of looking at cities and city differences out of context, an approach all too common in both urban geography and urban economics. Accordingly, we determined that a broader appreciation of the social, economic, and political environments that produced the urban areas of Canada and the United States was essential. Having established the context, we plunged ahead, guided in part by this contextual knowledge, to develop additional comparative "facts" and to strive for a fuller understanding of the depth and meaning of the urban differences that were uncovered. The process was cyclical, moving back and forth between cities and context, with each phase of the cycle causing us to ask new questions about the just completed phase. The loop is endless and must be extended. However, the level of our current knowledge allows a stepping down from this iterative merry-go-round to report on our findings before reboarding to search for the elusive golden circle.

At this point, some cautionary words and an expression of some limitations are needed in order not to mislead the reader about the substance that follows. Immediately apparent upon probing the first half of this book is our awesomely large topic. Cities themselves are complex and unfathomable enough. However, we attempt to situate the city in its cultural context. Entire books, even entire fields of study, essay to treat adequately what we of necessity deal with in a single paragraph or section. The American or Canadian federal system is one example of a subject we deal with in a matter of pages, but about which there exists an enormous and growing literature. Similarly, the notion of the American "melting pot" and the Canadian "mosaic," which we address in a portion of a chapter, has deservedly attracted the attention of a myriad of scholars, generating popular as well as scholarly articles and books.

Clearly, limitations of space and time prevent us from even approaching a complete discussion of the contextual issues we raise. Rather, by sifting, presenting, and synthesizing what we consider to be important findings of others, new and interesting insights into the nature of the differences between Canadian and U.S. cities are obtained. This interpretation and synthesis of the work of others is fraught with dangers, and herein lies the caution. First, not being experts in these varied fields, we cannot lay claim to either the depth or breadth of knowledge of other researchers but only hope to have drawn from the best and most appropriate studies. Second, we also hope for a proper interpretation and understanding of this work. While we are not steeped in the knowledge and traditions of these cognate areas of study, we can appreciate them through our own work as urban researchers, since the contexts are not independent of or unaffected by the urban reality. Moreover, considerable help from colleagues in various related fields has made us more comfortable in drawing the contextual pictures.

One last caveat needs explicit statement. We write this book about Canadian and American cities from an anglophone perspective. The francophone cultural presence in Canada is a major differentiating cross-national factor, yet one that regrettably is largely beyond our competence and clear comprehension. We acknowledge this limitation of our work and upon our perspective (too often glossed over by others), denying us and you the reader, the insights of the francophone perception and intelligence. It is frustrating to recognize that there is a social fact so central to shaping Canada and its urban areas that we cannot fully interpret within a Canadian or North American context.

We have updated some of the statistics in this book to incorporate the new census data. However, because of changes in definitions, changes in the formats in which data are presented, and the scattering of needed items throughout a host of sources, this is no easy or straightforward task. It would require considerable effort and time, given the scale and range of data which we use. As the reader will observe from looking at the findings of Chapters 7 through 9, the volume and complexity of the statistical analyses for data already in hand from the 1970s posed an enormous challenge. To repeat these analyses for even a selected number of variables for the 1980 and 1981 data represents a task beyond our present resources. In any event, it is our conviction that many of our essential findings will remain unchanged when a re-examination utilizing the 1980 and 1981 data is undertaken. That challenge lies ahead.

Our goal is to increase the understanding of the nature of cities. Specifically, we are concerned with cities in North America and with developing insights into the distinctiveness of Canadian cities compared with their American counterparts. We also seek to provide the empirical basis for improving our understanding about cities. If fundamental differences become apparent between cities that appear similar, as do those in Canada and the United States, then more effective theories are needed to explain urban phenomena. Given this increased understanding of urban differences and of Canadian and American cities, our final goal is to provide the knowledge base for more sensitive, appropriate and effective context-specific urban policies in both countries.

A study as broad ranging as this draws on intellectual and financial resources beyond the scope of the two authors. On the intellectual front we want to acknowledge and publicly thank colleagues John Agnew and Don Meinig at Syracuse University, Jonathan Mark of the City of Vancouver, and Lawrence D. Jones and David Ley at the University of British Columbia. David Elkins in Political Science, Allan Smith in History and Don Paterson in Economic History, all at the University of British Columbia, helped greatly to reduce our ignorance in their respective areas. The book has also benefited from the constructive critiques of three anonymous reviewers and the valuable editorial advice, assistance and support of Brian Scrivener of UBC Press.

Financial support over a number of years has been pieced together from a variety of sources enabling us to hire a number of part-time research assistants.

Foremost among these financial backers is the Social Sciences and Humanities Research Council of Canada (SSHRCC) who provided us with a research grant in 1980 to get this project launched successfully. SSHRCC also supported Michael Goldberg with two leave fellowships during 1979/80 and again in 1984/85 during which time he could pursue this study. John Mercer was the recipient in 1983 of full-time summer support via a Senior Fellowship in Canadian Studies from the Department of External Affairs of the Government of Canada. At different times, the Real Estate Council of British Columbia has provided assistance to carry on portions of the study, as has the Humanities-Social Sciences Committee of the University of British Columbia. Finally, computer services were made available to us on a large scale by the Computing Centre of the University of British Columbia and, more modestly, by Syracuse University. Both our institutions have given us needed space and secretarial and clerical assistance over the years of this undertaking.

We want to acknowledge the able research assistance at various points in this research by: Kevin Johnston, Greg Gardiner, Ralph Sebralla, Eric Lum, Carol Smith, Karen Eng, Peter Horwood, Roland Ebelt, and Judy Fountain at U.B.C.; and by Martha Drake at Syracuse. Guy Young at U.B.C. provided invaluable last minute data collection and proofreading help. Extraordinary secretarial help was provided by Mabel Yee at U.B.C.; Pamela Walker typed portions of the manuscript at Syracuse. Ultimately, the chore of putting together a readable draft and subsequent changes into publishable form fell to the Word Processing Centre in the Faculty of Commerce and Business Administration at U.B.C. and its Supervisor, Ms. Lori Thomas. Regrettably, space limits our ability to thank each member of the Word Processing Centre individually, but virtually all of the people in the Centre helped us with this manuscript at one time or another. This effort could not have seen the light of day without their exceptional help. We acknowledge their vital role and apologize for the volume of work that we imposed upon them, often with little lead time. Cartographic assistance in the form of drafting charts and figures was ably provided by Mr. Michael Kirchoff at Syracuse.

Despite the lengthy support cast who deserve to take much credit for this study, we cannot apportion any of the blame for errors and omissions—that responsibility is ours. We thank all of the aforementioned and others too numerous to name for their help, and we thank you the reader for your forebearance with what follows.

Finally, but most importantly, we wish to acknowledge the support, encouragement and forebearance of our respective families. We hope our spouses and daughters will find that the time taken from them to enable us to do this work has proved to be worthwhile and that they will share in the sense of accomplishment. Their patience and understanding have been strong foundations for us both.

1

ON COMPARING AMERICAN AND CANADIAN CITIES

The boundary between Canada and the United States is typically a human creation; it is physically invisible, geographically illogical, militarily indefensible and emotionally inescapable.
Hugh Keenleyside

INTRODUCTION: THE NORTH AMERICAN CITY AND THE CONTINENTALIST IDEA

At the western terminus of "the world's longest undefended border," the Peace Arch marks the boundary between Canada and the United States. Across its top is written, "Brethren Dwelling In Unity—Children Of A Common Mother." As with many siblings, the unity is more hoped for than actual, and the common bonds often mask individual differences and personalities. Such is very much the case when considering things Canadian and things American, where the smaller and junior sibling goes largely unnoticed, often assumed to be a lesser version of the senior. The consequences for the second child can be significant with much of his or her life spent in the shadow of the older child, striving, often in vain, to establish his or her own identity.

In the discussions and analyses that follow, we are concerned with the implications for urban studies of homogenizing Canada and the United States into an American-dominated conception of North America. In particular, we will be concerned with the concept of the North American City that has evolved over the past decade or so and which represents the logical consequence of such an homogenization when brought to bear on the study of cities in Canada and the United States.

The notion of the North American City is initially attractive. After all, Canada and the United States are now politically stable, predominantly English-speaking democracies growing out of the English legal tradition (excepting Quebec), occupying vast land areas, and relatively youthful in comparison with European and Asian societies. Additionally, both are nations of immigrants, the aboriginal populations long since having been overwhelmed by the sweep of European settlers. Despite its larger land mass, Canada is generally viewed, particularly by Americans, as a smaller version of the United States, in keeping with its smaller population. In this vein, Andrei Gromyko has purportedly observed that Canada is the boring second violin in the American symphony.

So blurred is the border between Canada and the United States and so great is the ignorance about Canada by Americans that one almost wonders why we should even consider critiquing the notion of the North American City or North American anything else for that matter. Canadian author Walter Stewart set out a decade ago to travel around the United States to ascertain American views about Canada. The following selections bear humorous, but sad, witness to the lack of Canadian distinctiveness in the eyes of many Americans.[1]

You never hear anything bad about Canada, that's one thing. In fact, I guess it's the only thing.
                    English major, University of Indiana, Bloomington

I just think of Canada as that great orange expanse north of us.
                    Marine biology student, University of Hawaii, Honolulu

Canada, that's up north, near New York state, isn't it? Only, it's not a state, it's a whole country. Is that right? Do I win a prize?
                    Liquor store clerk, Albuquerque, New Mexico

A lot of people speak French and a lot of other people don't. And those that don't don't like those that do. I read that in the paper.
                    Security guard, Banning, California

We went up to the border once, but they wouldn't let my Dad through with his rifle and pistol, so we had to come back, 'cause he wouldn't go anywhere without a gun, he needs it for protection. Why would they do that to him?
                    Mechanic, Napa, California

They don't have any heroes, and not much history.
                    History student, University of Rochester, New York

Canada is absolutely vital to this country. There is no nation in the world
that can compare with Canada as a safe, reliable supply of needed
resources. Political stability is there, the resources are there, the friend-
ship is there, and the need for American dollars is there. It's all there.
                    Research assistant, oil company, New York, New York

I think if we need it and they won't give it to us, we should just take it.
                    National guardsman, Fremont, Ohio

These last two comments are particularly germane to the present discussion as they reflect the "continentalist" view of North America in rather stark
form. In essence, North America is viewed as a basically homogeneous unit
largely reflecting American values and needs in keeping with the dominant
position of the United States in North America. Mexico is usually ignored
altogether in this conception.

Such an homogenized view of North America is not at all inappropriate if,
in fact, Canada and the United States are substantially similar entities. As we
will demonstrate below, this is not the case — Canada and the United States
are different nations and places, with distinct economic, political, social and
value systems, albeit both capitalist. Furthermore, we reason that if the
societies differ so markedly, then why should one expect the cities which
evolve within these societies to be undifferentiable?

The prevalence of the "North American" construct has important consequences for Canada beyond the immediate and future policy issues raised by
the foregoing comments about Canada's energy and natural resources. It
extends to the manner in which Canadians view Canada and themselves
increasingly through a "North American" lens. A continentalist perspective
is sensible if Canada is essentially similar to the United States. If, on the
other hand, significant differences do exist between U.S. and Canadian
institutions, then homogenizing Canada into "North America" is not especially instructive and may be quite misleading and, in the extreme, even
dangerous. By extension, this work challenges the broader concept of
"continentalizing" Canada and the transfer of research and policy formula-
tions from the one country to the other without a careful understanding of
the context into which quintessentially American constructs are to be injected.

The case in point is the concept of the "North American City," advanced
by Maurice Yeates and Barry Garner and others and the focus of this book.[2]
It is acknowledged that among these writers, Yeates and Garner, for example,
have increasingly paid attention to contrasts between Canadian and Ameri-

can cities in their widely used text, *The North American City* — compare the first edition with the 1980 third edition. There is a movement in the urban literature toward a more sensitive appreciation of context and of Canadian and American urban differences. The need for a separate treatment is argued in other recent work,[3] notably *The Geography of American Cities*, wherein Palm states:

> The book focuses on cities in the United States. Canadian examples are generally not included in this book for a very important reason. Although the history of urban development in Canada has many similarities to that of the United States, there are significant differences in the histories of the two nations, and more important, in their governmental structures, ethnic development, and general ideologies. Since this book argues that an understanding of a set of cities requires a detailed understanding of the political economy, the ethnic background, and the attitudes toward cities, cross-national differences in these circumstances would complicate the comparison of urban structure. The book asserts that cities in the United States are a product of circumstances within this country; and that other circumstances would probably have produced different urban structures.[4]

Elsewhere Palm has commented positively on the air of excitement in urban geographical research generated by articles focusing on studies of urban form and development processes and their relationship to a specific cultural context. Specifically, she characterizes our initial research as "an important first step in the understanding of the ways in which demographic and political-economic processes constrain and shape urban form."[5]

Taking the continentalist thesis literally, there should be an homogeneous set of characteristics and processes that describe and govern the growth and structure of urban areas in both the United States and Canada. However, if Canadian cities are substantially different from those in the United States, then generalization from the U.S. to Canada becomes difficult and quite possibly counter-productive. One useful illustration is provided by the brief reign of U.S.-style urban renewal provisions in Canada's *National Housing Act* from 1964 to 1969, introduced in the belief that Canadian cities faced pressures and problems similar to those in the U.S. There was little prior concern given to the possibility that U.S.-derived policies were inappropriate. A review of the Canadian experience does demonstrate the inapplicability of these U.S.-style urban renewal measures. It also calls into question the utility of such uncritical transfers of policies and theories from one urban system to another, even when these systems appear to be so similar.[6]

Embodied in the book are the results of analyses of urban change and structure for the 277 Standard Metropolitan Statistical Areas (SMSAs) of the

United States and for the 40 principal urban areas in Canada for which comparable data are available.[7] The social, economic and political context of the two national urban systems is also explored. The central tenet of the argument is that cities evolve within the cultural framework of the societies within which they are located. In their spatial and architectural forms, they are manifestations of deeply rooted cultural processes which encompass economic elements as well. Thus, cities and city dwellers are more than just products of a prevailing economic system. It should be possible to separate cultural processes into social, economic and political categories. These categories would include both the underlying institutions and their integration into functioning systems. While this is useful, the interrelatedness of phenomena which we label economic, social and political must be borne in mind.

In recognizing that cities express the dominant, or hegemonic, culture in which they are located, we reject the "city as mirror" notion, a widely held conception frequently expressed by urbanists. Cities are not simply game boards upon which one culture constructs "monopolyville" while another creates "equalityville." As a real place, each city has an urban form within which people live. This setting, together with the surrounding territory that constitutes the urban region or field and other cities frequently visited, affects our behavior in terms of daily living. Beyond this immediate interaction, the experience of living in particular settings helps shape culture. In the aggregate, daily life and urban experience affirm the dominant culture for many. On the other hand, through their experience, others come to view society and the city very differently from the majority through their patterns of living. In seeking change, this group comes to represent an emerging culture (some writers label this a counterculture). Risking reification, the emerging culture modifies or supplants the dominant culture. A new urban form will eventually result as the city continues to manifest the dominant culture. If supplanted, the previously dominant culture becomes residual. Its heritage is still found in elements of the urban form, however, coexisting alongside expressions of the new or modified culture.

While this is a more complex way of thinking about cities, it is a necessary recognition of the interactive nature of the city-culture relationship. Cultures are continually being made or remade — they are neither received tradition nor disembodied organic entities. The making of a culture lies in a human experience which is always place-specific — for most, and especially for Canadians and Americans, this place is the city and particular cities at that. Equally, the making of towns and cities occurs in a cultural context. At the risk of oversimplification, we try to illustrate this interactive conception diagrammatically. The cultural context is broken down into constituent parts and placed in relation to the development of cities within regions and also to the structure of the metropolitan area itself; this is what Urban Systems entails (see Chart 1-1).

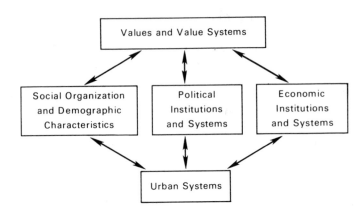

CHART 1—1   Inter-relationships between Values and Value Systems, Functional Structures, and Urban Systems

The philosophy or, perhaps more accurately, the vision of continentalism is neither new nor confined to a limited set of activities. As we have noted elsewhere:

> Historically, American interests sought to create a North American State. Presently, there are strong continental linkages in economic activity: the U.S.-Canada Auto Pact, energy transfers, and the penetration by U.S. corporations in certain sectors of the Canadian economy. In the social sphere, the border is easily crossed by various forms of media, family and social networks and other forms of interaction such as recreational pursuits.[8]

The practice of continental thinking can have deleterious effects. In his book on the short-lived Progressive Conservative administration of 1979, Simpson recounts how Prime Minister Joe Clark's key American-trained economic advisors urged upon the Cabinet policies which had been utilized successfully in the U.S. Their inability to recognize the important contextual difference ultimately led to failed policy initiatives.[9]

Too vigorous an application of continentalism is checked, however, by two kinds of literature. One, written mostly by Canadians, is at pains to establish a separate and distinct Canadian identity, while the other examines Canadian-American relations and gives due recognition to Canadian perspectives and experiences which are different from those of the United States. Until recently, there was not such a check on the utilization of the North American city concept. This book and the research upon which it rests should give pause for a careful reconsideration of this continentalist concept without necessarily implying that the concept has no merit.

Drawing distinctions between cities in Canada and those in the United States is particularly useful at this juncture, since the process of urbanization which has been vitally important in the transformation of Canadian and American societies and landscapes is exhibiting a new form. Metropolitan growth which has been so pervasive in the two countries (as in other advanced nations) appears to be at an end, with markedly reduced rates of population increase for principal metropolitan centers and a real decline in certain instances becoming apparent in the United States but not yet on any scale in Canada. While it may be premature to talk about de-urbanization or counter-urbanization, there seems to be little doubt that we are entering a new phase in the continuing evolution of the human settlement systems on this continent, but with distinct differences between Canada and the United States.[10] It is therefore timely to revise our conceptual frameworks.

By placing Canadian and American cities in a comparative perspective, we should be able to discern important differences and also add to our knowledge about each set of cities separately. As Marc Bloch, a famous comparativist, once put it: "Correctly understood, the primary interest of the comparative method is ... the observation of differences, whether they are original or the results of divergent developments from a common origin."[11] Such work has been suggested for some time for Canadian cities, as is succinctly put by Kerr in a review of Nader's two-volume *Cities of Canada*:

> Nor does he at any time stand back and comment on relationships of Canadian cities to others in the Western world. Is there a distinctive Canadian city? Are the qualities of Vancouver, Quebec, St. John and Regina similar enough to warrant their segregation in a general typology or are they simply part of a larger basket of North American cities?[12]

Others have attempted comparative empirical research on urban structure in North America, but in a limited and somewhat crude fashion.[13] Nothing, however, has been attempted on the present scale.

THE COMPARATIVE METHOD AND OUR OBJECTIVES

Put simply, we have two objectives, both closely related to the comparative method employed here and in earlier work.[14] The first is to treat an important theoretical issue that has arisen in comparative analyses of cities and the city building process. Certain theorists argue that cities and city systems in advanced countries should be expected to reveal similarities in urban structure and in the underlying process of urbanization because they are dominated by a particular capitalist economic order and associated modes of behavior.[15] The paramountcy of the economic order is central to this view; cities are seen as important nodal elements in the spatial arrangements and interconnections at both the level of the national and regional economies. The location of jobs in urban areas induces labor in-migration, and thus the social and demographic composition of urban populations fundamentally derives from the urban economic system. Differences in urban form and development are to be expected as a result of different national contexts, although recent literature seems to ascribe a remarkably similar role to the state in capitalist societies irrespective of context.[16] However, these are viewed as surficial configurations of no great substance, given the similarity of the more basic economic order. Indeed, in certain Marxist analyses, the whole superstructure of a society, including its broadly defined culture, is seen as derivative and as being determined by the base which, as Raymond Williams observes,[17] is characterized largely in economic terms. Ironically, these normative value-based Marxist analyses share a common perspective with positivist and supposedly objective views that have prevailed in urban geography and urban economics.[18] Both fundamentally subscribe to an economic (or materialist) determinism which assigns culture to an insignificant secondary role and places either the economic system (capitalism for the Marxists) or rational economic behavior (for the economists) in a paramount position.

An alternative view would advance a form of cultural determinacy. Superstructure might be thought of as being limited to social, political and cultural institutions, their agents and members; culture would then typically embody such things as art, literature, theater, or the visual arts. Here, we wish to use culture in a broader sense as comprising the central beliefs, values and meanings that people hold and which affect the way in which they organize their institutions and relations, both among themselves, between themselves and other groups, and among institutions. Thus, culture has a determining effect upon the nature of these socially constructed institutions, their agents and members. Culture in this sense also influences the way in which a people see themselves, a kind of self-portrait, and thus can give rise to the concept of a national character. Although partly mystical, this concept may have the capacity to be self-fulfilling, since people often act in accordance with the ways they believe they should.

One could go further and argue that the economic order is culturally determined since the economic institutions and the rules drawn up for their operation are human creations and very much influenced by our values. For example, the culture of one society may permit it to treat the land as something that can be subdivided, the rights to parts of which may be owned individually and exchanged in a complex commodified manner. In another society, the land may be something indivisible, held in temporary steward-ship by the group on behalf of some creator and for the enjoyment of unborn generations and for which exchange in a market sense is unthinkable. These societies would most likely create and sustain different economic orders and different institutions relating to land and have contrasting social relations.

A more culturally sensitive view would be less likely to treat urban differences as phenomena that transcend national or regional boundaries and would wish to pursue, as we do here, the roots of such differences and their substantive meaning. Much too depends on the scale of the interpretation. What may be dismissed by the universalist or practising continentalist as superficial differences of no great consequence may well constitute the daily lived-in reality for numerous city dwellers who, were they able to engage in comparative reflection, would probably retort that the differences were experientially real and of major importance to them. We develop this theme later when we consider the differential attractiveness of inner-city residen-tial areas in Canada and the U.S. and its implications for central-city popula-tion and household characteristics in the two countries.

Why might urban differences occur between the cities of two nations which are seen as economically so similar? An explanation may lie in two not necessarily exclusive directions. One might be that the designation of the two economic orders as similar, in that they are mature or advanced capital-ist states, is too crude and masks the fact that urban differences are a reflection of deeper and more subtle differences in the economic systems. The other direction is to attribute urban differences to a more comprehen-sive set of factors than solely economic ones. This is the path pursued here. In so doing, we hope to add revealing insights to the central theoretical issue outlined. Specifically, do observed differences in urban structure in advanced market economies signify minor and essentially inconsequential departures from underlying structural similarities, or do they signify the existence, importance and perhaps centrality of non-economic processes that shape cities and create markedly different living conditions for city dwellers and, in fact, markedly different cities?

Our second objective is to raise basic questions about the nature of Canadian and American societies and how these may be manifested in their principal urban areas. Our empirical analyses provide the ingredients for asking such questions. These questions in turn yield the building blocks upon which improved theories of urban form and development can be framed.

In prefacing a recent study of comparative analysis in the field of urban planning, Masser succinctly sums up the benefits of the approach: "Over the last few years, the idea of cross-national comparative research has become increasingly attractive because of the opportunities that it provides for analysts to test emerging theories under new circumstances and for practitioners to consider the lessons from other people's experience."[19] In his view, cross-national comparative analyses also have the potential to stimulate the development of new and better theory.[20] Our present efforts aim to realize these kinds of benefits.

In view of the benefits arising from comparative research, it is curious that there has been relatively little attention paid to the approach until now. Harloe could write only a few years ago that "there has been little consideration given to systematic comparative work, although its importance is generally recognized."[21] He goes on: "Far more needs to be done if the validity of the claims that patterns of urban development are essentially linked to characteristics of basic modes of production and of their associated class conflicts is to be firmly established and if these theories are to be further developed."[22] A leading comparative urban scholar, John Walton, concluded in a recent review that urban social science has undergone a revolution and that a new paradigm is being elaborated. He observes, however, that most of this work is not really comparative and that further developments "will depend on full use of the comparative imagination."[23] If these views are authoritative, then there is much to recommend comparative urban studies, regardless of discipline. But is comparative work essential? We believe so.

A comparative approach (or imagination to use Walton's term) could help avoid the serious theoretical errors that arise from over-generalization from specific cultural contexts. American "liberal" social scientists have been particularly guilty in this respect. The British urban geographer Robson has noted the limitations that face the application of essentially American urban theory to British cities—the cultural context is different, causal processes are structured differently (housing provision and consumption is one good example), and the urban form is different.[24] We have been critical previously of American geographer Brian Berry's insensitivity to important Canadian-American urban differences, since he continues to cling to the concept of the North American city, allowing that such differences that do arise are attributable to the deep-seated racism in American culture.[25] Comparative analysis challenges his over-generalization that the public sector has performed as poorly in urban Canada as it has in the United States. To argue that "economic and political power, vested in the claims of ownership and property, is widely dispersed and competitively exercised"[26] is simply erroneous in the case of Canada, where economic and political power is highly concentrated.[27] Such an argument is also dubious at best for the United States.

It is not only "liberal" social scientists who incorporate elements from one specific country at an unjustifiable level of generality in theories or syntheses. As Harloe notes, "radical" (read Marxist) social theorists such as Lojkine and Castells have abstracted elements from the French context and injudiciously over-generalized from these.[28] Theorizing about the state, with all of its implications for urban study, suffers similarly. The nature and development of the state has been and continues to be quite different among modern capitalist societies. For example, the federal system operates quite differently in Canada than in the United States or Australia—in each country, local government, especially urban government, operates in a different political culture. Urban governments are organized in geographically different ways, different fiscal characteristics are apparent, and powers in land and housing markets are exercised differently. Only comparative work reveals this. What appears self-evident and expectable in one context is a problem requiring explanation in another.

A comparative methodology also has considerable ability to generate new questions and issues otherwise overlooked in extant theories. The discovery of unsuspected variation leads to the redefinition of problems,[29] giving new importance and context to facts yielded by apparently unrelated local studies. Comparative analysis is also essential to support the proposition that cultures are being made and remade: the signifying system requires continuous realization. Although British colonial settlement and English liberalism were common antecedents to the formation of culture in Canada and the United States, different political cultures and social histories have resulted in contrasting urban experiences; in short, different outcomes can and did derive from similar antecedents. Phrased somewhat differently, the continentalist concept with which our discussion began is, under the scrutiny of comparative analysis, fraught with omissions and over-generalization.

2

VALUES AND CULTURE: A CONTEXT FOR COMPARING AMERICAN AND CANADIAN CITIES

Our purpose in this chapter is to discuss certain values and attitudes which differentiate Americans from Canadians comparatively. We restrict our examination to values and attitudes having a connection to the various processes which shape the nature of cities. For example, it has been asserted that Americans are "risk-takers" and "competitive," more so than "conservative" Canadians. This would presumably mean that on some scale or measure, they would rate or place "competition" or "competitive behavior" more highly than Canadians. A more competitive milieu could reasonably be anticipated as having an effect on the city-building process. One consequence could well be a greater profusion of smaller construction and development companies as entrepreneurs seek to get in on the action more than in less competitive contexts.

Here too we focus on social (some might say civic or public) values rather than personal or professional values, recognizing their inseparability. We will be concerned with selected values and attitudes that seem to be widely held in a society. As majority values, part of the mainstream consensus, these positions with respect to phenomena, including institutions and appropriate or "proper" modes of behavior, may be thought of as dominant or hegemonic. However, the simultaneous co-existence of "old-fashioned" values and new values must be acknowledged.[1] Though these values are not those of powerful individuals, legislators, or opinion-makers, we do not gainsay their influence or deny that their values may become encoded in value systems.[2] Rather, they are the social values by which the mass of people live, selecting and interpreting experience and events in a particular time and place.

If values are to be connected to the surface features of our worlds and specifically in our case to cities, they must be possessed of some stability over time, beyond expressions of transitory opinion.[3] This therefore requires an historical perspective. Given our goals, an appropriate example is the position Canadians take on the matter of North American integration. A key element binding Canada economically and politically to the United States has been an immense amount of direct investment by American-controlled corporations in Canada. This is well known. But the proportion of Canadians who believe that this is a good thing ranged from a high of 64 per cent (in 1970) to a low of 45 per cent only four years later.[4] Lately (1983), this proportion has risen to 62 per cent under severe recessionary conditions. Reading opinion polls taken in any given year—"how is the mood of the country shifting?"—led to policy actions that were perceived to be "popular" with the Canadian electorate. For instance, the government's nationalization in the energy field was based on such assessment of popular support. There is clearly a favorable attitude towards American investment on the part of a majority of Canadians. Equally, there is a sizable minority who, over time, view American investment as "a bad thing." It is the existence of this persistent divergence that is of more importance than any particular up or down turn in current opinion. How these attitudes relate to the more general attitudes of Canadians towards America (as an object of affection or liking) or the centrality of "national independence" as part of some value system cannot be directly answered.

While it is true that pro-American sentiment has risen substantially in the last decade, an historical perspective reminds us that in the nineteenth century the United States was probably the country most feared by Canadians. Both militarily and politically Canada was in opposition to America. Equally, an historical view reminds us that Americans were early engaged in nation-building. Though hardly an exercise in mass participation, Americans were self-consciously and publicly deciding what sort of place and society America was to be. Similarly important decisions were being made within what constituted a set of colonies in British North America in the mid-nineteenth century. The Canada of 1867 was created in opposition to and as a counter-vailing force to American interests on the continent, but very much within the colonial framework of the British Empire (in Chapter 5 we pursue the development of federalism in more detail). Thus, while "national independence" was of early importance in America, and nation-building as a process has been complete for some time, it could be argued that Canada is still caught up in that latter process and that national independence has been less important than national unity as both a value and a goal. Contrasting the continuing search for a "Canadian identity" with the rather well-defined "American character" is of direct concern.

Values and culture are transmitted from generation to generation, each new one being socialized into prevailing values or value systems. These values and the contemporary hegemonic culture are refashioned in light of the experience of groups and individuals so that what is passed on is changed, a change often associated with conflict. As scholars have reflected and expounded on the nature of specific societies and their major features, they have uncovered important values that were deeply and widely adhered to, the lineaments of which can still be traced in contemporary society.[5] In some of this work, the concept of "national character" has been invoked.[6] We reject the notion that the values and attitudes of a people can be sensibly reduced to one or more average or modal positions or traits. We prefer to think of dominant attitudes and values and a hegemonic culture. Nevertheless, the various dimensions that make up a portrait of a people as created by "national character" writers have entered popular mythology, becoming in a self-fulfilling way a basis for action. When young Americans are socialized into a world where Americans are thought, or believed, to have more self-confidence than others, many appear to have accepted this, often uncritically, and acted in a manner consistent with this state of mind.

Following a discussion of national character, we move to a more specific comparison of selected features of American and Canadian society, some of which have arisen from the national character literature, others of which have emerged from functional sociology and its use of pattern variables as a conceptual device. This is not an endorsement on our part of this particular school of sociology but simply a recognition that an early influential but flawed comparative analysis of value differences employed this approach.[7] In outline form, these dimensions are as follows:

Canada		United States
Deferential Behavior	vs.	Assertive Behavior
Collective	vs.	"Frontier" Individualism
Respect for Authority	vs.	Distrust of Authority
Elitist/Oligarchic	vs.	Egalitarian/Democratic
Self-restraint	vs.	Self-indulgence
Social Liberalism	vs.	Economic Conservatism
Cautious/Evolutionary	vs.	Dynamic/Experimental
Peace/Order/Good Government	vs.	Pursuit of Happiness

In the final part of the chapter, we attempt to draw out and briefly highlight some central themes of special importance to the study of cities in North America. We discuss privatism as against collectivism, especially as this relates to the appropriate role of government or the state. Some attention is also given to the mythologies surrounding private enterprise. We compare and contrast assimilationist tendencies with those that sustain diversity and ethnic or regional rather than national identity. And lastly, we focus on rights and responsibilities and property and propriety.

DIFFERENCES IN NATIONAL CHARACTER

From the national character literature a number of salient themes emerge. Consider first Britannic continuity in Canada, meaning that there is a continuing link and affinity between the United Kingdom and Canada. This idea is employed to differentiate Canada from the whole of North America.[8] While an important and useful notion, it would be a mistake to over-emphasize it; there are many non-British influences at work upon Canada and Canadians. Furthermore, there is no denying that Canadians are and see themselves as North Americans. Yet the revolutionary creation of the American republic caused many Americans living in the dissenting regions to reaffirm their loyalty to the monarchy and Britain. As is well known, the loyalists subsequently moved north in the thousands, settling primarily in Upper Canada (now Ontario) and New Brunswick. The infusion of these political refugees generated settlements, some of which have become leading cities. Thus, long before Confederation there was a significant element in the North American population which cherished, even romanticized, Britain and British ways of doing things.[9] At the same time they resented bitterly the fact of "America" and its "aggressive" ways and distrusted its expansionary intentions.

The "Anglophiles" found themselves sharing a territory with a "Canadien" population which was determined to maintain its identity, or better yet enlarge upon it, within a predominantly and increasingly anglophone continent. This was relatively easy to do. The British colonial authorities, being limited in military power and resources, really had little option but to permit Canadien elites to control and develop the social life of their community consistent with their own purposes. Survival of the francophone community was of the highest priority. The community required nurturing and was accompanied by a growing realization that the group was more important than any individual members.[10] The British-American group also had a survival mentality: preservation in North America of the British fact was an important collective goal.

The two groups co-existed uneasily. A sense of inferiority grew amongst elements of the subjugated francophones. The deportation of the Acadians in 1755 was a blunt reminder of the fragility of the francophone situation.[11] Over the longer period, this sense of inferiority came to rest upon economic inequalities in Quebec. Anglophones became dominant in the spheres of commerce and industry, and the wealth thus created was distributed in a way that emphasized the cultural gulf within an embryonic Canada.[12] Thus, one of the great and enduring dualities of Canadian life can be discerned even before the country or nation-state was formed.

The uneasy co-existence of these two groups, each so concerned with its own survival as a distinct identity, meant that Canada was, for almost a century and a half, bicultural in a way that America most certainly was not. Nevertheless, the British were dominant in numerous respects, and thus it is the Britannic continuity which was important within the nation as a whole. This continuity has been replenished constantly through immigration from the mother country, while the French continuity had little subsequent nourishment.

What has this continuity meant? According to some, Canadians partake of quintessentially British values.[13] While this may be true to some extent, it must be remembered that actions consistent with these imported values occur in a place: Canada and its locales. The interplay between inherited values and attitudes and the experience of daily life in particular places and regions resulted in distinctively Canadian values, attitudes and actions.

Maintenance of order and the public peace is one example of a social situation that is highly desired in Britain and Canada; the rights of individuals are secondary to this end. Canadians are more constrained than Americans by laws and bureaucratic rules designed to protect the larger collectivity.[14] Americans have considerably more freedom to pursue their individual goals protected by a fabled constitution based on individual rights. Canadians, as a consequence of Britannic continuity, are more respectful of authority and hold a greater conviction that governments will act responsibly on their behalf. Thus, we would expect a greater trust of "the government" in Canada, a view which finds considerable support in claims, assertions and research findings (see Chapter 5).

On a different level, Britannic continuity should result in a wealth of British symbols in Canada. This is decidedly the case, even in Quebec. In contrast, the devotion of Americans to republicanism leads to a rejection of monarchical symbols and a profusion of Greek and Roman nomenclature and symbols alongside distinctively American ones, such as the eagle and the flag. Alan Gowans has suggested that the architecture of public buildings in Canada bears a British imprint, whereas American public buildings bear a strong resemblance to "classical temples."[15] At the level of the cityscape, Canadian cities express a British flavor in names, symbols and the quality and cleanliness of public spaces.[16]

Ironically, at the time of the revolutionary break with Britain, English writers were major contributors to the universal and rational modes of thought to which Americans turned as they developed and interpreted their own society and territory. The reliance upon universal norms led to a national identity conceived in terms of liberty and equality. This linkage to mostly English theorizing on the nature of man, civil society and government was facilitated by a common language and the social dominance of Anglo-Saxons in the republic's first century. It was further intensified by the enormously popular associations between post-Civil War liberalism, owing much again to British liberalism, individualism, free enterprise and competition. Later, these concepts were seized upon by new immigrant groups who were also making a decisive break with their past. What the new United States lacked was a conservative or "tory" tradition strong enough to counter this individualistic juggernaut: that tradition had been displaced northwards with the disgruntled loyalists.[17]

Thus, despite the break, there was a strong British influence on American political thought and on the emerging American national identity. On a different level, if there is one style of living that has long been favored by affluent American elites, especially in the longer settled regions of the country, it is that of the English landed gentry.[18] To the extent that elites provide role models, this Anglophilia is an important undercurrent in American society.

Government, or to use more recent terminology, the public sector, has long been viewed as being a more important element of Canadian life than in the United States. The power of the state, as exercised through the bureaucracy, was mobilized to preserve the embryonic nation on more than one occasion, ranging from military action to legislation in such spheres as economic development, continental trade and ecclesiastical relations. The pervasiveness of government has led some interpreters to declare that "the Canadian middle class man was a bureaucratic man."[19] Special or vested interests were protected by state action. Reformist elements, drawing inspiration largely from the U.S. (which was perceived by them as progressive, open and pluralistic with boundless opportunities for individual freedom and enterprise) could not alter substantially the oligarchic, sometimes monopolistic nature of society. Clearly, government in Canada has long supported capitalism; some would say it has been subservient to capitalist interests.[20] At the same time, it has developed an active economic role for itself through the agency of public (or crown) corporations. There has not been sustained and effective opposition to this. Rather, there has been pressure from interest groups for the formation of crown corporations which, by the nature of their existence and actions, begin to command wider public support. Despite much talk of privatization, many public corporations survive and new ones continue to be created both by federal and provincial authorities. This public sector visibility in a diversity of activities enhances the role of the state, which with public support gives Canada a more collectivist look, one that can reasonably be judged to be different from the more private entrepreneurial and individualistic tenor of social and economic life in the United States.

Government, then, is something which appears to be highly valued by many Canadians, a view which is part of historical and current experience. For the majority of Canadians, the government may well be the first thing they think of in terms of solving problems rather than the last. This might be interpreted as part of a mutuality central to Canadian thinking and practice, born of a struggle to survive in a difficult environment. Canadians may now have the technical sophistication necessary to master that environment, but the mutuality rooted in an earlier time may still be an important value. This notion of surviving in relation to the environment by, as it were, entering into a contract with the environment is important in Canadian life and letters.[21]

It is useful to think of Canada as an "organic society," a concept advanced by philosopher Leslie Armour, in which the individual is not against or above society but rather interrelated with it.[22] An organic society is one in which "the parts work together to form an intelligible whole in which each has a unique place."[23] Mutual interest and dependence and the idea of a common good transcending individuals' self-interest have a place in such a society. Importantly, this conception of the organic society is neither so homogeneous nor so narrow as to preclude a variety of cultures and differing ways of life. Furthermore, this notion rests not upon some naive or imagined harmony but upon never-ending tensions between constituent parts. Though stressful, the fluidity and uncertainty may be more beneficial to a community than complacency and implicit consensus about the nature of a society's received and dominant institutions and values. It is possible that the United States approaches this latter condition, for example, in its veneration of principles enunciated two centuries ago and embodied in the Constitution.

In Canada, the collectivism incorporated in the conservative tradition and in varied and successful socialist movements can perhaps be understood in terms of the organic society notion. This political philosophy stands in marked contrast to individualist philosophy, popular in the United States; it also stands distinct from Marxian philosophy which ascribes dominance to the economic order and material conditions. In the United States, government is widely portrayed as something that shackles needlessly those individuals who are driving aggressively towards their goals in the spirit of a competitive free enterprise system. American civil society and individuals are not seen as having a co-operative relationship with the state. Rather, the state is seen as an impediment in domestic affairs. Instead of being turned to first in problem-solving, it is more likely to be considered as the last resort.

The debate about Canadian identity reveals an uncertainty about "who we are," especially in comparison to what appears to be a well-developed and confident self-portrait in America. Part of this is reflected in the very strong regional affinities expressed in Canada. These affinities are dramatically intensified by the postwar emergence of provincial authorities as strong and at times truculent players in the national pastime, better known as federal-provincial relations.[24] Thus, a deep-rooted and meaningful regionalism finds expression in anti-centralist feelings, articulated as provincial government animosity toward federal officials, both elected and appointed, and their policies.[25] When George Woodcock tartly observed that uniformity and unity are not the same thing nor equally desirable, he was underscoring his conception of the nature of Canada as a multi-faceted, regionally based diversity which a nascent centralizing nationalism could not, and indeed should not, readily weld together into a uniform national identity.[26] A well-developed regionalism, while celebrated by some, does pose a challenge to the conduct of both political and economic life. For example, as Pierre Trudeau wrote prior to his political career: "The advantage as well as the peril of federalism is that it permits the development of a regional consensus based on regional values; so federalism is bound to fail if the nationalism it cultivates is unable to generate a national image which has immensely more appeal than the regional ones."[27] Again, there are persistent regional inequalities that cannot be readily, if ever, resolved without a mobilization of national will and resources. Woodcock and others would remind us, however, that these inequalities are not entirely the result of regional variation in the resource base but arose historically from the exercise of power by a central elite which has benefited from the creation of a nation with a strong core and weaker peripheries.

The American national character exudes a greater self-confidence and an assuredness that the United States, its governmental system and way of life are, simply, the best. Thus, Americans are imbued with a missionary zeal to bring this formula to the developing nations of the world and to counterpose it against the "Communist/Totalitarian" model. The older societies of Europe are left to their own political-economic devices, since it is thought that mass popular culture, quintessentially American, will bind these societies to the American way. The national identity and self-image are strong and have developed in conjunction with regionalism, though the latter is more politically muted than in Canada.[28] While not incompatible, regionalism cannot challenge nationalism. Any tendency in such a direction would be labelled "sectionalism," and preservation of the Union would then be elevated to the highest priority. Devotees of a strong and active regionalism in America can always contemplate the specific instance of the South and secession. It is interesting to note here that Canadian federal authorities claimed they would not exercise military power to prevent Quebec leaving the Confederation if such a decision was arrived at under proper legal circumstance.

DIMENSIONS OF VALUE DIFFERENCES

Lipset, in his comparison of Canadian and American societies, identified a number of pattern variables. Since his views have been both cited approv-

ingly and roundly criticized, his analysis has obviously elicited very divergent reactions.[29] Lipset himself once observed that "to demonstrate that
such differences [in value patterns] really exist would involve considerable
research."[30] We agree with critics such as Truman and Horowitz that Lipset
just did not do enough basic research initially and that his interpretations of
existing evidence seem more designed to support his contentions than other
equally plausible interpretations. Some of the hard, grinding research that
Lipset, Truman, Horowitz and others called for has now been done. Below
we briefly counterpose this more recent work against the assertions of
difference arising from Lipset and others.

Before doing so, however, it must be stressed that the dimensions of value
differences as set out in the introduction to this chapter are far from being
independent. If a society is oligarchic in nature with a small number of
interlocking elites, a characterization of Canadian society supported by the
research of Porter and Clement,[31] then it becomes relatively easy to identify
and affix responsibility on authority, both public and private. If, despite
occasional rebellious tendencies, the majority are successfully socialized
into accepting these elites as acting in the common good, then respect for
authority will be evidenced, likely through deferential behavior toward
authority or its representatives.[32] Part of this socialization hinges upon elites
convincing masses that the former are the legitimate instruments of achieving and maintaining an ordered society with public peace, honest and
efficacious government, and a sense of the common weal as goals which
both groups have in common. In short, there is an alleged mutual benefit in
achieving these goals by means of established elites and institutions.

Furthermore, to the extent that the well-being of the group or community
is accorded equivalent stature to that of individuals, a collective spirit will
influence behavior, encouraging restraint in the willful pursuit of individual
goals. Since government is seen as having a legitimate role in advancing
communitarian objectives, an interventionist strategy by public agents can
be anticipated, giving rise to the view that the country is socially liberal.

There now exists a modest research literature that allows at least a
preliminary judgment on whether or not these dimensions do discriminate
between Americans and Canadians and also whether or not the characterizations of Lipset and others are accurate. Cross-national survey evidence
allows a more informed position to be taken than the previous reliance upon
impressionistic evidence and fragments of objective empirical data open to
varying interpretations. Using data from the late 1960s, Arnold and Barnes
compared the responses of large national samples to over 200 questionnaire
items common to both surveys.[33] Given some technical survey design issues,
the data were analyzed on a male-female categorical basis in both countries.
Of particular interest is the attempt in this study to compare intranational

versus international differences, permitting a consideration of whether or not respondents in central and eastern Canada and those in the eastern U.S. had more in common with each other than with their western co-nationals. Also of special interest was their attempt to examine the within-country variance compared to between-country variance. A reasonable position on cross-national comparisons is that even if significant differences are identified between, in this case, Canada and the United States, the variations within each country are of more fundamental importance. In this analysis, the same regions that we use later in our empirical analysis of cities were employed.

While the results need to be treated with some caution since the stability of these views over time has not yet been demonstrated, some of the extensive battery of items bear on the value dimensions we are considering. The findings contradict conventional wisdom. Instead of Canadians being more conservative in value orientation, Americans were found to be significantly more non-permissive and morally conservative. Related to this was a greater emphasis upon spiritual values in the American respondents. When one considers the socio-political importance of various "moral" movements in America in recent years, these results are not too surprising. The popular notion of Americans as risk-takers was not supported, there being no cross-national difference in the desire for security. American consumers were much more inclined to use credit instruments and to enter into debt to a substantial degree. This is a form of risk-taking, but the difference is likely more apparent than real. The U.S. federal government is effectively subsidizing credit purchases by permitting interest payments on credit debt as a tax deduction. This institutional practice, not allowed in Canada, is in itself revealing.

A cluster of items casts some light on individualism. The results are consistent with the belief that there is a greater degree of individualism in America as distinct from greater collectivism in Canada. Despite this, it is an error to ignore the public or communitarian life that certainly exists in American cities, towns and villages. Arnold and Barnes found that a greater community involvement was evident among Americans than Canadians, which they took as a possible indicator of collectivism, which runs contrary to the comparativist literature. There is a question of scale here. Collectivist tendencies in Canada may be greater at regional and national levels. We interpret this particular finding instead as being consistent with a stronger American sense of localism and municipal autonomy, which is an expression of a highly privatized society.

Another finding was that significant differences between Canada and the U.S. occurred more often than ones between the east and west by a factor of seven. Thus, cross-national differences are far more likely to exist. Taking those scales with significant cross-national differences, less than 10 per cent had significant regional differences in both countries. Some scales revealed significant differences by region within one country but not the other. Overall, more than half of the scales with a significant cross-national difference showed no statistically significant regional differences whatsoever. While the evidence is far from conclusive, one could not assert with confidence that the within country variation is of more importance than the between country variation, as some would like to believe.

Another set of survey evidence is provided in the work of Gordon Fearn, who examined mass survey data, again from the 1968-70 period.[34] In general terms, this study supports the proposition that there exists a set of social attitudes which are distinctively Canadian and demonstrably different from American attitudes. One proviso is that francophones are seriously underrepresented in the sample of Canadian survey respondents. In discussing this same study, however, Armour asserts with conviction that other information (unfortunately not summarized or cited) would show that francophone respondents would buttress the concept of the organic society as revealed through Fearn's findings.[35] Fearn found a number of important differences. Compared to Americans, Canadians were less strongly attached to individual achievement, private property and work, and in terms of rewards for effort, they expected more reciprocity. In a related vein, they perceived their society as being more nepotistic than that of the U.S., a position consistent with the notion of an oligarchic culture. Nepotism apparently does not give rise to much public indignation, let alone outrage in Canada. It might evoke contempt in America, for if Americans perceived a powerful oligarchy, its existence would transgress the popular mystique surrounding equality, freedom of choice, and a classless society. Interestingly, in these survey data, Canadians do perceive more of a class structure in their country than Americans do in theirs. These survey data also reveal a Canadian population which is more skeptical of government and its officials and less likely to participate in voluntary and civic work than the American respondents. The latter finding is consistent with that of Arnold and Barnes on the same issue. A lack of voluntarism is understandable if Canadians expect that government should take care of "problems." However, the skepticism tapped in this survey tends to run counter to other survey evidence which shows Canadians to have a higher level of trust in government and believe that its behavior will be beneficent. This mode of research is frequently at odds with itself since the specific wording of survey questions has much to do with the contradictory findings that are often obtained. Finally, Canadians exhibited a greater degree of family solidarity than Americans. Some would likely interpret this as evidence of higher conservatism in Canada. There is historical evidence that Canadians, especially those imperialists brilliantly dissected by Berger,[36] doubted seriously the future of the family in their southern neighbor. Contemporary evidence points in a similar direction. A study of personal values in Canada and the United States indicates clearly that the domain of "Love/Marriage" is much more important in contributing to the general quality of life in Canada than in the U.S. (based on representative national samples in 1977 and 1971 respectively).[37]

The greater degree of individualism in America evidenced by Fearn's study is reinforced by a study of social bonding in six nations, including the U.S. and Canada.[38] In terms of self-restraint and concern for others the American respondents scored the lowest of six national groups (Canada, China, India, Japan, Norway and the U.S.A.). They were also the highest by a significant margin in self-indulgence. In contrast, the Canadian respondents scored the lowest of all on self-indulgence and were higher than the Americans on self-restraint and concern for others. Furthermore, in contrast to the dominant American value orientation, individual progressive action, Canadians adhered most strongly to a societal orientation. These findings, although needing further substantiation, will not surprise many Canadians. One recent study of how Canadians view Americans summarized the view in this way: "corrupt, conceited, inconsiderate, disrespectful of authority, fixated on status."[39] There was a definite sense of there being an "American style" of human relations.

While we have chosen to emphasize social values, it seems to us that it is inevitable that personal values are an important influence on social values as are the values of elites. Thus, these various sets of survey data provide a perspective not only on mass values and attitudes but also indirectly on social values. They permit a reassessment of Lipset's characterizations using the pattern-variable approach. Indeed, this kind of evidence constitutes a better test of the comparativists' propositions concerning national character, value systems and orientations than the information Lipset and others originally used. Thus, Atkinson and Murray's findings, for example, challenge Lipset's implied notion that there would be greater materialism in the United States.[40] Materialism, as measured by the importance of financial concerns, is not at all different in Canada and the U.S. However, there is one notable difference between the two countries that emerged in Atkinson and Murray's work: the love and marriage (family) value domain in Canada far outweighs financial concerns in terms of the overall quality of life, whereas in America financial concerns are given as much weight as family, work and leisure. Another of Atkinson and Murray's conclusions worth restating relates to social relationships, which are more highly valued in Canada, implying a greater level of caring for others; this ties in well with Stark's findings on social bonding. An earlier conception of America as "the achieving society" is supported by the cross-national comparison of mass values since work experiences are a much more prominant value domain in America than Canada.[41] Because status and achievement are closely associated with work in capitalist societies, this finding would lend credence to the belief that Americans are more status conscious and achievement oriented than are Canadians.

There does not appear to exist a systematic cross-national comparison of Canadian and American attitudes towards racial and ethnic minorities and social diversity within a population. Thus, with respect to prejudice and tolerance, we must draw on scant cross-national attitudinal items, on several which were not designed as comparisons, and on the risky drawing of behavioral inferences from non-behavioral data.[42] We can point to some empirical differences between the two countries in how people react to the social fact of race in a residential context (see Table 2-1). Canadians have also shown less propensity for moving if "colored people came to live in great numbers in your area."

From a comparison of racial prejudice in Britain and Canada, it appeared as if Canadians (at least a Toronto sample) were more accepting of persons such as East Indians and Blacks as a neighbor or a relative.[43] However, on a scale of racial prejudice, the distribution of the Toronto respondents in terms of their degree of prejudice was quite similar to that of the United Kingdom respondents. This suggests that situational determinants are important. If conditions in Toronto or other Canadian cities were more like those in British or American cities, one might expect a higher level of racial antipathy. A comparison of American and Canadian ethnic and racial rankings based on perceived social standing did not reveal any marked difference in the relative position of various groups.[44] Non-white persons are very clearly at the bottom in both countries. Furthermore, racism and housing discrimination against blacks, other non-whites and native Indians in Canadian cities certainly exists.[45] Given Canada's record in ethnic and race relations, one has to admit the possibility that if non-whites were as significant an urban minority as they are in many U.S. urban contexts, one might then find less willingness among Canadians to accept them as near-neighbors.

Nevertheless, racial relations in the U.S. have been widely documented as being extremely discriminatory and violent. The limited cross-national attitudinal data do suggest a more tolerant Canadian population, bearing in mind the caveat concerning situational conditions. A widespread acceptance of structural and cultural pluralism among immigrant minorities has been noted for Canada, allegedly because of the bicultural nature of the early colonial experience and the lesser pressures on the various immigrants to assimilate to Canadian ways, compared to assimilationist pressures in the U.S.[46] This is an issue to which we will return on more than one occasion in this book.

CONCLUSION

A number of themes arise from our selective review of values and culture in a cross-national context. These themes recur in the following chapters which more directly consider the social-demographic structure, economic organization and political institutions. There is always a risk in creating polar opposites for it invariably over-simplifies a situation. Such dichotomies can be useful, however, in drawing attention to where real communities or groups are located on some imagined continuum.

Individualism and Collectivism

This particular polarity might well be retitled Privatism and the Public Good. It concerns the primacy a people ascribe to certain values, the manner of their behavior consistent with these values, and the nature and practices of the institutions they create. For many scholars and commentators the celebration of the individual and the pervasive dominance of individualism is something that sets America apart as a place and as a society.[47] It certainly contrasts with a conception of Canada in which private interests and personal freedom exist in some kind of harmonious relationship with the imperatives of group maintenance: individual and social needs co-exist in a dynamic balance. The group orientation both within Canada and in the context of intra-continental relations (Canadians as a group vis-à-vis Americans) is of profound importance: "There is little doubt that the most impressive characteristic of Canadian social behaviour is our national, social and cultural dualism."[48] This orientation gives rise to the collectivism noted in many facets of Canadian life, which means that the public interest or good has become as important as the individual good.[49]

From this distinction, another important theme arises. What is the proper role of government? Historically and at present, the various governments in Canada have played a primary role or have functioned in partnership with private interests in many walks of life. Public and private interests historically, as in nineteenth-century railway expansion, and presently, as in suburban land development, tend to overlap. But there are times when these interests do not readily coincide. Governments have taken firm action on communitarian grounds and have intervened in market contexts on a scale that is hardly conceivable and probably politically impossible in the United States. Indeed, the interventionist tradition in the public sector in Canada gives rise to a particular federalism, an enduring trait of which has been friction and conflict between central and regional governments over their proper roles in many spheres. Even the most casual of observers would notice the relatively tranquil federal-state relations in the U.S.

In the United States, the government's role seems to be viewed in a different light. The primacy of private enterprise and initiative is not challenged; rather it is to be supported, with the government absorbing costs to make the engines of capitalism run ever more smoothly and profitably. Domestically, the larger policy debate hinges on the extent of public sector involvement in social issues and their solution. Here, there are genuine shades of difference within the American polity, but even under "liberal" Democratic administrations, state interventionism has not reached the level seen in Canada. Other opinion, currently in the ascendancy politically, seeks an even more circumscribed role for "big government" in a range of social programs but not in other important arenas, such as military expenditure, infrastructure for regional development and tax incentives for business.[50]

But one must approach these matters skeptically. Things are rarely as simple and clear as they seem. The collective orientation that exists in Canada does not mean Canada is a socialist country or is even tending in that direction, the electoral successes of the socialist New Democratic Party not withstanding. In fact, there is considerable evidence of privatism in Canada. Who could disagree with Allan Gotlieb, Canada's Ambassador to the U.S., when he states: "The fact is that in Canada as in the United States, the private sector has been and will remain the driving force behind economic development."[51] There is a good deal of mythology surrounding the role of government in America. The government has increasingly been involved in economic matters, periodically legislating, regulating and requiring private interests to respond to the dictates of the state. Public expenditures, particularly but not exclusively by the federal government, have transformed the face of America. Patterns of urban decline and regional growth have a relationship to many of these federally initiated public programs. As we will argue in more detail later, highway expenditures for freeway development had negative impacts on central-city residential areas. Again, who can doubt the necessity of massive public investment in water control, water supply and irrigation facilities for urban and regional growth to have attained present levels in California and other parts of the arid West? Private capital has been important in the growth of Florida, but so too has public investment in the space program. Significant private interests have benefited enormously from the strategic disbursement of federal largesse and protectionist legislation, no less in America than in Canada. What is not so immediately apparent is the plethora of public enterprises, or crown corporations, that exist in Canada.

Assimilation and Multiculturalism

There is a tendency in Canada to be more accepting of ethnic and racial differences and to permit, even encourage, their retention. Despite this, at various times in its history, Canada's residents have exhibited a decided intolerance. Asians were not welcome in British Columbia, and those already there were consistently devalued as human beings; Ku Klux Klan chapters flourished in parts of Canada; European Jews were callously denied entry at a time when a humanitarian response was vitally needed; anglophones (especially Orangemen) despised francophones, and vice versa. Set against this imperfect record, there is the increasingly multicultural and multi-racial nature of Canada's immigrants. Upon arrival, they find a society confused and troubled about its sense of purpose and direction and its identity. In the effort to hold the federation together, differences must be allowed full expression, and no group should be excluded. Thus, individuals are welcomed for what they can contribute to the mosaic; one must belong to some ethnic group to be patched into the mosaic. Equally welcome, we must observe, is the capital that often accompanies them or their skilled labor power—Canada is after all a capitalist society.

This stands in marked contrast to what has generally been an assimilationist posture in America, where there has been a deep-seated suspicion of differences and puzzlement over the retention of old ways and customs. "New people for a new land and the greatest democracy on earth" was much more the watchword. Immigrants had to be remade into Americans, which presupposed that an American identity existed. It did: at the risk of a stereotype, it was, and is, the free man, and later woman, who would be successful by dint of hard work and keen competition. In this romantic but very marketable vision, there were a number of freedoms: freedom of expression, of religion, of franchise, and perhaps for an entrepreneurial society most importantly, freedom to choose from what have been perceived as boundless opportunities. Social pressures and institutional practices, notably through the state-run schools, free from religious overtones, resulted in considerable conformity with this vision or its variants: off with the old and on with the new.

Now, it would be foolish to ignore assimilating processes at work in Canada, which certainly existed and continue to function. But linguistic and religious differences are generally accepted within an institutional context that would be difficult to imagine occurring in America. The state maintains separate English-language public schools in Quebec: one cannot conceive of California having Hispanic-language public schools. In Ontario, separate Catholic public schools are maintained alongside the secular public schools and have been maintained in separate and almost equal form for years. In the

U.S., to circumvent the separation of church and state, the notion of tax credits for fee-paying parents with children in private schools is advocated, but no direct action has yet been taken.

Finally, the pressure to homogenize America and Americans, related to the creation of large national markets for the retailing of goods and services, has worked against strong regional identities persisting in the U.S. These regional identities certainly exist and are not likely to fade away. Geographers and others write sensibly and with insight about Midwesterners, Californians and their respective locales, and indeed schools of regional scholarship are becoming increasingly respectable. But the political system does not reinforce regional identities and scholarship as it tends to in Canada. The remarkable postwar growth of all provincial administrations builds on regional allegiances and gives them a new and fuller expression; in urban terms, the provincial expansion is manifested in numerous central office towers devoted to public administration, part of the growth of the service economy. Thus, while geographers and others may think of the Prairies, there are important differences between the attitudes and postures of an Albertan of the last decade and a Saskatchewan resident attuned to the pragmatic socialism of that province. This does not discount their identification with Western Canada as against Central Canada or "the East." In contrast, one would hesitate before drawing such a distinction between residents of Montana and North Dakota.

Property Rights, Individual Responsibilities and Proper Behavior

The last theme revolves around a series of interrelated features. Until recently, Canadians had no Bill of Rights which guaranteed individual rights. There was a quasi-constitution in the form of the British North America Act, a piece of British legislation, and rights were protected through the body of Common and Statute Law. Here the Britannic continuity was very much in evidence. All authority ultimately resided in the Crown and its agents. Bureaucratic order was assured because individuals relied on the Crown to protect them and their rights which had arisen through convention. Thus, there was little sense in challenging this order as long as it was perceived to be acting fairly; challenges in the form of rebellions did arise, but they were perfunctory and fairly easily turned aside.[52] When the most obvious alternative was a lawless and disrespectful America—as superior Canadians were wont to portray it—why abandon the devil you know?[53]

Individual responsibilities did exist in Canada, but, following the notion of the organic society, the individual had a substantial obligation to the larger social group along with the responsibility to oneself. Thus, anti-social behavior was in a sense violence against oneself. This, together with a derivative respect for law and authority recognizing the latter's historic protectionist role, was likely a contributor to the more law-abiding nature of Canadians, at least with respect to crimes against persons. Proper behavior is perhaps easier to instill in Canadians than Americans. The latter seem to require more laws to achieve this effect. As Myrdal perceptively noted: "To demand and legislate all sorts of laws against this or that is just as much part of American freedom as to disobey the laws when they are enacted."[54]

For many, it is one of the chief glories of the American system that individual rights are enshrined in and protected by the Constitution, a document that has taken on enormous significance in America, especially in the sphere of social policy and state interventionism. Americans therefore do not have to rely upon appropriate behavior by government agents for their personal rights: they can demand that treatment conform with what is constitutionally prescribed. Of major significance for urban development in both countries is the constitutional protection of property rights in America, which is consistent with a society committed to individualism, and the absence of any similar protection of such rights in Canada. Even with the making of a new constitution and lobbying to this end, property rights were not constitutionally protected in Canada, and they remain vested in the Crown, a position consistent with the notion that the state has as its mandate the maintenance of the well-being of the civil society rather than the further-ance of individual liberty, happiness and economic gain. The implications of this difference for the control and development of urban land use will be elaborated in a later chapter.

Attitudinal indicators of the differences in what individual rights and responsibilities might mean in the two countries are to be found in the right to possess firearms and in the conception of appropriate punishment for crimes. Over a ten-year period, approximately three-quarters of Americans favored requiring the issuance of a police permit before a gun purchase could be made.[55] For one year in Canada for which there is a similar response, the proportion was 86 per cent. An overwhelming majority (80 per cent) of Canadians would forbid the possession of handguns, except for the police and other authorized persons, but only a minority of Americans (41 per cent) would take this position. Even when a law is passed in America forbidding the carrying of a concealed firearm, as in New York State, it is unenforceable. When laws are broken, Canadians demand stronger punish-ment.[56] Could this be because they subconsciously see the criminal act as violating the co-operative relationship between the individual and society? Or is the explanation again situational? With higher crime levels clearly apparent and experienced, Americans may have a lesser confidence in the deterrent effect of punitive sentences.

Veneration of authority figures in Canada, we might note whimsically, has

reached the point that one of the few national symbols recognizable throughout the world, courtesy of Hollywood, is the Mountie, a member of a
paramilitary federal police force, who paradoxically functions as the local
peace enforcement officer in over two hundred municipalities, including
some within the large metropolitan areas. Sadly, the image of American law
enforcement officers is not vested with much stature as a national symbol;
even the G-men have fallen on hard times.

SOME FURTHER URBAN IMPLICATIONS

Despite the difficulty of drawing conclusions from socio-cultural analysis
and essays, there does seem to be a consensus that Canadians are more
accepting of authority figures than Americans. These figures constitute an
important element in the Canadian elite, a widely studied group. Nowhere is
the central and enduring nature of the Canadian establishment more clearly
revealed in the landscape than in the replication of upper-class suburbs at
the edge of the nineteenth-century Canadian city under the control of the
builders of the Canadian Pacific Railway. In a number of cities, notably
Vancouver, Calgary, Winnipeg and Montreal, CPR planners created what
they thought should be the ideal residential landscape for the civic elite,
including the upper managerial echelons of the railroad. This uniformity,
which is still evident as these districts have been maintained as high-status
residential areas through land-use controls implemented by sympathetic
civic administrators, has resulted in a phenomenon that is far less common in
American cities—the location in what is now the inner area of the city of a
highly valued residential location with single-family homes in a countrified
setting.

A second element in our argument follows from the conception of Canada
as an organic society, predicated on material interest and dependence, as
contrasted with a society where individual self-interest remains paramount.
This is revealed in the nature and history of the development of co-operative
housing in the respective urban centers. Though still a minority feature in
the overall urban housing stock, increasing numbers of co-operative housing
units have been built in Canada with both federal and provincial assistance
in most of the principal urban centers since 1973. This subsidized housing is
mostly built on a "not for profit" basis, so that when someone moves out of
the co-operative, he or she does not, and does not expect to, make a capital
gain on the exchange of his or her personal residence. In contrast, co-operative
housing in America is largely of the market type, where, as in other forms of
property ownership, the individual seeks and hopes for a capital gain upon
resale. The U.S. federal government, despite its history of subsidizing housing,

has never promoted co-operative housing as has been done by all levels of the public sector in Canada.

Pursuing the individualistic-collectivistic distinction leads to the position that governments in Canada have acted on communitarian grounds more often and with greater effect than in the United States. One of the sharpest contrasts is in the provision of health care, with Canada having what is undoubtedly viewed in the American context as "socialized medicine." One might expect therefore a rather different geographic pattern in the provision of medical services within cities. While there is little in the way of direct cross-national evidence, the work of deVise on the social and spatial inequalities in the provision of health care in the American city and the recent work of Rosenberg suggest some cross-national differences.[57] In short, the welfare state takes many forms within the city, and we would expect it to be more evident in the Canadian city than in the U.S. This greater collective sense may also be reflected in the provision of public open space and recreation facilities. Contrast what generally appears to be a low level of park provision by suburban municipalities in the U.S., a lack which is offset by private clubs and private play equipment on generally larger suburban lots, with a high quality of park provision in many Canadian suburban municipalities, rivalling in certain instances, the established parks of the central city.

TABLE 2-1
RACIAL CHANGE AND RESIDENTIAL RELOCATION

	Yes, Definitely		Per cent Answer[1] Yes, Might		No	
	Canada	USA[2]	Canada	USA	Canada	USA
1963	3	20	5	25	91	55
1965		13		22		65
1966		13		21		66
1967		12		23		65
1969	4		6		90	
1975	3		6		91	

[1]The question posed was "If colored people came to live next door, would you move your home?"
[2]The question is put only to white people in the USA.

Source: Alex C. Michalos, *North American Social Report: Volume 5, Economics, Religion and Morality* (Boston: D. Reidel, 1982), Table 32, 206.

3

SOCIAL AND DEMOGRAPHIC STRUCTURES IN CANADA AND THE UNITED STATES

There are a number of broad but interrelated purposes to this chapter. The first is to compare the ethnic and racial character of the two societies, giving explicit attention to religion and language as they serve to further differentiate Canada from the United States. This particular comparison also necessitates consideration of immigration. Although immigration is a common and important process, in terms of its impact on evolving social structures and increasingly upon cities, some important distinctions emerge. Secondly, we comment upon class structure. Neither society is thought to be "class-ridden" in comparison to those in Europe, for example. Indeed, American society has been characterized as "classless", although this view has been criticized as being an almost self-fulfilling requirement of an open, fluid society permitting upward social mobility. It should be obvious, but it can stand repeating, that the class structure in the two countries is not independent of the ethnic and racial composition of the two populations. Our third purpose is to compare demographic characteristics in the light of population trends since World War II and especially those of the last two decades. Finally, a commentary is provided on the relative levels of satisfaction-dissatisfaction with life in cities in Canada and the United States. Such a concluding commentary is far from gratuitous since one's feelings about the places in which one lives, about oneself and about one's society and country are really inseparable. These matters provide some keys to an understanding of ethnic and racial residential segregation, of neighborhoods, of housing patterns and of residential movement and urban decline, to list but a few important urban phenomena. This chapter challenges the popular position that these two countries have "quite similar societies (and economies)."[1]

IMMIGRANTS AND IMMIGRATION

For the student of cities and societies in North America, immigration is a central process. The ethnic, racial, linguistic and religious diversity of both American and Canadian society is perhaps the most obvious outcome of centuries of immigration. Persistent tension between resident populations and newcomers is another. Immigration is therefore an important foundation for understanding both societies. Furthermore, in the last century, immigrants have overwhelmingly been destined for urban locations, contributing greatly to rapid growth. Both countries have had a similar experience; since immigrants are primarily interested in material advancement and greater freedom from religious, economic or political persecution, the city is the key destination. In the last twenty years, immigrant streams have been particularly biased towards the largest metropolitan areas. In these receiving cities there has been a profound transformation in the degree of variability in social life. It is to such places as New York, Chicago, Los Angeles, the San Francisco Bay Area, Toronto, Vancouver and Montreal that the word cosmopolitan most aptly applies.

Immigration is not an uncontrolled or undirected process, entry having been controlled for decades. Who gets in and in what numbers is a function of bureaucratic decision-making in the implementation of immigration policies.[2] The most glaring exception is the illegal immigration into the United States, mostly but not entirely Hispanic, from and through Mexico. There are a probably significant but unknown number of illegal immigrants in major Canadian metropolitan areas, especially Toronto. But it is unlikely that these illegals approximate in scale the American situation. Despite this important exception, selective controls and the administrative organization of the immigration process have been the source of an important cross-national difference in terms of the composition of the immigrant groups.

It is incontestable that until recently Canadian immigration policy has encouraged and favored immigration from Britain and to a lesser extent from the United States. This is much less the case in the United States where immigrants from Britain, while preferred and not unimportant either in numbers or subsequent influence, were only one national group amongst many. Only once since 1900 has the percentage of immigrants to the U.S. from Great Britain been more than 10 per cent (12.8 per cent in 1930), whereas in Canada the lowest that proportion has ever been since 1900 is 12.5 per cent (coincidentally also in 1930).

Although there have been major changes in Canadian immigration policies in the last fifteen years, Britain remains a leading source country. In 1982, for example, immigrants from Britain were almost double those from the next leading source country—the U.S.A.—and accounted for about 13 per cent of all immigrants. As this relatively low proportion, in historic terms, indicates, the immigration stream is more diverse than previously.

There are a number of important consequences that follow from this historic bias. The first is that the Britannic continuity has been maintained. The second is that the anglophone population has been reinforced in a manner quite different from the francophone one. It is more than likely that most of these British newcomers would hold little sympathy for or understanding of French-Canadian aspirations. This would buttress existing antipathies among English-speaking Canadians. A third consequence has been a more or less steady inflow of people with a democratic socialist ideology. The history of Canada's socialist movements shows British immigrants figuring prominently. This strand has been of value in developing socialist political parties in Canada and in their electoral success in contrast to the experience in the United States where socialism was more readily labelled "foreign" and "bolshevik," one factor contributing to its political vulnerability and demise.

In sum, Canada remains much more "British" than the U.S. partly as a consequence of differences in immigration policies. In ancestral terms, the two Canadian charter groups still account in 1981 for two-thirds of the population (40 per cent British and 26 per cent French—although this is an historic low for the British component).

The immigration data reveal a notable, absolute and proportional increase in non-European immigration. The diversity of source countries is shown in recent tabulations (Table 3-1). A predominantly bicultural Canada, having already absorbed a substantial, even spectacular, Italian immigration in the 1951 to 1971 period (to the degree that Italian now ranks as Canada's third most spoken language), now faces a significant non-white migration stream. While the total number of non-whites is still relatively small in relation to the total population (combining various categories of persons yields a proportion of 3.1 in 1971 and 5.0 in 1981), their visibility and urban concentration makes resident Canadians aware of a new dimension in the immigrant stream—race relations rather than purely ethnic ones become increasingly important.[3]

One must be careful in suggesting this new dimension in the immigrant flow as an important difference between the two societies. Most Canadians undoubtedly think of America's race relations as not only problematic but domestic in nature, the legacy of the colonial importation of labor. But the proportion of immigrants from predominantly non-white countries has also risen sharply in the U.S. in recent years, adding to and diversifying the non-white population in America. In 1978, for example, there were about 310,000 immigrants who might be classed as non-white. This represents an increase of roughly 110 per cent over 1970 data. But these numbers pale into relative insignificance when we observe that America's non-white population in 1980 was approximately 36.5 million. Herein does lie a central cross-national difference — the legal immigration process, at least at the national level, now has a relatively modest aggregate impact in the U.S. and is only locationally important to the extent that non-white immigrants cluster in specific urban places, such as Koreans in Los Angeles but, interestingly, not the Thais.[4] In Canada, however, the shift in immigration source regions has been instrumental in creating a meaningful, albeit non-homogeneous, non-white minority in the national context and engendering new ethnic residential and working patterns within certain metropolitan areas, such as Toronto and Vancouver, while by-passing others, such as Halifax or Quebec City.

Two further points direct us to additional cross-national differences in social composition. The increase in ethnic diversity in Canada after World War II, consequent upon the relative decline of Britain and the U.S. as the dominant sources of immigrants, meant an increasing strain on the conception of Canada as a bicultural society or nation. The growing clamor from ethnic groups outside the two charter groups encouraged the federal government to adopt the position that Canada is a multicultural society. This was officially encoded in policy statements, the creation of a minor federal ministry for multiculturalism, and modest budget appropriations. This framework was being put in place at the very time when immigrant policies were resulting in an even greater multicultural presence emerging in the 1970s. Although pluralism is valued in America, it is not officially promulgated and fostered by federal expenditures.

The second point is that the immigration process affects the two societies differently because of population scale difference. Data from Michalos are again helpful—they show that the standardized immigration rate in Canada from 1964 to 1974 was almost four times that of the United States.[5] Even prior to 1926, when the U.S. sharply curtailed immigration, Canada was, in a sense, even more of an immigrant society than the U.S.—"While the United States had ninety-two people to absorb each immigrant, Canada had only sixteen" (this was in 1912).[6] But many immigrants were British, more readily accepted than the polyglot arrivals at Ellis Island and elsewhere in the United States. Foreign immigration produced nativist movements in both countries. However, in political and experiential terms, the American nativists had a more negative impact on the newcomers than did their Canadian counterparts.

It is in this sense of coping with the newcomers that one can assert that Canada is more of an immigrant society. In proportional terms, newcomers as a meaningful social category bulk larger in Canada than they do in the U.S. Thus, for Canadians and their institutions immigration poses more of a challenge to the indigenous capacity to absorb the influx, bearing in mind that some of the influx is and always has been bound for the U.S.—for many, Canada is but a stepping stone. This social challenge has grown in recent decades, and the multiculturalist position is one response, growing instances of racial discrimination another. Equally important is the realization that at any given time, newcomers are a modest proportion of the total population. As Kalbach and McVey demonstrate, only in the first decade of this century were immigrants ever more than 20 per cent of the population.[7] But these statistics must be tempered with the knowledge that many in the host population are only one or two generations away from newcomers. In this, Canada and the United States are quite similar in nature but different in degree. The relatively large proportion of immigrants in Canada's population is a contributory factor to an understanding of cross-national differences in ethnicity. As will be seen in the next section, the greater importance of ethnic categories and identities in Canada is in part a function of this need to incorporate a proportionally significant number of newcomers.

ETHNICITY

A more pervasive sense of ethnicity differentiates Canadian and American society. There is unfortunately no systematic cross-national comparison on which to base this assertion. Rather, it rests upon a synthesis of certain sociological and other literature. The meaning and measurement of ethnicity are contentious matters, and the non-specialist must tread warily. Certain key questions quickly arise. We have seen the relatively greater impact of immigration in demographic terms alone in Canada. The higher rate of immigration has been a powerful feature in maintaining an effective demand for inner city residences, especially in cities like Toronto and Vancouver which continue to be leading destinations. In some instances, the extended immigrant family is ideally matched with an older housing stock built for a larger family than is now found in Canadian cities,[8] as in the U.S. and elsewhere. Is a sense of ethnic identity maintained through such immigration, and is it actively reflected in the urban landscape, as in the federal policy of multiculturalism? In contrast, is ethnicity fading as a relevant social fact in the U.S., and are ethnic areas in the U.S. cities aging and becoming less "ethnic"?

At one level, the ethnic composition of Canadian society is readily determined through the decennial census. Given our previous discussion of immigration, the distribution and trends of the major ethnic categories should not be too surprising. From 1871 to 1981, there has been a systematic decline in the proportion of people of British and Irish ethnic origin, a fairly stable situation in terms of the French ethnic origin group, and a steady increase in the proportion of people who claim an ethnic origin different from the two so-called charter groups. Despite these changes, the British Isles group (though far from homogeneous and with strong antipathies, such as that between Irish and English) remains proportionately dominant. This ethnic group also dominates in other than demographic ways as numerous studies of Canada's elite have shown (see Chapter 2, n. 10). In contrast, French Canadians have been almost equalled demographically by what were once referred to as New Canadians — a most inadequate and misleading label.

This non-British, non-French group is not homogeneous. Post World War II immigration at least initially was predominantly European in character. In 1971, people of German origin, who have been the leading non-charter ethnic group since 1871, were more than twice as numerous as the next populous group— Italians. Those claiming Italian ethnic origin only moved into this position as recently as 1971, following two decades during which their number increased by 380 per cent, from roughly 150,000 to about 730,000. There has also been an Asian presence in Canada since the late nineteenth century. This group, though modest in numbers, occasioned considerable hostility and discriminatory legislation, mostly in British Columbia where the Chinese, Japanese and Sikhs congregated. Of late, this category has increased dramatically, by about 290 per cent from 1951 to 1971. It is important to differentiate within this category between Chinese from the Crown Colony of Hong Kong, from the People's Republic of China, and from Taiwan, as well as between immigrants from the Indian subcontinent— Sikhs, Hindus and others.

There is however a certain unreality about these data. For the Canadian resident whose male ancestor came from Scotland or the Rhine Palatinate in the mid-nineteenth century, what does this ethnic origin mean? Perhaps it means a great deal, not much, or even nothing. Furthermore, the denial of the matrilineal ethnic origin is arbitrary—in cultural terms, that particular ethnicity may be much more important, such as in transmission of folkways. In the 1981 census, officialdom has relented by not restricting ethnic origin to the paternal side. Also, multiple ethnic origin responses were retained for tabulation for the first time. Although this option was available, just over 90 per cent of the population identified with a single ethnic origin. Is it that old habits die hard or that there are indeed strong affinities to a unique ethnic identity? For answers to these and other questions of ethnic identity one must go beyond the census, to surveys and attitudinal investigations.

Before doing so, it should be noted that, in contrast, the American census-takers appear to have believed that ethnic measurement was too difficult or that to ask Americans about their ethnic origins was almost un-American.[9] Whatever the reason, no question on ethnicity was asked until 1980, when persons were asked to self-identify their ancestry group. Multiple responses were retained for tabulation so that dominant multiple groups could be identified. The results are interesting and provide a rough comparison with Canadian data. Single group identifiers only accounted for 52 per cent of the population (see Table 3-2). The multiple ancestry group contained just under one-third of all persons. The remainder, about 17 per cent, included those not reporting an ancestry group and those responding "American." As in Canada, the leading single ethnic group was English, but only one-tenth so responded in the U.S. compared to about one-quarter in Canada. However, one must take into account the fact that "English and others" was one of the top three multiple ancestry groups in the U.S. (the others being "Irish and others," second, and "German and others," first). On balance, it is likely that the British ethnic group, excluding the Irish, is more important in Canada. Italians on the other hand are a more important group in the United States. Their single ancestry group equals that in Canada, proportionately speaking, and "Italians and others" is a significant but not leading multiple ancestry category. Although the data are not collected in a directly comparable fashion, there is little doubt that Jewish people are demographically more important in the U.S. Thus, despite the need for further detailing, we would still conclude that there is a cross-national difference in the ethnic composition.

But we are also left grasping at the meaningfulness of these ethnic labels. Is ethnicity mythical in nature, its legendary but unverifiable character obscuring more important cleavages such as race and class? All we can do here is to encapsulate, in a limited way, the principal views in both countries.[10] Conventional theory suggests that the strong and continuous pressures to conform and assimilate that were part of nation-building in the United States broke down ethnic identity—people came to think of themselves as Americans. The ethos of individualism to which the immigrant was already receptive, having moved outside the cultural hearth, further encouraged a decline in group identity. Recently, a contrary view has emerged which argues that ethnicity is persistent and important. Diversity was and is an important element of the American social experience—the "unmeltable ethnics" are seen as one dimension of American pluralism. Alternatively, ethnicity is seen as a conscious and active choice, even an affectation perhaps, something that can be put off or taken up again. Such a rise in ethnic awareness among whites is apparent in the face of growing demands by some black Americans to be treated as an ethnic group. In a society supposedly characterized by individualism, blacks, above all, are not likely to be treated on an individual basis but as stereotypical members of a group, and a low-status one at that.

In Canada a different situation seems to have prevailed.[11] The European immigrant, who was quickly categorized as a member of a national group, arrived in a society where the group was enormously important—language, above all, was the membership card. In an important study, Allan Smith emphasizes the importance of the group in the ascendancy of the ethnic idea.[12] But important cleavages were discernible. Some of these were religious in nature, such as between Scotch-Irish Protestant and Irish Catholic, others were locational, such as between Italians from the north of Italy and those from the south, while still others were temporal, such as between German Jews and East European or Russian Jews. To a degree, the group identity was externally imposed as a result of the inability of the receiving population to differentiate sufficiently between the immigrant sub-groups.[13]

While it is true that this occurred in both Canada and the United States, a prominent Canadian ethnic scholar notes an important difference. For Isajiw, the concept of an ethnic boundary which defines the group is useful, and he extends this notion by conceptualizing a double boundary "[one] from within, maintained by the socialization process, and a boundary from without established by the process of intergroup relations."[14] The critical cross-national difference lies in the externally imposed boundaries. He implies that there is a difference in how various ethnic groups are perceived and identified by residents of the two host societies; of special importance is the view held, and the labels used, by the existing elites.

A comparative perspective on how residents view ethnic groups is available. A few years ago, the sociologist Pineo observed that there is no consensus concerning the status condition of ethnic groups either amongst Canadian or American scholars.[15] Since the respondents in the Canadian survey were separated into English-speaking and French-speaking, an interesting comparison within Canada is also available. There is a high degree of similarity between the ratings of ethnic groups by English-speaking Canadians and a sample of U.S. residents. There is one notable difference, however, consistent with a point made elsewhere in this chapter—English-speaking Canadians ascribe a superior ethnic status to those labelled British. There is no evidence of such exceptional status ranking in U.S. studies, nor is there an equivalent to the colloquial term "English-Canadian." Relatedly, Pineo reports that among English-speaking Canadians, English Catholics exhibited more difference from the overall rankings than for other compositional categories. This reinforces the notion that religion matters a good deal—an issue we take up later. French-speaking respondents developed a ranking system substantially different from that of anglophones. Thus, if one were to compare cross-nationally with no separation within the categories "Canadian" and American, a difference in ethnic rankings would emerge. At a gross level, this would seem to support Isajiw's position. But one wonders if the within-nation variations are not more important than the between-nation differences. Nevertheless, important cross-national differences in the social world of ethnics persist, despite some obvious commonalities of experience for newcomers with a distinctive national origin. In commenting on the Ukrainian experience, Isajiw conveys this well:

> Ukrainian immigrants, both in the U.S. and in Canada, entered the social structure of the respective societies at its bottom. However, there are many important differences in the way Ukrainians entered the two societies. These differences have to do with the type of occupations they have been funnelled into, the state of economic development of the two countries, the role that the governments played in bringing immigrants into the country, prevalent ideologies of assimilation and patterns of dealing with ethnic prejudices.[16]

We return finally and briefly to multiculturalism. Multiculturalism has been enshrined in Canadian federal public policy, and publicly supported cultural pluralism is manifest at both provincial and local levels. Whether or not this is simply good politics and devoid of real meaning or a true reflection of an important dimension of social life is for the specialists to debate.[17] Taking the phenomenon at face value, we can say that ethnicity and the associated diversity or pluralism are officially valued. Ethnic identification, according to certain surveys, is widespread—nationally, over 30 and 40 per cent respectively, of the third and second generation, identify themselves as ethnic or "hyphenated" Canadians.[18] Activities designed to promote multiculturalism such as parades, festivals, and, more significantly, "heritage" language programs have the potential to heighten a sense of ethnicity. They reinforce the external boundaries by emphasizing "cultural differences" among Canadians, and they support the internal boundary by aiding the socialization process. Whether or not this is desirable will continue to be debated.

In the United States, ethnicity is a concept contested amongst scholars, and there is no official recognition of cultural or ethnic pluralism at the federal level. Indeed, as ethnic diversity increases in the United States, we witness a re-emergence of an "America first" sentiment, one that could become more widespread.[19] One urban illustration is found in Dade County, Florida, which contains the City of Miami and constitutes a large part of the Miami metropolitan area. With an exceptionally high voter turnout, a referendum was passed in 1980 prohibiting languages other than English in official business. Also prohibited is the use of county funds "for promoting any culture other than that of the United States." Implicit in this position, adopted in a county where about 40 per cent of the residents are Spanish-speaking, is the dominance of English and the existence of a national culture. In Canada, the linguistic dominance of English is continuously confronted by French-English bilingualism and unilingual French speakers. Secondly, if Canada has a national culture, a collective self-portrait, it is likely to be intrinsically more fragmented than that of its self-confident, powerful neighbor.

In contrast to such an explicit public reaction, it is fair to say that on balance that the arrival of new people in Canadian cities has been accommodated and, paradoxically, that ethnic residential segregation is neither feared nor despised. While we know of no systematic comparable data, it is our suspicion that immigrant Canadians may have less desire to move out of somewhat ethnic districts for the more heterogeneous suburbs than their American counterparts. The pitfalls of generalizing about ethnic residential segregation in urban areas are illustrated by Agocs's study of Detroit and by Driedger's work in Winnipeg.[20] Both demonstrate quite different patterns of settlement and community development, depending upon ethnic group. There is little evidence that there is any universal pattern of ethnic residence or that assimilation necessarily implies dispersal to the suburbs. Reviewing a scattering of local case studies leads us to conclude tentatively that a higher degree of ethnic residential segregation persists in Canadian cities. Other than for black and Hispanic populations, segregation is generally declining for American ethnics— the ethnic community may persist, but pronounced residential clustering seems now to be less of a prerequisite. As long as the principal organizational elements of ethnic communities in Canada are located in the central cities, there is a powerful element fostering positive household growth, offsetting suburbanization, and checking so-called counter-urbanization.

LANGUAGE

Language is an important social differentiator. Canada is officially a bilingual state, while the United States is unilingual and remains determinedly so. Despite the rapid increase in Hispanic-speaking peoples in the United States, the concept of official bilingualism still is marginal—as one commentator noted, "it is very limited in scope and grudgingly granted".[21] The Hispanic population is simply one of the the latest in a long line of non-English-speaking groups to take up residence in the United States. They, as were their predecessors, are subject to public, institutional and market pressures to use English as soon as possible. By the third or fourth generation, Spanish has almost completely been lost among Chicanos, and language shift is promoted by the transfer of school pupils from bilingual to monolingual classes as soon as their English skills permit. This stands in contrast to the Canadian experience, most notably of course in Quebec. In Quebec, the retention of language across many generations is supported by a dual school system designed to educate francophones and anglophones in their native language throughout their education. In Quebec and to a much more limited extent elsewhere, post-secondary education is also available totally in French.

The existence of two official languages in Canada results in a major social cleavage; no such substantial linguistic division exists in the United States. This rift is expressed in geographic, economic and political ways, all of which are interrelated. Geographically, the most striking feature is the pronounced regional concentration of francophones, overwhelmingly in Quebec with significant outlying clusters in Northern and Eastern Ontario and in New Brunswick, where the culturally distinctive Acadians see themselves as different from the Quebecois.[22] This historic concentration has been a necessary condition for the preservation of the language. The language has been seen, even more than religion, as the symbol and instrument for the survival of the "French fact" in North America. Formerly appropriated as a central goal by the Catholic Church, survival is now in the hands of the state, which controls the educational system and.has passed legislation intended to make French the language of work and not just the language of home and the street. Language becomes even more enmeshed with politics because of the geographic correspondence between the regional concentration of francophones and an increasingly activist Quebec state.

But language is also a major and divisive national political issue. The attempts of the federal government, especially under Pierre Trudeau's leadership, to create a more truly bilingual federal state and to protect the language rights of francophones outside Quebec have met with resentment, although successes have been achieved. New Brunswick has become an officially bilingual province, and Manitoba has sought to restore bilingualism and language rights which were arbitrarily revoked by a predominantly anglophone power structure in the late nineteenth century. French radio and television services have been established in a number of major metropolitan centers, changing in a modest way the ambiance of these places. Ottawa, the federal capital, is more of a bilingual place than formerly, and the incorporation of Hull, in Quebec, with Ottawa into the National Capital Region, together with expansion of federal offices into Hull, has only served to accentuate this. Nevertheless, English remains dominant among the majority of the public service sector, even there.

It is not necessary here to detail the resentments expressed by many anglophones and non-English-speaking immigrants. The latter cannot understand the historical and current necessity for the preservation and promotion of French. They resent its advancement and "special status"—for them, Canada is an English-speaking country, and they are more concerned about the preservation and use of their own language than French, it being foreign and remote from their daily experience unless they have migrated to Quebec. Increasingly, the Quebec government is forcing immigrants toward French and away from English, which had been the preferred choice for the majority of immigrants.

Given that most immigrants have chosen to reside in Canada's major cities, Montreal emerges as a unique place within Canada, even North America. The great majority of Quebec's anglophones dwell in the Montreal metropolitan area and remain largely residentially separate from the French-speaking population.[23] This duality is complicated by the various immigrant groups, themselves bi- or tri-lingual. Thus, the pattern of residential segregation is both ethnic and linguistic, since the new immigrants have clustered, at least initially, in a geographic and cultural niche between the anglophone and the francophone populations. Although the bulk of the immigrant population adopted English, in the main they were and are socially and economically separate from the Anglo-Scottish and Anglo-American elites which have controlled the entrepreneurial and financial empires based in Montreal.

In one of Canada's principal metropolitan centers and in a variety of lesser industrial and resource towns in Quebec, language intertwines with class — an important relationship that inexplicably eludes some neo-Marxist anglophone writers on class.[24] English-speaking elites by virtue of their class dominance had little reason to learn French. In their own social sphere they were unilingual, and in the world of work they could be sure that their francophone subordinates would of necessity become bilingual. Even outside the corporate/industrial context, English was often dominant in services and retailing—for example, in Montreal's downtown.[25] French could be used, however, in certain occupational groupings that primarily served French residential sectors. Beyond Montreal, however, francophones predominate, and the existence of a significant unilingual population not restricted to the working class is a distinctive social fact. In sum, language use and its socio-political and economic contexts differentiates Canada from America. Understanding bilingualism in Canada does not mean one understands Spanish-English bilingualism in the U.S., and explanatory transfer would be inappropriate. Language in Canada is no mere epiphenomenal cultural issue to be explained away by overly deterministic thinking. The consequences of this social fact which constitutes a major cleavage are as profound for Canada and particularly urban Quebec as race relations are a vitally important issue for urban America.

RELIGION

Religion for many people is an important part of social life. For some, it is the anchor for their spiritual and social life; for an increasing number of others it is irrelevant. In certain respects, important cross-national differences exist between Canada and the U.S. on religious matters. Despite recent attempts to connect religious values with organized politics, America is characterized by a legal separation of secular and religious life, following the First Amendment of the Constitution. The separation has not been as sharp nor as clear as the statute mandates. Nevertheless, it is an important principle, and one that remains deeply etched in Americans' beliefs about the nature of their society.

There is no such separation in Canada in terms of legal declarations, either during the colonial era or in more recent decades. Canada was long viewed by Canadians as "a Christian society with Anglo Saxon Protestant and French Catholic spheres of influence."[26] This is another social dimension of the fundamental duality. Yet, this characterization has come under pressure from at least three directions: the decline in religious identification in historically important denominations; the increasing number of non-French Catholics; and the growth of other non-Protestant and non-Catholic denominations. Again, the impact of immigration on the last two is profound. It is clear that at least historically English-French tensions were amplified by religious antipathies. That Quebec was Catholic and Ontario Protestant, even Orange in important instances, has prevented, among other things, a sense of cohesion and common cause within the working class in central Canada. The religious identification of an important element of organized labor in Quebec has further accentuated this split.[27]

The difference in the status of religion in relation to the state is reflected in the absence of a question on religious affiliation in the American census in contrast to its presence in the Canadian one. Thus, other, more idiosyncratic sources must be relied on for the U.S., making comparison difficult. Michalos does attempt such a comparison.[28] His data, although weak for the U.S., indicate that Canada is a much more Catholic country than the U.S. but is decidedly less Jewish. This is particularly the case with Catholicism when private survey takers asked for a statement on religious preference. What this difference means is difficult to say, especially in terms of its meaning for cities, since U.S. data are difficult to obtain on a systematic basis.

One consequence of note in Canada, especially evident in certain cities, is the existence of publicly supported but separate school systems, the separation being based on religious grounds. While there seems to be in the United States, at a highly impressionistic level, growth in popular support for this kind of dual public school system, it has yet to be attempted. Not every province maintains such a system, but outside of Quebec, the most extensive dual system exists in Ontario. The two-and-one-half million Catholics in that province are served by fifty separate school boards registering some 430,000 elementary students. Under the British North America Act, the Catholic school boards received full public financing for an elementary education system.[29] In Metropolitan Toronto and a few other urban centers the boards received additional support for grades 9 and 10. In 1984, the Ontario government announced that it will move to full financing of the Catholic schools, placing the separate school system on an equal footing with the public, non-denominational schools in response to the changed political reality of an increasingly immigrant Catholic composition of the Ontario urban population, especially in Toronto.

Interestingly, given the difference in separation between secular and religious life noted above, more Americans consider themselves to be very religious than Canadians (26 per cent to 14 per cent) and seem to value religion more highly.[30] In terms of church attendance, however, less than ideal data show no cross-national difference of substance during the past decade, although there was such a difference as recently as the 1960s. Where a striking difference does arise is in the American fundamentalism that is expressed in opinion sampling on religious beliefs. This is quite possibly related to a greater moral and perhaps even political conservatism evident in the U.S.[31]

RACE

There is hardly a more divisive social fact in America than race and race relations. The white-black duality is as important to Americans as the French-English duality is to Canadians. Although parallels are not especially helpful and can in fact mislead, there is no doubt that a "them and us" mentality with potential for violent confrontation has developed in both countries as a result of these deep cleavages.

It is not our purpose to review the extent of racial divisiveness in America. From classic studies such as Myrdal's *The American Dilemma* to presidential commissions such as the *National Advisory Commission on Civil Disorders*, the extent of racial discrimination in American social life and its consequences are well known. Despite evidence from public opinion sampling of a growing racial tolerance among white Americans,[32] various institutional practices have proven to be remarkably persistent. Of particular interest is the functioning of urban housing markets. American housing economists still argue over the importance of racial discrimination in housing markets.[33] It would appear from a small but growing literature that this is one issue to which Canadian urbanists will have to devote increased attention.

Although racial and ethnic cleavages are important in both countries, the geographical distribution of the key groups involved is strikingly different. The regional concentration of francophones in Canada means that only in a few distinctive regions is there a great deal of contact; this, as we asserted, is what makes Montreal so fascinating to an urbanist, yet strangely neglected by many anglophone urbanists. In contrast, non-whites in America, and particularly blacks, are not as concentrated regionally. The classic or "traditional South" does remain racially distinctive because of a sizable rural black population, not found to any significant extent in other regions (Table 3-3), but blacks and other non-whites live in significant numbers in the principal metropolitan centers throughout America. Hence, the potential for contact is great compared to French/English language contact in metropolitan Canada. But this potential is counter-acted by the sharp residential separation by race within metropolitan centers. The black population is still overwhelmingly concentrated in the central cities of the metropolitan regions and even within specific neighborhoods of these cities. The ghetto districts, square mile upon square mile of almost solidly black residences, are perhaps the clearest geographic expression of this duality. Despite convincing evidence of an increased racial tolerance in America, the geographic separation of the races by residence means that in the everyday world of private consumption, a largely segregated society exists.

An important national survey of the quality of community life attests to this and further documents the difficulty of overcoming this geographic separation within American cities.[34] Almost 90 per cent of the white respondents lived in predominantly white neighborhoods, and a majority of black respondents (55 per cent) lived in all or mostly minority districts. While about one-third of the black respondents said they lived in neighborhoods which were racially balanced, it must be borne in mind that some were districts in transition, destined to become almost exclusively black in composition. The persistence of this segregation by residence seems likely when white Americans overwhelmingly state that they prefer white neighborhoods (75 per cent), whereas only a quarter of the black respondents prefer mostly or all black neighborhoods. Taking racially balanced neighborhoods as a crude indicator of integration, such a neighborhood is clearly desired by blacks (57.2 per cent) but *not* by whites (only 15.5 per cent). Action on the part of blacks, especially those in the middle class, to move into these elusive neighborhoods is continually frustrated by white avoidance of such areas. This engenders a new round of racially motivated musical chairs, and when the music stops, the racial separation by residential districts in cities persists.

There is probably greater racial contact at work and in the schools than in the residential districts. However, this integration was achieved only with federal intervention through legal instruments. School integration has been politically damaging to the Democratic Party because of its identification as pro-busing, and it has also led to that classic privatist response, withdrawal.[35] This withdrawal occurs both from public schools to various private schools, with soaring enrolments resulting for some of the latter and accelerated pupil declines for the former, and from the residential districts of the cities to almost racially pure suburbs with predominantly white school enrolments.

In the previous chapter, we saw some evidence that Canadians were more racially tolerant than Americans. But the situational differences are so great that it may be relatively easy for Canadians to express tolerant attitudes. Future action or practice in concrete situations may be very different from responses to abstract questions. Nevertheless, Canada is becoming a more racially diverse society, and its multiracial character is most evident in its central cities. But in Toronto, as Kalbach has demonstrated, the combined West Indian and Negro group is less segregated residentially than certain other groups.[36] More casual empirical evidence from centers such as Edmonton and Winnipeg suggests that white Canadians shun residential areas with increasing concentrations of Asian Indians and native peoples.[37] The consequent formation of small ghettoes cannot be entirely discounted. In subsequent chapters, we present some data on the non-white proportion in Canadian cities in comparison to those in the U.S. During the last decade, the non-white proportions in fact have grown substantially in the principal metropolitan centers. To illustrate, the Asian percentage of metropolitan Vancouver's population has risen from 3.1 per cent in 1961, to 5.4 per cent in 1971, to 8.2 per cent in 1981. In addition to non-white immigration, there has been a marked urban increase in another element of the non-white population — native peoples. Certain places are much more affected than others; proportionately, the most important concentrations are in the inner cities of Winnipeg and Regina. Conditions there are approaching those of such American cities as Minneapolis, Oklahoma City, Tulsa and Albuquerque, which contain groupings of urban Indians.

While this is a pronounced and visible change within Canada, chiefly in the big cities, a balanced view reminds us that Canada is overwhelmingly a white country. Non-whites tend to be viewed more as another ethnic group than as a discrete racial category, and reference is made to immigration issues rather than social class matters within the country.[38] Here, then, is another marked cross-national contrast, since race and class are inextricably mingled within America. Furthermore, race is an important variable in the demographic structure of American society, particularly in the metropolitan component. In short, race is a vitally important compositional category in America and is historically important. In Canada, it has only recently emerged as a category with much significance and even now pales beside the linguistic and religious cleavages.[39]

CLASS STRUCTURE

For those who claim a basic similarity between American and Canadian societies, the question of class structure is a central one. One element in understanding class structure is the societal distribution of income and, more broadly, wealth. Marked inequalities in these distributions could be expected to provide a basis for groups to differentiate themselves in terms that constitute a basis for class identification. A decision on whether or not the Canadian income distribution is more or less equal than the American one depends, as is often the case, on measurement. From one source, we are told that in 1951 and 1975 the Canadian distribution is "slightly less skewed" (that is, less unequal) than the U.S. distribution.[40] Taken over more instances from 1965 to 1974, another conclusion is that American family incomes were distributed more unequally than Canadian incomes.[41] A different measure of income inequality (the Gini coefficient) yields an opposite conclusion— namely, that the Canadian distribution is more unequal.[42] Obviously, no firm judgment can be made on this issue.

In the context of class, wealth is more important than income. On this important variable data are scanty. For example, Michalos could only compare U.S. data from 1962 with Canadian data from 1970, and he concluded that with reference to the upper and lower fifths of wealth-holders, "the United States almost certainly has greater disparity than Canada," a statement that is surprisingly bold given the data base.[43] What is certainly true is that in both countries wealth is more unequally distributed than income. These views are confirmed by other comparative data, though these are very limited in nature.[44]

In Canada at least these inequalities may have worsened slightly. Most commentators note the stability of the income distribution over time; since 1951 the proportion of income received by various income classes has changed little. But Moscovitch notes that the proportion of incomes received by the bottom fifth declined from 4.4 per cent to 3.8 per cent (1951 versus 1977), while in the uppermost fifth of incomes the proportion remained relatively constant.[45] Again we find that share ownership (one indicator of wealth) has become less diffused over time: in 1970 a mere 12.3 per cent of individuals and families held publicly traded stock holdings, and this had declined to 8.5 per cent by 1977.

Another perspective on inequality is gleaned from a comparison of certain aspects of poverty in the two countries. From the inception of the concept of a poverty line or "cutoff," the Canadian low-income cutoff has been higher than that in the U.S.[46] What is clear from data collected by Leman is that Canada has consistently maintained its poverty line far closer to the popular conception of what is needed to "get along" than has the U.S.

What this means is not entirely clear because in both countries the average income assistance paid to a family of four is less than the line—but these assistance payments are averaged across states and provinces, whereas the poverty lines are based on urban families in Canada and non-farm families in the U.S. The data are of some interest, but their utility is limited. One important difference which confounds measurement in this area is the fact that in Canada health benefits are available to all regardless of income, whereas publicly supported health coverage is only available to targetted groups, including the poor, in the U.S. Another is the universal provision of Family Allowances in Canada; this program is of particular benefit to all mother-headed families and to families which are below the poverty line yet receive no other benefits.

It is necessary to point out that class structure in Canada has long been seen as owing much to the relative position of ethno-linguistic groups, whereas in America the important social cleavage reflected in the class structure is largely racial in nature. There is little doubt that anglophones have earned more than francophones, even when doing similar jobs.[47] Controlling for educational differences, it is equally clear that workers of British ethnic origin have earned more than those of French ethnic origin. Also, many immigrant members of ethno-linguistic groups other than the two charter groups start "at the bottom" and so can be expected to earn even less than francophones.

Other analyses have emphasized the importance of ethnicity for understanding social status, based on an analysis of the relationship between occupational and ethnic groups. This latter relationship is said to distinguish Canada from the U.S. Re-analysis suggests that, except for a few groups, ethnicity may be of decreasing importance in terms of who works at what occupations.[48] This cautious comparison (based on 1950s data) with U.S. findings further asserts that levels of ethnic occupational differentiation are not in fact strikingly different. After reviewing a number of studies, Darroch concludes that it is an exaggeration to state that ethnic affiliations are a primary factor sustaining class structures. But, he concedes that entrance and membership in Canada's elite is strongly related to ethnic affiliation— Canada's elite is disproportionately British in terms of ethnic origin. Non-British and non-French individuals have become members of various elites, however, as the economies of the more diverse Western provinces have grown rapidly in recent years. Equally, the recent recession has removed some of these new players from the scene—the "old money" survives.

If a relatively small country like Canada has a complex class structure, how then to approach the United States? Rather than attempt to describe the class structure with objective measures, we will simply touch on two points. There is a considerable literature in American social science and social planning that deals with what is now called the underclass—this group is overwhelmingly non-white, is demographically youthful, has generally low levels of formal schooling and high drop-out rates, is extremely marginal in terms of labor force participation, and tends to reside in urban districts with high crime rates, poor quality housing and public services that are perceived as inadequate. One of the implications for our later urban analysis is that the geographic concentration of this underclass is related to the high levels of crime in American central cities, especially in inner-city ghetto districts. The tragedy of casual violence is daily fare in the media, as are reports of arson, decay and abandonment. These are popularly associated with minorities. Regrettably, only too often is causality readily imputed to blacks, Puerto Ricans and others—an extensive literature on white fears concerning neighborhood quality and the impact on property values when black households move in is the basis for this judgment. Violent responses to these in-movements have been widely documented. A second implication worth noting is that because of the concentration of the underclass in the central-city, the aggregate income of the central city population is depressed, thereby accentuating the central city/suburban income disparity. This disparity has been acknowledged in numerous studies; we also investigate this matter comparatively (in Chapter 7). Despite the urban influx of native Indians who share some of these characteristics, Canada simply has no substantive equivalent to this underclass. As we will see in the next section, the life chances of many members of this underclass are severely compromised by changes in black family structures.

The second point is that a characterization of America's elite remains somewhat elusive in comparison to the consensus that surrounds the work of Porter and subsequently Clement and others in Canada. Some contest the existence of a powerful ruling class and claim that there is a more diffuse, plural power structure in both economic and political terms.[49] Others hold to the conception of a ruling class rooted in the military-industrial complex aided and abetted by a willing state apparatus, including elected officials up to the level of the presidency.[50] Without taking a position on the merits of power structure/ruling class analysis in the U.S., we would simply say that the lack of consensus contrasts with the clearer sense of a definable and identifiable Canadian elite—a stronger sense of hierarchy, at least at the top, may well exist in Canada.

Before leaving the matter of class structure, we need to consider subjective notions of class in the two countries. Another perspective on the existence of social classes emerges when representative samples are asked about the existence of classes and the extent of their identification with a particular class category. There is little evidence on class consciousness in Canada; however, one reliable cross-national comparison is possible with respect to class identification.[51] There was essentially no difference between American and Canadian respondents in their identification with five given classes in surveys carried out in the mid-1960s (Table 3-4). The Canadian research underscores the importance of religion as a differentiating factor in Canadian society. It was found that in general there was a stronger relationship between socioeconomic status and class identification among Protestants than either francophone or anglophone Catholics. Furthermore, while occupation was the best predictor of class identification for Protestant respondents, it was family income in the case of Catholics. A recent formulation of class structure in Canada (based on the 1979 Survey of Social Change in Canada) is provided by Harris.[52] While it cannot be directly compared to U.S. data, it serves to caution us that the class identifications shown in Table 3-4 may be far from stable. Harris reports a relatively small middle class (13.2 per cent) and a surprisingly large working class proportion (50.4 per cent); these results do seem at variance with popular notions of Canada. More research must be done to express more concretely the notion of class structure in the two countries.

DEMOGRAPHIC STRUCTURE[53]

One basic demographic attribute is the rate of national population growth. In the postwar period, the Canadian population has grown at a faster rate than that of the United States (Table 3-5). To the extent that there is an "official" position on this issue, in Canada it is that it is a non-issue. In contrast, American views, at least as embodied in a presidential commission's report, are that "continued population growth . . . is definitely not in the interest of promoting the quality of life in the nation."[54] This, however, is a Canute-like position, opposing the apparently inevitable.

In terms of an age-sex profile, the recent national population structure is examined comparatively by Michalos.[55] About the only notable minor difference is that Canada has a more youthful population, partly a function of its immigration policies. However, within the U.S., there is an important racial dimension to key demographic variables. Minority populations are in general younger than the white population. Thus, Canada with an overwhelmingly white population is more youthful than the majority white American population. The youthfulness of black and Hispanic groups has some interesting long-run implications in the U.S. in terms of, for example, partisan politics in certain regions, household formation and housing demand and labor force participation.

Through the 1960s and 1970s, natural increase in the two countries has been somewhat different in the aggregate. Crude birth rates have fluctuated within a few points of one another; in the 1950s, Canada's average birth rates exceeded those of the U.S. (Table 3-6). Death rates have consistently been about 2 points per 1000 people lower in Canada, consistent with a younger population, but both exhibit a similar downward trend. What is of greater importance is the common experience of a sharp decline in fertility in the last twenty years. Again with a younger population and a proportionately higher rate of immigration, it is not surprising to find the Canadian rate generally, but not always, higher than the U.S. rate (Table 3-7). Both countries have seen a virtual halving of the total fertility rate. Although there has been a recent small increase, this rate (and other measures of fertility) is at an historic low. Having large numbers of children no longer appears either desirable or sensible to many women. A growing number of married couples remain childless. Moreover, further delaying of childbirth, an increasingly common practice, can lead to a point of no return.

We need to recall the importance of certain social characteristics already emphasized in this chapter. Two of the most important social groups in America are Hispanics and black Americans. Both have fertility levels higher than the total population while experiencing the same pronounced decline in the last two decades. The Hispanic rate is about 50 per cent higher than the U.S. average for all women; with increasing immigration, legal and illegal, and a largely Catholic population, it will probably remain substantially higher for a considerably longer period.[56] Thus, those regions of the U.S. with a concentration of Hispanics—the Southwest, Florida, New York, New Jersey and Illinois—and their cities will experience a higher rate of population growth than they would otherwise. Black fertility has historically been higher than white. There is little doubt that this is the result of the over-representation of black women in the lower class—black women with college degrees actually have a fertility rate lower than their white counterparts.[57] If unwanted births among black females could be reduced and teenage pregnancies substantially lowered, then one might see an increasing black-white convergence with respect to fertility. Over time, this could reduce the relatively large pool of black youths, a predominantly urban group that faces a serious problem in terms of employability, but this is not seen as a necessarily desirable solution among minority activists.

In Canada, the fertility experience of Quebec's population is truly remarkable.[58] As we noted previously, only through a natural increase fueled by the highest fertility of any region has the francophone population sustained itself. But in a forty-year period, and particularly during the last two decades, Quebec went from being the province with the highest reproduction rate to the lowest. There has always been a clear difference in fertility by religious affiliation, Catholics having a higher level than Protestants, thus explaining Quebec's preeminent position. But the social and economic transformations in Quebec have altered the cultural context within which couples make their child-bearing decisions. Despite the strictures of Catholicism, contraception and abortion are practiced. Nevertheless, among the major denominations Canada-wide, Roman Catholics still have the highest fertility level.

These changes in fertility should be seen in relation to marriage and family life and structure. In Canada and the United States, the institution of marriage has undergone broadly similar changes but with differences in particulars. Following World War II, the marriage rate increased dramatically in both countries. From the peak years of 1946 and 1947, in Canada it declined steadily to 1963 and then rose again just as steadily until 1972, when another declining trend set in. The first decline has its explanation in the smaller cohorts of persons born during the Depression moving into the "marrying" years. The economic recession of the early 1960s also took its toll. The second and more recent decline may indicate a change in traditional marriage patterns— alternative forms of living other than marriage are growing in popularity and acceptability. The U.S. experience is somewhat different; the marriage rate remained relatively high during the 1950s and 1960s before it declined sharply in the 1970s. The reasons are complex, but again the increasing numbers of alternative forms of cohabitation and the growing attractions of single life come into play. In short, in both societies the imperative to marry has weakened.

Another common social feature in family life is the extraordinary increase in divorce rates in both countries in recent years. Despite a similarity in trend, there are important differences. The rate has been persistently higher in the U.S., and the marked increase took place earlier. Legislative changes facilitating divorce in Canada were not made until 1968; only subsequently did the rate rise. Recently, both countries have experienced some slowing in the rate of increase in the divorce rate, and a decline in the total number of divorces has been observed in the U.S. Part of the reason for a cross-national difference in divorce rates is the persistently higher divorce rates experienced by two key American social groups—blacks and Hispanics. Also, the higher proportion of Roman Catholics in the Canadian population likely acts as a partial check against divorce. Remarriage has become increasingly common in both countries, especially in the U.S., but the prospects for marital bliss are not always realized—in the U.S., about one-third of white children and one-half of black children whose mothers remarry witness the breakup of that marriage before the children become adults.[59] Family life becomes much more complicated in many remarriage situations, and this could be a contributing factor to high divorce rates among remarriages.

With more women remaining unmarried and engaging in other forms of cohabitation and the drop in the marital fertility rate, a rise in the proportion of children born outside legal marriage is not unexpected. But the increase in America has been very sharp; furthermore, it is racially skewed and socially disturbing. By 1980 almost one-fifth of all babies were born to unmarried mothers. In contrast, from 1940 to 1960, the proportion did not exceed 6 per cent.[60] The racial difference is acute; for non-whites, the proportion of births to unwed mothers is close to 50 per cent, but it is only 11 per cent for whites. Even more staggering is the 50 point spread between black and white teenage mothers (85 per cent versus 33 per cent in 1980). These mothers have difficulty in completing formal schooling and often lack the skills demanded in contemporary labor markets. These new single-parent families will undoubtedly face difficult economic circumstances in the future. They will most likely live in slum properties or in public housing projects, depend on public income transfers, and be geographically over-represented in central-city ghettoes. While illegitimacy has increased in Canada in the last twenty years, the level has consistently been and remains lower than that for the U.S., even for the latter's white population. Furthermore, the rate of increase over, for example, the 1964-73 period was also lower in Canada.[61]

The number of births has been adversely affected by a greater number of abortions. At first glance, a clear cross-national difference exists. Well into the last decade, the abortion rate was twice as high in the U.S. as in Canada; again Canada's higher proportion of Catholics is probably a relevant factor. But interestingly, on a few attitudinal items related to abortion issues, there was essentially no cross-national difference in the proportion of responses that could be considered pro-abortion. Across the continent, abortion rates have continued to rise.[62] When one realizes that there were 300 abortions for every 1000 live births in the U.S. in 1980, the political saliency of this phenomenon in recent American elections is more understandable. In Canada too, while the rate has remained lower, abortion has become a divisive social issue. Attempts to open abortion clinics in Toronto and Winnipeg have sparked fierce controversy and legal action. It has also been shown that the more liberal availability of abortions in the United States attracts Canadian women, swelling the U.S. rate—one recent estimate yielded a total of 2300 abortions outside Manitoba, mostly in the U.S., compared to 1700 performed in Manitoba hospitals (1982 data).[63] Thus, the cross-national difference in abortion rates needs to be qualified.

Another important and common change in family life is that married women work outside the home in proportions that were undreamed of but a few decades ago. In the U.S., for example, a little over one-tenth of all married women participated in the labor force in 1940—by 1982 this proportion had reached 50 per cent.[64] Despite an initial lag (in 1961 the participation rate for Canadian married women was 22.2, more or less equivalent to the 1948 U.S. rate), Canadian married women now participate in the labor force at a level equivalent to that for their U.S. counterparts.[65] The motivations seem quite similar: a combination of family financial need, especially in the lower income strata, and a desire on the part of educated women to gain personal satisfaction from the world of work.

These various demographic characteristics which we have touched on combine to produce new patterns in family and household structure. While husband and wife families are still the dominant type, there has been a significant increase in single-parent families—without a high level of remarriage after divorce, this type would have increased even more.

Comparatively, there is a consistent and growing difference in family structure. Over the last two decades, the proportion of husband and wife families dropped by only two percentage points in Canada (Table 3-8). There was a clear but modest upward trend in single-parent families, almost entirely in female-headed families. These changes have been more pronounced in the United States, largely because of marked changes within black families. For white American families, the shifts have only been marginally greater than for Canadian families. But for black families there has been an extraordinary twenty point drop in the proportion of husband-wife families and a corresponding increase in the proportion of single-parent families, almost entirely female-headed.

As of 1980, for example, there were 2.5 million black families which were female-headed. It does not take too much imagination to anticipate the likely future of the hundreds of thousands of children in such families when one takes into account the joint effects of the poverty of women (relative to men) and the poverty of blacks (relative to whites). This is a sensitive and worsening social problem that Canada simply does not face in either scale or nature, none of which is to belittle or underestimate the serious problems facing poor Canadian families with female heads and disadvantaged children. In particular, we should ask what is the likely effective demand of such families in urban housing markets which have seen dramatic price volatility in recent years, even for rental units, probably the preferred tenure. The weakness of their demand means that many become tenants of the state. The population of public housing projects, especially in American central cities, is increasingly characterized by female-headed households and large numbers of youths, many tied to gangs.

To make this important issue a little more specific in terms of cities, but maintaining the comparative perspective, we have ranked a selection of the largest central cities in the U.S. and Canada with respect to the proportion of households which are headed by a lone female parent (Table 3-9). What is striking is the range in this proportion across only eighteen cities. The three Canadian cities occur in the lower half of the distribution, just below the median. Below that figure the American cities are all in the West or in Texas — interestingly, Toronto belongs more in this group than its geographical location would suggest.

Family size has also declined recently, and this is strongly correlated with a decline in the average number of children per family. There is no significant cross-national difference on this point. One cannot, however, simply extrapolate from this a demand for smaller housing units. While family size may decrease, with increasing family incomes there may be a strong demand for more residential space per capita. The fact that developers have recently built proportionately more smaller single-family dwellings than in the 1960s probably has as much to do with land costs, the costs of space heating and the desire to keep the finished unit affordable for middle-income families as with shrinking families.

One sees something of the same social change when looking at household structure. Despite a significant growth in non-family households, families still account for about three-quarters of all households—the family proportion is marginally higher in Canada (Table 3-10). The growth in non-family households is mostly attributable to the explosion in one-person households. In Canada, for example, one-person households increased from just under 600,000 to over 1.2 million in the ten years from 1966 to 1976 and by 1976 accounted for 17 per cent of all households. Somewhat similarly, in the U.S. we find that, as a proportion of all households, one-person households increased by almost 10 percentage points in the last twenty years.

One-person households are themselves demographically distinctive. Many are elderly, maintaining independent living quarters rather than rejoining their adult children or moving to a group home. Others are the by-product of the boomlet in divorces; these are more likely to be male since the typical break-up tends to leave the woman with the children and the single-family home. Yet others are young, well educated and sufficiently well paid to maintain their own place, be it an apartment, condominium or even a single-family home.

America has a somewhat more aged population than does Canada, and with higher divorce rates and a greater proportion of one-person households, it should come as no surprise to find that the number of persons per household is smaller in the U.S. than in Canada. There has been a steady common decline in household size over the last two decades.

To sum up this section on demography we can make several broad statements. In general, both countries have undergone a similar demographic experience. Both have witnessed a sharp drop in fertility, to the degree that their populations are incapable of reproducing themselves without immigration (assuming no upturn in fertility). Families have declined in importance, and there has been a significant increase in non-family households— the rise in numbers and proportion of one-person households has been particularly dramatic. Despite considerable similarities, some interesting cross-national differences still emerge. It appears that the conventional family is declining less rapidly in Canada. Secondly, such social trends as rising divorce, abortion and illegitimacy rates have had less effect in Canada, though they are not inconsequential. Finally, far less than America is Canada characterized by major social divisions on racial and sociolinguistic criteria which are reinforced by divergent demographic circumstances.

These national demographic changes carry with them the seeds of change within cities, some of which are already observable. Here we can but highlight a few of the more significant that bear directly on our analyses.

The family structure long thought of as typical, husband and wife with children, still remains a dominant demographic and consumption unit, despite widely publicized increases in non-family households. For such families, a quality of living environment for the pursuit of their goals and raising the children is a major priority. The growth of smaller non-family households has had its impact in housing markets. Childless couples, for example, have been a significant component of the gentrification process leading to residential and social change in selected inner-city districts. This is something that is common to both Canadian and American cities. Also common is the rapid increase in one-person households, with a somewhat greater occurrence in the U.S. One might expect this to translate into a higher demand for rental apartments in U.S. cities, but there are strong countervailing forces, not the least of which is the pronounced American demand for ownership of single units. The generally higher cost of residential land in most Canadian cities, where values are bid up in response to demands for central area living, which is generally perceived to be more attractive than its American counterpart, results in a well-developed supply of high-rise apartment units. Thus, just how a national demographic trend works on through to specific urban developments depends in part on interaction effects with other factors and the specific contexts of particular cities.

At the same time, societies and communities can respond to broadly similar demographic trends differently. A case in point is the provision of subsidized housing for the growing numbers of elderly households, often single women. Research by Mercer documents the strong public sector response in one Canadian metropolitan area.[66] The desire of the elderly to find senior citizen projects located in the inner parts of Vancouver, a pattern repeated in other cities, is contrasted with the fearful character of elderly life in certain U.S. urban contexts. When the police have to escort the elderly to do their shopping, as has happened in New York City, or when the elderly whites feel trapped and frightened in their racially changing districts with few options to move, one realizes that these are situations far less likely to exist, if at all, in the Canadian city.

QUALITY OF SOCIAL LIFE

Just as societies are compared and categorized with respect to economic indicators, so too are they increasingly compared with respect to "quality of life" measures or social indicators. At the national scale, the recent impressive work of Michalos comparing Canadian and American societies is path-breaking. While we make use of certain of the many individual indicators reported in his study, the overall conclusion is also worth quoting here:

> On the basis of an examination of over 135 social indicators and over 1659 indicator values, it seems fair to say that the quality of life in the 1964-74 period was comparatively or relatively higher in Canada than in the United States.[67]

If this is the case, then where do cities and metropolitan areas fit into the picture? There does not exist a systematic cross-national comparative study using respondents in both countries with similarly worded questions on quality of life items. However, we can make use here of two recent surveys in both countries to obtain a cross-national comparative perspective on how Canadians and Americans view their cities.[68] Both surveys were done in 1977-78, and both were undertaken for federal agencies (the Department of Housing and Urban Development in the U.S. and the now abolished Ministry of State for Urban Affairs in Canada). In the Canadian survey, 11,061 persons who lived in twenty-three metropolitan centers were interviewed. In the American survey, 7,074 persons were interviewed, including residents of metropolitan areas (both central cities and suburbs), towns outside the metropolitan areas, and rural districts (metropolitan residents comprised 70 per cent of the sample).

Canadian residents expressed a consistently positive degree of satisfaction with their cities. On a scale of 1 (lowest) to 11 (highest) no metropolitan area scored less than 7.06 (6 being the neutral value); the maximum was 8.92 indicating only modest variation between the cities (the mean score was 8.2). Another measure, the index of attraction, confirmed the view that metropolitan areas are seen by Canadians as satisfactory places within which to live. A point worth emphasizing is that in those metropolitan areas for which attraction scores are available for suburban districts beyond the central-city boundary, five of the seven showed higher scores for the outer part of the central city than in the suburban neighborhoods. More generally, scores within the cities tended to increase outward from the downtown area. In general, however, people were satisfied with the neighborhood in which they live.

The American data are intriguing. When asked to compare "Large Cities,"

"Suburbs," and places in nonmetropolitan areas, the "Large Cities" are perceived as having by far the most crime, the worst housing, the worst schools and being the worst place to raise children. However, they were seen to have positive features, scoring well on employment opportunities, health care facilities, shopping and public transportation. A clear inference is that one can have the best of both worlds by living in the suburbs, which are viewed extremely positively and which provide ready access to the opportunities of the large cities by way of extensive urban freeway systems. Despite this overall view of the large cities, the central cities are viewed positively *by those who live there.* When asked about their overall feelings, the average response lay between "usually satisfied" and "pleased" on a 7-point scale. Nevertheless, a notable proportion of central-city residents, about one-third, expected to move "in the next two or three years." Given what we know about residential moves within American cities, a substantial proportion of these city dwellers will move out to the suburbs and beyond.

This is confirmed by the survey itself. When asked about their first choice of places to live, respondents chose small to medium nonmetropolitan communities first (31.0 per cent), suburbs next (26.6 per cent), then rural areas (24.7 per cent), followed last by large cities (16.1 per cent).

We know from data presented earlier in this chapter that family households still represent almost three-quarters of American households. Thus, the appropriate environment for raising a family is likely to be significant to millions. Large cities are not seen as being suitable for raising children, and this view is especially strongly held by suburban residents and those living outside metropolitan areas. Of all respondents, four-fifths rated large cities as the worst place to raise children with this proportion rising to around 90 per cent amongst those who live outside the central cities. Looking ahead to when their children are grown up, respondents were much less likely to express support for large cities as the preferred location for their children. Those questioned said overwhelmingly that they wanted their children to live in a community like the one in which the respondents themselves lived. However, the proportion that said this was the lowest in the case of those already living in large cities (38.3 per cent); in most other areas, the proportion was around 70 per cent. Furthermore, if people said they would prefer to see their grown-up children live in some other place, very few selected large cities when asked to specify what they would mean for "other place." The dominant choices were rural areas and small communities in the suburbs. Finally, and relatedly, there is a wide consensus among Americans that large cities have the worst public schools (62 per cent of respondents said so), whereas the best public schools were believed to be in the suburbs (39 per cent) and medium to small nonmetropolitan communities (32 per cent). Interestingly, despite the obvious residential attraction of rural areas, they are not seen as having good schools—this could be a partial deterrent on nonmetropolitan population growth in specific locations. One comes away from this evidence which, we stress, is not directly comparable in nature, with a clear sense of an important cross-national difference, one which is in the same direction as the overall conclusion of Michalos. Canadians do not abhor cities, are satisfied with living in them, and even in certain instances rate the outer parts of cities as better places to live than suburban districts. In sharp contrast, while the present residents of American central cities also evince satisfaction with living in the city, there is an extremely negative view of the American city held by suburbanites and residents of nonmetropolitan America. Even the large city residents expect to move out (the others could hardly be expected to move in), and they are less enamored of their community as a place to raise children or for their grown-up children in the future. This supports the view that it will be much more difficult for the large American central cities to retain their population, specifically family-oriented households, than for the Canadian central cities. These central city differences in perceived livability are of major significance, as will become apparent in an empirical analysis of urban areas discussed in Chapters 7 through 9.

TABLE 3-1
LEADING SOURCE COUNTRIES FOR IMMIGRANTS: CANADA AND THE U.S.

CANADA

1951	1968	1979	1982
Britain	Britain	Vietnam	Britain
Germany	USA	Britain	USA
Italy	Italy	USA	Poland
Netherlands	Germany	Hong Kong	India
Poland	Hong Kong	India	Hong Kong
France	France	Laos	Vietnam
USA	Austria	Philippines	Philippines
Belgium	Greece	Portugal	Federal Republic
Yugoslavia	Portugal	Jamaica	of Germany
Denmark	Yugoslavia	China	China
			Guyana

USA

1951	1968	1975	1979
Germany	Cuba	Mexico	Mexico
Canada	Mexico	Philippines	Philippines
Great Britain	Canada	West Indies[1]	Korea
Austria	West Indies	Korea	Cuba
Italy	Great Britain	Canada	Other West Indies
Mexico	Italy	Vietnam	India
West Indies	Germany	India	Dominican Republic
France	Philippines	Dominican Republic	Hong Kong
Greece	Portugal	Hong Kong	Great Britain
Ireland	Hong Kong	Great Britain	Portugal

[1]This category included Cuba at this time.

Source: U.S. Bureau of the Census, *Statistical Abstract of the United States: 1984*, 104th ed. (Washington, DC, 1983); Department of Employment and Immigration Canada, 1979, *Immigration Statistics*, Cat. No. WH-5-006 (Ottawa: Minister of Supply and Services Canada, 1981); Department of Employment and Immigration Canada, 1982, *Immigration Statistics*, Cat. No. MP22-1-1982 (Ottawa: Minister of Supply and Services Canada, 1984); Warren E. Kalbach and Wayne W. McVey, *The Demographic Bases of Canadian Society*, 2nd ed. (Toronto: McGraw-Hill Ryerson, 1979); U.S. Bureau of the Census, *Statistical Abstract of the United States: 1954*, 75th ed. (Washington, DC, 1954).

TABLE 3-2
U.S. POPULATION BY ANCESTRY GROUP: 1980

Single Ancestry Group	52.33
English	10.48
German	7.92
Irish	4.56
Italian	3.04
Polish	1.68
French	1.35
Dutch	0.62
Russian	0.61
Swedish	0.57
Scottish	0.52
Hungarian	0.32
Greek	0.27
Ukrainian	0.17
Other	19.39
Multiple Ancestry Group	30.78
Ancestry Not Specified	16.88
Ancestry Not Reported	10.20

Source: U.S. Bureau of the Census, *Statistical Abstract of the United States: 1984*, 104th ed. (Washington, DC, 1983).

TABLE 3-3
REGIONAL PATTERN IN THE BLACK PROPORTION OF THE
AMERICAN POPULATION: 1970 AND 1980

	1970	1980
New England	3.3	3.9
Middle Atlantic	10.6	11.9
East North Central	9.6	10.9
West North Central	4.3	4.6
South Atlantic	20.8	20.7
East South Central	20.1	19.6
West South Central	15.6	14.8
Mountain	2.2	2.4
Pacific	5.7	6.3

Source: U.S. Bureau of the Census, *Statistical Abstract of the United States: 1984*, 104th ed. (Washington, DC, 1983); U.S. Bureau of the Census, *Statistical Abstract of the United States: 1971*, 92nd ed. (Washington, DC, 1971).

TABLE 3-4
CLASS IDENTIFICATION BY SURVEY RESPONDENTS IN NATIONAL SAMPLES[1]

	USA (1964 survey)	CANADA (1965 survey)
Upper class	2.0	2.0
Upper-middle class	17.0	13.0
Middle class	44.0	50.0
Working class	34.0	31.0
Lower class	2.0	2.0
No such thing	1.0	1.0

[1]The respective sample sizes were 793 for Canada and 918 for the U.S.A., giving a much higher sampling fraction in the Canadian survey.

Source: P.C. Pineo and J.C. Goyder, "Social Class Identification of National Sub-Groups," in J.E. Curtis and W.G. Scott, eds., *Social Stratification: Canada* (Scarborough, Ont.: Prentice-Hall, 1973), 187-96.

TABLE 3-5
AVERAGE ANNUAL RATE OF GROWTH
BETWEEN PERIOD[1]

	USA	CANADA
1940/1941		
	1.0	1.0
1950/1951		
	1.7	1.7
1955/1956		
	1.8	2.8
1960/1961		
	1.6	2.5
1965/1966		
	1.2	1.9
1970/1971		
	1.3	1.5
1975/1976		
	1.0	1.3
1980/1981		

[1]U.S. figures are for 0 and 5 years; those for Canada are for 1 and 6 years.

Source: U.S. Bureau of the Census, *Statistical Abstract of the United States: 1984*, 104th ed. (Washington, DC, 1983); Department of Finance, Canada, *Economic Review, April 7, 1984* (Ottawa: Minister of Supply and Services Canada, 1984).

TABLE 3-6
CRUDE BIRTH RATE: NUMBER OF BIRTHS PER 1000 POPULATION

	USA	CANADA
1950	23.9	27.1
1955	24.9	28.2
1960	23.8	26.8
1965	19.6	21.3
1970	18.2	17.5
1975	14.6	15.8
1976	14.5	15.6
1977	15.1	15.6
1978	15.0	15.2
1979	15.4	15.4
1980	15.9	15.4
1981	15.9	15.2
1982	16.0	15.1

Source: U.S. Bureau of the Census, *Statistical Abstract of the United States: 1984* (Washington, DC: 1983); Department of Finance, Canada, *Economic Review, April 7, 1984* (Ottawa: Minister of Supply and Services Canada, 1984).

TABLE 3-7
FERTILITY RATE: CANADA AND THE UNITED STATES

	CANADA	USA
1961	3840	1768
1966	2812	2721
1971	2187	2267
1972	2024	2022
1973	1931	1879
1974	1875	1835
1975	1852	1774
1976	1825	1738
1977	1806	1790
1978	1757	1760
1979	1764	1808
1980	1746	1840
1981	1704	1815
1982	1694	n.a.

Source: U.S. Bureau of the Census, *Statistical Abstract of the United States: 1984*, 104th ed. (Washington, DC, 1983); Statistics Canada, *Canada Yearbook, 1980-81* (Ottawa: Minister of Supply and Services Canada, 1981); U.S. Bureau of the Census, *Statistical Abstract of the United States: 1963*, 84th ed. (Washington, DC, 1963); Statistics Canada, *Births and Death*, Vital Statistics 1982/1980/1978, Cat. No. 84-204, Vol. 1.

TABLE 3-8
FAMILIES BY FAMILY STRUCTURE

CANADA	1961	1966	1971	1976	1981
Husband and wife	91.6	91.8	90.6	90.2	88.7
Single-parent	8.4	8.2	9.4	9.8	11.3
Male	1.8	1.6	2.0	1.7	2.0
Female	6.6	6.6	7.5	8.1	9.3

USA	1960	1970	1975	1980	1981
White					
Husband and wife	88.7	88.7	86.9	85.7	85.1
Single-parent	11.3	11.3	13.1	14.4	14.9
Male	2.6	2.3	2.6	2.8	3.0
Female	8.7	9.0	10.5	11.6	11.9
Black and Oriental					
Husband and wife	73.6	68.0	60.9	55.5	55.7
Single-parent	26.4	32.0	39.2	44.4	46.3
Male	4.0	3.7	3.9	4.1	4.6
Female	22.4	28.3	35.3	40.3	41.7
Black Households (millions)					
Total	4.2	4.9	5.5	6.2	6.3
Married Couples	3.1	3.3	3.3	3.4	3.4
Male, Single-parent	0.17	0.18	0.21	0.26	0.29
Female, Single-parent	0.95	1.4	1.9	2.5	2.6

Source: Statistics Canada, *Canada Yearbook 1980-81* (Ottawa: Minister of Supply and Services Canada, 1981); Statistics Canada, *1981 Census of Canada*, Cat. No. 92-905, Tables 1-5; Statistics Canada, *Canada Yearbook 1973* (Ottawa: Minister of Industry, Trade and Commerce, 1973); U.S. Bureau of the Census, *Current Population Reports*, Series P-20.

TABLE 3-9
SELECTED CENTRAL CITIES RANKED BY PROPORTION
OF HOUSEHOLDS HEADED BY FEMALE SINGLE PARENT[1]

Detroit	22.50
Baltimore	21.86
Washington, D.C.	19.29
Cleveland	18.97
Philadelphia	18.53
Chicago	17.90
New York	16.60
Boston	16.20
Pittsburgh	15.50
Milwaukee	15.47
Montreal	15.18
Los Angeles	12.79
Toronto	12.66
Edmonton	12.60
Dallas	12.37
Vancouver	11.82
Houston	11.50
San Diego	10.59
San Francisco	9.95
Seattle	9.11

[1]U.S. data are for 1980; Canadian data are for 1981.

Source: Statistics Canada, *1981 Census of Canada*, Cat. No. 95-943, Vol. 3, Profile Series B; U.S. Bureau of the Census, *U.S. Census of Population and Housing 1980*, Table P1, Cat. No. 2551-2, 1984.

TABLE 3-10
HOUSEHOLDS BY FAMILY STRUCTURE

	Family Households		Non-family Households	
	USA	CANADA	USA	CANADA
1960/61	85.0	86.7	15.0	13.3
1965/66	83.3	84.5	16.7	15.5
1970/71	81.2	81.7	18.8	18.3
1975/76	78.1	78.6	21.8	21.4
1980/81	73.9	75.2	26.1	24.8

Source: Statistics Canada, *1981 Census of Canada*, Cat. No. 92-904, Table 2; Statistics Canada, *Canada Yearbook 1980-81* (Ottawa: Minister of Supply and Services Canada, 1981); U.S. Bureau of the Census, *Statistical Abstract of the United States: 1984*, 104th ed. (Washington, DC, 1983).

4

ECONOMIC ORGANIZATION AND ECONOMIC INSTITUTIONS IN CANADA AND THE UNITED STATES: THE FUEL FOR URBAN GROWTH AND CHANGE

INTRODUCTION: HISTORICAL OVERVIEW OF THE U.S. AND CANADIAN ECONOMIES

Perhaps to the surprise of many, the Canadian economy has fared extremely well as compared with other developed economies, not just in the past decade, but over the past century as well (Tables 4-1 and 4-2). In particular, the growth rates of the Canadian and U.S. economies over the period 1860 to approximately 1960 have been remarkably similar. Moreover, as shown by the level of aggregate income, the Canadian economy is large on a world scale, even though dwarfed by that of the U.S. In addition, in terms of the 1980 per capita gross domestic product, Canada ranked tenth among all developed countries.

These economic indicators mask certain crucial differences with the U.S. economy. To understand these we will begin by reviewing briefly the historical foundations of both the U.S. and Canadian economic systems and then proceed to discuss contemporary differences in economic organization and institutions in the two nations.

Early Performance and Structure of the Canadian and U.S. Economies

The Canadian economy early took on its resource-based character. Demands for natural resources originating in European urban markets led to the export of fish, fur and lumber. At first, the Atlantic fishery was the basis for economic activity. With more permanent settlements which functioned as entrepots, furs surpassed fish in exports to Europe. But by the nineteenth century, the principal exports were in the timber trade. Under conditions of increasing complexity, these few readily exportable resources generated the greatest share of income in the economy and induced capital and labor to enter the new colonies.[1]

This staple theory, as it has come to be called, has been a recurring theme in Canadian economic history through to the present.[2] Although still dependent on staples, the Canadian economy by the close of the nineteenth century had begun to take on the characteristics of modern industrial economies of the day. At mid-century, the Canadian economy was essentially agriculturally based with nearly one-third of gross national product (GNP) originating there (32.0 per cent), and with other primary products— mining, forestry and fishing— accounting for an additional 15 per cent (Table 4-3). By 1860 primary products accounted for just over half of GNP (50.2 per cent). Manufacturing in contrast provided less than one-fifth of GNP up to 1890, when its share started to increase, rising from a low of 15 per cent in 1860 to almost one-quarter in 1890. Thus, by the late Victorian era, Canada was moving toward a well-developed manufacturing and service sector.

However, this view is deceptive. Much of the modern manufacturing sector in Canada is related to primary products, such as lumber and wood products and metal-smelting, as revealed through Canadian exports and imports (Tables 4-4 and 4-5). The information on exports and imports since 1851 demonstrates clearly that Canada can be characterized as an exporter of primary and primary-manufactured goods and as an importer of finished manufactures such as textiles, machinery and chemicals. This reliance upon the extraction and export of resources, both raw and somewhat processed, has made the Canadian economy extremely sensitive to cyclical fluctuations in the world economy. Accordingly, the Canadian economy is less balanced and "developed" than conventional data imply.

Two other important aspects of Canadian economic development need to be explored before reviewing analogous data for the United States: the prominence of government or the public sector in the Canadian economy; and the dominance of foreign capital, not just foreign trade.

Data on government spending by various authorities are sketchy for the period before 1867 and Confederation. From then on, there are data available on federal government spending, but only after 1933 are there data series for total government expenditures in Canada. Consolidated expenditure data for all levels of government in Canada can be seen in context through the share of GNP represented by government. From 1870 to 1983 federal government spending as a proportion of GNP or of its definitional equivalent, gross national expenditures (GNE) rose from 3.5 per cent ($16.1 million of spending out of a total GNP/GNE of $459 million) to one-fifth ($79.8 billion of federal spending out of a total GNP of $388.6 billion). Moreover, other evidence reveals major public expenditures throughout the nineteenth century, particularly in large transportation projects such as canals and railroads.[3] In any event, in Canada government is a major force in the economy, particularly when contrasted with the U.S. (Table 4-6).

The Canadian economy has always been "open" in the sense that foreign trade has been an important component of total economic activity. The foreign role in Canadian "capital formation" (the accumulation of capital for production in the future) has been particularly important in shaping the Canadian economy and in providing Canada with some unique and difficult policy questions concerning the relationships between Canada's political economy and those of the United States and the rest of the world (Tables 4-7 and 4-8). It is clear that this pattern of massive foreign investment in, and ownership of, key economic sectors makes Canada look much more like an undeveloped rather than a developed and advanced nation.

The extent to which the Canadian economy is controlled by foreign capital is a crucial distinguishing feature between the national economies and cannot be overemphasized (Table 4-9). But Canadian capital has also made its own investments abroad. While one thinks of multi-national firms mostly in U.S. terms, Canada has its share. Indeed, these activities have expanded rapidly since 1960, highlighting the degree of economic integration between the two countries. Not surprisingly, they are focussed very much on the U.S., with almost half of the Canadian direct foreign investment concentrated there in 1980 ($16.4 billion out of a total of $25.8 billion of direct foreign investment by Canadians) (Table 4-10).

Some very significant differences emerge in the analysis of the economic development of the United States. The record of achievement of the U.S. economy since independence in 1776 is quite remarkable. In his text on U.S. economic history, Albert Niemi summarizes this experience:

> The United States has achieved a standard of living unparalleled in the world, and this has not been due to any single factor or isolated event, but instead it has resulted from an almost ideal combination of circumstances. In the early stages of development, the American economy was endowed with a rich natural resource base, a high land/labor ratio, a favorable mix of public and private enterprise, access to British capital and technology, selective inflow of European migration, and early transportation development; the joint operation of these and other favorable circumstances created a solid base for United States economic development.[4]

This statement has many elements that relate to Canada since both countries were blessed with extraordinary gifts of nature. But more favorable climate and resources allowed the U.S. to grow more rapidly. The scale of the U.S. economy in turn led to qualitative differences between the neighboring economies, as is reflected in industrial mix, foreign investment and foreign trade patterns, the roles of government, financial institutions and savings behavior, and in the growth of the urban systems, to name a few dimensions.

The economy of the United States changed quickly and dramatically. Thus, in the period 1869 to 1879 over 30 per cent of GNP was traceable to agriculture and mining.[5] By 1980 all primary industries together accounted for only 5 per cent of GNP (U.S.$99.9 billion out of a total of U.S.$2,174.0 billion of GNP). At the same time manufacturing rose from a share of 13.9 per cent in 1869 and 1879 to roughly one-quarter in 1980, while services (including business and personal services, finance, insurance and real estate, and government) rose from 30.8 per cent in 1869/1879 to 41.7 per cent a century later in 1980 (Table 4-11).

With the shift from agrarian primary producer to industrial mammoth came parallel shifts in the composition of imports and exports. Up through the early 1880s, export of crude materials and crude foodstuffs comprised more than half of total exports (59 per cent in 1881). By 1900 the proportion had dropped to 41 per cent, by 1920 to 35 per cent, and by 1970 it had fallen to only 17 per cent. Meanwhile, the export of manufactures (manufactured foodstuffs, semi-manufactures and finished manufactures) soared from 41 per cent in 1881 to 83 per cent in 1970. A similar transformation occurred in the structure of imports where reliance on manufactured goods declined and relatively greater quantities of natural resources and crude materials were imported (Table 4-12).

This remarkable evolution can also be gleaned from changes in the distribution of the labor force in major industries. From 1870 to 1982, the proportion of the work force employed in primary activities declined relentlessly from 47.4 per cent to 4.2 per cent, while the proportion in manufacturing climbed to a peak of nearly 30 per cent in 1950 from 21.7 per cent in 1870 and has declined steadily since 1950 to 20.4 per cent in 1982 (Table 4-13). It should be noted, moreover, that this latter proportion overstates the number of production workers considerably since the percentage of the blue-collar employees involved directly in production is falling steadily, down from 41.4 per cent in 1950 to 29.7 per cent in 1982 (Table 4-14). Perhaps the most striking change has been the movement into service industries, including government. In 1870 30.9 per cent of the employed labor force was involved in service industries; by 1982 the proportion had ballooned to 71.2 per cent.

Regardless of the indicator used, it is clear that since 1870 the U.S.

economy has undergone a radical transformation from an agricultural economy with a growing industrial base, to the world's largest and most complex economy. In the process it was the engine for filling in half a continent, absorbing extraordinary numbers of immigrants and generating an increase in per capita gross national product from $165 in 1869-73 to $13,239 in 1982, a staggering eighty-fold increase in just over a century.[6]

Expenditures by American federal, state and local governments have grown dramatically from 4.4 per cent of GNP in 1869 and 1879 to 38.0 per cent of GNP in 1982 (Table 4-6). As government's role has changed from that of the provider of national security and defense and education, to the current role of provider of a broad array of services, this has brought about an expanded and complex economic presence. Comparing the U.S. pattern of expenditures (Table 4-15) with that in Canada (Table 4-16) reveals how differently the two societies allocate their scarce resources: U.S. defense spending and the Canadian "social safety net" stand out as clear differences.

Finally, we turn to the international capital relations of the United States. Through World War I, the U.S. was a net importer of capital, particularly during the period 1870-1900 when it was experiencing unprecedented growth in manufacturing and extending its railroad system across the continent. However, by the post-World War I era, the U.S. had become a net international creditor, a position which it has expanded considerably and continuously since. In terms of international investment, as of 1982, the U.S. had direct investments of just over U.S.$221 billion, just under a quarter of which, U.S.$44.5 billion, was invested in Canada—more than in any other country. In contrast, the total direct investment of foreigners in the U.S. amounted to only U.S.$68.4 billion in 1980, or 0.9 per cent of total corporate assets, in stark contrast with the equivalent figure for Canada which is in excess of 25 per cent (Table 4-17). Thus, while the U.S. is an active investor abroad and a recipient of foreign investment funds, the net impact of direct investment in the U.S. by foreigners is small compared with that of U.S. direct foreign investment in other countries, most notably Canada. It is also worth noting that portfolio investment in the U.S. is continually two to three times larger than direct investment, whereas in Canada, portfolio investment—stocks, bonds and other securities—only caught direct investment in plant, equipment and real property in 1978, also implying a significant difference between the two countries (Table 4-7 and Chart 4-1).

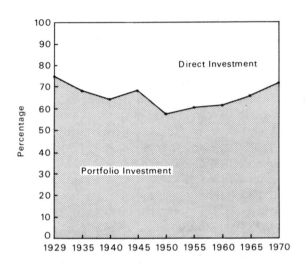

CHART 4—1   Percentage Distribution of Foreign Long-term Investment in the United States, by Type, 1930-1970.
*(Source: Historical Abstracts of the U.S.: Colonial Times to 1970, pp.
868-69)*

One further measure of the minor role played by foreign activity in the
U.S. economy can be derived from the volume of international trade and its
relation to U.S. GNP. In 1900, total U.S. exports amounted to roughly
U.S.$1.4 billion or approximately 7 per cent of GNP. Exports had risen by
1982 to just over U.S.$208 billion, still only a small fraction of U.S. economic
activity (6.8 per cent of GNP). To compare, Canada had $0.18 billion of
exports in 1900 out of a GNP of $1.05 billion (18 per cent). In 1983, however,
Canada exported $91.0 billion of goods and services out of a total GNP of
CDN$388.7 billion. In other words, one-fourth of the Canadian GNP is
accounted for by exports (Tables 4-18 and 4-19 and Chart 4-2).

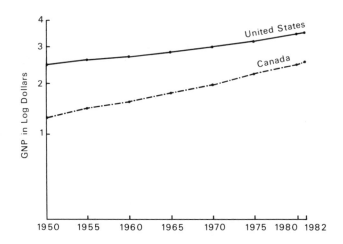

CHART 4—2   Gross National Product,[1] Canada and the U.S.,
1950-1983.

*(Source: Economic Review (Canada), 1984, p. 134; Statistical Abstract
of the U.S., 1984, p. 448)*

1. The data, originally reported in billions of dollars have been
logarithmically transformed for ease of visual display.

In sum, over the past two centuries the U.S. has had a remarkable
economic record. Not only has it achieved extraordinary growth and diversity in its own economic activities, but it has increasingly broadened its role
in foreign economies. At the same time, because of the scale of the domestic
economy, the U.S. still finds itself relatively independent of world trade,
despite the large volume of direct American investment abroad and the large
absolute volume of its foreign trade. There is increased concern, though,
about the growing U.S. trade deficit and its foreign and domestic impact.[7]
This stands in marked contrast to Canada's role in the international economy and the role of the international economy in Canada, as will be stressed
shortly.

THE U.S. AND CANADIAN ECONOMIES: SIMILARITIES AND DIFFERENCES

The foregoing discussion set out in broad terms some key features in the evolution of the U.S. and Canadian economies over the past century. From this, a number of similarities and differences can be discerned and expanded upon. These provide essential context for understanding the economic milieu within which Canadian and U.S. cities developed. Given the close ties between the urbanization and industrialization/development processes, economic differences between the two countries should provide important clues for exploring differences in the structure and functioning of urban areas in Canada and the U.S.

Similarities in Economic Organization and Institutions in Canada and the U.S.

Both Canada and the United States are advanced capitalist societies, characterized by different degrees of government participation in economic and social life. They share other readily apparent, and some not so apparent, similarities. These similarities have been all too frequently sufficiently obvious to deter the exploration for deeper-seated differences. It is the very nature of these similarities and their breadth that have, in our opinion, led people in the past to conclude uncritically that the U.S. and Canada are fundamentally similar and therefore subject to broad generalization. This is far from the case.

Both the U.S. and Canada are highly urbanized and economically advanced market economies. Nearly three-quarters of the population in each country is classified as urban, though the timing and pace of urbanization has been different (Chart 4-3). While the two countries are now almost equally urbanized, it is only in the post-World War II era that Canada began to approach the levels of urbanization experienced in the United States, in part a function of the later development of the Canadian urban-industrial economy. Some of the data reviewed in the first part of this chapter provide additional evidence of the paths to economic development in the two countries.

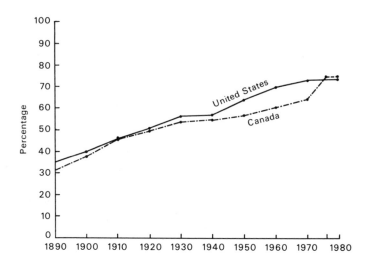

CHART 4—3   Per Cent of Population Living in Urban Areas, Canada[1]
and the U.S., 1890-1980.

(Source: Historical Statistics of Canada [2nd ed., 1983], A67-74; *Census
of Canada, 1981, Cat. No. 92-901; Historical Abstract of the U.S.;
Colonial Times to 1970,* p. 11; Statistical Abstract of the U.S., 1984, p.
xvii)

1. For Canada, census information is gathered in the first year of a
decade (i.e., 1891, 1901, etc.)

Specifically, by the dawn of the 1980s primary activity accounted for a
scant 5 per cent of GNP (Tables 4-3 and 4-11). Both nations are now
dominated by the tertiary service industries and employment (Tables 4-20
and 4-14), which comprise roughly two-thirds of GNP presently. Tables 4-1
and 4-2 also showed that Canada and the United States were among the most
buoyant economies over the century prior to 1960, experiencing, with Japan,
the most rapid rates of real economic growth of any nations in the world. The
result by 1980 was that Canada and the U.S. possessed among the highest
standards of living (Table 4-2). The achievements of both economies in
transforming large regions and in absorbing mass immigration are remarkable.
Yet, despite this similarity, the countries have shown significant differences
in economic performance and structure.

Differences in Economic Organization and Scale

Despite similar physical sizes, the U.S. dwarfs Canada in terms of the scale of its output and of its population, for which a 10:1 ratio is a good first approximation. The present Canadian population of roughly 25 million is just over one-tenth of the 240 million people in the U.S. Similarly, 1982 U.S. GNP of US$3,073.0 billion was roughly 10 times Canada's GNP of CDN$356.6 billion.

These scale effects lead to important qualitative differences in the economic institutions and economic organization of the two nations. First and most important, the size of U.S. markets permits a more self-contained U.S. economic system. American manufacturers, in particular, can operate plants of sufficient size to realize economies of scale and density from the American marketplace alone. Remember that both exports and imports represent less than one-tenth of U.S. GNP (1982), but for Canada are more than one-quarter (1983), making Canada much more dependent upon foreign trade. Smaller and highly dispersed markets, save those in Ontario and Quebec, make large production runs difficult. In addition, transportation costs to service these geographically dispersed markets add to the costs of domestically produced goods and services. Often, foreign goods and services are substituted at a lower unit cost.

The differential role of trade in the two economies is the first consequence of the cross-national difference in scale of population and therefore of markets. A second and related one is the dramatic qualitative difference in the goods traded. In general, Canada is still characterized by the phrase "a hewer of wood and drawer of water." Canadian exports are dominated by resource-based materials and imports by manufactures. The situation in the U.S. is the reverse. Consider that in 1983 over 60 per cent of Canada's exports were comprised of raw materials and secondary manufactures while just over one-third were in the high value-added categories of machinery and equipment. This contrasts markedly with 1983 imports with almost two-thirds being machinery, equipment and other finished manufactures (80 per cent of which came from the United States), and one-third crude or semi-finished materials.

Turning to the U.S., almost a mirror-image emerges. In 1982 U.S. exports of foods, feeds, beverages and industrial supplies and materials represented 38 per cent of all exports, while the remainder spanned the whole range of machinery, equipment and consumer manufactures (Table 4-21). On the import side, the situation was similar. For 1982, 45 per cent of U.S. imports were in the categories of crude and semi-finished materials and 55 per cent were in finished manufactures and machinery and equipment. This reinforces the characterization of Canada as an exporter of primary materials and an importer of finished and high value-added manufactures, while the U.S. is in the more enviable position of being much more self-sufficient and of selling high value-added finished products and buying crude and semi-finished materials. This pattern of dependence on trade and especially on the importation of finished products and the export of crude and semi-finished products puts Canada in a unique position among the developed and advanced industrial nations of the world. Despite its high standard of living and remarkable growth over the past century, the Canadian economy, in Wallace Clement's words, is still only "semi-developed."[8] As we will indicate, this has implications for the urban system and the functional character of certain Canadian cities.

Transportation and Communication and the Filling In of North America

In settling a land mass of nearly 20,000,000 square kilometers, the development of transportation and communication systems of previously unknown scale had to be achieved. In the U.S. the network developed very differently from that in Canada. The means of expansion across the continent are instructive and highly relevant for understanding the cities of the two countries.[9]

Great prominence is accorded the railroads in both Canadian and American economic history. However, as modern economic historians of both countries are quick to point out, railroads represented but a stage in the evolution of North America's transportation system. In macrocosm, this expansion across the North American continent as a result of transportation and communication improvements parallels the internal expansion and extension of cities on this continent: increasing residential densities and rising land values encourage transportation investments to bring more land into the effective land supply, facilitating outward expansion and additional waves of transportation and communication investment and population movement.

Three significant areas of difference can be discerned in the transportation/communication "revolution" in Canada and the United States: scale, timing, and underlying rationale. As is to be expected, the scale of transportation and communication investments in the U.S. was much greater than that in Canada. Additionally, the timing of these improvements tended to be earlier. Finally, and of particular importance, the underlying rationale in the U.S. for continued expansion across the continent was provided by the claim of "Manifest Destiny" and the growth of the capitalist system in the United States, while much of Canadian expansion can be seen as defensive in light of American westward movement with sporadic northerly thrusts.

At a continental scale, the very different pace of nation-building and associated settlement is revealed by simply noting the land areas of the two countries since their respective foundings (1790 and 1867). From its inception, the U.S. was significantly larger than Canada (891,800 square miles in 1790 compared with Canada's 384,600 square miles in 1867). The Louisiana Territory (in 1803), Texas-New Mexico-Arizona and Washington and Oregon (in the 1840s) and Alaska (in the 1860s) were quickly added. By the time of Canadian Confederation in 1867, the geographic boundaries of the continental United States were fixed.

Whereas the U.S. expanded across the continent through purchase or outright military conquest, Canada grew through the successive ceding of territory by Great Britain, starting with the original four provinces of New Brunswick, Nova Scotia, Lower and Upper Canada (thereafter Quebec and Ontario) and then adding Manitoba and the Northwest and Yukon Territories (1870), British Columbia (1871), Alberta and Saskatchewan (1905) and Newfoundland and Labrador (1949). Westward development in Canada was in part fueled by the influx of immigrants and the desire for additional arable land and in part by the desire to stave off the American taking of lands north of the 49th parallel. This was the case in British Columbia, where the residents of the Crown Colony of British Columbia required that the Dominion of Canada build a transcontinental railroad within ten years. The railroad was needed to ensure an east-west link with the Dominion rather than north-south links, and it represents perhaps the clearest and most dramatic example of defensive expansion practiced by Canada.[10]

To implement these different approaches to territorial expansion, contrasting approaches to transportation and communication investment were adopted, reflecting, in part, prevailing ideologies and, in part, the scales of undertaking. Beginning with plank roads, then canals, railroads, highways and airports, quite distinctive methods of financing, building and administering these transportation improvements evolved in the two countries. To generalize, the U.S. was characterized by more private financing, development and management than was Canada. Notable exceptions can be cited; the massive public schemes for funding the Erie Canal in New York state and the Mainline Canal in Pennsylvania in the 1830s, as well as the enormous subsidies provided to railroad companies by federal government land grants in the West. In Canada, governmental involvement often extended beyond subsidizing construction, as the Dominion did on a lavish scale with land and construction grants to the Canadian Pacific Railway, to the management and operation of transportation investments and systems. Notable illustrations include the federally owned Canadian National Railways (CNR), the National Harbours Board (NHB), the airport system (Ministry of Transport) as well as the early canals and the St. Lawrence Seaway project (though here again U.S. government investment and management is present, providing an exception to the generalization).[11]

The scale differences in the development of transportation and communication infrastructure in Canada and the U.S. are striking. For example, by 1850, less than two decades after the introduction of the railroad in the U.S., there were some 9,000 miles of track, rising to 31,000 in 1860 and reaching 53,000 by 1870. Railroad mileage peaked at 430,000 in 1930 and has declined steadily to its present level of roughly 300,000 miles.

In Canada, construction and completion of the transcontinental rail link took place almost two decades later than in the U.S. Hence, we see both a different scale and later development. At mid-century, Canada had a paltry 66 miles of track in operation. By 1860 this figure had risen to 2,000 miles and by 1870 to 2,600 (roughly one-twentieth of the U.S. total). With the admission of British Columbia to Confederation, railroad track mileage soared as the transcontinental system began to take shape. Reaching 13,000 miles in 1890, it peaked at just over 60,000 miles in 1974, though the basic configuration has not appreciably changed since the mid-1950's; the exceptions are developments in British Columbia and Alberta continuing to the present. Thus, despite a later start, the Canadian railroad network has been developed by the public sector so that it is relatively larger and more important than its American counterpart; U.S. trackage is less than five times that in Canada.

Some additional comments concerning the national rail systems are worth making. First, despite similar funding in the nineteenth century (largely through the sale of stocks and bonds abroad, particularly in Great Britain), during the twentieth century U.S. railroads have largely continued as private companies (the exceptions being AMTRAK and CONRAIL), whereas the biggest and most technologically advanced railroad in Canada, the CNR, is in public hands. Also, considerable public railroad expenditures continue to be made in Western Canada by the provinces of Alberta and British Columbia. There is provincial involvement in Quebec and Ontario as well, on a smaller scale, but with similar ends—opening up resource-rich hinterlands and servicing the resource towns created by the new transportation routes. A second key difference lies in the much closer relationship between the development of the railroad and the evolution of the Canadian national settlement system. Indeed, from Sault Ste. Marie, Ontario, west, all major communities lie on either the CPR or the CNR. Thus, the role of the railroad in forming and, through service, maintaining the settlement pattern in Canada is much more apparent than in the U.S., where air, water and highways had at least an equal role in the present distribution of the U.S. population, especially through highway building in the post-World War II period.

Highways provide a striking instance of the degree of difference between the present transportation systems in Canada and the U.S. First, the highway network in the latter is much more extensive and has grown more quickly than that in Canada. Beginning with the first U.S. data, in 1904 there were 154,000 miles of paved roads.[12] By 1981 a total of 3,853,000 miles of road were recorded in the U.S., one-sixth of which lay within municipal boundaries and over 86 per cent of which were paved. In contrast, Canada had a total of 382,000 miles of road in 1928 (the first year for which complete data are available) of which a mere 7,700 miles were paved (2.0 per cent), 56,400 were surfaced with gravel or stone and 320,000 miles were earth, of which half were improved and half were unimproved. By 1974, Canada recorded a total of 537,000 miles of road of which almost two-thirds were under municipal jurisdiction, but only about one-quarter were paved, and a fifth had no surfacing whatsoever. Canada's paved road mileage figure of 144,000 represents a scant 4.5 per cent of the U.S. figure; in other words, the U.S. has twenty-two times the amount of paved road mileage, which understates the total since there are many more multi-lane roads in the U.S. than in Canada. Differences persist when we look at motor vehicle registrations, though they are less dramatic. For instance, in 1977 there were 143.8 million registered motor vehicles (excluding tractors) in the U.S., while in Canada there were only 12.5 million motor vehicles registered, or one-twelfth of the U.S. figure.

The road system in Canada has been the one form of transport that has not received significant federal funding, the major exception being the Trans-Canada highway. In contrast, highways have been the predominant area for U.S. federal government transportation investment. For example, in 1976, the Canadian federal government transferred a total of $70 million to provincial, territorial and local governments for road maintenance and construction. In marked contrast, the U.S. federal government contributed $9,198 million for highway construction and maintenance and administration in 1977, or 130 times the Canadian federal government total. The impacts of such massive spending on the access network in the U.S. have been equally massive. As will be seen in Chapter 7, the form and spatial organization of urban areas in the U.S. and Canada differ greatly, in part as a result of differences in their urban transportation systems.

Comparable data do not exist for air travel in Canada and the U.S. In summary, both nations rely heavily on air carriers to service vast distances, and both have established extensive nation-wide air networks.

Once again, significant differences are hidden by looking at data alone. Most significant is the distinctive role played by the Canadian government in air traffic in Canada compared with a much lesser role played by the U.S. Both governments licence and regulate, or deregulate, air traffic. However, the Canadian government, through the Ministry of Transport, operates and plans all major airports in Canada. In the U.S., local government airport authorities have this responsibility. Of greater importance is the presence of Air Canada. This publicly owned airline accounts for more than one-half of

funds for urban development have been considerably more abundant and more stable in Canada since the 1967-69 mortgage market deregulation than they have in the U.S. This has undoubtedly contributed in some measure to the relatively greater stability of Canadian cities to be discussed in later chapters. Ample sources of private capital have enabled Canadian cities and their central neighborhoods to reinvest in their building stock and maintain their fiscal, physical and economic health.[17]

The Role of the Public Sector

Probably the most striking and consistent difference between Canadian and American value systems is the sentiment toward government. Americans express great concern about and distrust of government. Canadians, in contrast, place considerable trust in government and in its civil servants. This fundamental divergence in values must figure prominently in any discussion of the economic institutions and structures of the two countries.

A fascinating picture emerges. Despite the generally perceived view that Canada is more "socialist" than the U.S. because there is more state involvement in the economic system, the perception does not stand close scrutiny. While it is certainly true that Canadians are less wary of government involvement in the economy and more accepting of government economic initiatives, it is not the case that the public sector is in fact consistently more heavily involved in the economy than is the U.S. government. The style of intervention, however, does differ considerably, as does public acceptance. Thus, one finds strange inconsistencies in the American approach, such as the previously noted involvement in mortgage and capital markets. This particular intervention has come under criticism recently. In attempting to regulate savings and mortgage interest rates, rather than letting them find their own levels through the marketplace as in Canada, considerable instability was introduced into U.S. mortgage markets. Such intervention might even be termed "socialistic." Other anomalies will be touched on shortly, such as the massive subsidies for urban and interregional expansion through federal highway and water resource funds, funds which are not available in Canada where the urban system has had to grow much more out of its own and local developer resource bases.[18]

Governments are important economic actors as a result of their capacity to raise and spend revenues. Firstly, considering spending, *all* levels of government in Canada spent CDN$168.7 billion or CDN$6,930 per capita in 1982; this represented just under half of the GNP. In that same year, *all* levels of government in the U.S. spent US$1,167.7 billion or US$5,040 per capita; furthermore, this spending amounted to 38 per cent of U.S. GNP. By both measures, government spending in Canada is, in proportionate terms, 24.4 per cent greater than in the U.S. (Table 4-6).

Two other comparisons shed light on the relative roles of government in the two countries. The public sector has become an important employer in national, regional and metropolitan economies. In the U.S. there were a total of 15,803,000 government employees in 1982, each serving 14.6 Americans. In Canada, equivalent figures for 1982 show a total of 647,000 government employees or one employee for each 38.1 Canadians. In other words, there were just over two and one-half times as many government employees in the U.S. per capita as in Canada, an unexpected outcome given the divergent attitudes toward government in the two countries. These data, it should be noted, are not strictly comparable since the Canadian figures include military personnel but exclude crown corporations employees, while the U.S. figures include the employees of publicly owned enterprises like TVA but do not include the two million military service personnel.

Lastly, consider the contentious issue of the public debt. Unmatured debt by all levels of government in Canada in 1981 amounted to CDN$168.1 billion or CDN$6,906 per capita or a staggering 86.9 per cent of 1981 GNP. In the U.S., all levels of government realized debts in 1981 of US$1,368 billion or US$6,037 per capita or 46.3 per cent of GNP. These figures are not strictly comparable because Canadian debt figures include the debt of crown corporations.

Synthesizing this leaves a very muddied impression. On some dimensions Canada is indeed much more dominated by government. However, on other dimensions such as the number of governmental units and government employees, it is the U.S. that is clearly a more governed society. What can be concluded is this: it is difficult to make categorical statements about the relative degree of government involvement in the economic systems of the two countries despite prevailing myths of free enterprise in the U.S. and public enterprise in Canada.

This last point is worth stressing. If there is one significant difference between U.S. and Canadian governments, it is the willingness, and corresponding public acceptance, of Canadian governments at all levels to engage in public enterprise activities which would be considered inappropriate in the U.S. Such leading crown corporations as Air Canada, CNR, and PetroCanada come immediately to mind. Herschel Hardin, in a stimulating book, *A Nation Unaware*,[19] makes this point repeatedly: whereas Americans have demonstrated a particular and unparalleled ability in the realm of private enterprise, Canada's "genius" with respect to economic organization and innovation lies in public enterprise.

When we look at cities and government roles in cities, there is an enthusiasm for public enterprise development in Canada that is distinct from analogous undertakings in the U.S. and which has had significantly different impacts on Canada's cities. For example, one of the key considerations in moving the headquarters of the government-owned Insurance Corporation of British Columbia (ICBC) was its impact on urban form. A close-in suburban location was chosen for its consistency with a regional development plan, thus seeking to enhance the general public good and not the more limited corporate objectives of ICBC. Similar collectivist goals were achieved by the location of Saskatchewan's provincially owned potash company offices in Saskatoon and not Regina in order to help stimulate the Saskatoon office sector and promote its urban core. The two million square-foot PetroCanada building in Calgary had similar social goals and a visible impact on downtown Calgary. At the level of the urban street, PetroCanada service stations also provide symbolic evidence of public enterprise for Canadians, who are urged by billboards to "pump their money back into Canada."

Branch Plants and Multinationals

Earlier in this chapter considerable attention was paid to the international trading and investment positions of the Canadian and U.S. economies. Two central and critical differences emerged from these explorations: the Canadian economy is much more dependent upon foreign trade and on foreign capital, making it much more subject to external control than is the U.S. economy. Relatedly, the U.S. economy is the principal purchaser of Canadian exports (primarily raw and semi-finished materials), is the principal seller of Canada's imports (primarily manufactured and finished goods) and is the principal foreign owner of Canadian productive capacity. The share of foreign ownership of non-financial corporate businesses in the U.S. is so small that it is scarcely a concern in contrast to the Canadian situation (Tables 4-9 and 4-19). In sum, the Canadian economy is much more vulnerable to foreign influences, not just through its dependence upon trade, but equally through the enormous share of Canadian productive capacity controlled by foreigners, particularly Americans.

This massive and asymmetrical set of economic linkages between the Canadian and U.S. economies has attracted much attention, primarily in Canada as one would expect. Nevertheless, there is a growing parallel interest in the "last bastion of free enterprise" now that a number of large Canadian urban development, cablevision and conglomerate companies have cast their eyes, and their financial resources, south of the 49th parallel in recent years. At the same time, Canada has taken steps to increase domestic control of key sectors; the National Energy Program in the petroleum and natural gas sector is probably the most well known and politically contentious example. The Foreign Investment Review Agency (FIRA) was visible, if less effective, in promoting and regulating Canadian ownership of Canadian enterprises. Despite a considerable body of restrictive legislation in the U.S. and despite the miniscule proportion of foreign ownership of U.S. assets, the foreign ownership issue is rapidly becoming important there.

Extant research has dealt with several facets of the foreign ownership issue. Those receiving attention are: i) foreign control of the Canadian economy; ii) branch plants and loss of research-and-development and administrative autonomy; iii) natural resource depletion; iv) elites and elite linkages which are foreign and externally oriented; v) local economic impacts, often urban in their specific geographic context. Of particular interest to this study are the local impacts, but obviously these cannot be readily separated from the others. A brief review of these issues will prove helpful.

Ardent economic nationalists decry the loss of Canadian economic autonomy and the resulting helplessness in a complex and highly integrated Western economic system. They emphasize the consequences of foreign control for production methods, plant size and efficiency.[20] Their studies do establish that the Canadian economy is critically influenced by foreign direct investment, particularly in manufacturing and petroleum and especially by American firms.

In response to the evidence and subsequent political pressure, the federal government, as noted, initiated a number of policies to stem the tide. Market conditions have had their effect, too. Canadian enterprises have been reacquired by domestic interests as their foreign owners found operating in Canada too expensive or too different from operating in the U.S. or elsewhere.[21] Data are not yet available to show the effects of these changes during the early 1980s, but in all likelihood they will alter the picture outlined in this chapter. So too will the policies of the Progressive Conservative government in Ottawa; for example, FIRA has been replaced by the more encouraging *Investment Canada* agency.

Viewed historically, the present circumstance is ironic, since much of the thrust for foreign ownership of Canadian productive resources arose out of the highly nationalistic National Policy of 1879 propounded by Sir John A. Macdonald and advocated as the basis for a strong domestic economy.[22] As Macdonald observed in an 1878 House of Commons debate:

> We have no manufacturers here. We have no workpeople; our work people have gone off to the United States. . . . These Canadian artisans are adding to the strength, to the power, and to the wealth of a foreign nation instead of adding to ours. Our workpeople in this country. . . are suffering for want of employment. . . . if Canada had had a judicious system of taxation (tariffs) they would be toiling and doing well in their own country.[23]

Facing highly restrictive tariff barriers, foreign firms invested directly in plant, equipment and resource extraction to get behind these barriers and reach a growing Canadian market—a logical extension of the U.S. market. This shift from what Marr and Paterson term "portfolio investment" to "direct investment" accelerated as a result of the National Policy and escalated dramatically after World War II as foreign firms expanded their Canadian operations and established new ones. Thus, as often happens, well conceived policies in economics wind up being not only ineffective but also rather counterproductive. In this instance, a nationalistic economic policy to promote economic development led over the ensuing century to a progressive takeover of the domestic economy by foreign interests.

The direct control over Canadian productive capacity and investment decisions is worrisome enough. Compounding the seriousness of the situation, the political power that goes with economic power also devolved to foreign interests. Naturally, they sought to protect their investments, making the Canadian political system vulnerable to external interests to a degree not acceptable elsewhere, especially in the U.S. The loss of central office functions and with them entrepreneurial initiative, research-and-development spending, and autonomy all take their toll of the Canadian economic system and have been discussed widely in the academic and the popular literature.[24]

Turning finally to the consequences of external control of Canadian enterprises on local economies and urban development, Robert Parry in his classic study *Galt, U.S.A.* traces the evolution of U.S. purchases of Canadian establishments in the Ontario manufacturing center of Galt and the consequences for its local economy and urban development.[25] Clearly, branch plant openings, closings and expansions or contractions have enormous consequences for local economies and for the management of urban development in affected areas. When such plants are controlled locally, there is a *quid pro quo* that can be established which explicitly acknowledges the overlap and conflict of the public and the private interest. When ownership is removed, not just to another locale but to another country, a very different *quid pro quo* evolves, one which is much more likely to favor the private as opposed to the public interest. In microcosm, the vulnerability of the Canadian economic system is repeated at the local level. With the pace of urban development so sensitive to investment decisions in these foreign-controlled activities, it is perhaps not surprising that the local public sector has sought an active autonomous role in urban development.

URBAN ECONOMIES: DIVERGENT APPROACHES TO URBAN DEVELOPMENT

The relative roles of government in the two economies provide a useful point of departure for comparing urban development processes in Canada

and the United States. Three themes are pursued, each relating to government and urban development and revealing the differing types and perceptions of public sector involvement.

First, the federal structure (discussed in more detail in Chapter 5) in the
two nations is very different indeed. Paradoxically, the U.S., with its anti-
involvement mythology and its Jeffersonian ideals of strong local and weak
central governments, emerges as the nation in which an expansionary central government has played a major role in urban affairs, whereas the
generally more "interventionist" Canadian federal government plays a minor
role in urban affairs, leaving the major role to the provinces.[26] It can also be
argued that at the local level, Canadian municipalities have generally been
more active and less passive than their American equivalents.

Secondly, we will see Canadian involvement in urban development not
just in a subsidy role but also in profit-making public enterprises, a form
noted previously at the federal and provincial levels. This latter orientation
provides for very different kinds of direct intervention in urban development,
as often as not through the market itself as well as through more traditional
regulatory instruments such as zoning and subdivision controls.[27]

Third, and finally, Canadian provincial governments have demonstrated
an ingenuity and willingness to experiment with new local governmental
forms in a manner virtually unknown in the U.S. This is particularly apparent in the varieties of regional governmental experiments in several provinces,
again fully consistent with the greater acceptance of government as a positive actor in economic affairs in Canada. Discussion of this theme is reserved
to Chapters 5 and 8.

The first two themes will be explored in the context of the two principal
kinds of urban development guidance carried out by local governments in
both Canada and the U.S.: regulatory guidance through zoning, subdivision
and growth management/environmental controls; and direct government
investment and enterprise.

Regulatory controls of urban development

In general, in both countries these controls are local in nature, emanating
from counties and municipalities in the United States and from municipalities,
counties and regional governments in Canada. There are some important
exceptions to this generalization.

First, the role of the U.S. federal government in urban affairs in general
and in regulatory issues specifically is vastly greater than the corresponding
role of the Canadian federal government. For example, the Canadian federal
government has no direct role, and only a minor indirect role, in the urban
development process itself, a subject treated in the next chapter. In this

lesser capacity, it provides monies for mortgages and mortgage insurance and for some servicing of land by municipalities and provinces. In the U.S., in contrast, the federal role is significant and in some instances pivotal. Specifically, the entry of the federal government into urban development by way of the Environmental Protection Agency and the related legislation results in a leverage over urban development not available to Ottawa.[28] Federal concerns about air-sheds, watersheds and ecologically sensitive areas have enabled the federal government in the U.S. to establish urban development guidelines and set standards for air and water pollution and for the protection of ecologically sensitive areas such as wetlands and shorelines. The U.S. government through recent changes in tax policy has tended to promote preservation and reuse of historic and landmark buildings, just as in earlier decades it promoted urban renewal and new construction through tax and subsidy schemes. School aid and busing have also had significant impacts on the patterns of U.S. urban and suburban development, again without parallel in Canada.

Considering the range of development controls exercised by local governments in the two countries, a very different picture emerges. Canadian local governments have been able to be far more aggressive and innovative. The scope for such controls in Canada derives from a very different legal and institutional base from that in the U.S. and follows directly from differing social and political conceptions of private property and of property rights in the two countries. A brief review of the concept and institution of property in Canada and the U.S. is now in order. This done, some consequences of the contrasting conceptions of property as an institution can be explored by examining the kinds of land use and urban development controls that are possible in the two nations.

In a technical sense, no individual person or corporate entity in Canada owns land. The Queen, as monarch, through federal, provincial and local crown ownership, is the sole "owner" of land in Canada. Individuals and corporations do own interests in land such as fee simple rights to occupy, use and sell land, consistent with societal controls, and can also own leasehold rights and other legal interests such as easements. However, ownership, and the implied right to use and develop land for private purposes that flows from ownership, is vested with the Crown in its several manifestations. As a result, in Canada the control and use of land is a societal or crown responsibility from the start.[29] Interestingly, the Canadian *Charter of Rights and Freedoms* (enacted in 1982) explicitly excluded property rights from among the enumerated and protected rights, a completely consistent outcome in light of past precedent (see Chapter 5 for additional discussion on this point).

This treatment of land contrasts markedly with that in the United States, where property rights are explicitly vested in the individual owner through the fifth and fourteenth amendments to the U.S. Constitution, which ensure that real property rights cannot be taken away and that real property can only be taken under eminent domain with due process and with due cause.[30] As a result, such legislation as the British Columbia *Limited Access Highways Act*, wherein the B.C. Highways Department as an agent of the Crown can seize up to 5 per cent of an individual's land *without* any compensation whatsoever is unimaginable in the United States. Similarly the *B.C. Land Commission Act* which "froze" all farmland in agricultural use, again without any compensation, is also unimaginable in the context of U.S. land use and urban development law.

However, as noted previously, where Canadian governments have much greater ability to control land use and urban development, the role played by the Canadian federal government in this process is minimal. Under Sections 92(8) (Municipal Institutions) and 92(13) (Property and Civil Rights) of the original *British North America Act*, and continued under *The Constitution Act, 1982*, the provinces have the exclusive rights to govern cities and regulate property. Thus, such federal intrusions into the urban development process as are commonplace in the U.S. are inconceivable in Canada. More specifically, such U.S. legislation as the *National Environmental Policy Act* (1969), The *Coastal Zone Management Act* (1971), the *Clean Air Act of 1970 with 1977 Amendments*, and the *Federal Water Pollution Control Act of 1972*, which together give the U.S. federal government significant powers to regulate urban development where it conflicts with the purposes of the above acts, would be considered well outside the federal domain in Canada. The much talked about *National Land Use Act* of the early and mid-1970s could never have been introduced into the Canadian federal parliament, it being so clearly outside the purview of Canadian federal responsibility.[31]

Ironically, therefore, it is in the U.S. where federal activities in relation to urban land markets are most vigorous despite prevailing myths of private property rights, preference for small government and general abhorrence of government intervention into markets, especially local markets such as those in real property. As the plethora of court battles of the 1970s attest, efforts to bring urban development and land use under tighter controls were met by exceptionally strong opposition at all levels, though the federal legislation bore up best against these challenges. In Canada, on the other hand, the myriad of locally based land-use and urban-development controls enacted during the 1960s and 1970s has remained virtually untouched by the courts. With local governments having been delegated the responsibility and authority to regulate land use and urban development by their respective provinces, public officials can act directly to regulate the pace and character of urban growth without having to circumvent constitutional protection of individually vested real property rights. They utilize stringent subdivision controls and servicing standards, downzoning, heritage and historical preservation and the protection of agricultural and sensitive lands. Such convoluted and contentious growth controlling devices as sewer and water moratoria, exclusionary zoning and development rights, transfers and limitations are much less common.

In summary, Canadian local governments have much greater direct power to regulate urban development than do their American equivalents, given the absence of broadly based constitutional guarantees of property rights. At the federal level, however, it is the U.S. central government that has exercised the larger role. With Canadian provincial and local governments (including here regional governments) having more freedom to control urban growth and land use, together with marked inter-provincial differences in planning legislation, we see a diversity of land-use controlling strategies and regulations in Canada that is without an equivalent in the United States.[32] Moreover, much of the simplicity of the Canadian approach is obviated by the U.S. Constitution and the body of law erected upon it.

Government Investment in Urban Development: The economic consequences of the differences in regulating urban development and land use in Canadian and U.S. cities are significant. Of equal significance is direct public involvement in the urban development process itself and in the provision of needed public utilities and transportation. Here again, major differences between Canadian and American practices exist. In general, Canadian cities and the provinces are much less hesitant about becoming directly involved, often as an entrepreneur, than is the case in the U.S. In addition, and again consistent with the preceding discussion, in Canada the federal government has a relatively minor role, particularly when compared with the scale of U.S. federal government in funding urban development and its attendant infrastructure.

Some recent examples serve to amplify the point. First, the resurgence of interest in public transit provides a good starting point. To begin with, public transit in Canada never did experience the ridership declines registered in the U.S. in the heyday of freeway and suburban development, in part because of the much less extensive freeway programs in Canada.[33] Starting from a higher ridership base, Canadian cities during the past decade or so have financed their transit systems in a radically different fashion from cities in the U.S., largely because of the absence of direct Canadian federal financing.

With the first energy "crisis" in 1973, greater attention was focussed in the U.S. on transit as a means for conserving scarce energy resources. The Ford Administration redirected federal funds from highways to rapid transit and committed in excess of US$10 billion to rapid transit construction.[34] The details and thrust of this program were remarkably similar to the freeway boom of the 1950s and 1960s—only the transportation mode and technology changed. Beneficiaries of such federal funding include the extensions to the Massachusetts Bay Transportation Authority subway in Cambridge, Massachusetts, at a cost of over US$1 billion for less than 4 miles of added line; the 100+ mile Washington METRO system at a cost in excess of US$8 billion; the Metropolitan Atlanta Rapid Transit System (MARTA) with a cost in excess of US$3 billion; and numerous smaller systems such as those in Detroit and Cleveland. In all cases, large-scale federal funds were crucial to project financing.

Recent Canadian experience is quite different. In 1978 Edmonton, Alberta, opened a 7.2 kilometer light rail transit system using German streetcars, with roughly 2 kilometers underground below the city center and the remainder at grade on "rented" railroad tracks with street level crossings. The system was in operation for the 1978 Commonwealth Games, at a cost of under CDN$70 million, paid for by the city and the province of Alberta.

Calgary, Alberta, shortly followed suit and opened its own 12.4 km light rail transit system in 1981, again using German streetcars, rented track and downtown Calgary streets. The Calgary system is largely financed by the city of Calgary with provincial assistance. Again, as in Edmonton, land use controls promote intensive development in station areas to focus future growth in those areas with superior access and well served by other public and private investments, such as community centers and shopping.[35]

The last example is provided by the Advanced Light Rail Transit (ALRT) now under construction in the Greater Vancouver region. This is a more ambitious project with 30 to 32 kilometers of trackage and automatically controlled light rail vehicles running on elevated guideways. This system is projected to cost about CDN$1 billion. The cost is financed by the Province of British Columbia as well as by a CDN$60 million grant from the Canadian federal government on the pretext that there is great export potential for this system, Vancouver being a prototype.

In short, there is much greater local input to the planning, development and financing of transit investments in Canada than there is in the U.S., where the federal government takes such a large and central position.[36]

This greater willingness of local governments to involve themselves directly in urban development in Canada is apparent from some other examples as well. For example, the cities of Red Deer, Alberta, Prince George, B.C., and Saskatoon, Saskatchewan, are all actively involved in the subdivision and servicing of residential land in direct competition with the private sector and without any public subsidy. The city of Vancouver has taken a very entrepreneurial stance in its development of the centrally located former industrial slum, False Creek, turning it into a booming housing area with more than 3,000 housing units built on city lands during the past seven or eight years and an additional 1,000+ units built on adjacent underutilized residential and industrial lands. The city has also subdivided and serviced a large subdivision in the southeastern part of the city and sold or leased parcels to developers, increasing the tax base and recovering all costs while making modest profits.

This self-financing locally based civic entrepreneurial activity should be contrasted with federally financed and heavily subsidized urban renewal schemes in the U.S. The oft criticized Urban Renewal schemes of the 1950s and 1960s are a caricature of this type of intervention. Such direct market involvement in profitable activities is however unlikely to be acceptable in the U.S., and thus government is largely confined to subsidized and non-market urban investments.

SUMMARY

To put the foregoing in perspective, it is clear that the U.S. and Canadian economies, economic elites and economic establishments are closely linked. It is also very clear that there are significant differences in the structure, function and scale of the two economies. Their histories also differ in important ways. One point that cannot be disputed is the magnitude and complexity of the economic linkages that connect the Canadian and American economies. But these linkages are not symmetrical. The U.S. clearly dominates these economic relations at all levels. Recent Canadian efforts to balance the linkages better have met with considerable resistance from both the U.S. government and from U.S. firms. The move by U.S. government to bring charges against Canada under the terms of the General Agreement on Tariffs and Trade (GATT) for the *Foreign Investment Review Act* and the growing resentment of Canadian takeovers of U.S. firms in selected industries provide evidence of the discomfort being experienced in economic relations as redress is sought to for the asymmetry of past and present economic interactions between the two countries.

TABLE 4-1
COMPARISON OF LONG-RUN TRENDS IN ECONOMIC DEVELOPMENT:
GROWTH OF REAL NATIONAL PRODUCT, POPULATION, AND REAL
PER-CAPITA PRODUCT PER DECADE, SELECTED COUNTRIES

Country Period (1)	Real National Product (2)	Population (3)	Real Product Per Capita (4)
Canada			
1870-74 to 1960-62	40.7	19.1	18.1
England and Wales-United Kingdom			
1700 to 1780	5.3	3.2	2.0
1780 to 1881	28.2	13.1	13.4
1855-59 to 1957-59	21.1	6.1	14.1
France			
1841-50 to 1960-62	20.8	2.5	17.9
Germany-West Germany			
1851-55 to 1871-75	17.6	7.7	9.2
1871-75 to 1960-62	31.1	11.2	17.9
Netherlands			
1900-04 to 1960-62	29.7	14.3	13.5
Switzerland			
1809-99 to 1957-59	25.7	8.3	16.1
Denmark			
1870-74 to 1960-62	31.8	10.4	19.4
Norway			
1865-74 to 1960-62	29.0	8.4	19.0
Sweden			
1861-65 to 1960-62	36.9	6.7	28.3
Italy			
1861-65 to 1898-1902	9.7	6.8	2.7
1898-1902 to 1960-62	26.8	6.8	18.7
United States			
1889 to 1960-62	42.5	21.6	17.2
Australia			
1861-65 to 1959-62	34.1	24.2	8.0
Japan			
1879-81 to 1959-61	42.0	12.3	26.4
European Russia-U.S.S.R.			
1860 to 1913	30.2	13.8	14.4
1913 to 1958	35.7	6.4	27.4
1928 to 1958	53.8	6.9	43.9

Source: William L. Marr and Donald G. Paterson, *Canada: An Economic History* (Toronto: Macmillan, 1980), 9. Reproduced by permission.

TABLE 4-2
RELATIVE SIZE OF SIXTEEN ECONOMIES, 1980
(Gross Domestic Product, GDP, in U.S. dollars at current
prices and exchange rates)

Country	GDP	GDP Per Capita
	($ billions)	($)
Canada	253.34	10,582
U.S.A.	2,587.10	11,364
U.K.	522.86	9,335
France	651.88	12,136
Germany	819.12	13,305
Italy	393.95	6,906
Japan	1,036.16	8,873
Belgium	116.48	11,816
Netherlands	167.63	11,851
Australia	148.05	10,129
Switzerland	101.46	15,922
Austria	76.98	10,251
Sweden	122.75	14,761
Denmark	66.38	12,952
Norway	57.29	14,019
Finland	49.90	10,440

Source: OECD, *Historical Statistics, 1960-1980* (Paris: OECD, 1983), 14-16.

TABLE 4-3
SECTORAL DISTRIBUTION OF CANADIAN GNP, 1851-1980
(in per cent)

	Primary Sector			Secondary Sector				
Year	Agriculture	Other[1]	Total	Manufacturing	Construction	Total	Tertiary[2] Sector	Other[3]
(1)	(2)	(3)	(4)	(5)	(6)	(7)	(8)	(9)
1851	32.0	14.8	46.8	18.3	4.2	22.5	18.9	11.8
1860	38.2	12.0	50.2	15.0	4.1	19.1	19.7	11.0
1870	33.3	11.6	44.9	19.0	3.0	22.0	20.9	12.2
1880	32.0	11.5	43.5	18.9	3.8	22.7	22.4	11.4
1890	27.0	9.6	36.6	23.5	4.5	28.1	26.7	8.6
1900	26.7	9.8	36.5	20.8	4.2	25.0	29.4	9.1
1910	22.8	7.4	30.2	22.7	5.1	27.8	33.6	8.4
1920	19.4	7.2	26.6	24.1	5.5	29.7	35.3	8.4
1930	11.0	4.8	15.9	21.7	4.4	26.1	52.3	5.7
1940	10.3	7.3	17.6	24.1	2.8	26.9	45.7	9.8
1950	9.5	6.1	15.6	26.2	4.9	31.1	44.6	8.7
1960	4.8	5.3	9.6	23.2	4.8	28.0	51.0	11.4
1970	3.4	5.0	8.4	23.3	6.3	29.6	62.0	
1980	3.3	7.9	11.2	20.7	5.9	26.6	62.2	

[1]Includes forestry, fishing and trapping, mining, quarrying, and oil wells.

[2]Includes transport and communications storage, utilities, wholesale and retail trade, finance, insurance and real estate, public administration and personal services

[3]From 1851 to 1920 inclusive this category includes rents, net indirect taxes, and net investment income. For later years it includes net income paid to non-residents.

Source: Marr and Paterson, *Canada*, 22, (for 1851-1970); and *National Income and Product Accounts* (Ottawa: Statistics Canada, 1982) (for 1980).

TABLE 4-4
COMPOSITION OF CANADIAN EXPORTS AND IMPORTS BY VALUE, 1851-1960
(percentage of total)

	1851	1860	1870	1880	1890	1900	1910	1920	1930	1940	1950	1960
	(1)	(2)	(3)	(4)	(5)	(6)	(7)	(8)	(9)	(10)	(11)	(12)
Exports:												
Agricultural Products	23.5	38.1	14.9	38.1	15.7	14.7	30.7	33.6	36.6	31.4	34.4	26.7
Animals and Their Products	11.8	19.0	23.9	28.8	40.4	38.4	25.5	25.3	10.5	31.4	34.4	26.7
Fibres and Textiles	—	—	1.5	1.4	1.1	1.1	0.7	2.7	0.8	2.0	1.0	1.0
Wood, Wood Products & Paper	52.9	33.3	34.3	20.9	28.1	18.6	20.4	17.3	28.9	29.5	38.6	37.2
Iron and Its Products	—	—	1.5	1.6	1.1	2.3	3.6	6.6	5.6	10.9	9.5	14.2
Non-ferrous Metals	—	2.4	1.5	1.6	2.2	18.6	12.4	4.4	10.9	16.5	15.9	28.4
Non-metallic Minerals	—	2.4	3.0	1.7	4.5	4.0	3.6	2.4	2.7	2.9	3.6	7.9
Chemicals	—	—	—	—	1.1	0.6	1.1	1.8	1.9	2.6	3.5	5.6
Others	11.8	4.8	19.4	5.8	5.6	1.7	1.8	5.8	2.2	4.3	1.7	2.0
TOTAL	100.0	100.0	100.0	100.0	100.0	100.0	100.0	100.0	100.0	100.0	100.0	100.0
Imports:												
Agricultural Products	22.2	31.1	26.2	21.2	21.4	21.3	17.4	22.7	19.0	15.2	16.5	13.4
Animals and Their Products	18.5	8.9	7.1	9.2	7.1	7.9	6.8	8.9	5.9	15.2	16.5	13.4
Fibres and Textiles	25.9	31.1	20.2	32.1	25.9	21.3	19.4	21.8	14.8	14.3	11.5	7.8
Wood, Wood Products & Paper	3.7	2.2	—	4.1	4.5	4.5	6.0	4.0	5.0	3.6	3.0	4.6
Iron and Its Products	14.8	11.1	11.9	13.9	13.4	16.9	20.3	17.6	22.3	29.2	30.8	37.3
Non-ferrous Metals	—	—	1.2	1.4	3.6	3.9	6.2	4.9	6.6	7.0	6.9	8.7
Non-metallic Minerals	3.7	4.4	4.8	6.8	12.5	11.8	11.7	11.5	16.4	15.7	19.2	12.1
Chemicals	—	2.2	2.4	3.3	3.6	3.4	2.7	2.8	3.7	5.1	5.1	6.3
Others	11.1	8.9	26.2	8.7	8.0	9.0	9.3	5.8	6.3	10.0	7.0	10.0
TOTAL	100.0	100.0	100.0	100.0	100.0	100.0	100.0	100.0	100.0	100.0	100.0	100.0

Note: The above are calculated from data which are in current-value terms. For the years prior to 1930 they cover all exports and imports whereas the most recent calculations are based on the adjusted declared value of domestic exports and imports.

Source Marr and Paterson, *Canada*, 17. Reproduced by permission.

TABLE 4-5
EXPORTS AND IMPORTS BY MERCHANDISE GROUP, CANADA, 1965-1983
(percentage of total)

	1965	1970	1975	1980	1983
Exports:					
Wheat	9.6	4.1	6.1	5.1	5.1
Animals and Other Edible Products	9.9	7.0	6.4	5.8	6.3
Ores and Concentrates	9.8	9.0	6.7	5.5	3.2
Crude Petroleum and Natural Gas	4.4	5.1	12.4	9.0	8.2
Other Crude Materials	5.9	4.2	4.7	4.8	4.5
Lumber	5.6	3.9	2.9	4.4	4.4
Woodpulp	5.6	4.7	5.5	5.1	3.4
Newsprint	9.9	6.6	5.2	4.8	4.4
Fabricated Metals	13.0	11.9	7.4	10.7	7.8
Other fabricated materials	8.4	7.8	8.6	13.6	13.1
Motor vehicles and parts	4.1	20.8	19.3	14.3	23.4
Other machinery and equipment	9.3	9.9	10.2	11.2	10.7
Consumer goods and miscellaneous	1.8	2.5	2.2	3.5	2.9
Re-exports	2.8	2.5	2.3	2.2	2.7
TOTAL	100.0	100.0	100.0	100.0	100.0
Imports:					
Animals and Edible Products	8.9	8.0	7.7	6.9	6.6
Crude Petroleum	3.6	3.0	9.5	10.0	4.3
Other Crude Materials	8.0	5.4	5.1	6.4	5.2
Fabricated Materials	24.5	20.7	17.1	18.3	18.5
Motor Vehicles and Parts	13.0	23.3	23.7	19.6	25.6
Other Machinery and Equipment	29.8	28.6	26.8	28.5	28.2
Other End Products and Miscellaneous	12.1	11.0	10.0	10.2	11.7
TOTAL	100.0	100.0	100.0	100.0	100.0

Source: Department of Finance Canada, *Economic Review, April 1984*, (Ottawa: Minister of Supply and Services Canada, 1984), 204-205.

TABLE 4-6
TOTAL GOVERNMENT AND FEDERAL GOVERNMENT TOTAL
EXPENDITURES AS PERCENTAGES OF GROSS NATIONAL PRODUCT,
1969-1982

	Average 1969-74	1975	1976	1977	1978	1979	1980	1981	1982
Total Government[1]									
Canada	36.7	41.3	40.0	41.1	41.7	40.2	41.9	42.7	47.3
United States	32.4	35.7	34.9	33.9	33.1	33.0	35.1	35.6	38.0
Federal Government[2]									
Canada	14.9	17.3	16.3	16.8	17.2	16.3	17.2	18.1	20.8
United States	17.5	19.4	19.0	18.6	18.0	18.2	19.9	20.9	22.8

[1]Includes all levels of government and the social security system, but excludes public corporations and public financial institutions.

[2]Net of transfers to other levels of government.

Source: Economic Review, 1984, 179.

TABLE 4-7
PERCENTAGE DISTRIBUTION OF FOREIGN LONG-TERM INVESTMENT
IN CANADA,
BY SOURCE AND TYPE, 1930-1980

	Source		Type		
Year	United States	United Kingdom	Direct Investment	Portfolio Investment	Miscellaneous Investment
1930	61.2	36.3	31.9	64.2	3.9
1933	61.0	36.4	31.9	64.4	3.7
1939	60.0	35.8	33.2	62.7	4.1
1945	70.3	24.7	38.3	57.7	4.0
1955	76.1	17.6	57.1	38.1	4.8
1965	79.0	11.9	58.6	34.1	7.3
1970	79.1	9.2	59.7	33.6	6.7
1975	76.5	8.2	54.0	40.7	5.3
1976	73.7	7.7	49.1	45.9	5.0
1977	71.8	7.4	47.7	47.4	4.9
1978	71.1	7.1	46.8	48.7	4.5
1979	69.9	7.0	47.0	48.9	4.1
1980	69.4	6.7	47.8	48.1	4.1

Source: Statistics Canada, *Canada's International Investment Position (1979 and1980),* 1983, Cat. No. 67-202, 59-61.

TABLE 4-8
BOOK VALUE OF FOREIGN DIRECT INVESTMENT IN CANADA, BY SOURCE,
1945-1980

Year	Total	Percentage		
		United States	United Kingdom	Others
	(millions of dollars)			
1945	2,713	84.9	12.8	2.3
1950	3,975	86.2	11.8	2.0
1955	7,728	84.3	11.5	4.2
1960	12,872	82.0	11.9	6.1
1965	17,356	81.0	11.7	7.3
1970	26,423	81.0	9.5	9.5
1975	37,389	79.3	9.7	11.0
1976	40,311	79.2	9.8	11.0
1977	43,683	79.5	9.4	11.1
1978	48,228	79.5	9.3	11.2
1979	54,260	78.8	9.5	11.7
1980	61,637	79.0	8.6	12.4

Source: Statistics Canada, *Canada's International Investment Position (1979 and 1980)*, 1983, Cat. No. 67-202, 58.

TABLE 4-9
BOOK VALUE, OWNERSHIP AND CONTROL OF CAPITAL EMPLOYED IN CANADIAN NON-FINANCIAL INDUSTRIES, SELECTED YEARS

Item and Year	OWNERSHIP						CONTROL					
	Investment Owned In			Percentage of Capital Employed Owned In			Investment Controlled In			Percentage of Capital Employed Controlled In		
	Canada $billion	U.S. $billion	Other Countries $billion	Canada %	U.S. %	Other Countries %	Canada $billion	U.S. $billion	Other Countries $billion	Canada %	U.S. %	Other Countries %
Manufacturing												
1971	12.7	11.7	2.3	47	44	9	11.2	11.7	3.8	42	44	14
1979	32.8	24.3	4.9	53	39	8	30.5	24.4	7.1	49	39	12
1982										51	38	11
Petroleum & Natural Gas												
1971	5.6	6.5	1.5	41	48	11	3.1	8.3	2.2	23	61	16
1979	18.9	14.1	3.5	52	38	10	17.3	14.7	4.6	47	40	13
1982										55	35	10
Mining and Smelting												
1971	3.1	3.4	0.7	43	47	10	2.1	4.3	0.8	29	59	12
1979	7.1	5.0	1.9	51	36	13	6.9	5.1	2.0	49	37	14
1982										57	31	12
Railways												
1971	5.1	0.4	0.5	85	7	8	6.0	0.1	—	98	2	—
1979	4.6	1.1	0.7	71	18	11	6.3	0.1	—	99	1	—
1982										99	1	—
Other Utilities												
1971	19.2	3.9	0.5	81	17	2	21.9	1.0	0.7	93	4	3
1979	47.6	11.4	5.0	74	18	8	61.7	2.2	0.1	96	4	—
1982										97	3	—
Total												
1971	64.6	22.3	6.2	66	28	6	62.7	26.9	8.5	64	27	9
1979	156.4	59.4	17.3	67	26	7	168.1	50.1	15.0	72	22	6
1982										74	20	6

Sources: Statistics Canada, Canada's International Investment Positon (1979 and 1980), 1983, Cat. No. 67-202, pp. 96-102; Canada Yearbook, 1980-81 (Ottawa: Minister of Supply and Services 1982) 882-83.

TABLE 4-10

CANADIAN LONG-TERM INVESTMENT ABROAD,[1] BY COUNTRY AND BY TYPE OF INVESTMENT, SELECTED YEARS, 1951-80

(million dollars)

Location and type of investment	1951	1960	1970	1975	1980
United States					
Direct investment	912	1,618	3,262	5,559	16,395
Stocks	289	827	2,115	3.030	6,840
Bonds	87	120	224	217	375
Miscellaneous investment	9	18	234	556	1,208
Government of Canada credits[2]	—	—	26	—	
Government of Canada subscriptions to international investment agencies	—	—	—	—	
Total, United States	1,297	2,583	5,861	9,362	24,818
United Kingdom					
Direct investment	74	257	586	1,019	2,405
Portfolio investment					
Stocks	17	26	60	85	90
Bonds	17	16	20	48	80
Miscellaneous investment	13	18	74	256	219
Government of Canada credits[3]	1,394	1,092	1,017	909	827
Government of Canada subscriptions to international investment agencies	—	—	—	—	—
Total, United Kingdom	1,515	1,409	1,757	2,317	3,621
Other countries					
Direct investment	180	592	2,340	3,948	7,000
Portfolio investment					
Stocks	161	197	170	425	1,025
Bonds	38	129	230	467	470
Miscellaneous investment	-80	-54	669	2,890	7,099
Government of Canada credits[4]	528	370	447	1,403	2,714
Government of Canada subscriptions to international investment agencies	66	85	268	663	1.726
Total, other countries[5]	893	1,319	4,124	9,796	20,034
All countries					
Direct investment	1,166	2,467	6,188	10,526	25,800
Portfolio investment					
Stocks	467	1,050	2,345	3,540	7,955
Bonds	142	265	474	732	925
Miscellaneous investments	-58	-18	977	3,702	8,526
Government of Canada credits[4]	1,922	1,462	1,490	2,312	3,541
Government of Canada subscriptions to international investment agencies	66	85	268	663	1,726
Total, all countries	3,705	5,311	11,742	21,475	48,473

[1]Figures include the equity of non-residents abroad of Canadian companies, but exclude investment of insurance companies and banks (held mainly, against liabilities to non-residents).

[2]Medium-term non-marketable United States government securities acquired under the Columbia River Treaty arrangements are shown from 1964.

[3]Includes deferred interest on the United Kingdom 1946 loan agreement starting from 1956 and amounting to $116 million in 1976.

[4]Includes United Nations bonds from 1962, which amounted to $3 million in 1976.

[5]Includes other Commonwealth countries.

Source: Canada Yearbook, 1980-81, 877-78; Statistics Canada, Canada International Investment Position, 1979 and 1980, 42-43.

TABLE 4-11

U.S. NATIONAL INCOME, BY INDUSTRIAL ORIGIN, IN CURRENT PRICES: 1930 TO 1980

(in billions of U.S. dollars)

Year	Total	Agriculture, Forestry, and fisheries	Mining	Contract construction	Manufacturing	Wholesale and retail trade	Finance, insurance, and real estate	Transportation	Communications and public utilities	Services	Government and government enterprises	Rest of the world
1930	75.7	6.2	1.6	3.2	18.2	12.2	10.6	5.6	2.8	9.2	5.3	0.7
1940	81.6	6.2	1.9	2.6	22.3	14.3	8.2	5.0	3.1	8.9	8.8	0.4
1950	241.9	17.9	5.0	11.8	74.4	42.7	21.8	13.3	7.2	3.1	23.5	1.2
1960	414.5	16.9	5.7	20.8	125.8	64.4	45.8	18.2	17.2	44.5	52.9	2.4
1970	800.5	25.6	7.7	42.8	217.5	121.3	89.9	29.8	31.5	102.9	126.9	4.6
1980	2,174.0	61.4	38.5	107.2	526.5	316.6	290.9	80.4	90.9	310.0	306.3	45.3

Sources: Statistical Abstract of the U.S., Selected Years; Historical Statistics of the U.S. (Colonial Times to 1970), Washington, DC: U.S. Government Printing Office, 1973).

TABLE 4-12

VALUE OF U.S. MERCHANDISE EXPORTS AND IMPORTS, BY ECONOMIC CLASSES: 1850-1970

(in millions of dollars)

Year	EXPORTS						IMPORTS					
	Total	Crude materials	Crude Foodstuffs	Manufactured foodstuffs[1]	Semimanufactures[2]	Finished manufactures[2]	Total	Crude materials	Crude foodstuffs	Manufactured foodstuffs[1]	Semimanufactures	Finished manufactures
1850	135	84	8	20	6	17	174	13	18	21	26	95
1860	316	217	12	39	13	36	354	40	46	60	35	172
1870	377	214	42	51	14	56	436	57	54	96	56	174
1880	824	243	266	193	29	93	668	142	100	118	111	197
1890	845	309	132	225	46	133	789	180	128	133	117	231
1900	1,371	340	226	320	153	332	850	282	98	133	134	203
1910	1,710	574	110	259	268	499	1,557	578	145	182	285	368
1920	8,080	1,883	918	1,117	958	3,205	5,278	1,784	578	1,238	802	877
1930	3,781	829	179	363	513	1,898	3,061	1,002	400	293	608	757
1940	3,934	464	74	167	900	2,330	2,541	1,011	285	277	559	409
1950	9,864	1,886	760	634	1,121	5,741	8,743	2,465	1,750	898	2,172	1,558
1960	19,459	2,588	1,645	1,117	3,535	10,574	15,068	3,012	1,720	1,566	3,493	5,276
1970	42,029	4,492	2,748	1,921	6,866	26,001	39,963	4,129	2,580	3,523	7,268	22,463

[1]Includes beverages

[2]Beginning 1950, for security reasons, a small amount of semimanufacturers included with finished manufactures.
General imports through 1933; thereafter, imports for consumption. For years ending June 30, 1850-1915; thereafter, calendar years.)

Source: *Historical Statistics of the U.S. (1820-1970)* 889-90; *Statistical Abstract of the U.S.,* Selected Years

TABLE 4-13

PERCENTAGE DISTRIBUTION OF THE EMPLOYED LABOR FORCE, UNITED STATES, BY MAJOR INDUSTRY, 1870-1982

	1870	1880	1890	1900	1910	1920	1930	1940	1950	1960	1970	1980	1982
Agriculture	47.4	44.4	39.2	40.6	36.3	28.0	26.3	20.7	13.2	7.3	3.8	3.1	3.0
Mining	—[1]	—[1]	—[1]	2.5	3.1	3.1	2.5	2.2	1.7	1.2	0.9	1.1	1.2
Construction	—[1]	—[1]	—[1]	4.5	3.9	2.2	3.4	3.2	4.5	4.9	4.6	4.7	4.2
Manufacturing	21.7	21.8	24.4	21.4	23.0	28.1	24.0	26.9	29.3	28.7	26.4	21.8	20.4
Transportation, Communication, and Public Utilities	[2]	[2]	[2]	8.9	9.9	11.3	9.2	7.4	7.7	6.9	6.1	5.5	5.5
Wholesale and Retail Trade	9.5	10.8	14.3	9.8	10.5	10.5	14.5	16.5	18.0	19.5	20.3	21.8	22.1
Finance, Insurance, and Real Estate	[3]	[3]	[3]	1.2	1.4	2.4	3.7	3.7	3.7	4.6	5.0	5.5	5.8
Services	21.4	23.0	22.1	6.8	7.1	8.1	8.5	9.0	10.3	12.7	15.9	19.2	20.7
Government	[3]	[3]	[3]	4.3	4.8	6.3	7.9	10.4	11.6	14.2	17.0	17.4	17.1

[1]Included in Manufacturing
[2]Transportation included in Wholesale and Retail Trade; Communication and Public Utilities included in Services
[3]Included in Services

Source: Niemi, *U.S. Economic History,* *14*; U.S. Census Bureau, *Business Statistics: Supplement to the Survey of Current Business* (Washington, DC: U.S. Government Printing Office, 1982), 45-57.

TABLE 4-14
PERCENTAGE DISTRIBUTION OF THE U.S. EMPLOYED LABOR FORCE, BY MAJOR OCCUPATION, 1900-1982

Occupation	1900	1910	1920	1930	1940	1950	1960	1970	1980	1982
White-Collar	17.6%	21.3%	25.0%	29.4%	31.3%	36.6%	43.1%	48.3%	52.2%	53.7%
Professional and Technical	4.3	4.7	5.4	6.8	7.5	8.6	11.2	14.2	16.1	17.0
Managerial	5.9	6.6	6.6	7.4	7.3	8.7	10.6	10.5	11.2	11.5
Clerical	3.0	5.3	8.0	8.9	9.6	12.3	14.7	17.4	18.6	18.5
Sales	4.5	4.7	4.9	6.3	6.7	7.0	6.6	6.2	6.3	6.6
Blue-Collar	35.8	38.2	40.1	39.6	39.8	41.4	39.7	35.3	31.7	29.7
Craftsmen	10.6	11.6	13.0	12.8	12.0	14.2	13.8	12.9	12.9	12.3
Operatives	12.8	14.6	15.6	15.8	18.4	20.4	20.1	17.7	14.2	12.9
Laborers, excluding Farm	12.5	12.0	11.6	11.0	9.4	6.6	5.8	4.7	4.6	4.5
Services	9.1	9.6	7.9	9.8	11.7	10.5	10.9	12.4	13.3	13.8
Farm	37.5	30.9	27.0	21.2	17.4	11.8	6.4	4.0	2.8	2.7

Source: Niemi, *U.S Economic History*, 14; *Statistical Abstract of the U.S.* (1984), 417.

TABLE 4-15

UNITED STATES GOVERNMENT FINAL CONSUMPTION EXPENDITURE

(according to purpose at current prices)[1]

(millions of dollars)

Expenditure Purpose	1965	%	1970	%	1975	%	1980	%
General public services	13030	11	19154	10	32985	11	56831	12
Defense	49895	42	74077	39	87916	30	143281	30
Education	23471	20	44882	24	79305	27	124045	26
Health	4963	4	9057	5	18122	6	28640	6
Social security and welfare services	1700	2	3641	2	8516	3	16124	3
Housing and community amenities	3273	3	4754	3	8854	3	14691	3
Other community and social services	883	1	1863	1	3720	1	5875	1
Economic services	17992	15	27574	15	41203	14	63443	14
Other purposes	2221	2	4504	2	10813	4	18593	4
Total Outlays	117428	100	189506	100	291434	100	471523	100

[1]Totals may not add due to rounding.

Source: OECD, *National Accounts of OECD Countries* (Paris: Organization for Economic Cooperation and Development, 1982).

TABLE 4-16

CANADIAN FEDERAL GOVERNMENT EXPENDITURE BY AREA OF SPENDING[1]

(millions of dollars)

	1976/77	%	1979/80	%	1982/83	%
Energy	1,631	4	2,362	5	3,008	4
Economic development	4,739	12	5,371	10	8,546	11
Social affairs	18,605	46	22,690	44	31,993	40
Justice and legal	773	2	1,037	2	1,536	2
Fiscal arrangements	3,184	8	3,635	7	5,663	7
External affairs and aid	1,123	3	1,404	3	2,043	2
Defense	3,382	8	4,389	8	6,990	9
Parliament	73	—	99	—	167	—
Services to government	2,150	5	2,333	5	2,880	4
Sub-total	35,660	88	43,320	84	62,826	79
Public debt	4,721	12	8,524	16	16,971	21
Total outlays	40,381	100	51,844	100	79,797	100

[1]Figures for all years are on a consistent basis; the Post Office is treated as a crown corporation and is not included here.

Source: Economic Review, 1984, 184.

TABLE 4-17
BOOK VALUE OF FOREIGN DIRECT INVESTMENT
IN THE U.S., BY SOURCE, 1937-1982

Year	Total (millions of dollars)	Percentage			
		Canada	United Kingdom	Netherlands	Other
1937	1,882	24.6	44.3	9.5	21.6
1941	2,312	22.9	30.8	14.5	31.8
1950	3,391	30.3	34.4	9.8	25.5
1955	5,076	30.4	34.5	12.1	23.0
1960	6,910	28.0	32.5	13.7	25.8
1965	8,797	27.1	32.4	14.8	25.7
1970	13,270	23.5	31.1	16.2	29.2
1975	27,662	19.3	22.9	19.3	38.5
1980	68,351	14.7	17.9	24.7	42.7
1982	101,844	9.6	22.9	21.1	46.4

Source: Historical Statistics of the U.S., Series U47-74; *Statistical Abstract of the U.S., 1984*, 822.

TABLE 4-18
MAJOR TRADING PARTNERS OF THE UNITED STATES, 1950-1982
(millions of dollars)

	Exports				
	1950	1960	1970	1980	1982
Americas	$4,902	$7,684	$15,612	$74,114	$67,312
Canada	2,039	3,810	9,079	35,395	33,720
Mexico	526	831	1,704	15,145	11,817
Brazil	365	464	840	4,343	3,423
Europe	3,306	7,398	14,817	67,512	60,054
United Kingdom	548	1,487	2,536	12,694	10,645
France	475	699	1,483	7,485	7,110
Germany	441	1,272	2,741	10,960	9,291
Asia	1,539	4,186	10,027	60,168	64,822
Japan	418	1,447	4,652	20,790	20,966
Australia and Oceania	151	514	1,189	4,876	5,700
Africa	376	793	1,580	9,060	10,271
TOTAL	10,274	20,575	43,225	215,730	208,159

	Imports				
	1950	1960	1970	1980	1982
America	5,063	6,864	16,928	78,687	84,467
Canada	1,960	2,901	11,092	41,459	46,477
Mexico	315	443	1,219	12,580	15,566
Brazil	715	570	670	3,715	4,285
Europe	1,449	4,268	11,395	46,602	52,346
United Kingdom	335	993	2,194	9,842	13,095
France	132	396	942	5,265	5,545
Germany	104	897	3,127	11;693	11,975
Asia	1,638	2,721	9,621	80,299	85,170
Japan	182	1,149	5,875	30,714	37,744
Australia and Oceania	208	266	871	3,392	3,131
Africa	494	534	1,113	34,410	17,770
TOTAL	8,852	14,653	39,928	243,390	242,884

Source: Niemi, *U.S. Economic History*, 373; *Statistical Abstract of the U.S.*, *1984*, 834

TABLE 4-19
MAJOR TRADING PARTNERS OF CANADA 1950-1983
(millions of dollars)

			EXPORTS		
	1950	1960	1970	1980	1983
Americas		3,190	11,391	50,663	69,295
United States	2,021	2,935	10,641	46,825	66,333
Western Europe		1,518	3,083	11,064	7,834
United Kingdom	470	915	1,480	3,193	2,509
Eastern Europe		39	169	2,123	2,122
Middle East		25	124	1,117	1,446
Asia		294	1,274	7,448	8,706
Japan	20	178	793	4,370	4,762
Australia and Oceania		125	244	790	610
Africa		76	173	1,054	950
TOTAL		5,267	16,458	74,259	90,964

			IMPORTS		
	1950	1960	1970	1980	1983
Americas		4,114	10,596	52,423	57,918
United States	2,130	3,693	9,905	48,414	54,103
Western Europe		961	1,948	6,989	7,527
United Kingdom	404	589	738	1,971	1,810
Eastern Europe		14	75	306	250
Middle East		107	104	3,016	865
Asia		211	865	5,025	7,828
Japan	12	110	582	2,792	4,409
Australia and Oceania		52	199	686	521
Africa		33	153	534	678
TOTAL		5,492	13,940	68,979	75,587

Source: Statistics Canada, *Exports: Merchandise Trade*, Cat. No. 65-202, Annual, and *Imports: Merchandise Trade*, Cat. No. 65-203, Annual; various editions.

TABLE 4-20
PERCENTAGE DISTRIBUTION OF EMPLOYEES, BY MAJOR INDUSTRY, CANADA,
1961-1982
(excluding agricultural employment)

	1961	1965	1970	1975	1980	1982
Mining	2.3	2.0	1.9	1.7	1.9	1.8
Construction	6.0	6.5	5.6	5.7	5.1	4.6
Manufacturing	27.7	27.6	25.0	22.3	20.9	19.2
Transportation, storage and communications	12.3	11.1	10.1	9.7	9.5	9.3
Trade	16.1	16.0	16.4	17.5	17.5	17.7
Finance, insurance and real estate	4.2	4.3	4.6	5.4	5.8	6.0
Community, business and personal services	22.9	24.6	28.5	29.3	31.2	33.3
Government, including defence	7.1	6.5	6.8	7.5	7.2	7.3

Source: Economic Review, 1984, 163.

TABLE 4-21
PERCENTAGE DISTRIBUTION OF U.S. DOMESTIC EXPORTS AND GENERAL IMPORTS,
BY BROAD COMMODITY GROUPS: 1960-1982

Commodity Group	1960	1965	1970	1975	1980	1982
Exports:						
Food and live animals	13.2	14.7	10.2	14.6	12.8	11.6
Beverages and tobacco	2.4	1.9	1.6	1.2	1.2	1.5
Crude materials, inedible	13.7	10.5	10.8	9.2	11.0	9.3
Mineral fuels and related materials	4.1	3.5	3.7	4.2	3.7	6.1
Chemicals	8.7	8.8	9.0	8.2	9.6	9.6
Machinery and transport equipment	34.3	37.3	42.0	43.0	39.1	42.1
Other manufactured goods	18.7	18.0	17.9	15.6	17.8	15.8
General imports:						
Food and live animals	19.9	16.1	13.5	8.8	6.4	5.9
Beverages and tobacco	2.6	2.6	2.1	1.5	1.1	1.4
Crude materials, inedible	18.3	14.5	8.3	5.8	4.3	3.5
Mineral fuels and related materials	10.5	10.4	7.7	27.5	33.9	26.8
Chemicals	5.3	3.6	3.6	3.8	3.5	3.9
Machinery and transport equipment	9.7	13.8	28.0	24.4	24.7	30.1
Other manufactured goods	30.3	35.1	33.3	24.9	22.9	25.1

Source: Statistical Abstract of the United States, 1984, (Washington, DC: U.S. Government
Printing Office, 1984), 838, Table No. 1474.

TABLE 4-22
PERSONAL SAVINGS AS PERCENTAGE OF PERSONAL DISPOSABLE INCOME

Year	Canada	United States
1950	5.6	5.3
1955	4.1	5.4
1960	3.3	4.9
1965	5.5	6.4
1970	5.3	7.4
1974	9.9	8.5
1975	10.9	8.6
1976	9.2	6.9
1977	9.1	5.9
1978	10.8	6.1
1979	11.3	5.9
1980	12.1	6.0
1981	13.8	6.6
1982	15.1	5.8
1983	12.9	5.0

Source: Economic Review, 1984, 142; National Income and Product Accounts of the U.S. (1929-76); U.S. Business Statistics, 1982, 2.

5

POLITICAL STRUCTURE, CULTURE AND
INSTITUTIONS IN CANADA AND THE U.S.

INTRODUCTION: APPARENT SIMILARITIES; DEEP-SEATED DIFFERENCES

There are four broadly cited features of the Canadian and American political systems that have been used to demonstrate the similarities between
these systems. It is observed that both Canada and the United States are long
established and stable democracies; spawned by the English legal tradition;
federal in structure; and typified by strong regional differences. If to these
initial similarities are added the economic and social commonalities, we
should expect to find similar political systems with similar political values
and political cultures. Such is far from the case. Chapter 2 suggests some
basic value differences between Americans and Canadians; this chapter
explores the manifestation of these in the political workings of the two
countries.

Each similarity bears closer scrutiny. Beneath the surface lie fundamental
differences in political structure, culture and functioning. Given the present
interest in divergences between Canadian and U.S. cities, the political
setting within which cities, and local governments more generally, operate is
of direct interest. More to the point, an understanding of the political
systems and structures in Canada and the United States lays the groundwork
for a proper appreciation of urban government and of the urban development process itself, this process being highly political in nature and therefore
influenced by deeper-seated cultural values about the role of government in
the two countries. Accordingly, we will examine briefly some of the relevant
political history in each nation and then move on to explore differences in
the two political systems.

THE REVOLUTION/EVOLUTION DICHOTOMY AND ITS IMPLICATIONS

A convenient point of departure can be found in the colonial history of the two nations and in their approaches to independence. Of particular interest will be the complex of negotiations and forces from which the respective initial constitutions of Canada and the United States were derived: the *British North America Act* of 1867 (hereafter the B.N.A. Act) and the U.S. Constitution of 1787.[1] Given these forces and statutes, the subsequent evolution of the federal political systems in each country can be better comprehended.

Much has been made of the revolutionary aspects of the American experience in contrast to Canada's evolutionary history.[2] This revolutionary/evolutionary dichotomy is probably overdrawn and fails to include central elements of the early experiences of both Canada and the United States, most particularly the experience just prior to the drafting of the respective constitutions and the pressures and events that shaped those charters. However, the dichotomy is useful for exploring Canadian and American political institutions.

In 1963, the sociologist Lipset compared a range of values in four English-speaking democracies: Canada, the United States, Australia and the United Kingdom. This comparison drew on Parsons's pattern variables across four continua: elitism-equalitarianism; ascription-achievement; particularism-universalism; diffuseness-specificity. Lipset's work provided a basis for our prior discussion of values in Canada and America (Chapter 2); it anchors our overview of the political systems that interact with these value patterns. It is clear from the results of his analysis (Table 5-1) that Great Britain and the United States occupy opposite ends of his dimensions.[3] In seeking to explain these differences, Lipset suggests that an understanding lies in part in the revolutionary history of the United States as opposed to the evolutionary history of Canada; Britain in these terms has remained largely static and therefore reflects its older aristocratic traditions.

This work and its extensions have received much attention and significant critiques.[4] The issue is clearly oversimplified both in terms of the dimensions of comparison employed and the evidence used to substantiate the case, a point stressed in earlier comments. But the revolution/evolution dichotomy remains potentially useful for comparative work on Canada and the U.S.

Because Canada did not sever its ties with Great Britain through revolution, its political institutions and values, Lipset argues, do not represent a discrete break with the past but have evolved slowly from the colonial experience in the context of North American geography and the frontier.[5] This theme has a range of interesting implications for political institutions and cultures in the two countries. For example, we would anticipate that the U.S. federal system was designed to be a radical break with its past and the highly centralized governmental forms of Georgian England. In Canada we would anticipate a federal design which is more conservative and more consistent with the British unitary parliamentary system. Examining the political cultures cross-nationally, we would expect similarly open political institutions in America, whereas those in Canada should be more elitist and closed. The American focus on the individual should contrast with greater collective feeling in Canada. We explore each by reviewing federalism and its development in Canada and the United States in the following section and then subsequently look at political culture, broadly defined, in each nation.

THE ROOTS OF CANADIAN AND AMERICAN FEDERALISM AND THE RESULTING FEDERAL POLITICAL SYSTEMS AND INSTITUTIONS

The development of the federal systems in Canada and the United States provides an appropriate format for examining the evolution/revolution argument. Focussing on federalism also allows us to construct a unifying thread that can be followed in our subsequent discussions of broader issues related to the political institutions and cultures in these countries. Federalism, finally, forces us to address one of the basic political problems faced by any society: how the rights and needs of the individual unit are traded off against the rights of the larger society whether the individual unit be a person, a neighborhood, a city or a province/state/region.

Seen in this context, federal institutions are much more than merely established relations, laws and customs between states or provinces and the national government. Rather, federalism is a means for institutionalizing at a high level the constant tensions inherent in all open political systems between tendencies to centralize for the good of the nation or the larger social unit and tendencies to decentralize for the good of specific local, provincial/state or regional populations. These countervailing centrifugal and centripetal forces are at the heart of any federal system. We trace here how Canada and the United States have come to deal with and accommodate these forces.

This accommodation has a particularly long and important history in the United States, antedating the War of Independence and stretching back into the colonial past. In his compelling study of the dualisms in early American life, Michael Kammen (calling them "biformities") observes:

The Federalist mind tended toward bisociative patterns of thought, in part, because of the very nature of the problems faced after Independence. Localism versus centralism was a critical issue; and as Benjamin Rush reported, "half the people think the government too strong, and the other half too weak." John Adams felt compelled to reply that "in the hands of aristocrats it has been too strong without being sufficiently wise or just. In the hands of democrats it has been too strong without being either wise or just."[6]

Henry Steele Commager, a dean of American historians, focuses on the importance of the pull of individualism and the corresponding pull of authority: "In a larger sense, this issue of particularism and nationalism is part of a very ancient issue in politics, one of the oldest, one of the most persistent, and one of the most difficult of all political questions: the question of the reconciliation of liberty and order."[7]

Canada and the United States have sought to resolve, or at least to acknowledge and deal with, the tensions inherent to federalism quite differently; each has evolved a distinctive federalism arising out of the different paths followed from colony to nation. What follows is a brief review of these paths and the constitution-writing that each undertook to create a federal state.

The United States of America was born out of seven years of revolution against Great Britain. Out of that historic struggle was fashioned the American constitution at the Constitutional Convention of 1787, four years after the 1783 Treaty of Yorktown which ended the War of Independence. The major trade-offs facing the Founding Fathers were rooted in the biformities noted earlier. They were also rooted firmly in the political realities of the day and of the Constitutional Convention itself.

A struggle of central importance was that between democracy—rule by the people—and liberty, as expressed in the ability to exercise rights, particularly property rights. In his classic analysis of American politics, Richard Hofstadter asserts that this is at the root of the problem faced by the Founding Fathers:

> It is ironical that the Constitution, which Americans venerate so deeply, is based upon a political theory that at one crucial point stands in direct antithesis to the main stream of American democratic faith. Modern American folklore assumes that democracy and liberty are all but identical, and when democratic writers take the trouble to make the distinction, they usually assume that democracy is necessary to liberty. But the Founding Fathers thought that the liberty with which they were most concerned was menaced by democracy. In their minds liberty was linked not to democracy but to property.[8]

They were caught in the thick of a paradox which derived directly from their view of man: "They thought man was a creature of rapacious self-interest, and yet they wanted him to be free—free, in essence, to contend, to engage in an umpired strife, to use property to get property."[10]

At the Convention, this tension was embodied in the debate over the relative strengths of the States and the soon-to-be-formed Nation. The resulting federal system was a radical departure from the past. In summarizing the resolution of the trade-off between state and national rights, Gibbins observes:

> The American federal system provided a means by which territorial state governments were preserved, and through which territorial interests could be represented within the national government. It is important to point out, however, that the adoption of federalism was based as much on the desire to fragment and thus limit government as it was on the recognition of territorial interests meriting constitutional protection.

The U.S. Constitution reflected the biformities that plagued the age. It sought to accommodate these by creating a national entity that was held in check by the states and by an intricate series of checks and balances built into the structure of American government. These checks and balances derived from splitting governmental function into executive, legislative and judicial branches where the judiciary was seen as a referee of sorts in the inescapable battles between all governments and the people, between the federal government and the states, and between the legislature (the House of Representatives and the Senate which jointly comprise the Congress) and the executive branch (the president and the administrative departments needed to carry out the federal government's role). In view of the fears of the Founding Fathers about "excessive" democracy and potential oppression by the central government, the balance of power was carefully weighted in favor of the states and the people through the Bill of Rights which were the first ten amendments to the U.S. Constitution. This initial conception of strong states and a weak central government was to change dramatically during the next two centuries as a result of judicial decisions and the changing nature of the American economy.

All of the foregoing contrasts markedly with the Canadian experience, which as we surmised at the outset was a much less radical experiment in governing than was the U.S. Constitution. Until 1982, Canada had no formal constitution in the American sense, in keeping with the British model. In Britain the supremacy of Parliament is taken as a fundamental tenet of government, and therefore there can be no power to supersede it. A written constitution which limits parliamentary power, such as that in the United States, is therefore inconsistent with British parliamentary democracy. In addition, Canada existed as an act of the British Parliament (the B.N.A. Act, 1867, with its numerous amendments) up through 1982 when the Canadian constitution was "repatriated" and made an act of the Canadian Parliament (*The Constitution Act of 1982*).[11]

Unlike the U.S. Constitution, the B.N.A. Act was concerned only with creating the Dominion of Canada and in allocating powers among the federal and provincial parliaments. In keeping with British practice, these parliaments were to be supreme, and therefore it was unthinkable that anything approaching the American Bill of Rights which protected individuals from governments would be a part of the act of Parliament that created Canada. Thus, it was noted early on that Canada would have a "constitution" like that of Britain.[12] Moreover, consistent with Canada's roots in a unitary and not in a federal state, it was initially envisioned that there would be a strong dominion government with relatively weak provinces, the reverse of the original American design.

The B.N.A. Act was born out of British concern that there be a relatively strong and autonomous colony to protect imperial interests against American expansionism. The American doctrine of Manifest Destiny, wherein it was seen as an American right or more properly American duty to control the entire North American continent, had already led to significant losses of British territory to the U.S.—Oregon and Washington—with threats of losing the entire area west of Ontario. Pressure to acknowledge and preserve provincial rights came primarily from two sources: French-speaking Quebec (then known as Lower Canada) and the autonomous provinces of Nova Scotia and New Brunswick. Thus, the drafters of the B.N.A. Act had to contend with the trade-off between federal power and provincial autonomy analogous to that faced by the Founding Fathers in the U.S. concerning states' rights. However, the Canadian Fathers of Confederation did not have to contend with American fears of government in general or with the need to limit powers of government in favor of individual rights. This relatively more favorable disposition toward government persists to this day in Canada.

To effectuate the creation of the Dominion, the Fathers of Confederation met in Charlottetown, Prince Edward Island, in 1864 and in Quebec City in 1865. The resulting Quebec Resolutions formed the basis for the B.N.A. Act. Interestingly, and again in great contrast with the United States, only the legislatures of the existing provinces voted on the Resolutions. There was no large-scale public debate sought, nor did any arise.[13] Clearly, the dynamics, and the final substance as well, differed greatly from the experience in the United States eighty years earlier. This is not to say that the American experience escaped the Fathers of Confederation. Quite the reverse is true, for the American constitution and the Civil War that resulted from American-style federalism were uppermost in the minds of the Fathers of Confederation, providing a model to be avoided.[14]

Accordingly, the B.N.A. Act foresaw a strong central government with weak provinces. The rights of the provinces were largely to be confined to those areas of a "merely local or private Nature"[15] reflecting the need to maintain French institutions and education in Quebec. As in the U.S., initial designs have been greatly transformed both through judicial decisions and through economic and social change during the past century.

Despite the intentions of both the framers of the U.S. Constitution and of the contributors to the B.N.A. Act, the passage of time and forces well beyond the vision of even these visionaries have led to contrasting federal systems and institutions in Canada and the United States. However, they are also quite different from the initial conceptions in each country, being the reverse of the original designs; the U.S. presently has a much more highly centralized form of federalism with a vastly more powerful federal government than does Canada. Let us look briefly at how these unexpected turns of events came about.

That the U.S. Constitution was created to effectuate national union while maintaining state autonomy is apparent from the Tenth Amendment to the Constitution: "The powers not delegated to the United States by the Constitution, nor prohibited by it to the States, are reserved to the States respectively or to the people."[16] However, judicial actions altered permanently the relationships between the federal government and the states. In a series of decisions in the first two decades of the nineteenth century, Marshall's Supreme Court invalidated federal (*Marbury v. Madison* in 1803) and state (*Fletcher v. Peck* in 1810) statutes by declaring them unconstitutional. Additionally, through a very flexible interpretation of the so-called Commerce Clause (Article I, Section 8(3) "Congress shall have the power to regulate commerce with foreign nations, and among the several States, and with Indian tribes"), the Marshall Court also began tilting the balance of power toward the federal government, a process which continues to the present.[17]

Several other factors led to the enormous growth of power of the federal government in the United States. The Civil War of 1861-65 demonstrated lastingly that states did not have the right to secede and that the national government remains supreme. The Sixteenth Amendment (1913) gave Congress the "power to lay and collect taxes on incomes, from whatever source derived, without apportionment among the several States, and without regard to any census enumeration,"[18] thereby greatly enhancing the ability of the federal government to raise taxes and putting the states at a severe disadvantage in this regard. Two world wars and the Great Depression further gave opportunities for the federal government to extend its scope and power, as did the host of civil rights cases of the 1950s, 1960s and 1970s.

As a result of these factors, a view that the national government should not be subject to unalterable constitutional restraints prevailed. Accordingly, a federal system has unfolded wherein the central government is dominant, with strong homogenizing forces affecting the practice of politics and with federal actions permeating the entire political system.[19]

In Canada a very different scenario has unfolded. Early hopes by the Fathers of Confederation, particularly those of Sir John A. Macdonald, that the Dominion of Canada would be dominated by the central government with minimal protection of provincial rights were dashed with a series of decisions by the Judicial Committee of the Privy Council in London, the British Law Lords then being the arbiters of Canadian legal disputes. The result of these decisions, commencing with *Maritime Bank v. Receiver General of New Brunswick* (1892), was a strengthening of the provincial role. It was left to Viscount Haldane in the 1920s to firmly establish provincial rights.

The general federal power to enact laws for "the Peace, Order and Good Government of Canada" was deemed only to exist in emergencies. "The Regulation of Trade and Commerce," a Parliamentary power of great inclusivity, was simultaneously narrowly defined. In contrast, provincial authority over "Property and Civil Rights" was made an impediment to federal actions.[20] Thus, the apparent favoring of the federal parliament under the B.N.A. Act, intended to limit the scope for provincial action, was counterbalanced. Macdonald had hoped the important "Peace, Order and Good Government" clause would disarm sectional dissent which in America had led to the Civil War, general and residual powers being assigned to the central government and not to state, that is, provincial, governments as in America.[21]

Other matters have greatly expanded the importance of the provinces relative to the federal government. Given the strict construction by the Law Lords that in essence Sections 91 and 92 of the B.N.A. Act allocated powers exclusively either to the federal parliament or to the provincial legislatures, and furthermore that these allocations were not permissive of involvement of the other level of government without express permission by the other level of government, the provinces wound up with control of urban affairs, education and resources, while the federal government exercised control of foreign trade and affairs and broad matters for regulating the Canadian economy, along with a range of lesser duties.[22] Since Confederation it has been cities, education and resources that have been major growth sectors in Canada, and these sectors have been reserved for the provinces. The federal government is constrained from acting directly in these sectors and accordingly has lost influence in these areas in contrast to the situation in the United States. The resource issue has been particularly important, with provinces, both in the West and in the Atlantic region, being impelled to claim sovereignty over these valuable and important sources of revenue and growth.[23]

The Canadian federal system has found itself evolving very much along the lines set in the U.S. Constitution, whereas the U.S. federal system has moved more and more in the direction that Macdonald envisaged for Canada. Gibbins summarizes this state of affairs ably with a schematic diagram and a comment.

> The American and Canadian federal systems cannot be placed on this continuum with any exactitude. It is difficult to be precise about the federal balance between national and territorial governments in 1787 or 1867, and it is impossible to be so today. However, the direction of change that has taken place over time is much less ambiguous. The irony is that Canadians today have a federal system not far removed in spirit from the early American model, whereas the American federal system has evolved toward the Canadian model laid out in 1867. The evolutionary path followed by Canada has been toward the federal model explicitly rejected in 1867, and in the welter of proposals for constitutional change that have appeared over the last decade there is little support for reversing this evolutionary course.[24]

Evolution of the American and Canadian Federal Systems

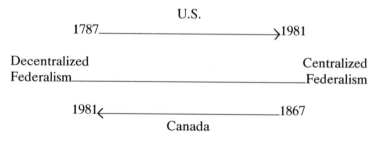

While the causes for this historical inversion might remain elusive, it is possible to observe that the Canadian system today is much more contentious and open-ended than its American counterpart. In Canada, there is a constant tension between the federal and provincial governments and a dynamic equilibrium that is in a constant state of flux, compared with the American system in which there is no sign of halting the supremacy of the federal government or even of curtailing it in any significant way. In both countries these current trends are unlikely to change greatly in future. In the U.S., the power and resources of the national government are simply too great and the body of jurisprudence upon which this dominance is built is overwhelming. In Canada, the on-going regional pulls are driven not just by past judicial precedents and by resource revenues, but also by partisan politics: the Liberals have supported "centripetal Federalism" and the Progressive Conservatives provincial rights.[25]

In sum, on closer inspection the federalism practiced in the United States differs greatly from that practiced in Canada. Different institutions in turn drive and are driven by these differences. The much lesser role of the Canadian government in urban affairs is a notable element in the differences in the two federal systems and will be of signal importance later in the consideration of the implications of these differences for urban development and urban differences in the two nations.[26] An example should help clarify the point.

The Ministry of State for Urban Affairs (MSUA) was created in 1971, underwent a number of internal reorganizations, and was abolished in March 1979. This ministry was a radical institutional innovation in Canadian terms. Unlike the traditional ministries, it had no executive authority, being intended to increase "flexibility" and the Cabinet's capacity to make policy decisions. It had a broad mandate which quickly gave rise to contradictory internal impulses. More specifically, it was intended to coordinate the urban-related activities of federal agencies and departments, to promote comprehensive urban policy by supporting relevant federal programs and policies, and to consult with the provinces and their municipalities and other interest groups. This mandate at once required MSUA to function within the closed, "club-like" atmosphere of senior bureaucratic decisionmaking in Ottawa, to implement and promote independent urban research, and to reach out in an open way to the provinces, municipalities and other interested parties.

MSUA failed to demonstrate to anyone's satisfaction that it could co-ordinate urban-related policy, quickly running afoul of entrenched and powerful interests, at the Central Mortgage and Housing Corporation and the Ministry of Transport in particular. It raised false expectations amongst the municipalities, and it seemed to confirm provincial suspicions of a larger federal role in urban development. Its demise has been analysed in detail by various scholars, including Feldman and Milch, who state:

MSUA was also doomed from the outset because it was caught in the escalating conflict between federal and provincial establishments. The provinces feared the Ministry of State as the opening wedge in a federal campaign to gain control over urban affairs; only the weaker and poorer provincial governments chose to deal with MSUA, at least during the first crucial years.[27]

In the absence of a strong federal urban presence, Canadian provinces and cities have had to fend for themselves. Direct federal input into urban transportation is lacking in Canada, as emphasized earlier. So are the massive federal urban subsidies and direct transfers to local governments

Canadians to accept government involvement in the economy (Table 5-7). The findings on efficacy might be seen as reflecting deeper-seated attitudes in the U.S. and Canada concerning self-assuredness and differing perceptions among Americans and Canadians about their own abilities to act independently or to provide leadership in general. Survey data in fact do support the notion that Americans perceive themselves as more independent and self-assured than Canadians (Table 5-8).

The foregoing likely reflect the considerably greater degree of optimism exhibited by Americans when compared with their northern neighbors, which suggests that Americans seem to feel much more in control of their own futures and circumstances than do Canadians, an impression which is supported by the data set out in Tables 5-6 and 5-7 on attitudes toward socialism and economic liberalism. In Chapters 2 and 4, we also saw a much greater tendency on the part of Canadians toward collective economic action than is prevalent in the United States.

The underlying and strong acceptance of government intervention in Canada stands in stark contrast to American attitudes and has attracted a great deal of attention from researchers. The deferential character of the Canadian public has been particularly curious, and likely upsetting as well, to American observers, given the enormous stress placed in the United States on individualism and on resistance to government intervention.[31] Interestingly, despite expressing a lower degree of political efficacy, Canadians, in fact, participate more broadly in politics than do Americans (Table 5-9), an anomalous finding for a people who view government as not being responsive and catering more to "big interests" than to all the people (the converse of American views). Again, it must be stressed that the concept of political culture used here is a product of American social science and its application in Canada needs to be assessed cautiously.

The preceding elements of differences between Canadian and American political culture point to additional differences in political organization between the two countries. In view of American egalitarian beliefs, it is not surprising to find divergences in the manifestation of national identity or national "character" American and Canadian-style. So pervasive is the belief in the "American way of life" that the American character has tended to coalesce about this unitary idea of government and the supremacy of the American democratic forms and institutions. The widespread acceptance of this view almost overshadows the federal nature of the American nation since regional or state concerns appear to be overwhelmed by the sense of nationhood.[32] In Canada, perhaps one of the few unifying symbols, in contrast, is the perennial clash of federal and provincial governments. In short, the U.S. federation is more static in the sense that the respective roles of the states and the federal government have long since been decided, recent federal revenue-sharing and current proposals notwithstanding, with the federal government paramount. The Canadian confederation, on the other hand, is dynamic and fluid, with the locus of power shifting among the various governments over time from one issue to the next, federal-provincial tensions being key elements in the evolving Canadian identity.

There are important features in the U.S. system which provide for and thus encourage the rights of the individual to prosper. In Canada some of the disorder that would normally ensue given the weaker federal role is offset by the nature of the legal and legislative system. These features of both countries are also essential expressions of deep-seated attitudes toward government and politics more generally.

Built into the American system of government is a much-studied system of checks and balances provided by the legislative, executive and judicial branches of government. The federal structure itself was seen as providing a further check within the legislative sphere by splitting legislative functions among the states and the federal government. Furthermore, since it is the American people who are popularly believed to hold ultimate power in the United States, the written constitution and particularly certain amendments to it reserve to the people rights which transcend the rights of governments formed in their name. This basic check on government maintains much of the initial spirit of the U.S. federal system and provides for redress through the courts should the legislative or executive branches usurp too much power. The ability, potential or realized, to challenge government serves to restore balance and prevents the unlimited growth of power by the federal, or any other, level of government. Finally, the Congress itself with its two houses and nearly six hundred legislators provides further centrifugal force away from a total dominance of political affairs by the executive branch of the federal government. The notorious weakness of U.S. political parties means that a great deal of political brokerage can take place in Congress; compromise and refinement can be introduced into legislation, weakening the tendency of the federal government toward total domination of U.S. political life.

Turning to Canada we see an analogous set of political institutions which provide the essential glue to keep the Canadian federation from becoming unstuck. First, the *Constitution Act, 1982* continues the B.N.A. Act function of allocating powers to the federal and provincial legislatures, and in so doing it sets limits on provincial domination of the Canadian federal system. Moreover, the parliamentary system provides the federal government with a powerful and highly centralized institution, the federal cabinet, with which to challenge the ten provinces and thus provide countervailing centripetal forces to the provincial centrifugal forces. Finally, and perhaps most importantly, the overarching Canadian attitude toward collective behavior provides the federal government with an element of legitimacy since federal action is the ultimate in Canadian collectivity. In fact, as Elkins and Simeon have shown, Canadians seem to feel strongly about both their own provinces and about the entity Canada.[34] A dual "allegiance" is evident (Table 5-10).[35] Thus, in Canada there are a number of forces keeping a dynamic balance between central and non-central powers, although the forces and the balance itself differ markedly from those in the U.S.

This dynamic balance between the federal and provincial governments provides an interesting analog for metropolitan government, particularly for reform movements. When combined with predispositions toward active government, the Canadian model, built on shifting and dynamic equilibria, has led to experiments for governing urban areas that would be largely unacceptable in the United States. Thus, differences in attitudes towards government and in the functioning of the political system have significant implications for the governance of urban areas and, therefore, for the development of metropolitan regions in Canada and the United States. While we dwell at some length on local government structure, reform and finances in Chapter 8, a brief sketch of the reform issue is useful here to provide a link between the national-level analysis of this chapter and the urban analyses that follow in Chapters 7 through 9.

Beginning with metropolitan Toronto in 1954, Canadian provinces initiated a number of changes to provide for better metropolitan government in a series of efforts to promote efficiency in the provision of urban infrastructure and services, to avoid needless and often harmful competition among local neighboring communities for "tax base," and simultaneously to protect local input.[36] In Toronto, a two-tier government was initially created by the province of Ontario: thirteen municipal governments with local planning and service responsibilities; one Metro Toronto municipality with regional functions such as transportation and property assessment. Subsequent changes resulted in a widened metropolitan scope including police protection and pollution control and the reduction of the lower tier municipal governments to the present six. The result has been a system of local urban government that mirrors the Canadian federal system by explicitly dealing with the trade-offs between local autonomy and metropolitan efficiency. The shifting balance of these trade-offs is reminiscent of that at the national level between the federal and provincial governments.

Later, local government fragmentation and some of the observable differences between Canadian and American metropolitan areas in local government are discussed. At this stage it should be noted that these differences derive in no small way from the differences in political institutions and values that have been the focus of the present chapter. Canadian provinces have been much more willing and able to impose metropolitan government than have American states. As a result, virtually every major Canadian metropolitan region is governed in part by some form of metropolitan-wide government. Only a handful of analogous governments can be identified in the U.S., reflecting an American predilection for local autonomy and a fear of centralized governmental structures. Quite clearly, we can anticipate different patterns of urban development, different revenue and expenditure patterns at the local level, and differences in local government relations with states/provinces and the respective national governments. Indeed, the empirical work that follows in Chapters 7 through 9 highlights significant differences in all of these spheres between Canadian and American urban areas.

Deference, Collective Action and Private Property: Transcendant Differences in Political Values Between Canadians and Americans

"Peace, Order and Good Government" were, as noted earlier, the rationale for the British North America Act's distribution of powers to the federal and provincial parliaments.[37] In contrast stands the American "life, liberty and the pursuit of happiness." Many authors have pointed to this difference as an indicator of deeper-seated attitudes toward government in the affairs of citizens.[38] The deference to authority that Canadian society has exhibited over the past century or more has been traced all the way back to the country's conservative anti-revolutionary roots and the United Empire Loyalists,[39] as noted in Chapter 2. This relatively greater deferential behavior of Canadians has a number of implications for the different structure and conduct of government and politics in Canada.

First, Americans, going back to Thomas Jefferson and other drafters of the U.S. Constitution, feared bureaucratic control of their "life, liberty and pursuit of happiness." The Jeffersonian model, and the one operating in many places in the U.S. today, "solved" the problem through the election of an extraordinary range of public officials. For instance, it is still commonplace to elect judges, assessors, controllers, sheriffs and even county clerks in many American jurisdictions. The theory of such practices is that bureaucracies will be accountable to the public through direct election. This remains debatable.

Canada demonstrates the Britannic continuity alluded to earlier by establishing powerful and generally well-staffed bureaucracies which are accountable to political masters, be they municipal councils or provincial or federal ministers of the Crown. The relatively greater role played by bureaucrats in Canada would be anathema to most Americans as would be the broad discretionary powers wielded by senior officials.

Given the relatively greater degree of elitism in Canada, it is not surprising to find that recruitment of the ruling senior bureaucrats relies much more heavily than in the United States on socio-economic elites. Research by Presthus and Monopoli (Table 5-11) confirmed that the bureaucratic elites in the two countries are from different social backgrounds, with many more Canadian administrators coming from the upper-middle and upper class.[40] Additional evidence is provided by Campbell.[41] His work suggests that American bureaucrats are more likely to come from blue-collar backgrounds (23 per cent compared with 14 per cent in Canada) and to have fathers whose educational attainment is lower. These cross-national findings should not be confused with other work by Campbell which demonstrated that, over time, senior federal officials in Canada were being drawn from less prestigious social backgrounds.[42] On a U.S.-Canada comparative base, it is the case that Canadian senior bureaucrats tend to be drawn from more elite social backgrounds than their American colleagues.

In keeping with this more elitist orientation in Canada, and the general feeling that it is appropriate for these elites to administer the nation and the provinces, is the view among senior civil servants in Canada that they do in fact run the country (Table 5-12). Canadian bureaucrats have a much greater sense of control.

The greater acceptance of the actions of non-elected public officials is matched in Canada by much greater freedom of action in the absence of the constraints of a binding written constitution. The recently proclaimed *Constitution Act, 1982* is a step toward providing Canadians with some of the procedural and substantive protection accorded American citizens, which, if taken to the U.S. limit, would surely curtail both legislative and bureaucratic autonomy.[43] There are several factors, however, that are likely to militate against the evolution of the new Canadian Charter of Rights and Freedoms into a northern version of the U.S. Constitution. All relate closely to the very deference under discussion. First, there is the historic unwillingness of the Canadian judiciary to interpret issues broadly, unlike their American counterparts. As a result, it is reasonably likely that Canadian legislatures will be handed back highly contentious issues for legislative, not judicial, action in stark contrast with recent U.S. jurisprudence. Second, the Canadian Charter of Rights and Freedoms is a compromise—to be expected in such a federal-provincial environment as that which exists in Canada—and is not necessarily binding on the provinces. Third, the long history of litigiousness that has characterized U.S. constitutional battles is lacking in Canada. It is reasonable to expect therefore that given greater deference, greater conservatism of the judiciary, and greater willingness of parliaments in Canada to cope with issues, the political route to social change will continue to dominate. This contrasts with the U.S., where the judiciary has played a central role in bringing about social and political change in the absence of action by federal or state legislatures (witness the evolution of civil rights enforcement since the historic 1954 Brown decision).[44]

In short, it is clear that Canadians do not dread government involvement and are willing to tolerate a much broader range of government controls and interventions in markets and in the lives of citizens than would be tolerable in the U.S. One area where this is especially apparent is in the quasi-public sector of crown corporations.[45] The range of "public enterprises" from the mammoth Air Canada and Canadian National Railways down to Regina's community owned Saskatchewan Roughriders football team is vast. In between are at least four provincially owned railroads, a provincially controlled national airline (controlled interestingly enough by "Conservative" Alberta), municipal telephone systems (e.g., in Edmonton), municipal power companies (e.g., New Westminster, B.C.), and on and on. Such diversity and depth of involvement by the public sector in the national and regional economies would likely be unsettling to most Americans. While public enterprises are not unknown in the U.S. and are more powerful and efficacious than is commonly recognized,[46] the prevalence and visibility of crown corporations mark Canada as having a distinctive public sector within a North American context.[47] It points towards a very different political environment within which Canadians see their governments functioning at all levels as compared with that which Americans perceive. Of particular importance is the acceptance of government involvement in the economy, not just through regulation and taxation as in the U.S., but also through direct government action. This was supported in Chapter 4 with reference to economic values and institutions, for which there is a very different kind of economy in Canada, in part as a result of this greater willingness on the part of Canadians to accept government as an active element in the economy and the marketplace.

SUMMARY

Three themes that emerged in this chapter indicate that in Canada there is greater acceptance of government involvement in economic affairs than in the United States. In the U.S., there is a greater role for federal government relative to the states as compared with that of the Canadian federal government relative to the provinces. In the U.S., there is greater stress on the pursuit of individual goal, and there is a correspondingly greater interest in collective action in Canada.[48]

The next chapter presents the implications of these generalizations for urban development in Canada and the United States. Here, it suffices to observe again a number of very significant differences relating to the political systems of the two countries, differences that reinforce those already identified with respect to values, demographic and social structure, and economic institutions and structure. In short, Canada is very different from the United States. It now remains to set out what this means for cities.

TABLE 5-1
TENTATIVE ESTIMATES OF RELATIVE RANKINGS OF THE FOUR ENGLISH-SPEAKING
DEMOCRACIES ACCORDING TO STRENGTH OF CERTAIN PATTERN VARIABLES
(rankings according to first term in polarity)

Polarity	United States	Australia	Canada	Great Britain
Elitism-Equalitarianism	3	4	2	1
Ascription-Achievement	4	2.5	2.5	1
Particularism-Universalism	4	2	3	1
Diffuseness-Specificity	4	2.5	2.5	1

Source: Seymour M. Lipset, "The Value Patterns of Democracy: A Case Study in Comparative Analysis," *American Sociological Review* 28, no. 4, (1963), 521.

TABLE 5-2
FREQUENCY OF INTERACTION WITH INTEREST GROUPS,
UNITED STATES VS. CANADIAN LEGISLATORS
(per cent)

Interaction	United States		Canada	
	Federal	State	Federal	Provincial
High[1]	72	94	42	58
Medium[2]	25	5	29	32
Low[3]	3	1	29	11
(n)	(100)	(149)	(141)	(127)

[1] "frequently" (twice a week)
[2] "occasionally"
[3] "seldom" or "rarely"

Source: R. Presthus, "Aspects of Political Culture and Legislative Behavior," in Robert Presthus, ed., *Cross-National Perspectives: United States and Canada* (Leiden: E.J. Brill, 1977), 12.

TABLE 5-3
COMPARATIVE POLITICAL EFFICACY,
UNITED STATES VS. CANADIAN LEGISLATORS[1]
(per cent)

Political efficacy[1]	United States		Canada	
	Federal	State	Federal	Provincial
High	57	35	28	36
Medium	41	56	53	43
Low	2	9	19	21
(n)	(92)	(147)	(135)	(118)

[1] "Efficacy" is based upon the following items: "The old saying, 'You can't fight city hall' is still basically true"; "Most decisions in business and government are made by a small group that pretty well runs things"; "The average man doesn't have much chance to get ahead today"; 'Anyone in this country who wants to, has a chance to have his say about important issues." Although the 'average man doesn't have ...' item is often used as an alienation item, it emerged as part of this index through cluster analysis.

Source: R. Presthus, *Cross-National Perspectives*, 18.

TABLE 5-4
COMPARATIVE POLITICAL EFFICACY,
BY SENIOR BUREAUCRATS IN CANADA AND THE UNITED STATES[1]
(per cent)

Political efficacy	United States		Canada	
	Federal	State	Federal	Provincial
High	61	45	37	31
Medium	22	28	37	30
Low	17	27	26	39
(n)	(87)	(160)	(89)	(119)

[1] Efficacy is based on these items: "The old saying, 'you can't fight city hall' is still basically true"; "Most decisions in business and government are made by a small group that pretty well runs things"; "Anyone in this country who wants to, has a chance to have his say about important issues."

Source: Robert Presthus and William Monopoli, "Bureaucracy in the United States and Canada: Social, Attitudinal, and Behavioral Variables," in Presthus, *Cross-National Perspectives*, 183.

TABLE 5-5
POLITICAL TRUST (% CYNICAL)[1]

	Canada		United States		
	1968	1965	1972	1968	1964
Government Wastes Money	46%	38%	68%	61%	48%
People in Government Crooked	27%	27%	38%	20%	30%
Government Run by Big Interests	90%	83%	59%	44%	30%
People in Government Smart	49%	57%	42%	39%	28%
Trust Government to do Right	39%	39%	46%	37%	22%
Average	50%	49%	51%	40%	32%

[1] For political trust questions, the entry in each cell is the per cent giving a cynical response. No political trust questions were asked in a 1970s Canadian study.

Source: Nathaniel Beck and John C. Pierce. "Political Involvement and Party Allegiances in Canada and the United States," in Presthus, *Cross-National Perspectives*, 39.

TABLE 5-6
ECONOMIC LIBERALISM, UNITED STATES VS. CANADIAN LEGISLATORS
(per cent)

Economic Liberalism[1]	United States		Canada	
	Federal	State	Federal	Provincial
High	21	25	56	63
Medium	55	53	43	37
Low	24	22	–	–
(n)	(90)	(147)	(122)	(117)

[1] "Economic liberalism" is defined here by the following items: 'That government which governs least governs best' (reverse scored); 'Economic security for every man, woman and child is worth striving for, even if it means socialism'; 'If unemployment is high government should spend money to create jobs'; 'A national medicare plan is necessary to ensure that everyone receives adequate health care'; 'More federal aid to education is desirable if we are going to adequately meet present and future educational needs in this country'.

Source: Presthus, *Cross-National Perspectives*, 13.

TABLE 5-7
PERSONALITY DIMENSION: INDIVIDUALIST-COLLECTIVIST,
PERSONALITY TRAIT: SOCIALISTIC

Personality Items	Mean Level of Agreement[1]	
	Canada	U.S.
The government in Ottawa (Washington) is too big and powerful	40	54[2]
The government should guarantee everyone at least $3,000 per year whether he works or not	36	14[2]
Communism is the greatest peril in the world today[3]	54	70[2]

[1] 0 = definitely disagree; 20 = generally disagree; 40 = moderately disagree; 60 = moderately agree; 80 = generally agree; 100 = definitely agree.

[2] Difference is statistically significant at the 0.001 level and in agreement with the comparative literature.

[3] Males only

Source: Stephen J. Arnold and Douglas J. Tigert, "Canadians and Americans: A Comparative Analysis," *International Journal of Comparative Sociology* 15 (1974), 81.

TABLE 5-8
PERSONALITY DIMENSION: INDIVIDUALIST-COLLECTIVIST,
PERSONALITY TRAIT: SELF-ASSURED

Personality Items	Mean Level of Agreement[1]	
	Canada	U.S.
I am more independent than most people	62	66[2]
I like to be considered a leader	39	53[2]
People come to see me more often than I go to them for information about products and brands[4]	42	51[2]
I think I have more self-confidence than most people[3]	53	59[2]
I think I have a lot of personal ability	71	74[2]
I hate to lose at anything	48	61[2]

[1] 0 = definitely disagree; 20 = generally disagree; 40 = moderately disagree; 60 = moderately agree; 80 = generally agree; 100 = definitely agree.

[2] Difference is statistically significant at the 0.001 level and in agreement with the comparative literature.

[3] Males only

[4] Females only

Source: Arnold and Tigert, "Canadians and Americans," 78.

TABLE 5-9
REPORTED POLITICAL PARTICIPATION IN THE UNITED STATES AND CANADA[1]

Political Activity	United States			Canada		
	1972	1968	1964	1974	1968	1965
Read Newspapers Often	37%	49%	47%	43%	—	—
Tried to Convince Others	32%	34%	31%	23-34%[2]	—	23%
Attended Rally, Meeting	9%	9%	9%	19-32%[2]	—	15%
Did Party Work	5%	5%	5%	11-17%	—	5%
Displayed Sticker	14%	15%	16%	16-21%	—	—
Voted[3]	75%	76%	78%	85%	86%	81%

[1] The entry in each cell is the percentage of the sample in that year reporting that they engaged in that political activity.

[2] On these activities the questions in the two countries were asked differently. In the Canadian study, individuals were given the opportunity to indicate the frequency with which they participated in the activity, while in the American studies the response alternatives were simply yes or no. The first figure in the Canadian percentages excludes respondents saying they "seldom" or "never" participated in the activity. The second figure excludes only those individuals who said they "never" participated in the activity.

[3] Looking at national voting statistics since 1945 Ivor Crewe finds that the United States only experienced a mean voting turnout that has declined by 2.2% over the three decades 1940s/1950s to 1970s compared to Canada's 2.9% increase. Absolute levels of turnout are not comparable because of differences in methods of calculating turnout percentages in Canada and the United States. See Ivor Crewe, "Electoral Participation," in David Butler, Howard R. Penniman, and Austin Ranney, ed., *Democracy at the Polls: A Comparative Study of Competitive National Elections* (Washington, D.C.: American Enterprise Institute, 1981), 233-37.

Source: Beck and Pierce, "Political Involvement," 25.

TABLE 5-10
RELATIVE ATTRACTIVENESS OF CANADA AND THE PROVINCES
BY PROVINCE/LANGUAGE GROUPS (1974)[1]

	Percentage Most Oriented to Provinces	Percentage Most Oriented Nationally	Mean Scores	Standard Deviations	N
National	4.9%	18.4%	3.64	1.70	2383
Newfoundland	5.9%	3.9%	2.74	1.47	90
P.E.I.	4.2%	2.1%	2.89	1.45	84
Nova Scotia	1.7%	10.9%	3.45	1.48	147
New Brunswick	4.3%	21.5%	4.01	1.65	85
Ontario	0.9%	25.9%	4.29	1.44	651
Manitoba	5.3%	18.6%	3.79	1.69	108
Saskatchewan	6.9%	12.9%	3.53	1.72	94
Alberta	12.0%	6.3%	2.72	1.68	166
B.C.	6.0%	13.5%	3.42	1.67	242
Quebec English	1.5%	37.9%	4.78	1.37	126
Quebec French	9.3%	11.6%	3.21	1.78	531
Non-Quebec French	1.7%	20.0%	3.61	1.65	59

[1] This index compares "Canada in general" to "your province in general", "Canada as a place to live" to "your province as a place to live", and "Canadian government" to "government in your province". The range is 0-6, with zero being most favourable to your province, and six being most nationally oriented. Percentages do not add to 100 because of the omission of scores 1-5.

Source: David J. Elkins and Richard Simeon, *Small Worlds: Provinces and Parties in Canadian Political Life* (Toronto: Methuen, 1980), 17.

TABLE 5-11
SOCIAL CLASS STATUS AMONG CANADIAN AND AMERICAN ADMINISTRATORS
(per cent)

| | Administrators | |
	U.S.	Canada
Upper	49	74
Upper-middle	48	22
Middle	3	3
Lower-middle	0.5	0
Lower	0	0
(n)	261	214

Source: Presthus and Monopoli, "Bureaucracy in the U.S. and Canada," 178.

TABLE 5-12
OPINIONS OF ADMINISTRATORS CONCERNING INFLUENCE
(per cent)

| | United States | | Canada | |
	Federal	State	Federal	Provincial
Strongly agree	2	2	12	9
Agree	33	22	62	50
Don't know	14	20	8	15
Disagree	46	51	16	25
Strongly disagree	5	6	2	1
	(90)	(163)	(89)	(120)

Those surveyed were responding to the statement "senior civil servants are among the most influential groups in this country."

Source: Presthus and Monopoli, "Bureaucracy in the U.S. and Canada," 184.

6

URBAN FORM AND INSTITUTIONS IN CANADA AND THE UNITED STATES

To this point, we have been exploring differences beween Canada and the United States at an aggregate national or macro-level. This is consistent with our view that cities cannot be understood if they are studied out of the larger context within which they are situated. They inevitably bear the imprint of the nations and cultures within which they are formed.

It is the goal of this chapter to bridge the gap between the previous societal emphasis and the urban focus that follows. The purpose, therefore, is to sketch out some of the differences to be expected in Canadian and American cities in light of the foregoing observations about national differences. Because of the complex two-way interaction between cities and their larger cultural contexts, as exemplified by the macro-scale systems dealt with in the preceding chapters, an inquiry into the differences in urban places can yield potentially important insights into deeper-seated differences and problems in larger regional and national settings, a point ably advanced by the recent writings of Jane Jacobs.[1] This chapter will set the stage for subsequent chapters, which examine an array of urban differences in detail.

SOCIAL VALUES AND THEIR IMPLICATIONS

Our principal findings with regard to social values in the preceding chapters were these.

The value system of white Americans is such that residential integration on a local area basis is relatively rare. Black in-movement occasioned by a search for jobs and cheap, affordable housing helps to propel white out-migration when it is seen as the portent of an inevitable change in the local area. Black areas are generally avoided by whites seeking housing.

The net migration flows outwards are accentuated by the very high levels of crime in American central cities, these being in part a reflection of attitudes towards the rule of law, authority and public order. Historical context, daily experience and economic conditions are also relevant factors.

The declining significance of immigration from European sources and the possible erosion of ethnic identity mean that ethnic residential communities are less persistent or less likely to be established in American cities than in Canada. The potential for substantial offset to white and now black out-migration is less in the U.S. than in Canada.

Canadian value systems now attach considerable worth to ethnic enclaves and diversity and appear to be more accepting of other races as near neighbors. Massive net outflows of households are as yet unknown, and, in the aggregate, central-city population is growing.

The American emphasis on individualism and competition contrasts with the Canadian preference for collective and public action. Given such a fundamental value difference, relatively greater trust of government and ruling elites is found in Canada than in the United States.

Roles played by elites in the two countries differ also, with Canadian elites being more tolerated and also more powerful in general. This is in keeping with the relatively greater degree of deference shown in Canada to authority and the respect and desire for order.

In short, values tolerating ethnic and racial diversity and values which contribute to a less violent milieu play a role in maintaining the superior livability of the Canadian central city.

Accordingly, we should expect to find significant differences in the societal and household structure of Canadian and American central cities and their suburbs. Specifically, greater concentrations of families and middle-income households can reasonably be anticipated in Canadian central cities in comparison with those in the United States. Greater ethnic diversity in Canadian metropolitan areas (both central cities and suburbs) should also not be a surprise. Lower crime rates and a general perception of cities, particularly central areas, as being desirable and valued places to live should also serve to contrast Canadian and American urban areas. Indeed, two separate studies show that Canadians find urban living, in general, highly satisfying. The first study, done for the federal government, suggests very high degrees of satisfaction with urban life across the country.[2] A major concern of the 11,000 surveyed households was affordable housing for lower-income elderly groups, consistent with the notion of greater collectivist orientation among Canadians. The second study provided even more surprising results, in light of American perceptions of declining livability of central cities, since it demonstrated that over the decade of the 1960s Canadian central cities actually showed *increased* socio-economic status in comparison to *decreased* status for outlying suburban areas.[3] This finding not only suggests a striking difference from U.S. experience and media perceptions, but it also dramatically weakens one of the classic conceptions of urban growth as being typified by declines in central-city status over time and a continuing growth in the status and scale of suburban residential enclaves. In short, these studies support our earlier assertions that Canadians and Americans hold quite different values and perceptions about cities and city living, perceptions that imply the continued strength of Canadian cities as quality living and social environments, and conversely imply continuing struggle for central-city life in the United States. In fact, the American distaste and distrust for urban life have roots that stretch back before the founding of the republic, having been shored up over the centuries by a strong anti-urban intellectual tradition.[4] Moreover, this intellectual tradition has spilled over into everyday values, and the American public does not hold the city in high esteem.[5]

If the value base and attitudes towards cities in Canada are more positive, they have certainly been reinforced through a greater desire to plan and regulate cities than has been the case in the United States. As we saw when looking at political and economic institutions, the Canadian willingness to allow government intervention into various market sectors is at odds with cherished American values. It implies a much greater ability, however, to plan and control urban development in the interests of the society at large, creating, in principle, more livable cities. This would clearly interact with the more favorable Canadian disposition toward cities to continue to provide prized living environments in central cities.[6] We should also expect to see greater reliance in Canada on publicly provided urban services such as transit than is the case in the United States.

IMPLICATIONS OF DIFFERENCES IN ECONOMIC ORGANIZATION FOR URBAN FORM
AND STRUCTURE

As shown in Chapter 4, there are major differences between the Canadian and U.S. economies. Among the more obvious and important are: scale and complexity; industrial structure and role of manufacturing and resource industries; the roles of banks and commercial activities; and economic wealth and inequality. The U.S. is larger, more diversified, more complex, less dependent on resource developments and foreign trade, richer and clearly less tolerant of government involvement in economic matters.

In light of these economic differences we will be looking for deeper differences in urban form, structure and function. Particular attention will be focussed on differences in urban development patterns and transportation. Given the generally larger role for government direct and indirect intervention in the economy in Canada, we should expect to see much greater planning control exercised and as a result somewhat denser development with heavier reliance on public, as opposed to private, means of transportation. Given the relatively greater importance of income redistribution and welfare measures in Canada, we should also expect to see considerably less divergence between central city and suburban areas with respect to income and socioeconomic levels, Canadians it is reasoned being relatively more tolerant and accepting of government redistributive measures including housing assistance to lower-income households.

By extension, Canadian central cities should have relatively greater concentrations of economic activity, given the foregoing discussions about the perception of the central city as being a healthier and more desirable place to live and work than is the case with the American central city. Retail and wholesale trade, manufacturing and services should all exhibit less movement to the outer city in the Canadian context. In view of our repeated observations about different public sector roles, different local government fiscal policies should not be confounding either.

IMPLICATIONS OF DIFFERENCES IN POLITICAL CULTURE, VALUES AND INSTITUTIONS FOR URBAN DEVELOPMENT

Three themes relating to these issues emerged that have implications for urban development in Canada and the United States: greater acceptance of government involvement in economic affairs in Canada; a more dominant role for the federal government in the U.S. relative to the states compared with that for the Canadian federal government relative to the provinces; greater stress on the pursuit of individual goals in the U.S. and a correspondingly greater interest in collective action in Canada.[7]

Given the possibility of greater public involvement in urban development in Canada we should expect to see considerably greater attention paid to planning and development controls. In the absence of constitutional protection of property rights, governments at all levels in Canada should possess greater ability and willingness to intervene. The result of such planning involvement should be more compact and better planned cities in Canada. Costs of development should be higher in Canada, since municipalities and provinces have the legal right to pass on servicing and development costs to developers as well as the right to set high servicing standards. Such higher costs need not be uneconomic, however, as higher quality urban development with greater satisfaction and lower maintenance costs can ensue from such policies.[8]

The restricted role of the federal government in the Canadian confederation is particularly important when looking at urban development. Much of the initiative for urban policy in the United States has come from the federal government, and U.S. federal policies of freeway building, urban renewal and urban public housing have left considerable marks on the U.S. urban scene. There is only modest evidence that such federal interventions have been positive and much to suggest they have been negative.[9] In Canada, because of the much lesser federal role in urban development, cities and provinces have been left to fend for themselves, facing few, if any, of the problems faced by American cities such as urban blight, loss of middle-income and family households and population redistribution away from existing large metropolitan areas, especially those located in the historic American heartland.[10] All this is not to say that the Canadian federal government is without an important role or that it has not attempted to expand its role. Simply put, under the terms of the original B.N.A. Act and its judicial interpretations, and now the *Constitution Act*, federal urban policymaking has had to be minimal. Any federal initiative should have been taken in cooperation with the provinces and their creatures, the cities.[11] Unilateral federal actions became suspect and a source of tension.

Finally, the recurring myth of individual action in the U.S. led to what Warner has called "The Private City", and, more generally, to privatism with respect to the development and maintenance of cities. This contrasts with relatively greater stress in Canada on publicly provided goods and services. Differences in public transit patronage and automobile ownership and use between Canadian and American urban populations will serve to demonstrate Warner's thesis. Canadian cities should be more compact and have a different urban form from their American counterparts since extensive expansion has not been subsidized through federal highway programs in Canada and since Canadians expect and receive higher levels of public transit service.

An interesting extension of the American stress upon the individual instead of the society or group is seen in the number of governments in the U.S. It is ironic that a country with a long history of disliking government should have so many governments, but these are largely comprised of special-purpose districts and small municipalities, logical extensions of privatism where local governments can be seen as virtual private extensions of small population groups. Certainly, much of the debate on zoning and land-use controls in the U.S. has centered on exclusionary land-use control practices wherein municipalities seek to provide services to well-defined and relatively homogeneous social classes. Consider that in 1979 there were 79,913 governments in the United States for 223,880,000 people or one government for each 2,801 Americans. In Canada, in 1978, there were 4,740 governments for 23,483,000 people or an average of one government per

4,954 Canadians. In other words, there were nearly 80 per cent more governments per capita in the U.S. than in Canada. Interestingly, by 1982 there were just over 82,000 governmental units in America, a figure that is growing now at about 1 per cent per annum after three decades of decline. The fragmentation evident in the American urban system has provided almost individualized services to residents, but it has also made it difficult to deal effectively with regional, as opposed to local municipal, concerns, as would again be expected given the American private and individualistic ethic.[12]

In many U.S. municipalities, the scope of public services is limited, and private contracting for what are more commonly public services in the Canadian case, such as garbage collection or even fire protection, is more widespread, especially in suburban districts. The relative absence of public parks in these districts is compensated for by large, private, single-family lots complete with a range of private recreational paraphernalia.

CONCLUSION

In making this summary, the conclusions concerning contextual differences and their implications for urban development reflect both caution and boldness; caution because of the limited nature of some of the evidence, particularly with respect to values, and the tenuous nature of the connections that can be made to urban findings, and boldness because of the importance of the differences which have come to light in each of the four major macro-systems explored. These differences, as argued earlier, are intimately related to the urban differences between Canada and the United States that we seek to identify and understand.

The principal conclusions drawn from the research summarized here can be expressed usefully in terms of a public-private continuum. Canada and its cities generally lie towards the public end of such a dimension, and America and its cities lie towards the private end. The publicness of Canadian urban life is a manifestation of a greater collective orientation, while the privatism of urban America is a manifestation of individualism, highly possessive and materialistic at that. These attitudes are not absolutes, but questions of degree. There is clearly a sense of public life in American cities, and the evidence to date suggests that Americans are significantly more likely to be involved in community affairs than Canadians.[13] This is consistent with a stronger sense of localism and municipal autonomy, which is an expression of a highly privatized society. In this regard, the resistance in American cities to municipal integration is well known, and the thought of this being imposed by any of the states with no local say is anathema. Yet this kind of imposition has been common in Canada, especially in Ontario. The different responses to government intervention and control are numerous and striking.[14]

Equally, privatism is far from absent in Canada. One of the clearest instances of this is the very high level of home-ownership in a country where the home-owner cannot deduct interest payments on a mortgage or local property taxes from personal income for federal tax purposes, as can be done in the U.S., where it represents a massive federal intervention in the housing market and subsidy to property-owning classes. The Canadian home-ownership rate is 63 per cent (1981); the corresponding U.S. rate is 60 per cent (1983). Since 1960 the two rates have fluctuated within a few percentage points.[15] This, together with individual ownership of land and the very high level of consumption of consumer durables associated with property ownership, suggests that the highly urbanized Canadian society also has a pronounced privatized face. Nevertheless, individual interests in Canadian cities are more likely to give way to the rule of the state and to bureaucratic order than in the U.S., where freedom for the individual, with an implied absence of bureaucratic control, is to be preserved almost at all costs.

Another aspect of the publicness of Canadian cities is the prominence of the public enterprise as a leading urban institution and employer. The state intervenes in both direct and indirect manners in the urban economy: as employer, as regulator and as investor (in developing a public infrastructure). While the data examined next do not readily permit urban comparisons, the trend seems clear: Canadian cities are more closely governed and managed than are their U.S. counterparts. The focus of senior government intervention is also dramatically different. We argue that the U.S. federal government has been the major agent in key urban sectors across the nation. For example, its provision of urban freeways has benefitted auto-owning suburbanites, downtown and other private enterprises that employ these suburbanites, and the corporate interests that constitute the highway lobby in America. This intervention also served to transform fundamentally urban land markets, to decrease the accessibility advantages of the inner city, and to gut minority and poor neighborhoods around the city core.

In Canada, on the other hand, various federal administrations have been kept at a distance from the cities by aggressive provinces or by their own lack of interest. It bears repeating that there is a federal presence in all Canadian metropolitan areas. This presence is a function of both direct actions (waterfront redevelopments such as Harbourfront in Toronto) and indirect federal impacts (the housing finance policies of CMHC). Nevertheless, when approached comparatively, the Canadian federal role and the scale of its impact are far less than the equivalent role and impact of the U.S. federal government. It is the provinces which have been the dominant players in the urban transportation field but much more modestly, with less devastating results and with a mix of capital investments that has encouraged mass rather than, or as much as, private transportation. Thus, not only are the urban outcomes significantly different, reflecting a greater collective disposition, but the geographic orientations of Canadian civic politicians, interest groups and constituents are also different with respect to municipal affairs. They tend to look to provincial capitals and largely ignore Ottawa, whereas their American counterparts are much more oriented to Washington and less so to state capitals.

Canadian society has been asserted to be more ascriptive, more hierarchical and elitist than that of the U.S., where achievement is honored, structures are more diffuse and pluralism is almost an article of faith. These assertions may need to be rethought in light of the recent survey evidence presented earlier.[16] Furthermore, our review and interpretation contribute to this reappraisal. There is some evidence pointing towards greater tolerance in Canada of racial mixing residentially and of a greater desire to sustain a rich ethnic life in Canadian cities, even at the risk of weakening a sense of national identity. The attraction of the Canadian central city as a more livable place is indicated and is an important theme for our empirical analysis.

A value system that is more accepting of interpersonal differences, that contributes to a markedly lower level of personal violence and that prefers city living is a factor in the greater livability of most Canadian cities compared with the majority of their American counterparts. In a privatized society, solutions to problems are sought in a highly personalized fashion, one of the most prominent being withdrawal.[17] In America, conditions of life in many central cities and certain large metropolises are conducive to such a withdrawal. These conditions are not, however, simply part of the self-fulfilling behavioral outcomes that arise when people act upon their beliefs. They arise too from deeper structural tendencies or processes over which most individuals have very little control.

At the risk of breaking up closely interrelated concepts, we will examine empirically the following propositions, which can be used to differentiate between American and Canadian cities:

1. Beginning with the greater emphasis in Canada on collective action and multiculturalism, we can expect a more livable central city in Canada with less desire to shun central residential districts. This does not imply that Canadians do not value suburban living or even non-metropolitan exurbs. Rather, it is to emphasize the strong attraction of the central areas in Canadian cities for a broad range of social and demographic units.

2. This livability is related to a strikingly different cross-national social composition, reflecting different social histories in the two countries,

different public policies and social practices in ethnic and race relations, and different immigration experiences. These differences will be found at the urban level no less than at the national scale. Urban crime, for example, is simply one of a number of manifestations.

3. The strong desire expressed by Americans for suburban and quasi-rural living, combined with an affection for small, responsive local governments, is a contributory factor towards a more decentralized urban form. The social tensions of racially mixed but residentially segregated cities further impel the majority of white residents to seek out suburban areas with their pristine school districts. All this movement is underpinned by urban freeway systems which not only link suburbanites with the economic oppportunities and artistic/educational/cultural institutions in large cities but also enable the outer city to develop increasingly on its own, including an independent economic base. This decentralization theme should be reflected in metropolitan spatial structure and the location of economic activities in cities and suburbs.

4. Canadian cities, while exhibiting suburbanization, are anticipated to be more compact. This should be evident in the structure of the housing stock, in the geographic distribution of the population within metropolitan areas, and in a greater commitment to a public transportation system, which is often planned in conjunction with urban development to increase residential densities along and near major bus or trolley lines and rapid transit stations.

5. Our interpretation of political culture in the two countries and the cross-national contrast in the evolution of federalism points to two distinctive systems of intergovernmental relations. Thus, we anticipate a geographically different structure of local government in metropolitan areas in the two countries. Furthermore, patterns of governmental intervention in the urban public economy will also be different, and this should be apparent in urban public finance data.

6. Finally, if our thesis is correct that Canadian metropolitan centers are different in diverse and important ways from their American counterparts, then we should find that Canadian urban areas constitute a distinctive group within a North American framework, having more in common with each other than they do with cities in the U.S. In short, the border does matter for it is the territorial marker between two different places.

While Canadians and Americans are indeed North Americans by virtue of sharing the continent, they remain as different today as they have been in previous eras.[18] The monuments to this difference are the cities they have created and the settlement systems that have developed across this continent; it is to the empirical investigation of these places that we now turn.

7

URBAN FORM AND SOCIAL
CHARACTERISTICS

This chapter presents empirical evidence which, in the main, substanti-
ates the argument of the previous chapter. This evidence comes from a wide
cross-section of information, much of it drawn from public sources, especially the respective national censuses; this range is necessary in order to
capture a significant part of the complexity which characterizes the modern
city.[1]

In this chapter and the next, evidence is examined comparatively by
treating each variable as a single entity. Generally, data are cross-sectional
for one period of time (for example, from 1971 and 1976), and only rarely are
there data over a period of years. Chapter 9 presents the results of a more
complex sort of analysis that allows examination of a number of selected
variables and of how they relate with one another simultaneously.[2]

Organizationally, this chapter falls into three principal parts. Firstly, urban
form and access are discussed. This is followed by a section on demographic
and social characteristics, including population and household changes,
household structure, income measures, and race and ethnicity. Finally, the
metropolitan spatial structure of various economic activities—such as manufacturing or retailing—is analyzed. Here, the focus is on the degree of
decentralization as measured by the central-city share of an activity relative
to the metropolitan area as a whole. In Chapter 8, institutional facets of
urban structure are considered. Evidence on local government structure
and public finance are examined. By investigating urban form, demographic
and social variables, economic activity and political structure and public
finance, we believe we have captured and compared some of richness and

much of the complexity of urban areas in Canada and the United States.

It is also important to recognize the interrelationships among these important attributes of cities. Urban form or morphology is the manifestation of the interaction of complex economic, social and political processes. It is the setting within which many live out their lives, and, as the built environment, it plays a crucial role in the man-environment interrelationship which is central to the nature of those lives. The urban population as a mass inhabits this form and gives it meaning. Size, as measured by the number of people, is one of the first and most important facts noted about a place. Population growth is the delight of civic boosters heralding wealth and prosperity, while population decline is the harbinger of troubled times. Furthermore, it is the almost indescribable variety in the characteristics of urban populations that make the city an attractive social laboratory. Given present technologies of transportation and communications and preferences for ways of living and working, urban forms now exist where opportunities are typically concentrated in nodes and the population is dispersed with varying intensity throughout the urban area. These activity nodes and dispersed households must of necessity be periodically connected; thus, there is a demand for urban access, which itself is channeled through physical networks, such as roads and telephone cables, themselves part of the urban form.

Major activity nodes are increasingly found in more than one location in the modern metropolis. Urban regions, far less single-centered on the downtown or central business district than ever before, are increasingly polynuclear in form. Many of these new nodal concentrations are in the suburban parts of the metropolitan region, while the historic core dominates within the jurisdiction of the central city.[3] The public services and tax shelters afforded by certain suburban governments have been alleged to be a factor in the decentralization of economic activity from the central city. Certainly, the existence of suburban school districts, separate from those in the central city with their growing minority enrolments, has been one of a number of factors leading to the substantial suburbanization of population, especially in America. This is in itself a factor in promoting the decentralization of economic activity and a "looser" urban form. The functional unity of the urban region, reflected in the flow of metropolitan commuters along the transportation networks, stands in sharp contrast to the fragmented system of many units of local government, each with differing fiscal characteristics and services to property and people. This fragmentation differs markedly in degree between the United States and Canada, as we shall see in Chapter 8.

Before proceeding to a discussion of findings, it is necessary to comment on the cities used in the comparative analyses and on the dates of the data base. In a nutshell, it is very difficult, if not impossible, to compare all urban places in the two countries. As one works with smaller urban places with a population of 10,000 to 50,000, there is a greater likelihood that important data are missing. To limit oneself to the comparative study, alternatively, of two "paired" cities, one American and the other Canadian, causes other problems in the representativeness of the chosen pair. This is not to imply, however, that such studies are without merit since they do provide certain useful insights.[4] We ourselves engage in a modified form of paired comparison in our research. We chose a different focus in our work and dealt with the metropolitan centers of the two countries. This overcomes the problem of representativeness of paired urban comparisons, though clearly there is a bias toward large cities. However, the advantage of this focus is that comparable data are available, and the bulk of the national urban population is accounted for.[5]

Whichever spatial unit is employed, difficulties still remain in international comparison.[6] In the United States, the statistical unit most widely used and for which the largest data base is readily available is the Standard Metropolitan Statistical Area (SMSA). In Canada, the corresponding unit is the Census Metropolitan Area (CMA). But these units are defined with different core population thresholds of 50,000 and 100,000, respectively. To obtain an equivalent to the SMSAs of between 50,000 to 100,000, selected Canadian Census Agglomerations (CA) have been included if the core city was over 50,000 in population. One exception which we included in our data set was Lethbridge, Alberta. Although not designated a census agglomeration, it is a sizeable community (1981 population: 54,072) and a regional center in southern Alberta. This yielded a total set of 40 CMAs and CAs in Canada (1976) and 277 SMSAs in the United States (1975).[7] Selecting these particular units also allowed our work to be better connected to the bulk of existing research in both countries, this too having relied primarily on metropolitan areas as defined for census purposes.

By using the county as the basic spatial unit for the creation of an SMSA, extensive metropolitan areas are created in some cases, including much non-urban territory. Using the municipality as the basic spatial unit, the CMAs and CAs are, in general, smaller in area and more precisely bounded than their American counterparts.[8] This problem is partly offset by analyzing the constituent parts of a metropolitan area—the central city and the suburban ring. In carrying out the univariate analysis, we compare the statistics computed under three controls. By stratifying the metropolitan centers by population, by regional location and by a ratio which is the proportion of the central-city population to that of the local metropolitan area, it can be determined if these factors have any impact on observed cross-national differences. The third control also helps compensate for the overbounding problem.

URBAN FORM AND ACCESS

The first hypothesis to be examined is that Canadian cities have a more compact urban form than American cities of an equivalent size. Several different measures can be used to explore this hypothesis. Firstly, consider the proportion of the housing stock comprised of single detached units. Other things being equal, for two cities of roughly similar size a higher proportion of single-family units in the stock means that a larger geographic territory will be required to accommodate "land-consuming" detached units. There is a distinct U.S.-Canadian difference in urban housing stock composition for 1970-71 within both central cities and suburban belts (Table 7-1). These significant differences persist when both city size and the central-city-to-metropolitan population ratio are held constant. The compactness hypothesis cannot be discarded on this evidence.

To consider trends in housing stock composition at least to mid-decade, an estimate of the 1976 stock is formulated from building permit data (Table 7-2). The importance of single-family units in metropolitan Canada is declining in relative terms, since the proportion of single-family unit building permits is substantially less than was the proportion of the total housing stock share at the beginning of the decade. The building permit data support the notion that Canadian cities are more compact, even when holding city population size more or less constant.

A second and different kind of measure allows a further test of the notion of a more compact form. In urban studies, the population density gradient has been widely used as an indicator of urban form. It is a readily grasped measure of population concentration and dispersion within an urban area; the distribution of population is linked to the nature and geography of the housing stock. An extensive cross-national analysis of population density gradients for metropolitan areas produced two important results (Table 7-3). Firstly, there is no notable cross-national difference with respect to decentralization in urban areas. In both cases, central densities fell on average in half from 1950-51 to 1975-76. Again, for both sets of metropolitan areas, the density gradients also fell considerably on average during this interval. The decline was more pronounced in Canada than in the U.S., the density gradient values going from 0.93 to 0.42 (a 55 per cent change) in the former, and from 0.76 to 0.45 (a 41 per cent change) in the latter. Secondly, there persists a striking difference in central densities; Canadian central densities average twice the U.S. figure, even though there were broadly similar declines in central density values over time in both countries.[9]

Focusing on the recent period (Table 7-4), a consistent pattern is revealed with respect to the distribution of gradients by size of metropolitan population — Canadian density gradients are either similar to those in the U.S. (for the both smallest and largest places in 1975/76) or considerably steeper (for places between 500,000 and 1,000,000 population). These results indicate a different form in the urban areas of Canada compared with those in the U.S. Taken together, the roughly similar mean density gradients (0.42 for Canada in 1976 and 0.45 for the U.S. in 1975) and the substantially greater mean central densities in Canadian metropolitan areas imply a markedly more compact urban form in Canada.[10]

Another facet of the urban form relates to the physical characteristics of urban transportation systems. The dominant transportation feature of the modern city is the expressway. Indeed, as a landscape feature its construction has often been vigorously opposed in both Canada and the United States. We computed the number of expressway lane miles per capita (a standardized measure of capacity). Comparing this statistic showed that there were just over four times as many lane miles of urban expressway for each metropolitan resident in the U.S. as there were in Canada (Table 7-5)—a clear implication is that U.S. metropolitan areas are much more oriented to the automobile. Greater reliance on the automobile is attested to by a different statistic: the number of automobiles in operation. Over time, the U.S. per capita figure is consistently and approximately 50 per cent higher than the Canadian.

Perhaps the second most important physical element in urban transportation is the public or mass transit system, which itself may have several components — surface rail and subway with separate right-of-way or bus systems using expressways and city streets. Comparing metropolitan data, we found that Canadian mass transit systems had nearly 2.5 times the number of revenue miles per capita as their American counterparts, a statistically significant difference (Table 7-5). This intensity of service is particularly interesting because there is no appreciable difference in the proportion of the metropolitan area population served by public transit. Canadian transit systems therefore are much denser and serve their respective areas more intensively than equivalent systems in the United States. In short, Canadian cities appear to rely more heavily on a dense public transit system, whereas American urban areas rely much more upon extensive freeway networks.[11]

Urban Access

Urban access and movement patterns are inextricably linked with urban form. If, as has been suggested, Canadians live in more compact cities and are less dependent upon private transportation, this should be reflected in travel behavior and travel distance. Data on the mode of transportation to work (called "modal choice" by analysts) shows that U.S. commuters rely more on personal transportation, with nearly 85 per cent of the sample using automobiles compared with 66 per cent in Canada. Equally significant is the difference in public transportation usage, where one-quarter of Canadian commuters use public transportation while only one-eighth of U.S. commuters use this mode (Table 7-6).

The notion of a more geographically extensive metropolitan area in the United States would be supported if intraurban distances traveled were also greater. Census surveys of metropolitan journey-to-work trips in both countries provide clear evidence of the suspected difference. Work trip distances are consistently shorter in Canada. Interestingly, there appears to be little difference in work trip travel time. This implies a more congested commuting experience in Canada, something that is understandable given the comparative lack of freeways.

While the data on modal choice of transportation for the journey to work are derived from a sample of urban areas, a form of statistical control can be applied to determine the effects of city size or other factors on the observed cross-national difference. For each of Canada's three major metropolitan centers (Montreal, Toronto and Vancouver) a small subset of American metropolitan areas have been selected as pairs. Thus, to illustrate, metropolitan Toronto and Pittsburgh are of roughly similar size (for 1970/71), and the proportion that the central city constitutes of the metropolitan population is also broadly equivalent. Finally, they are within the same admittedly rather broad region of the continent—this regional "control" could be seen as a crude surrogate for city age or stage in urban development. The general logic shown in this illustration is followed in the other pairings. For example, all of the metropolitan areas paired with Vancouver are on the West Coast, are around one million in population (1975 data) and have roughly similar central-city-to-metropolitan population ratios. That such pairings are not straightforward is clear from the Montreal case where, to obtain more than one U.S. city (Baltimore), it became necessary to relax the regional control and include centers from regions of the U.S. other than the Northeast/Middle Atlantic. As this is an admittedly rough control, on occasion other centers are added to the pairings, depending on whether or not we are comparing metropolitan areas or the central cities. The cross-national differences on modal choice are very sharp and quite consistent with the more general metropolitan evidence (Table 7-7). The magnitude of the differences is thrown into sharp relief when one considers that Vancouver has a modal mix not unlike Chicago, a metropolitan area nearly seven times its size. The evidence from these and other cases suggests that there is a strong relationship between modal choice and city size, with the proportion favoring public transportation increasing as city size increases.

While the foregoing is far from a detailed analysis of urban transportation systems and journey-to-work behavior, partial evidence lends strong support to the argument that Canadian and U.S. urban areas are different. Canadian urban regions appear less dependent upon automobile transportation, contain more extensive (in terms of capacity) and more heavily utilized public transportation systems and are typified by shorter commuting trips. All of this is consistent with our compactness thesis and with the previous data pointing clearly and consistently to differences in urban form.

URBAN POPULATION AND SOCIAL COMPOSITION

We now compare the fundamental population and household shifts in the metropolitan areas of the two countries in the first half of the 1970s. In addition, we consider metropolitan social differentiation, which has been described generally by three constructs developed and widely used by urban researchers: socioeconomic status; stage in the life cycle; and racial or ethnic segregation. To represent each of these dimensions, household income, household structure, and the racial and national composition of the metropolitan areas are examined comparatively.[12]

The declines in metropolitan growth, and even absolute population loss in some instances, have been widely discussed in the United States. In earlier research, a pronounced difference was discovered between the two countries during the 1960s: a greater proportion of Canadian metropolitan areas experienced substantial population increases (over 20 per cent), and proportionately fewer places suffered an absolute loss.[13] From the most recent censuses in Canada and the United States, we can see that Canadian metropolitan areas are still growing more rapidly than their U.S. equivalents. Specifically, from 1971 to 1981 Canada's CMAs grew by 12.95 per cent compared with a 10.30 per cent increase in the American SMSAs. In the central cities, these differences were even more marked. For example, almost 40 per cent of U.S. central cities lost population compared to only 8 per cent in Canada.

But the first half of the 1970s showed a tendency for the differences in population change to converge for the two sets of metropolitan areas and the central cities; only in the suburbs did the difference of the 1960s persist (Table 7-8). A notable difference is revealed in the distribution of population changes. The Canadian cities are more homogeneous, whereas the U.S. metropolitan set contains both "losers" (15 per cent of all centers) and a number of "substantial gainers" (10 per cent of the centers had growth rates over 20 per cent).

Perhaps the most striking aspects of the analysis are, first, that almost half of Canada's central cities lost population in this period—a situation similar to the U.S. experience—and second, that suburbanization, as manifested by population growth in the balance, was more pronounced in Canada. In contrast, almost one-third of U.S. metropolitan suburbs either lost population or exhibited only modest growth (0-4.9 per cent).

An examination of population change by size of metropolitan area indicates that the effects of city size were most evident in the central cities but less in either suburban fringes or in metropolitan areas as a whole. Population loss was pronounced in the central cities of the largest metropolitan regions in both Canada and the United States. Also, the contrast in growth in the suburbs was less marked in these largest cities. Considerable growth was still evident, however, in the medium and smaller size Canadian centers, though with considerable variability.

A tempting conclusion might be that the well-known and frequently advanced "lag hypothesis" is being verified here; that is, that Canada is really similar to the United States but that trends established in the U.S., say in the 1960s, would not be detected in Canada until the 1970s. But this hypothesis cannot yet be accepted, even on demographic grounds. Analysis of migration patterns by age group in the central city of Vancouver, for example, has shown that the greatest amount of net out-migration (1971-76) occurs in the 0-10 age group, together with their parents. Furthermore, while the city lost population for the first time in a census period, households increased by some 4 per cent. What seems to be happening is that low- and middle-income families are being "priced out" of the costly central-city area and are relocating in suburban municipalities, a movement aided by a continuing outward shift of employment opportunities. Thus, while the net patterns of metropolitan population change in the two countries are converging, the underlying causes may be quite different. With the exception of select central areas of revitalization, few American families are being "priced-out"—they leave willingly to the suburbs and beyond for a better quality and safer environment.

These thoughts lead to an examination of patterns of household change and here a consistent difference emerges, although not always statistically significant at a very high level of confidence. In all these categories, household change in Canadian cities was greater than in the United States (Table 7-9). Again, there is more variability in the American data (except for the suburban ring), and the statistic that holds the greatest portent for the United States is that of absolute loss of households in 15 per cent of the central cities. This represents a major loss of purchasing power in the central municipality and an underutilized or even abandoned housing stock. As households leave, service enterprises follow or fail with a decline in effective demand; the cumulative effect is to erode the fiscal base of central-city administrations. At mid-decade, no Canadian city exhibited this profound loss. In those few instances which were close to a net loss in households by 1976, the decline in the number of households was offset by the fact that certain central cities were retaining or attracting affluent, two-income households moving into costly redeveloped or upgraded housing.

We have concluded so far that with reference to population change in metropolitan areas Canadian cities are becoming more similar to those in America. But the much greater variability and range of experience in the U.S. must not be overlooked and can be exemplified using data from the most recent 1980 and 1981 censuses. This range is evident from conditions in the New York, Cleveland and Buffalo metropolitan areas where the population declined by about 8 per cent in the 1970-80 decade while at the same time metropolitan centers in Florida, Texas and elsewhere experienced increases in excess of 50 and 60 per cent.

The Canadian experience, is, however, more modest—no metropolitan area's population grew by more than 50 per cent from 1971 to 1981, but the largest decline was just less than -5.0 per cent (Sudbury, Ontario). The phenomenon of population decline and an overall slowing of the metropolitan growth rate is most dramatically evident in central-city losses. The American experience has been widely documented. Even before the 1980 census was taken, urbanists noted "the current nationwide trend of absolute central city population decline."[14] On this point, the Canadian experience does differ, and the 1980/81 data reinforce this difference. Numerically, more central cities (twenty-two) gained population than lost it during the 1976-81 period, and in absolute terms, there was a net gain of just over 100,000 people. While there are central cities in the U.S. that are "gainers," they are being swamped nationwide by the massive hemorrhaging from America's leading urban centers. Thus, even while there is some convergence in the aggregate metropolitan experience, important differences persist. The recent Canadian experience is typified by less dramatic growth and declines and by healthier central cities in terms of population gain. This is not to ignore the fact that eighteen Canadian central cities did experience population loss during this period.

Although population decline is important, in terms of provincial/state to city fiscal transfers or changes in demands for specific services such as education, insufficient attention has been paid to changes in a fundamental demographic unit: the household, a unit of great significance in terms of demands for housing, consumer durables, personal and public services. It has already been shown that there were important differences in the amount and distribution of household change in the first half of the 1970s. We have argued previously that the greater average growth of households in Canadian metropolitan areas, including the central cities, is a result of the continued greater attractiveness of central-city residential areas in Canada. In turn, we linked this to a series of variables including neighborhood racial change, race relations, public safety, educational quality and the provision of municipal services under fiscal stress. On these issues, there are significant U.S.-Canadian differences which, we believe, arise in part from institutional practice and historical differences.

It is now possible to make this important comparison for the past decade, treating here only the "worst case" scenario—the central city. The results are striking and confirm our expectations (Table 7-10). No Canadian city is yet in a loss situation in terms of net household change. Eight of America's twenty largest metropolitan areas suffered a household loss in their central cities, while another six "stagnated" (where stagnation is defined as growing at less than 0.5 percent per annum). Of all Canadian metropolitan areas, only Montreal falls into this latter category. Language was likely acting in Montreal as an impediment to foreign immigration, which continued to replenish anglophone Canadian inner-city areas. Apprehension over separatism and economic decline accelerated the out-migration of both employment and English-speaking households from Montreal. This evidence constitutes another challenge to the lag hypothesis, for we must now be prepared to accept a lag of greater than ten years, if indeed there is a lag. We remain skeptical.

These conclusions are reinforced by comparing household change over the decade for the three dominant Canadian metropoles with their selected pairs (Table 7-11). Houston and San Diego are clearly in a class by themselves, bearing the full brunt of "sunbelt" growth. For the remainder, the Canadian cities show positive growth along with several U.S. regional centers (for example, San Francisco-Oakland, Seattle, Portland, Milwaukee). Other large American cities used as pairs show either a loss or else are stagnating. Considering household growth and decline at the metropolitan scale shows that suburban growth is still considerable in Canada's big three cities (the proportions range from 23.6 per cent to 28.4 per cent). Again Houston and San Diego exceed this, Baltimore and Portland are in the same range, but six American metropolitan areas are below or substantially below the lowest Canadian score (Toronto), while three others though similar to Toronto are considerably lower than Vancouver and Montreal.

Social Composition

In this section, the discussion is organized around three concepts which have been employed theoretically and empirically validated in urban studies: socioeconomic status, stage in the life cycle and racial or ethnic segregation. The measurement of these concepts and their use in urban analysis is not straightforward, nor is it without controversy.[15] We adopt a simple approach by selecting one or two measures as a diagnostic variable for these broad concepts rather than subjecting readers to a battery of fifty or more variables and the statistical manipulations that traditionally accompany such analysis.

Household income is used as a diagnostic variable for the socioeconomic status dimension and is expressed as a ratio of central-city household income to metropolitan household income. A ratio of less than 100 identifies a central city poorer than the metropolitan area as a whole, and ratios of over 100 express the converse. We argued in the preceding chapter that there would be greater geographic disparities in socioeconomic status within U.S. metropolitan areas than in Canadian ones. The evidence obtained from computing and comparing these ratios does not permit rejection of our position (Table 7-12). The U.S.-Canadian difference in either the mean or the median household income ratios is considerable; the distributions are also sharply different. While the Canadian cities form almost equal groups, they are relatively tightly clustered around the value of 98. Spatial disparities in affluence are far more sharply defined in metropolitan America: for example, 30 per cent of U.S. cities have ratios of less than 90 for mean household income, which rises to 48 per cent for median household income; in Canada, the equivalents are 10 and 14 per cent, respectively. Thus, the relative poverty of the American central city is clear, but this is not found to the same extent in Canadian cities. In seeking to update these figures to 1980/1981 considerable difficulty was encountered. Median household income data could not be found for central cities and metropolitan areas in the United States; only per capita income data were available. Using these, we found that the central city represented 93.1 per cent of the metropolitan area total for the U.S. on average in 1980, whereas in Canada in 1981 the central city represented 99.7 per cent of the metropolitan total, thus confirming, if with less detail, the findings shown in Table 7-12 for 1970/1971.

Much of the literature on the relative poverty of central-city districts and the affluence of suburbia is based on evidence from America's larger metropoles. Our analysis has demonstrated a meaningful difference comparing a much more varied range of metropolitan areas. To focus on the larger metropolitan centers, we employed again the paired comparisons for those places over one million in size. With one exception, each American area examined is substantially below its Canadian pair—the exception is San Diego, where there is relatively little central city-suburbia disparity (Table 7-13). The preponderance of the evidence in the controlled comparison supports the hypothesis concerning greater geographic disparity in status (as measured by income) between the central city and the suburbs in the United States.

The concept of stage in the life cycle is an important differentiator, since the demand for specific types of housing in particular locations varies along this dimension. It is analyzed by comparing the distribution of one- and two-person households (encompassing the elderly and a high proportion of young adults) and households comprising families with children still at home (Table 7-14). Familism, as manifested by family households, is more strongly associated with Canadian cities, particularly the central cities; the difference in the means for the metropolitan areas is statistically significant. These data confirm our general hypothesis. The widely documented and predominantly "white flight" from the U.S. central city to the suburbs, seeking affordable housing, jobs and racially pure school systems, has taken its toll so that by 1971, only 40 per cent of all households in the central city were families with children at home; given the racial character of urban America, many of these families would be non-white and female-headed. The Canadian equivalent of 57 per cent suggests a capacity to retain families. However, these 1971 data are prior to the rapid price increases in housing which have caused families of more modest means to look to the suburbs for cheaper housing. More affluent families, often with two incomes, remain and seek out the prestigious neighborhoods which are still centrally located in Canadian cities. Households with two or fewer persons are more characteristic of U.S. cities, and the differences are significant.

The perception of American central cities as unsafe, unhealthy and containing poor housing and inadequate schools rests on "big city" evidence, some of it quite anecdotal in nature. It follows that people acting on this perception seek out suburban havens as the "right place" in which to raise and educate their children. But it needs to be stated boldly that in many big cities there are decent, livable areas in which to raise youngsters. Equally, it is true that many families lack the economic stability and credit to compete effectively for suburban housing opportunities. They thus remain in the central city. The exercise of discriminatory practices has also hindered minority families, although there is now an increasingly important minority component in the suburbanization process. Does the evidence from the larger cities fit this interpretation? Or are larger Canadian cities not characteristically peopled by family households either? In no city are families with children at home the majority household type. But the Canadian cities have consistently higher proportions of this type—again only San Diego outscores its Canadian pair (Vancouver), and the difference is not large (Table 7-15). Even Houston, which has a high central-city-to-metropolitan population ratio compared to Montreal and hence contains much post-1960 suburban style housing, has a lower proportion of family households than Montreal. Although we are not able to explore this in detail, we are confident that the higher rate of immigration into the central city in Canada is part of the underlying cause. Even if a male immigrant arrives alone, the family often joins him later. For many, the central city in Canada is still the primary destination.[16]

In the discussion of income and household structure, the important variable of race has been introduced. The central importance of race in America and the degree to which it is interrelated with class are well known; these were discussed in some detail in Chapter 3. Likewise, Canada is known as a racially homogeneous society with a few localized exceptions. Thus, it would have bordered on the fatuous to hypothesize about cross-national racial differences. All we do is in a sense document the conventional wisdom; the results do show a difference of considerable magnitude (Table 7-16). More importantly, the social, economic and increasingly the political meaning of this difference in racial composition must be properly emphasized, but not to the degree stressed by urban analysts who use race to explain all cross-national differences.[17]

It should be remembered that there is substantial variability in the significant non-white populations of American cities; most non-whites are disproportionately concentrated in the central cities. Some cities have relatively small proportions, and, with a dramatic increase in non-white immigration into Canada, an interesting comparison unfolds. Since non-white is not exclusively black, especially in certain locations, it is not surprising that in 1970 Vancouver city had a higher proportion of non-whites than did Seattle, Portland or San Diego, largely as a result of Asian immigration. Toronto also outranked Minneapolis-St. Paul in 1970; with continuing non-white immigration, especially from the West Indies, Toronto's proportion in 1981 increased to 8.0 per cent for the metropolitan area and 11.0 per cent for the city of Toronto. In comparison, the city of Boston has 30.0 per cent non-white, while the Boston metropolitan area has 8.9 per cent non-whites (1980). Yet "ghettoization," or high levels of residential segregation, of non-whites is definitely not characteristic of most Canadian cities. It is, on the other hand, a pervasive feature of the American urban landscape.

If the city differences on race are not surprising for the most part, perhaps less well known is the degree to which immigration has had a remarkable effect on most Canadian cities in recent years. The notable exceptions are the largely French-speaking cities of Quebec, which attract relatively few foreign immigrants and which account for the consistently greater variability within the Canadian data.

The distribution of foreign born in the metropolitan population provides something of a mirror image of the non-white distributions (Table 7-16). Although the differences are not of the same magnitude, they have been shown to be statistically significant. In 1971, close to half the people in Toronto were foreign born—only Miami with its large Hispanic population, primarily Cuban, comes close. By 1981, the foreign born proportion in Miami was just over half for the city (53.7 per cent) and about one-third (35.6 per cent) at the metropolitan level. The corresponding values for Toronto are 43.0 per cent and 38.1 per cent. The noted travel writer and essayist Jan Morris recently described Toronto as "the emblematic immigrant destination of the late twentieth century."[18] Canadian cities, especially the larger ones, are in fact bulging with immigrants—a vitally important urban difference between Canada and the United States. We have seen, for example, that this has given rise to a new phrase, and new public policies, to challenge bilingualism and biculturalism— multiculturalism, which, for Morris, is the key word to typify contemporary Toronto. Perhaps more importantly, the streetscapes and ambience of many Canadian cities, at the level of daily experience, contrast markedly with the majority of U.S. cities where the impacts of recent immigrants have not been so evident. There are obvious exceptions—New York, East Los Angeles, the Bay Area would be some of the better known.

Controlling for Size, Geopolitical Structure, and Region

City Size: In the discussion of urban population and social composition, it was noted that controlling for size yielded an additional insight. Although the average population change was similar for the largest metropolitan areas in both countries, there was a higher level of population growth in intermediate and smaller Canadian centers, especially in their suburban areas. Does the application of a control for population size alter in a substantial way our prior conclusions based, firstly, on an across-the-board metropolitan systems comparison and, secondly, on the controlled-paired comparison for the "million-plus" metropolitan centers?

The key finding in the analysis of household change was not that the cross-national differences were large or significant but that they were consistently more positive in Canada, be it at the metropolitan, central-city or suburban scale. Controlling for size does not seriously alter this finding. Only in the largest central cities is the mean and median value lower in Canada—the explanation here again lies in the pronounced variability in the 36 American cases with a range of 52 points compared to a trifling 2 points for the 3 Canadian cases.

The greater intra-metropolitan income disparities noted for the U.S. persist at all levels of city size except for those of under 100,000. Here, the central cities are revealed to have a higher income relative to the remainder of the metropolitan area. A possible explanation is that the smaller SMSAs in the U.S. normally constitute a single county. In these smaller cities, higher-income residential districts have been maintained in the city, and the surrounding rural parts of the country, sporadically dotted with mobile home parks beyond the city boundary, have few status connotations to the small-city elites.

The singular attractiveness of the Canadian central city for families engaged in child-rearing is not sensitive to city size, except perhaps in the case of the largest cities. Although the difference narrows from the 17 points that characterize all other size classes, it remains a substantial 6 to 7 point difference in favor of Canada (here taking a normative position that a higher proportion on this variable is desirable). The greater "maturity" of the U.S. suburbs compared to the relative "youth" of Canadian suburbs is demonstrated at all levels of city size. Our 1970 data presage what has become known more recently in the U.S. as the "greying of suburbia," as parents whose children have left are burdened by large single-family detached homes, a lack of housing alternatives in relatively homogeneous housing districts and little desire to move into the central city with its attendant risks.

Given the magnitude of the cross-national difference in the non-white proportion of the population, the fact that adjusting for size does not remove the difference should not be surprising. It is true that in both countries there is a general tendency for the non-white proportion to decline as urban size decreases. Nevertheless, the central cities in Canada's million-plus areas have an average proportional representation more akin to that in America's under-100,000 areas, which may help explain why the smaller U.S. central cities have higher status compared to their suburbs than the larger cities in that country. A similar finding results when the foreign-born population is controlled for by size. The striking difference persists at all levels of size. Here too, another difference emerges. While there is a regular decline in the proportion of foreign born as urban size decreases in the U.S., this relationship is less strong in Canada although the general direction of the relationship is also negative.

To sum up, then, there is little evidence when controlling for size that would cause us to modify our conclusions on differences in population, household dynamics or the various facets of social composition and status.

Geopolitical Structure: It is possible that some of the observed differences are a function of the proportion that the central city represents of the metropolitan area. For example, one might argue that because the Canadian cities as a whole have higher central-city-to-metropolitan population ratios and because they thus contain more people and housing that would likely be considered "suburban" (beyond the city limits) in America, it is this artifact that brings about the lower income disparities in metropolitan Canada.

A quick perusal is all that it takes to reveal that the racial and foreign-born differences are completely insensitive to this control. Also, the key finding that families with children at home are proportionately more important as a household type in Canadian cities is not invalidated by this control. It is true, however, that in the lowest ratio category, there is no difference— the mean value for the two Canadian cities in this category (Toronto and Victoria) is essentially the same as that for the 39 American cases in this lowest category. Also, considering again the results on the controlled-paired comparisons on this variable, we are not prepared to qualify our conclusion in any substantial way.

Considering the status disparity conclusions, some of the difference could be attributable to this basic structural condition. Recall that the lower the ratio, the greater the disparity. In both countries there is a clear and consistent relationship—as the central-city proportion rises, the income disparity of the suburbs to the central city lessens and even reverses, so that in the highest ratio category, the city populations tend to have higher incomes than the suburban residents. The poverty of the rural-urban fringe for smaller urban places is being demonstrated here. Thus, we should anticipate that because Canada has more metropolitan areas with higher ratios, some of the difference, which was in its favor, should "wash out" under this control. It does and even is reversed on the median household income variable. For the mean household income variable, the disparity ratio is higher for Canada but often not by much. It should be borne in mind that in the overall analysis our interpretation placed more stress on the nature of the distribution of the disparity ratios than on the cross-national differences that were apparent. While individual metropolitan scores may be a function of their geopolitical structure, that structure is not a statistical artifact but is itself a fundamental difference requiring an explanation.

Finally, with respect to demographic change, the control has the effect of reducing the cross-national difference in only a few categories. For instance, there was an overall similarity in the amount of household change in the central city—the control does not alter this substantively. The most obvious differences were to be found in the Canadian suburbs. This too is not affected by the control except in one category, where the central-city population is 70 per cent or more of the metropolitan population.

These tend to be smaller cities, and here we find considerable household growth in American suburbs: the median is 17.6 per cent to the Canadian 14.0 per cent—not a large difference but in the opposite direction from the others. For population change, the control tends to sharpen the central-city difference observed in the overall analysis—namely that losses tended to be greater in the Canadian case. This remains true for all levels of the control variable, and there is some tendency for these differences to be slightly greater than the overall values. The consistently higher population growth in the Canadian suburbs remains at all levels of the control variable.

On balance, this particular controlling for geopolitical structure leads only to a more cautious position on whether or not there is a real and basic difference in metropolitan income disparities between the two countries. For all other variables examined, the effects of the geopolitical structure upon the differences observed are sufficiently minor that no major revision of our conclusions is required. In the main, the range of evidence here makes our central arguments even more credible.

Regional Pattern: There are some intriguing geographical issues that can be partly addressed by analyzing by region the variables on urban form, population and household change, and social composition. In broad terms, both countries were settled and developed under European domination in an east to west progression. It is therefore valid, to a point, to talk about the older cities of the east in comparison to the newer cities of the west. We have suggested that there should be some systematic regional patterning to certain of the variables.

Part of the popular, and academic, convention on the settlement and development of North America is that the "natural grain" and hence orientation of the continent is north-south. Hence, cities of western Canada, it has been suggested, have more in common with other Pacific or "mountain/high plains" cities than they do with cities in eastern or central Canada. The border is seen as artificial, somehow cutting across these allegedly natural progressions, similarities and linkages.

While this issue is dealt with more fully in Chapter 9, some understanding can be gained through a regional comparison on selected variables. Looking at the metropolitan housing stock, it is clear that the higher proportion of single detached units in the U.S. areas occurs across the whole country compared to the corresponding regions in Canada, with only one exception— Atlantic Canada and New England—where there is no difference. There is a tendency for an east to west gradient in the U.S., although this is disrupted by a decline in the Far West. In Canada, once one moves out of Quebec (the uniqueness of its cities on this variable is dramatically clear), there is a somewhat surprising uniformity in the proportion across Ontario and the West; all are around two-thirds. While the regional pattern for American central cities is almost a mirror image of that for the metropolitan areas, the mirror is shattered by British Columbia. Here, a difference between B.C. on the one hand and Ontario and the remainder of the west on the other is clearly apparent. The B.C. central cities, with only 44 per cent of their stock in single detached units, not only differ from these other regions in Canada but also from the U.S. Pacific cities (at 68 per cent).

There is an interesting cross-national difference in the flow of additions to the housing stock. In metropolitan America, there is broad regional uniformity (the range between regions is 11 points) in terms of the proportion of single-unit permits, whereas in Canada there is pronounced regional variation (the range is 26 points). Duplex and row housing are a very important element in the additions in Atlantic Canada; one has to go to the Pacific Region of the U.S. to find the highest proportion in America. Apartment permits are proportionately highest in B.C., while the Pacific Region is one of the lowest in the U.S. These findings indicate neither a similarity in regional patterning nor much in the way of a cross-border similarity by region.

We have already shown that there are substantial differences in the urban transportation systems in the two countries. Other than New England, no region in the U.S. contains cities with the limited expressway capacity exhibited on the average in all the Canadian regions. While it is the case that the lowest capacities are in the U.S. Northeast and in Quebec and Atlantic Canada, the correspondence then begins to break down, since B.C. has the highest per capita figure in Canada whereas the Pacific Region in the U.S. ranks fourth out of the nine regions, the West South Central being premier in this element.

There has been a great deal said about interregional migration in both Canada and the United States. Our expectation that there would be a broad east-west positive trend in metropolitan population increase is substantiated — this is an important similarity in both countries. Given the greater regional diversity in growth in the U.S. and the fact that nearly all Canadians live in their "linear south," which in geophysical terms has more commonalities with the northern and western parts of the U.S., we should not be surprised to see this dominant trend disrupted by the exceptional growth in the Southeast, especially but not only in Florida.

Central-city population losses tend to be an eastern phenomenon in both countries with the exception of B.C., which, by showing a loss, is profoundly different from the corresponding Pacific Region in the U.S.; Prairie and Mountain cities are the highest in terms of population gain. Overall, there is some regional correspondence, although it should be noted that the cross-national differences observed in the suburbs persist. No matter which comparison is made, the population gain is always much higher in the Canadian case; Ontario, the Canadian region with the lowest score, is the most American, in a sense, on this variable.

The demographic differences between the two countries are more sharply focused through an examination of household change. At the metropolitan level, there is little between-region difference in Canada (from a high of 22 per cent to a low of 18 per cent). In the U.S., however, there is substantial regional variation with gains of only about 10 per cent in the Northeast and close to 25 per cent or greater in the cities of the South Atlantic, Mountain and Pacific Regions, a pattern largely mirrored in central-city household change. Canada's central cities do exhibit a similar east-west positive trend, but with a less steep slope. Eastern Canadian cities have scores greater than their regional counterparts in the U.S., but the opposite is true in the West.

In our previous discussion, we placed considerable emphasis on the variable, "families with children at home." The regional patterning of this variable is also different, with the trends going in roughly opposite directions. Secondly, the aggregate cross-national difference is also apparent for all regions in Canada compared to the U.S., except for B.C. With a one-third proportion, it is quite similar to its Pacific counterpart in the U.S.

Pursuing the social composition variables further, an interesting difference emerges in terms of the immigrant population. One could argue that there are two Canadas in terms of this variable—one containing cities that attract immigrants (B.C., Ontario and the Prairies) and one with cities that are not attractive destinations (Atlantic Canada and Quebec). There are two Americas also. However, it is the cities of the Northeast and the Pacific that attract and retain the immigrants; all other regions have extremely low proportions of foreign-born populations, especially the so-called "Deep South." Overall, most north-south comparisons on this variable reveal sharp differences. As one would expect given historical experience, B.C. cities have the highest proportion of non-whites, quite different from the rest of Canada. They are, in a sense, more American on this particular variable. The rest of Canada is uniformly low and very, very different from corresponding regions in the U.S.

In sum, our findings are not encouraging for those who think that there exists a regional typology of cities wherein there are West Coast cities, cities of the High Plains, or Great Lakes cities. It should be remembered that the bulk of the evidence from the controlled-paired comparisons also indicated more differences than similarities. Furthermore, the differences or similarities that were observed in the uncontrolled comparisons usually persist when regionally specific comparisons are made. It is true that on some urban form measures, cities of Atlantic Canada and those of New England have something in common. But sharp contrasts emerge as these regions are compared on demographic and compositional variables. What is apparent is that there is regional variation in both countries, with rather greater degrees of variation evident in the United States, a finding that is supported by other statistical evidence (see the standard deviations in many of the tables). While Quebec cities emerge as very distinctive within Canada, there is little in our findings to support the position that, without Quebec, "English" Canada is just the same as America. The evidence is simply to the contrary.

METROPOLITAN ECONOMIC ACTIVITY

Manufacturing

The evidence from a series of variables relating to the geography of manufacturing in metropolitan areas is, on balance, consistent with our principal argument. We have suggested that decentralization of economic activity from the central districts of Canadian metropolitan areas would be less than in the American setting. Our results support this position (Table 7-17). Within metropolitan areas, manufacturing plants and employment are proportionately more concentrated in Canadian central cities as a whole than in the U.S. This difference is particularly marked in the medium-sized urban areas of between 100,000 and 1 million people. In the million-plus category, the differences are again small, with a slight tendency for manufacturing to be more concentrated in the U.S. central cities.

Looking at these variables by region yields some further insight and reveals important differences (Table 7-18). America's traditional "manufacturing belt" has experienced stagnation and even loss in terms of population change (New York was the only state to show a population loss from 1970 to 1980). In the long dominant manufacturing activities, there has been a marked loss of employment, particularly in the lower skilled occupations. Closed factories, "mothballed" plants, and a decaying transportation infrastructure contribute to the negative image encapsulated in the media term "Rustbelt." Nevertheless, this region still remains the principal locus of such activity in the United States. Equally, in Canada, manufacturing activity is disproportionately concentrated in the southern Ontario/southern Quebec corridor, much to the chagrin of politicians and entrepreneurial elites in the hinterland regions of the country. Three census regions (New England, Middle Atlantic and East North Central) correspond crudely to the dominant manufacturing region in America. Within these regions, manufacturing activity is overwhelmingly suburban in location, whereas in the urban areas of Ontario and Quebec, roughly two-thirds of the plants and employment are still located in the central city. Within their respective countries, two cities epitomize the industrial heartland—Pittsburgh, Pennsylvania, and Hamilton, Ontario, both notable for steel and a not altogether deserved image as "lunchbucket" communities. The differences in terms of the metropolitan location of plants and employment are striking, as are the trends in employment (Table 7-19). Lest it be argued that this is a function of differences in city size in this particular instance, two other leading industrial centers somewhat closer in size to Hamilton are included in the comparison. The proportional size of the central city compared to the metropolitan area is also controlled. The striking differences remain for the most part. For Pittsburgh, a more appropriate comparison is with Toronto. The central-city shares of plants and employment are not very different, but the change data are revealing. Suburban growth is what differentiates Toronto from a declining Pittsburgh.

It has been widely asserted that manufacturing activity has been decentralizing within metropolitan areas in advanced market economies for some time. The aggregate evidence from urban Canada and America is consistent in this regard; it is also generally similar in direction—that is, negative (Table 7-20). But again important differences emerge. In looking at change we emphasize median values for there is a considerable range of experience, especially in the United States where the urban system again exhibits greater variability; this variability (and skewness too) tends to distort mean values. Considering central cities, in both countries there is a loss of manufacturing employment, but the magnitude is higher in the U.S. This remains true regardless of city size. However, it is worth noting that the central-city mean value is higher in the U.S. Examining the distribution of city values yields the answer. Almost half of the American central cities actually gained manufacturing employment in this period, with fourteen cities having dramatic increases in excess of 50 per cent; only one Canadian city enjoyed such growth. Equally, however, over one hundred cities, including nearly all the largest ones, regardless of regional location, declined. Many exhibited significant losses, given the base size of the manufacturing labor force. In Canada, on the other hand, only about one-quarter of the cities were gainers. However, where losses occurred, their magnitude was generally less than in the U.S.—no city lost more than 20 per cent of its manufacturing employment. In the U.S., twenty-five central cities suffered this substantial loss—about 12 per cent of all central cities. With respect to this trend, then, the Canadian cities show less variability and a less clear-cut regional patterning.

If the differences between Canadian and American central cities tend to be ones of degree and distribution, the differences in the suburban districts are more opposed in nature (Table 7-20). In aggregate and across all four city-size classes, the American median values for change in employment are negative, whereas in Canada they are all positive and substantially so. Only two areas, Kitchener and Halifax, exhibited suburban declines as opposed to 72 cases in the U.S.—40 per cent of all metropolitan areas. These data lend credence to an interpretation that a substantial amount of economic activity in America is relocating across regions and beyond boundaries of metropolitan areas. There is obviously considerable central-city growth, especially in smaller cities in regions favored by new investment, and this must not be overlooked. In Canada, manufacturing remains a predominantly metropolitan activity, with decentralization occurring to suburban locations.

Wholesaling

Just as the need for low-cost land on which to expand, and servicing by truck transportation rather than by rail, have significantly accelerated manufacturing decentralization, so too have these factors affected wholesaling activity, which has been long associated with central city locations, such as waterfronts and railroad terminals. Huge new suburban warehouses with cows grazing serenely in the background, undisturbed by the tractor-trailers with their containerized cargoes, attest to the new locations of wholesaling in both America and Canada.

Our expectation of differences here again rests on the notion that metropolitan deconcentration is proceeding at a much faster rate in the United States, leaving the central cities in an especially perilous situation. The aggregate evidence for this activity supports this position (Table 7-21). Whether one considers the location of wholesaling establishments, the incidence of sales or the distribution of wholesaling employment, Canadian central cities contain a significantly higher proportion of each than do American central cities. The greatest suburbanization of this activity has occurred in metropolitan Toronto, with a relatively modest port function on the central waterfront and an extensive freeway system, which has significantly improved access throughout the suburbs. There is a strong relationship between city size and the three variables examined here. In the million-plus category, there is only a marginal difference between the U.S. and Canadian metropolitan areas in the degree of central-city share. But in each of the other size classes, the Canadian central-city share is consistently higher, especially in the intermediate-sized metropolitan centers. Furthermore, as city size declines, the central-city share systematically increases for these wholesaling variables.

Wholesaling is a fairly common urban activity, and for a few centers it is a leading specialization. Port cities, as gateways and transshipment points, and key inland rail centers have historically been important foci of warehousing and wholesaling. To make our comparisons more concrete we compared leading centers in Canada—St. John's, Halifax, Winnipeg and Vancouver—with three important U.S. centers—Boston, Chicago and the San Francisco Bay Area (Table 7-22). The Canadian cases each have a substantially greater central-city share. Recognizing that this comparison could be affected by obvious size differentials, we selected other U.S. centers, controlling broadly for size and regional location. What is shown here is that regional effects are noteworthy. For the East Coast comparisons, the Canadian central-city share is generally greater, substantially so in the St. John's case. When one looks at the Plains/Prairies and West Coast comparisons, wholesaling is quite a bit less concentrated in the Canadian central cities. Indeed, here, the U.S. cases have a higher share. Local investigations and greater study are needed to explain this adequately.

Retailing

It has been clearly established in urban research that there is a strong geographical association between population and the location of retail

cal controls, we find that just over half the American cities have a central-city share value below the minimum Canadian value (again Toronto, at 47.8 per cent). These are exactly the same cities that fell below the minimum in the retail analysis. When the same distributional analysis is performed for both sets of cities, about one-third of all U.S. metropolitan centers (for establishments) and one-fifth (for sales) fall below the minimum Canadian value. This finding reinforces the close correspondence between the patterns for retailing and business and personal services.

There is also one quasi-public service that we investigated—hospital care. Here, the results are again consistent with our expectation (Table 7-29). For two variables, the number of hospitals and the total number of hospital beds, there are substantial differences in the central-city share between Canadian and American metropolitan regions. When city size is controlled for, some of the differences persist, but others do not. They persist in the intermediate-sized cases, but for both the million-plus urban areas and those under 100,000 the differences tend to be insignificant. Thus, any generalization about the decentralized nature of urban hospital provision must be qualified by reference to city size.

An additional caveat needs to be made. It could be argued that a better level of health care is provided by having a large proportion of hospitals and hospital beds in suburban areas, obviating lengthy trips to the central city. From this perspective, the Vancouver area is better served, with only 43.3 per cent of beds in the central city than any of its American "pairs" (Table 7-30). The Toronto and Montreal comparisons with their pairs are inconclusive. What needs to be remembered is that highly specialized hospitals and related medical services are more optimally located in central districts, often close to or in the central business district. This could account for the very high central-city shares in such places as Montreal and Minneapolis-St. Paul.

Controlling for Geopolitical Structure

As in previous sections, we have used the variable measuring the central-city proportion of the total metropolitan area as an indicator of metropolitan spatial structure. We have seen that there is an important difference in the geographical structure of Canadian and American cities. Therefore, our findings must again be reconsidered, controlling for the central-city-to-metropolitan ratio. For two manufacturing variables (plants and employment), the magnitude of cross-national differences narrows, but it does not disappear, especially in those instances where the city represents less than 30 per cent of the metropolitan population. Furthermore, while the differences decrease when controlling for central-city-to-metropolitan population ratio, the Canadian central-city share is nearly always the larger—consistent with our general argument. Examining the change in manufacturing employment under this control reveals the persistence of the most important difference— manufacturing growth in the Canadian suburbs and decline in the U.S. suburbs. Within the central city, the differences are less consistent in their pattern than when controlled for size.

Turning to the wholesaling variables, the evidence is that substantial differences are considerably muted by the effects of this control. Where the cross-national differences are minimal (only a few percentage points), they are probably not very important. However, it is again clear that the Canadian central-city share is consistently higher and in the case of the smaller ratio categories, more markedly so.

For the retail trade variables, establishments and sales, the effect of this particular control is less pronounced. With the exception of the largest ratio category, there are clear and consistent differences in the central-city share variable. With respect to change in retail sales in the central city, we noted a generally greater variability within the U.S. observations. This difference, which progressively weakened as city size decreased, also weakens and then reverses itself under the effects of this control. Examining the magnitude of the minimum values also suggests that, under this control, it is more difficult to sustain our original hypothesis that the decline in retail sales would be more marked in the U.S. case. Finally, for business and personal services, this control again tends to narrow the differences more than the city-size control. But the differences persist with some magnitude, especially for establishments in the lower ratio categories.

On balance, the application of this important control variable means that we must temper our initial conclusions concerning cross-national urban differences on these various economic measures. Nevertheless, important differences remain, and although the magnitude is often reduced, there is also a consistency to the direction of the differences. In short, the balance of the evidence suggests that our expectations cannot be rejected. The results of the numerous controlled-pair comparisons serve to reinforce our general conclusion that indeed Canadian and American cities differ significantly in their economic, social and spatial structure.

SUMMARY

The great majority of the results reported in this chapter support the propositions developed earlier concerning differences between Canadian and American metropolitan areas. It is tempting to talk of an American city and a Canadian city. But the evidence concerning the amount of variability in metropolitan characteristics in both countries makes this a suspect enterprise.

On balance, a picture is emerging of Canadian urban areas: as being more compact in form with a greater reliance upon public mass modes of travel; as experiencing a greater degree of suburbanization and higher levels of foreign immigration; as having a less racially diverse and less racially segregated population but as ethnically diverse as the U.S.; and as having lower status differences between the inner and outer cities with the former retaining their traditional family-oriented households. All this suggests that Canadian cities are indeed different from those in the United States, in these respects at least. Further evidence of additional differences are provided in the following chapter on urban government.

TABLE 7-1
SINGLE DETACHED UNITS AS PROPORTION OF HOUSING STOCK

Per cent of all housing units	USA (1970)			CANADA (1971)		
	Metro	Central City	Balance	Metro	Central City	Balance
mean	73.4*	64.9*	80.8**	57.1*	50.4*	72.1**
sd	10.3	14.8	9.0	14.0	18.9	14.9
n	257	257	254	36	36	32

  * significant at .001 level
 ** significant at .01 level
*** significant at .1 level

Source: U.S. Bureau of the Census, *County and City Data Book*, 1977; *U.S. Census of Population and Housing: 1970, Census Tracts, Final Reports*, PHC (1) Series, Table 4-2; Statistics Canada, *Census of Canada, 1971* (Ottawa: Minister of Supply and Services, 1973).

TABLE 7-2
DISTRIBUTION OF BUILDING PERMITS BY TYPE
(per cent)

Type	USA (1971-6)			CANADA (1971-6)		
	Metro	Central City	Balance	Metro	Central City	Balance
Single Units	55.3	37.0	68.5	42.7	27.2	59.0
Duplex	3.4	4.0	3.1	6.9	5.1	7.3
Row	3.5	4.0	3.3	7.7	9.1	6.9
Apartments	37.8	55.3	25.3	42.7	58.5	27.0

Source: U.S. Bureau of the Census, *Construction Reports—Housing Authorized by Building Permits and Public Contracts*, (annual); Statistics Canada, *Building Permits—Annual Summary* (Catalogue No. 64-203).

TABLE 7-3
DENSITY GRADIENTS AND CENTRAL DENSITIES
IN CANADIAN AND AMERICAN METROPOLITAN AREAS, 1950/51 TO 1975/76
(CMAs and SMSAs)

Population Size	Density Gradients	
	Canada (1941-76)	USA (1950-75)
Less than 250,000	0.91	0.80
250,000 to 500,000	0.63	0.55
500,000 and more	0.30	0.31

Year	Density Gradients		Mean Central Densities	
	Canada	USA	Canada	USA
1950/51	0.93	0.76	50,000	24,000
1960/61	0.67	0.60	33,000	17,000
1970/71	0.45	0.50	22,000	13,000
1975/76	0.42	0.45	20,000	11,000

Source: Barry Edmonston, Michael A. Goldberg and John Mercer, "Urban Form in Canada and The United States: An Examination of Urban Density Gradients," *Urban Studies* 22 (1985): 209-17.

TABLE 7-4
MEAN VALUES OF CENTRAL DENSITY AND DENSITY GRADIENT FOR
CANADIAN AND AMERICAN CITIES IN 1975-76, BY REGION AND
BY POPULATION SIZE

Region	Central Density	Density Gradient	Number
Canada			
Atlantic	24,000	0.53	3
Quebec	19,000	0.33	3
Ontario	17,000	0.41	9
Prairies	32,000	0.59	2
British Columbia	16,000	0.25	2
U.S.A.			
New England	12,000	0.30	12
Middle Atlantic	15,000	0.42	21
East North Central	11,000	0.46	45
West North Central	11,000	0.60	18
South Atlantic	9,200	0.35	37
East South Central	6,000	0.35	15
West South Central	13,000	0.57	35
Mountain	14,000	0.70	10
Pacific	9,500	0.35	13

Population Size	Central Density		Density Gradient	
	Canada	U.S.A.	Canada	U.S.A.
‹100,000	-	15,000	-	0.95
100,000 to 500,000	15,000	10,000	0.44	0.48
500,000 to 1,000,000	24,000	10,000	0.48	0.26
1,000,000+	31,000	16,000	0.24	0.19

Source: Edmonston, Goldberg and Mercer, "Urban Form," 216.

TABLE 7-5
URBAN TRANSPORTATION SYSTEMS[1]

Characteristic	USA	CANADA
Public Transit:		
a) Revenue miles per capita		
mean	8.7*	21.1*
sd	6.1	7.4
n	69	15
b) Service Area Population		
to Metropolitan Population		
mean	0.74	0.80
sd	0.19	0.24
n	63	15
Expressways:		
Lane miles per capita		
mean	0.0013	0.0003
sd	0.0029	0.0003
n	183	37

* significant at .001 level.

[1]The different sizes of n reflect different data sources and availability of data.

Source: 1) *Public Transit Data:*
American Public Transit Association, *Transit Operating Report, for Calendar Fiscal Year 1976* (APTA: Washington, DC); J. Sewell, "Public Transit in Canada: A Primer," *City Magazine* (May-June 1978), 40-55.

2) *Expressway Lane Miles:*
U.S. Department of Transportation, Federal Highway Administration, Highway Statistics Division, Washington, D.C., personal communication, January, 1979; Authors' survey of provincial Departments of Highways, 1978 and map estimates.

TABLE 7-6
MODE OF TRANSPORTATION FOR JOURNEY TO WORK IN METROPOLITAN AREAS[1]

Mode	USA				CANADA				
	1975 (n=21)	1976 (n=20)	1977 (n=20)	Average 1975-77 (n=61)	1976 (n=10)	1977 (n=10)	1978 (n=10)	1979 (n=10)	1980 (n=10)
Total Auto or Truck	85	80	91	86	64	65	65	66	67
Driving alone	68	62	72	67	45	48	48	48	49
Driving with passenger	5	4	4	4	7	6	6	7	7
Riding as passenger	7	7	7	7	11	11	10	11	10
Shares driving	6	6	7	6	n.a.	n.a.	n.a.	n.a.	n.a.
Public transit	12	19	7	13	26	25	26	25	25
Walking	5	5	4	5	8	8	8	8	8
Other	2	1	2	2	2	2	1	1	1

Source: U.S. Bureau of the Census, *Current Population Reports*, Series P-23, No. 68, "Selected Characteristics of Travel to Work in 21 Metropolitan Areas, 1975," and Series P-23, No. 72, "Selected Characteristics of Travel to Work in 20 Metropolitan Areas, 1976" (Washington, 1978); Statistics Canada, Education, Science and Culture Division, "Travel to Work Survey, November, 1976", Catalogue No. 81-001 (November, 1977), and "Travel to Work Survey, November 1977", Catalogue No. 87-001 (Sept., 1978) and series updates.

[1]Due to rounding, column totals may not add to 100%.

TABLE 7-7
MODAL CHOICE OF COMMUTERS FOR SELECTED CITIES

	Per cent Commuters		
	Using Auto/Truck	Driving Alone	Public Transp.
Montreal[1]	59	42	31
Toronto[1]	61	46	31
Vancouver[1]	75	62	18

	"Modal Choice of Commuters for Selected Cities"		
	Auto/Truck	Driving Alone	Public Transp.
Baltimore[3]	87	64	12
Minneapolis-St. Paul[4]	89	70	9
San Francisco-Oakland[3]	79	65	18
Pittsburgh[4]	86	68	13
St. Louis[3]	94	71	5
Washington[4]	84	58	15
Seattle[3]	90	72	8
Portland[2]	90	71	8
San Diego[2]	91	73	5

[1]All Canadian cities, average over 1975-77 inclusive
[2]Data for 1975
[3]Data for 1976
[4]Data for 1977

Source: See Table 7-6.

TABLE 7-8

POPULATION CHANGE IN AMERICAN AND CANADIAN METROPOLITAN AREAS: SUMMARY STATISTICS AND DISTRIBUTION OF CASES

Per cent change in population	USA (1970-75) Metro	Central City	Balance	CANADA (1971-76) Metro	Central City	Balance
-19.9 to 15.0		0.8				
-14.9 to -10.0		4.2	1.2		8.3	
- 9.9 to -5.0	0.8	19.2	0.4	2.8	13.9	
- 4.9 to 0.0	14.6	27.6	3.4	8.3	25.0	5.9
0.0 to 4.9	39.1	16.1	26.3	27.8	25.0	20.6
5.0 to 9.9	18.8	13.4	26.3	36.1	16.7	5.9
10.0 to 14.9	11.5	8.0	16.6	16.7	8.3	20.6
15.0 to 19.9	6.1	6.1	10.4	5.6	2.8	14.7
20.0 to 24.9	3.8	1.1	5.7	2.8		5.9
25.0 to 29.9	3.8	3.4	2.7			8.8
30.0 to 39.9	1.5	2.7			5.9	
40.0 to 49.9	0.4	2.3				
50.0 or more		1.6			1.8	
mean	7.1	2.2	11.2	6.3	0.9	19.1
sd	8.3	9.5	11.4	5.4	7.1	19.4
n	257	257	254	36	36	34

Source: U.S. Bureau of the Census, *County and City Data Book, 1977*; *U.S. Census of Population and Housing: 1970*, Census Tracts, Final Reports, PHC (1) Series, Table P-1; "1976 Survey of Buying Power", *Sales and Marketing Management* 117, no. 2 (26 July 1976); Statistics Canada, *Census of Canada: 1976*, Volume 1, Catalogue No. 92-806, Tables 6 and 7.

TABLE 7-9
HOUSEHOLD CHANGE IN AMERICAN AND CANADIAN METROPOLITAN AREAS:
SUMMARY STATISTICS AND DISTRIBUTION OF CASES

Per cent change in households	USA (1970-75)			CANADA (1971-76)		
	Metro	Central City	Balance	Metro	Central City	Balance
more than -15.0			1.2			
-14.9 to -10.0		1.2				
- 9.9 to - 5.0		3.1	1.9			3.4
- 4.9 to 0.0		10.8	1.5			
0.0 to 4.9	5.0	18.1	2.3		9.4	6.9
5.0 to 9.9	22.3	15.8	8.9	6.3	9.4	10.3
10.0 to 14.9	26.2	13.1	33.4	15.6	31.3	6.9
15.0 to 19.9	19.6	14.3	20.8	37.5	21.9	10.3
20.0 to 24.9	8.8	5.0	12.0	21.9	12.5	6.9
25.0 to 29.9	4.6	6.2	9.3	9.4	9.4	20.7
30.0 to 39.9	8.8	8.1	10.0	9.4	6.3	10.3
40.0 to 49.9	3.1	3.1	4.2			10.3
50.0 or more	1.5	1.5	5.0			13.7
mean	17.1	13.0	20.1	20.0	15.7	27.6
sd	11.1	13.5	14.9	6.7	7.9	20.3
n	257	257	254	32	32	30

Source: U.S. Bureau of the Census, *County and City Data Book, 1977*; *U.S. Census of Population and Housing: 1970*, Census Tracts, Final Reports, PHC (1) Series, Table P-1; "1976 Survey of Buying Power", *Sales and Marketing Management* 117, no. 2 (26 July 1976); Statistics Canada, *Census of Canada: 1976*, Volume 3, Catalogue No. 93-802, Tables 7 and 8; *Census of Canada: 1971*, Volume 2, Part 1, Catalogue No. 93-702, Tables 4, 5 and 6.

TABLE 7-10
DISTRIBUTION OF PERCENTAGE CHANGE IN DWELLING
UNITS (HOUSEHOLDS) IN CENTRAL CITIES,[1]
1970/71 to 1980/81

Percentage Change	USA (1970 to 1980)			CANADA (1971 to 1981)		
	n	Per cent	Cumulative Per cent	n	Per cent	Cumulative Per cent
100 or	1	0.4		0		
90 to 99	1	0.4	0.8	0		
80 to 89	6	2.2	3.0	0		
70 to 79	3	1.1	4.1	1	2.9	
60 to 69	7	2.5	6.6	0		2.9
50 to 59	13	4.7	11.3	0		2.9
40 to 49	19	6.9	18.2	8	23.5	26.4
30 to 39	27	9.8	28.0	7	20.6	47.0
20 to 29	50	18.1	46.1	9	26.5	73.5
10 to 19	52	18.8	64.9	7	20.6	94.1
0 to 9	72	26.1	91.0	2	5.9	100.0
0 to -9	22	8.0	99.0			
-10 or more	3	1.1	100.1			

Median 11.5 Median 29.7 (26.7)[1]
Mean 22.7 Mean 30.1 (27.1)[1]

[1] The 1971 base data have not been adjusted to ensure comparable area units with 1981. In some cases, this will inflate the amount of change. Cities where this is a major problem (e.g., Winnipeg) are omitted. To compensate, the median and mean are adjusted downward by a factor of 10 per cent. The U.S.-Canadian differences remain striking. For a more precise definition of "dwelling unit (household)," see the first source cited below.

Source: Statistics Canada, unpublished data (preliminary). U.S. Bureau of the Census, *1980 census of population: Standard Metropolitan Statistical Areas and Standard Consolidated Statistical Areas, 1980.* PC80 - SI 5. (Washington, D.C.: U.S. Government Printing Office, 1981)

TABLE 7-11
PER CENT CHANGE IN DWELLING UNITS (HOUSEHOLDS) FOR SELECTED
METROPOLITAN AREAS,
1971-1981

	City	Balance		City	Balance
Montreal	2.85	26.18	Baltimore	-0.31	22.03
			Minneapolis-		
			St. Paul	-5.15	
			Houston	24.31	29.90
			San Francisco-		
			Oakland	3.76	19.60
Toronto	2.65	23.58	Pittsburgh	-5.05	6.38
			St. Louis	-10.71	8.61
			Milwaukee	1.02	20.65
			Cleveland	-10.14	9.32
Vancouver	4.56	28.40	Seattle	4.33	13.26
			Portland	8.83	26.25
			San Diego	33.07	39.82

Source: See Table 7-10.

TABLE 7-12
CENTRAL CITY TO METROPOLITAN AREA INCOME RATIOS:
SUMMARY STATISTICS AND DISTRIBUTION OF CASES

Ratio	USA (1970)		CANADA (1971)	
	median household income	mean household income	median household income	mean household income
under 59	1.4			
60- 69	4.3	1.0		
70- 79	19.5	8.1		
80- 89	22.9	20.5	13.8	10.0
90- 99	31.0	41.0	44.8	36.7
100-109	15.2	24.8	41.4	53.3
110-119	1.9	2.4		
120-129	1.4	1.8		
130-139	1.0	0.5		
140-149	0.5			
150-159	1.0			
mean	91.1	93.2	97.6	98.0
sd	16.3	12.1	5.5	5.1
n	217	217	29	30

Source: U.S. Bureau of the Census, *Census of Population and Housing: 1970*, Census Tracts, Final Reports, PHC (1) Series, Table P-4; Statistics Canada, *Census of Canada: 1971*; Population and Housing Characteristics by Census Tracts, Catalogue No. 95-700 Series.

TABLE 7-13
CENTRAL CITY TO METROPOLITAN AREA INCOME RATIOS
FOR SELECTED CITIES
(1971 for Canada; 1970 for the U.S.)

	Median Household Income	Mean Household Income		Median Household Income	Mean Household Income
Montreal	85.8	86.1	Baltimore	78.3	81.2
			Minneapolis-St. Paul	71.6	78.4
			San Francisco-Oakland	76.9	82.9
Toronto	82.8	90.8	Pittsburgh	76.7	84.8
			St. Louis	67.9	72.8
			Washington	68.7	75.5
Vancouver	89.5	93.8	Seattle	79.3	85.8
			Portland	80.1	87.5
			San Diego	94.4	98.4

Source: See Table 7-12.

TABLE 7-14
HOUSEHOLD STRUCTURE

Type	USA (1970)			CANADA (1971)		
	Metro	Central City	Balance	Metro	Central City	Balance
% of one person households:						
mean	15.7*	20.5*	11.6*	12.5*	15.4*	7.8*
sd	3.3	4.5	3.8	3.4	5.7	3.9
n	217	217	215	32	32	27
% of two or fewer person households:						
mean	43.6*	50.0*	38.1*	37.5*	42.4*	28.5*
sd	6.0	6.6	10.4	6.1	9.4	11.9
n	217	217	215	32	32	28
% of households - families with children at home:						
mean	43.7*	40.1*	47.2*	59.4*	57.0*	63.1*
sd	5.6	6.7	11.3	5.4	11.5	17.5
n	217	217	215	32	32	29

* significant at the .001 level

Source: U.S. Bureau of the Census, *Census of Population and Housing: 1970*, Census Tracts, Final Reports, PHC (1) Series, Table P-1, H-1; Statistics Canada, *Census of Canada: 1971*, Volume 2, Part 1, Catalogue No. 93-762, Tables 4 and 5, and Volume 2, Part 2, Catalogue No. 93-715, Tables 16 and 17.

TABLE 7-15
HOUSEHOLD STRUCTURE: PER CENT OF HOUSEHOLDS WHICH ARE
FAMILIES WITH CHILDREN AT HOME, SELECTED CITIES, 1970/1971

Montreal	46.69	Baltimore	37.94
		Minneapolis-St. Paul	32.54
		San Francisco-Oakland	25.41
		Houston	45.50
Toronto	43.18	St. Louis	32.50
		Pittsburgh	33.09
		Milwaukee	39.36
		Cleveland	39.04
		Washington	31.64
Vancouver	37.65	Seattle	29.92
		Portland	31.07
		San Diego	39.18

Source: See Table 7-14.

TABLE 7-16
POPULATION BY RACE AND NATIVITY

Type	USA (1970)			CANADA (1971)		
	Metro	Central City	Balance	Metro	Central City	Balance
Per cent Population Non-white[1]						
mean	11.5*	17.1*	7.0*	1.2*	2.0*	0.7*
sd	9.7	13.9	8.4	1.0	2.6	0.7
n	217	217	215	36	36	21
Per cent Population Foreign Born						
mean	3.3*	4.1**	2.7*	14.6*	16.5**	11.3*
sd	3.4	4.6	3.0	8.9	11.0	8.9
n	217	217	215	33	33	31

* significant at .001 level
** significant at .01 level

[1]Non-white in Canada is the total of the following; Chinese, Japanese, Negro, Native Indian and West Indian. This approximates as closely as possible the definition of non-white in the U.S.

Source: U.S. Bureau of the Census, *Census of Population and Housing: 1970*, Census Tracts, Final Reports, PHC (1) Series, Table P-1 and P-2; Statistics Canada, *Census of Canada: 1971*, Volume 1, Part 3, Catalogue No. 92-723, Tables 5 and 6, and Catalogue No. 92-727, Tables 40 and 41.

TABLE 7-17
CENTRAL CITY SHARE OF MANUFACTURING PLANTS AND EMPLOYMENT, 1972,
BY SIZE OF METROPOLITAN AREA
(per cent)

| | Manufacturing Plants | | | Manufacturing Employment | |
	CANADA	USA		CANADA	USA
ALL			ALL		
Mean	71.5*	55.2*	Mean	68.9***	57.3***
Std. Dev.	19.4	19.8	Std. Dev.	25.6	23.5
Mdn.	69.0	53.0	Mdn.	72.0	57.0
SIZE			SIZE		
1,000,000+			1,000,000+		
Mean	48.6	47.7	Mean	42.2	46.2
Std. Dev.	15.2	16.8	Std. Dev.	14.9	18.2
Mdn.	50.0	47.8	Mdn.	45.0	46.7
.5 to 1M			.5 to 1M		
Mean	57.6	50.1	Mean	64.2	54.6
Std. Dev.	8.0	19.8	Std. Dev.	18.6	21.7
Mdn.	61.0	44.0	Mdn.	59.0	52.8
.1 to .5M			.1 to .5M		
Mean	78.4	55.0	Mean	71.3	58.1
Std. Dev.	19.3	19.0	Std. Dev.	29.2	24.1
Mdn.	81.0	54.0	Mdn.	73.0	58.8
‹ 100,000			‹ 100,000		
Mean	72.6	76.2	Mean	78.6	79.7
Std. Dev.	14.9	15.8	Std. Dev.	14.3	16.1
Mdn.	69.5	81.8	Mdn.	73.5	80.5

* significant at .001 level
*** significant at .1 level

Source: Authors' calculations

TABLE 7-18

CENTRAL CITY SHARE OF MANUFACTURING PLANTS AND EMPLOYMENT, 1972 BY REGION

(per cent)

	Manufacturing Plants				
	Atlantic	Quebec	Ontario	Prairie	B.C.
Mean	75.1	59.0	70.7	96.6	58.1
Std. Dev.	21.2	12.5	19.3	4.1	11.4
Mdn.	76.0	56.5	63.5	94.5	58.1

	New England	Mid Atlantic	East North Central	West North Central	South Atlantic	East South Central	West South Central	Mountain	Pacific
Mean	37.3	36.5	53.8	68.0	50.7	59.9	71.0	65.5	49.3
Std. Dev.	14.6	16.5	15.6	18.2	15.0	15.5	19.7	13.6	18.9
Mdn.	37.0	35.5	53.7	77.8	50.5	59.0	73.2	64.0	44.3

	Manufacturing Employment				
	Atlantic	Quebec	Ontario	Prairie	B.C
Mean	82.4	54.3	68.2	88.3	57.7
Std. Dev.	15.2	26.5	27.9	13.7	16.8
Mdn.	77.0	54.5	71.5	79.5	57.7

	New England	Mid Atlantic	East North Central	West North Central	South Atlantic	East South Central	West South Central	Mountain	Pacific
Mean	39.8	37.4	64.9	73.3	48.6	64.9	71.5	61.0	49.7
Std. Dev.	21.6	19.0	19.3	21.1	22.3	15.0	20.4	25.5	20.2
Mdn.	31.0	35.5	62.5	73.0	47.5	64.0	72.5	63.5	46.0

Source: Authors' calculations

TABLE 7-19

CENTRAL CITY SHARE OF MANUFACTURING PLANTS AND EMPLOYMENT, 1972, AND CHANGE IN EMPLOYMENT FOR SELECTED CITIES, 1967 TO 1972

(per cent)

	Central City Share		Change in Manufacturing Employment		
	Plants	Employment	City	Metro	Balance
Toronto	32.7	25.8	-17.7	6.8	19.2
Pittsburgh	29.6	23.7	-27.2	-12.3	-6.3
Hamilton, Ont.	63.4	84.7	-7.1	3.5	23.0
Akron, Ohio	39.4	53.5	-18.4	-6.5	12.4
Gary, Indiana	58.7	82.3	-8.6	-5.3	13.8

Source: Authors' calculations

TABLE 7-20
CHANGE IN MANUFACTURING EMPLOYMENT FOR METROPOLITAN AREA,
CENTRAL CITY AND BALANCE, 1967-72, BY SIZE OF METROPOLITAN AREA
(per cent)

	Metropolitan		Central City		Balance	
	CANADA	USA	CANADA	USA	CANADA	USA
ALL						
Mean	9.6	7.0	-1.3	8.3	53.0	10.5
Std. Dev.	30.1	30.3	26.3	28.8	92.0	40.3
Mdn.	1.5	-6.7	-7.8	-10.5	22.0	9.3
SIZE						
1,000,000+						
Mean	4.8	-3.0	-9.9	-6.8	16.9	2.4
Std. Dev.	5.3	15.6	6.9	18.5	7.1	20.6
Mdn.	6.0	-8.3	-8.0	-14.5	19.0	-3.8
.5 to 1M						
Mean	- 0.2	2.1	-9.2	5.4	19.9	11.5
Std. Dev.	3.5	16.0	3.7	30.2	8.3	34.3
Mdn.	-1.5	-4.8	-7.3	-9.0	22.0	11.8
.1 to .5						
Mean	3.7	9.7	-1.2	12.3	78.9	15.3
Std. Dev.	14.2	21.3	16.5	28.9	117.9	45.2
Mdn.	0.5	-6.6	-6.0	-9.5	27.5	-9.0
‹ 100,000						
Mean	—	10.8	3.1	18.5	—	15.2
Std. Dev.	—	20.6	40.1	34.1	—	33.0
Mdn.	—	-7.5	-10.0	-12.0	—	28.0

Source: Authors' calculations

TABLE 7-24
CENTRAL CITY SHARE OF RETAILING ESTABLISHMENTS
(UNINCORPORATED AND TOTAL), 1971 and 1972, BY SIZE OF METROPOLITAN AREA
(per cent)

	CANADA		USA	
	Unincorp.	Total	Unincorp.	Total
ALL				
Mean	70.9*	73.6*	50.8*	53.9*
Std. Dev.	18.5	17.7	19.5	19.6
Mdn.	66.5	70.3	48.3	51.4
SIZE				
1,000,000+				
Mean	51.3	49.2	39.0	40.1
Std. Dev.	4.4	5.8	15.3	15.4
Mdn.	49.0	49.0	39.5	40.0
.5 to 1M				
Mean	62.4	63.5	43.2	46.1
Std. Dev.	9.1	9.5	18.1	18.6
Mdn.	64.5	63.5	37.3	40.8
.1 to .5				
Mean	73.2	77.0	51.8	55.3
Std. Dev.	18.7	16.6	17.7	17.6
Mdn.	66.5	70.5	50.6	55.0
‹ 100,000				
Mean	75.1	78.1	74.8	77.9
Std. Dev.	19.8	18.1	17.1	15.7
Mdn.	74.0	77.8	76.8	81.0

* significant at .001 level

[1] An unincorporated retail establishment is defined by law and refers to the legal form of organization of the retail company (for multi-establishment companies) or of the retail establishment. Total includes both incorporated and unincorporated establishments.

Source: Authors' calculations

TABLE 7-25
CENTRAL CITY SHARE OF RETAIL ESTABLISHMENTS FOR SELECTED CITIES,
1971 AND 1972
(per cent)

Montreal	54.9	Baltimore	42.2
		Minneapolis-St. Paul	38.3
		San Francisco-Oakland	41.2
Toronto	43.3	Pittsburgh	22.2
		St. Louis	27.0
		Washington	25.7
Vancouver	49.5	Seattle	47.4
		Portland	44.7
		San Diego	49.0

Source: Authors' calculations

TABLE 7-26
CENTRAL CITY SHARES OF RETAIL SALES FOR CANADIAN URBANIZED AREAS
WITH LESS THAN 100,000 POPULATION, 1971
(per cent)

	Share of Sales
Brantford	80
Guelph	97
Kingston	70
Peterborough	95
Sarnia	70
Sault Sainte Marie	99
Sydney	58
Moncton	76
Shawnigan	55
Sherbrooke	96
Trois Rivieres	62
St. Jean	79
North Bay	100

Source: Authors' calculations

TABLE 7-27
CENTRAL CITY SHARE OF SERVICE SALES AND ESTABLISHMENTS,
1966/1967 AND 1971/1972,
BY SIZE OF METROPOLITAN AREA
(per cent)

| | Sales | | | | Establishments | |
| | CANADA | | USA | | CANADA | USA |
	1966	1971	1967	1972	1971	1972
ALL						
Mean	82.3*	81.9*	69.1*	65.9*	76.4*	56.9*
Std. Dev.	14.1	13.9	21.0	19.2	15.9	19.1
Mdn.	83.5	81.0	70.8	67.9	74.0	55.6
SIZE						
1,000,000+						
Mean	72.3	66.2	60.9	55.6	56.1	43.5
Std. Dev.	5.8	8.2	20.9	20.1	7.4	16.1
Mdn.	74.8	69.0	64.8	58.5	58.0	43.8
.5 to 1M						
Mean	75.9	71.6	64.6	61.8	66.1	50.5
Std. Dev.	9.9	13.7	19.5	19.8	9.1	18.5
Mdn.	71.5	69.5	63.3	57.0	63.5	44.0
.1 to .5M						
Mean	86.1	87.3	69.8	67.1	80.7	58.3
Std. Dev.	15.1	11.1	19.5	17.8	14.8	17.2
Mdn.	92.0	87.8	71.1	68.9	77.0	57.7
‹ 100,000						
Mean	83.0	82.3	86.0	81.1	79.1	78.8
Std. Dev.	14.9	14.6	26.1	16.0	16.2	15.6
Mdn.	84.5	81.0	89.0	86.2	76.0	82.0

* significant at .001 level

Source: Authors' calculations

TABLE 7-28
CENTRAL CITY SHARE OF SERVICE ESTABLISHMENTS AND SALES
FOR SELECTED CITIES,
1971 AND 1972
(per cent)

Establishments			
Montreal	62.1	Baltimore	44.0
		Minneapolis-St. Paul	44.8
		San Francisco-Oakland	44.2
Toronto	47.8	Pittsburgh	27.9
		St. Louis	27.8
		Washington	35.0
Vancouver	58.5	Seattle	54.8
		Portland	52.0
		San Diego	57.5

Sales			
Montreal	69.6	Baltimore	54.9
		Minneapolis-St. Paul	60.3
		San Francisco-Oakland	60.6
Toronto	56.9	Pittsburgh	53.8
		St. Louis	46.5
		Washington	42.3
Vancouver	72.2	Seattle	70.0
		Portland	69.4
		San Diego	71.6

Source: Authors' calculations

TABLE 7-29
CENTRAL CITY SHARE OF HOSPITALS AND HOSPITAL BEDS, 1975
(per cent)

	Hospitals		Hospital Beds	
	CANADA	USA	CANADA	USA
ALL				
Mean	86.7*	65.9*	89.6***	79.6***
Std. Dev.	19.0	23.1	17.1	19.3
Mdn.	99.6	65.0	99.6	81.0
SIZE				
1,000,000+				
Mean	60.4	50.8	58.3	59.1
Std. Dev.	8.9	16.4	14.6	21.4
Mdn.	55.3	51.5	59.0	60.5
.5 to 1M				
Mean	78.2	64.6	76.9	72.0
Std. Dev.	11.1	19.2	19.9	20.3
Mdn.	83.0	63.0	77.5	78.8
.1 to .5				
Mean	82.8	65.9	90.1	84.0
Std. Dev.	22.0	22.8	15.5	20.8
Mdn.	86.5	65.9	97.5	83.6
‹ 100,000				
Mean	100.0	91.8	100.0	94.0
Std. Dev.	0.0	17.4	0.0	17.7
Mdn.	100.0	99.9	100.0	99.9

* significant at .001 level
*** significant at .1 level

Source: Authors' calculations

TABLE 7-30
CENTRAL CITY SHARE OF HOSPITAL BEDS FOR SELECTED CITIES, 1975
(per cent)

Montreal	72.4	Baltimore	61.1
		Minneapolis-St. Paul	84.5
		San Francisco-Oakland	55.8
Toronto	59.3	Pittsburgh	51.5
		St. Louis	70.3
		Washington	60.5
Vancouver	43.3	Seattle	82.4
		Portland	70.6
		San Diego	59.6

Source: Authors' calculations

8

URBAN LOCAL GOVERNMENT:
STRUCTURE AND FINANCE

This chapter concentrates on selected aspects of local government in the metropolitan areas of the United States and Canada. The first part of the analysis focuses on what was once described as the "Urban Problem"—the division of the metropolitan region into numerous independent political-administrative units, each legally autonomous and often acting in an uncoordinated fashion. This condition, aptly described by the term fragmentation, is not examined in exhaustive detail, but rather as a source of further important cross-national differences.

The bulk of the chapter comprises a comparative treatment of urban public finance. This is a complex topic which, in Canada at least, has received relatively little attention.[1] We have selected various facets of city finances which allow us to extend our expectations about Canadian/American urban differences to the realm of urban government. The material is organized on the basis of three principal themes. The first and most important deals with sources of revenues. This discussion casts some light on the structure of local-central government interactions, which in turn helps us to understand partially the functioning of federalism in Canada and the United States, which, as we saw in Chapter 5, is an important source of differences between the two countries.

The second theme is that of expenditures—on what functions or services do urban governments spend their money and at what level do they spend (as expressed in per capita terms)? This section is restricted primarily to a discussion of protection services—policing and fire protection. Related to this is a cross-national comparison of urban crime, both matters touching directly on actual and perceived quality-of-life issues in urban areas. The third and final theme explored in this chapter is that of metropolitan fiscal disparities. Our expectation, as developed in Chapter 6, was that fiscal disparities would be more apparent and more acute in metropolitan America. A consequence of the fiscal pressures, particularly on central cities, is that their fiscal well-being has suffered. This is explored comparatively by using municipal bond ratings as an indicator of fiscal condition.

LOCAL GOVERNMENT STRUCTURE AND REFORM

Local Government Fragmentation

Following a discussion of the evolution of local governments in metropolitan areas in the two countries, we developed an hypothesis that the system of local government would be more fragmented in the United States. We should expect to find many more of what have been described as "toy governments" in metropolitan America, in keeping with our earlier discussion of individualism and atomistic local governments to serve individuals. To test this expectation, we computed an index of municipal fragmentation, which is the number of municipalities in a metropolitan area per thousand population resident in municipally governed areas. The interpretation of this ratio is that the higher is the score, the more fragmented is an area.

The Canadian mean score on this index is substantially lower than that for the U.S., and this difference is statistically significant (Table 8-1). The scores in Canada are also less widely dispersed (see the standard deviations), indicating a greater homogeneity than in the U.S. case. Further support for this important cross-national difference is obtained from examining the distribution of scores. The majority of Canadian scores are in the lower ranges of the distribution when compared to the U.S.; only 70 per cent of American metropolitan areas have scores less than the maximum Canadian score. Controlling for city size does not remove the difference. In every size class, the Canadian indices are substantially lower than the American ones. It is also worth noting that contrary to conventional wisdom, municipal fragmentation tends to decline as the metropolitan population increases; this holds for both countries.

In terms of the three largest Canadian metropolitan areas, there is quite a contrast on this measure. Montreal has a relatively high index, ranking a joint twelfth among the 34 metropolitan areas, whereas Toronto has a very low value for such a large metropolitan area and ranks a joint thirtieth— Vancouver occupies a middle rank (nineteenth). Part of the explanation for this is the particular circumstances under which local government evolved.

For example, the use of parishes as a geographical base for municipalities in Montreal certainly contributed to the numerical profusion. But another important factor is the geographical reorganization of municipal government in metropolitan Toronto, which greatly reduced the number of municipalities in that area. Given this context, the results of a controlled-paired comparison are not too surprising (Table 8-2). Toronto's index score is much lower than any of its pairs, but Montreal tends to be higher than the equivalent U.S. cities. Vancouver scores lower than two of its three matched cities. Overall, the three Canadian cases occur in the lower half of the distribution, thereby tending to support the overall conclusion that local government proliferation and balkanization is less severe in Canadian metropolitan areas.

It can be argued that, although useful, the index of municipal fragmentation does not capture the full extent of local government proliferation in urban regions. Not included in the computation are special-purpose district governments. This type of government, often providing only a single service or function, is common in U.S. metropolitan areas. Including independent school districts, special-purpose districts represented 58 per cent of metropolitan governmental units in 1972 and 55 per cent in 1977. The absence of a Canadian equivalent of the U.S. *Census of Governments* in itself reveals the fundamentally different and more decentralized nature of Canadian federalism. Therefore, it is not yet possible to compare fully the extent of local government fragmentation in Canadian metropolian areas. One detailed case study does permit the inclusion of Toronto in a listing of local governments by size of metropolitan area; with the exception of atypical Baltimore, Toronto has the smallest number of all local governments.[2] A further regionally based comparison is possible using Vancouver, Seattle, Portland and San Diego (Table 8-3). Again, the Canadian-U.S. difference is striking, with size being roughly controlled. This is additional, albeit limited, evidence that the amount of fragmentation is significantly different in the two countries.

Local Government Restructuring

Local government fragmentation has been seen in Canada as an impediment to the successful management of metropolitan areas—a view also widely held in the United States. But in contrast to the U.S. situation, there has been a reduction of fragmentation in urban Canada over the last twenty years as a result of provincial action. In many instances, provinces have unilaterally reformed local government structures, especially within the major metropolitan centers. While the two-tier federation of metropolitan Toronto is the most widely known example of this kind of reform and was a model for subsequent two-tiered governments in Ontario and elsewhere in Canada, the most dramatic debunking of the myth of local autonomy has come in Winnipeg, where twelve municipalities disappeared, in Cinderella-like fashion, at midnight 31 December, 1971 to be replaced by a single metropolitan-wide municipal government. The socialist provincial government in Manitoba did not hesitate to eliminate local units to achieve its own economic and political objectives, just as a nominally Conservative government in Ontario created the municipality of Metropolitan Toronto in 1953 and then eliminated seven autonomous suburbs in a consolidation of the lower tier in 1967. The fact that such interventions and restructurings have been implemented by administrations which apparently differ considerably ideologically suggests that such actions are based more on pragmatic considerations than on ideological positions for or against state intervention.

Such action by an American state government is practically unthinkable. Yet, the underlying economic motivations and objectives for reform are quite similar when one examines Canadian and American cases. In every instance, a more efficient government structure is desired—one that would not be an impediment to urban development and one that would efficiently provide services, including the infrastructure so critically necessary for successful private urban development.

The differential ability of the sovereign governments constitutionally responsible for local government to implement these restructurings is likely accounted for by political culture as examined in Chapters 2 and 5. The context of American political culture, encompassing a pervasive belief in local autonomy, results in a structural situation in which local government reform proposals travel a tortuous but ostensibly democratic road. Proponents must first obtain state legislative approval to proceed with a referendum process, and only then can they seek local voter approval directly for the specific proposal. In some cases double majorities are required for passage, in both the city and the suburban ring. The American political landscape is littered with the bleached bones of proposals that died at the hands of local voters— exceptions are rare, and when they occur, local autonomy still effectively guarantees the survival and continued power of independent suburban jurisdictions (Nashville, Indianapolis).

Canadian political culture, on the other hand, is much more accepting of greater direct control over, and intervention in, municipal affairs by provincial governments. Moreover, the lack of recourse to referenda on these restructurings is not perceived domestically to mean that political life is somehow less democratic in Canada. This is not to imply that there is passive acquiescence by local interests in these reorganizations. In some cases, there has been considerable local opposition to provincial restructuring proposals, but the energies of opponents have been spent largely in the provincially orchestrated public hearings and government-appointed commissions that are an integral part of the Canadian reform process.[3] Attempts to suborn members of the government majority, especially members from the affected communities, so that they can then oppose the provincial initiatives have been notably unsuccessful. The tight rein of the provincial authorities is further illustrated in the nature of the enabling legislation, which commonly grants the reformed governments little latitude to change their own structures independently but rather requires amendments to the provincial legislation. Even after restructuring, the provincial authorities remain dominant. Party discipline and the Canadian belief in "peace, order and good government" combine to make metropolitan government reform much easier, and more widespread, than is even imaginable in the United States with its very different political culture and values.

URBAN PUBLIC FINANCE

This section focuses on the varied sources from which governments obtain their revenues, on some aspects of expenditures and finally on fiscal disparities. The greater part deals with revenue sources for this helps in understanding inter-governmental relations, a key means for highlighting the very different ways in which federalism functions in the two nations.

Sources of Revenue

Urban governments, including central cities and suburban municipalities, obtain their revenues from two principal sources: transfers from other governments and their own resources. In general terms, it has been asserted that fiscal assistance from other governments, be they national, state or provincial, makes cities and suburban governments dependent on these outside agencies, and hence, increasing levels of such assistance can be viewed as a potential threat to municipal autonomy. Conversely, the more a unit of local government relies on its own revenue sources, the more autonomous it can be. If transfer programs are developed weakly or not at all, a city is essentially forced to rely on its own resources. In such circumstances, the quality and potential of the local tax base becomes critical. A city may have a degree of choice, however, if federal and state/provincial governments develop, perhaps independently, a battery of assistance programs. Although in the abstract a city could avoid being involved with these programs, the lure of outside dollars can mean that the principle of local autonomy is quickly eroded. Of course, it needs to be recognized that external assistance programs have often been developed after intense lobbying by local governments facing a stagnant or even declining tax base and increasing service demands and delivery costs on the expenditure side—the so-called fiscal squeeze. Opening up the local treasury to senior government largesse however, can be like the residents of Troy opening their city gates to welcome the Trojan Horse. Capital grants often bring in their train increased operating costs to be met by local taxpayers.

In previous chapters, we argued that local government autonomy was a more valued principle in the U.S. and that this should lead to greater fiscal reliance upon local resources than in Canada. However, and particularly for the central cities, we have also sketched a scenario of generally greater economic decline and social tension in the U.S. Thus, one would expect greater political demands from the American local level for a range of transfer programs. Hence, one should not be surprised to find such programs and their use increasingly compromising local autonomy, just as earlier American federalist principles were compromised to a strong central government.[4] In Canada, given the widespread perception that Canadian central cities are generally in a sound condition, one might expect higher levels of government to be more inclined to resist these demands, particularly since neither the government of Canada, nor the provincial governments, has any history of massive fiscal intervention in local governments akin to that in the United States.

In a federal system, there is always the issue of how the two senior levels of government will respond to local pressures. We have suggested that a major difference can be expected, with the federal level being paramount in the U.S. and the province in Canada being of greater importance than its analog, the state. To seek confirmation of our expectations we examine cross-sectionally a series of public-finance variables for the metropolitan centers. Before turning to the evidence, it must be remembered that the metropolitan unit of analysis employed in this study is not always a unit of local government; this is especially true in Canada, but less so in the United States where the SMSA is frequently one county. Whether that county acts as an urban government with a full complement of public services, however, is an open question. The residual category, "the balance," comprises many units of government in specific metropolitan areas. Recognizing the tremendous fiscal variation within this suburban ring and wishing to avoid over-generalization, the primary commentary is directed toward the central-city situation.

Consider first transfer payments. There is not a great deal of difference between metropolitan America and Canada in terms of the share of total revenues deriving from intergovernmental sources (Table 8-4). There was, however, a noticeable increase in the share attributable to transfer payments in the U.S. from 1972 to 1977; it may be possible to establish more definitively a trend once data from the most recent *1982 U.S. Census of Governments* are examined. Differences between Canada and the U.S. are more marked and increasingly so for the case of central cities. For both time periods, the U.S. cities are more reliant on transfer funds (for just over one-third of their revenues in 1977). If this share continues to rise, then some can surely argue that local autonomy is being compromised in certain respects. An interpretation consistent with these findings is that the central-city fiscal squeeze widely discussed in the U.S. is forcing cities to disregard the intangible notion of local autonomy and enter into a state of fiscal dependency. This is brought on by the fiscal and political difficulties encountered by city administrations seeking to raise ever more revenues from a limited or declining tax base. The substantially higher level of transfer payments to Canadian suburban governments suggests a continuing need to assist with infrastructural development in areas of growth— a condition which, as we have seen, is less prevalent in American suburbs.

As we predicted, there is a dramatic difference in the source of these intergovernmental transfers. Federal transfers as a proportion of total revenues and the federal share of all intergovernmental transfers are negligible in urban Canada, whereas they are of growing importance in urban America, especially for hard-pressed central cities.[5] In the U.S., it is not so much that the states have been supplanted but that the federal government has filled a gap, and aggressively so. In Canada, on the other hand, the federal role has remained circumscribed by constitutional norms and provinces zealously protecting their turf. Is this an important difference or just a minor wrinkle in the way the intergovernmental system works in two federal states? We believe it is important in terms of attitude and orientation. In the context of urban politics and what can be broadly termed civic or public affairs, the civic orientation in America is predominantly but not exclusively to Washington, whereas in Canada it is to the various provincial capitals. This reinforces an attitude that Ottawa is far removed and fairly unimportant while the regional capitals are at hand and are more important, an importance protected and fostered by the institutions of Canadian federalism itself. Washington is perceived as an extremely important place, by federal, state and local officials, and it possesses institutional means for maintaining and extending its importance.

However, the irrelevance of the Canadian federal government in local urban affairs can be overstated. Through its many departments and crown corporations, the federal government is an important agent in urban development and change. Nowhere is this more apparent than in transportation, where certain public facilities, such as airports, ports and railway stations, are operated by federal authorities or agents. Their operational and capital investment, or disinvestment, policies are clearly important in local affairs;

decision-making in Ottawa may be more crucial than that at the regional bureaucratic level. In housing finance and infrastructural assistance, a federal crown corporation, Canada Mortgage and Housing Corporation, has also been important in promoting certain lower-density styles of suburban development and in rehabilitating selected inner-city neighborhoods. Nonetheless, the breadth and scale of these federal roles and initiatives are dwarfed by comparable U.S. federal government powers.

There is an important distinction to be made within the category of transfer payments as we focus on intergovernmental relations. The distinction is between conditional and unconditional transfers. The latter are essentially unrestricted by the donor government, leaving municipalities to allocate these revenues freely and presumably in a manner consistent with local preferences. Conditional transfers are program specific; for example, a grant for sewer infrastructure would define clearly how the funds can be spent. In essence, the donor government dictates the expenditure patterns of the local government to a greater or lesser degree, depending on what proportion of the transfers are conditional.

In Canada, there is clearly a strong preference on the part of most provincial governments for conditional transfers. Data (1972-1975 inclusive) for specific cities from the *Report of the Tri-Level Task Force on Public Finance* show that, with the exception of Moncton, the unconditional or general-purpose proportion of all transfers is one-third or less (Table 8-5). Other studies using somewhat different data bases or focusing on all municipalities rather than solely metropolitan ones provide further evidence of the dominance of conditional transfers.[6] While there are some provinces that deviate from this pattern (British Columbia, New Brunswick and Prince Edward Island), the size of the predominantly unconditional transfers involved is small.

In the United States, both federal and state aid were predominantly categorical or conditional in nature in the 1960s. Following the introduction of general revenue-sharing and block-grants programs at the federal level in the 1970s, the conditional proportion of federal aid declined from 98 per cent in 1968 to 76 per cent in 1977.[7] Further progress in this direction appears to be limited. Speaking in 1980, a leading American authority, George Break, characterized federal aid as 10 per cent general-purpose grants (revenue sharing), 10 per cent broad-based grants (block grants), and 80 per cent categorical grants—as another speaker said, "categorical programs continue to dominate."[8] Break further observed that "general revenue sharing has been burdened with mandates and funded parsimoniously. Block grants have had too hard a time escaping from the categoricals folded into them or laid on them to prove what they could do."[9]

Paralleling developments at the federal level, there has been a growth in revenue sharing at the state level. A recent report identified twenty-three states with revenue-sharing equalization programs. These states are mostly in the West, with very few in the Northeast or North Central regions.[10] After the critically important categorical programs of education and welfare, general revenue sharing is the third most important form of state aid to local governments. Categorical programs remain dominant, however, in state to local transfers.

While a careful and systematic comparison of this matter remains to be done, it would appear that unconditional programs are still in the minority in most instances in Canada and the United States. If anything, Canadian provinces, especially the three previously identified, are more disposed to unrestricted municipal assistance than most American states, although generalization is difficult without a detailed state-to-province comparison. The lack of unconditional transfers by states is partly offset by their growth at the federal level in the U.S. through block-grant funding. However, this may have now reached a plateau. While the creation of new block grants has continued, such grants increasingly carry a considerable categorical burden, as Break has noted.

Also of importance is the manner in which urban governments raise revenues from their own resources. Here, a key instrument is the property tax. Traditionally, and in many different countries, local governments have relied heavily on this tax. As city governments have sought to increase their revenues, they have raised the property tax or mill rate. This tax has commonly been claimed to be one of the factors encouraging business activities to leave the central cities for lower tax locations in the suburbs or elsewhere. Loss of assessed property tax base only serves to put increased pressure on the remaining city property owners. Thus, American cities, with their declining areas, would need to find other mechanisms for raising revenues to reduce their reliance on the property tax. Canadian cities, with their generally expanding tax base, might behave in a more traditional way and rely on the property tax. In both cases, the flexibility provided by state/provincial or municipal laws or charters is of vital importance and must be recognized. A city government may want to use non-property tax mechanisms to raise revenues, but if the laws governing municipal practice do not allow this, it may reluctantly have to fall back on the property tax.

As expected with increasing transfers, taxes as a proportion of revenues declined in both Canadian and American central cities, markedly so in the case of Canada (Table 8-6). However, Canadian central cities also experienced a decline in transfers as a proportion of gross revenues, suggesting that Canadian municipalities are making more use of non-tax sources, such as sales of services or licensing charges. It is worth noting that while American metropolitan suburbs were raising fewer revenues from taxation, their Canadian counterparts were doing just the opposite.

The importance of the property tax for both sets of urban governments is confirmed but with some interesting differences. As expected, the property tax is the primary taxing instrument, for municipal authorities, but much more so in Canada (Table 8-7). American cities obtain just over one-third of their taxation revenues from other tax instruments, although the suburban ring has increasingly relied upon the property tax. In Canada, the property tax is clearly the dominant tax instrument in both the cities and the suburbs, with between 80 and 90 per cent of taxation revenues coming from this one source. In terms of gross revenues, however, the property tax is no longer as dominant a source, and a degree of convergence between urban Canada and the U.S. is evident for the central cities (Table 8-8). This is mostly a result of a substantial decline in reliance upon the property tax in Ontario.

Another perspective on the comparative importance of the property tax comes from per capita data (Table 8-9). Here, the differences are very clear and consistent — Canadian urban property owners pay substantially more (approximately double in 1971/72 and 1.5 times as much in 1976/77). However, one must take into account provincial grants to homeowners, which offset high nominal property taxes in a number of cases. Nevertheless, these data imply that Canadian city administrations are generating proportionately higher amounts of revenue from this source. This is substantiated by the per capita total gross revenue figures, which show that this statistic is substantially higher for Canadian cities in both 1971 and 1976 (Table 8-10). These data help explain why American visitors comment so favorably on the public infrastructure in Canadian cities — much more money is being spent. Americans could, of course, spend more and improve their own cities' physical plants. Recent successful anti-tax propositions in California and Massachusetts suggest otherwise. Also, American civic politicians perceive that raising tax rates will further drive property owners to the suburbs, yielding vacant buildings and diminished assessment rolls. While the difference is not stable over time, it appears that by 1976 the suburban belts in U.S. metropolitan areas were considerably better off in terms of revenues than their Canadian counterparts — much of this revenue, however, goes to high cost, labor-intensive schooling, with many other services receiving short shrift or being supplied on a private basis.

Expenditures

Given the data sources and problems of effecting comparisons, relatively little can be said about expenditures. Our findings do provide strong confirmation of one hypothesis — that American cities allocate a higher share of their expenditures for protection. For both time periods, this is clearly the case (Table 8-11). While the expenditure share is a useful indicator, of equal significance is the amount spent on a particular service (commonly measured in per capita or per household terms). With respect to police and fire expenditures, an interesting change is apparent (Table 8-12). From a situation in 1971 when little difference existed, a striking difference became obvious by 1976. Furthermore, the per capita expenditures have declined in the U.S. and risen sharply in Canada. Could it be that, despite higher crime rates, American central cities are less effectively policed? While questions of cause are always complex, perhaps the higher U.S. crime rates are a function of these lower expenditures.

An obvious inference to be drawn from these findings is that Canadian civic administrations spend more money, something that is to be expected knowing that Canadian urban revenues per capita were markedly higher. This is clearly demonstrated in per capita expenditure data, the difference being greater than one hundred dollars per capita in 1976 (Table 8-13). It is worth noting that the differences for the metropolitan area persist but are generally narrower. This indicates that expenditures per capita are higher in American suburbs, reinforcing the notion of the overall greater affluence of the suburban districts compared with the central city than is the case in Canada. Put another way, the social status gradient and its various correlates is less steep in the Canadian case, a point made earlier with other kinds of data, so that the Canadian central city and its suburbs share roughly equal social status, whereas in the United States status changes more markedly as one moves to the suburbs.

In an earlier discussion on the quality of life in cities, we noted that an important cross-national difference in terms of urban crime could be anticipated. We have shown that there are important differences in proportional and per capita expenditures on protection. How do these expenditures relate to levels of crime? Is the popular perception that Canadian cities are safer justified? The answer to the latter question depends on whether one refers to violent crime against persons or crimes against property. In the former case there are dramatically clear differences, but, and this may surprise some, on property crime there is a remarkable similarity in the rates.

Comparing the aggregate metropolitan statistics, violent crimes are over four times as high in the U.S.; this increases to a factor of six when the central cities are compared (Table 8-14). Even in the suburbs, which are rightly perceived to be safer than the core cities, the U.S. crime rate is more than four times higher than Canada's. Controlling for size, region, or the central-city-to-metropolitan population ratio does not remove these differences; the magnitudes remain extremely large under all controls. There are, however, two aspects of the violent crime data that the metropolitan centers have in common. In both countries there is a strong positive relationship between violent crime rates and metropolitan size. Secondly, there is a regional similarity in that within each country, metropolitan crime rates tend to be highest in those regions experiencing the most rapid growth.

Given the stark contrast in violent crime rates, the broad similarities in property crime rates is striking (Table 8-15). It is true that property crime rates are higher in American central cities and that this difference would seem to support popular perceptions. But the difference is not of a significant magnitude to be really meaningful. As with violent crime, property crime rates consistently decline as population decreases in the U.S. This is less true in Canada. What is remarkable is the close similarity between metropolitan areas of different size, with the exception being those in the 1/2 to 1 million class. To put it another way, you are almost as likely to have your residence broken into and your car or other property stolen in Trois Rivières as you are in Toronto. In both countries, however, there is again a common relationship between property crime rates and region — cities in the faster growing regions (British Columbia and the U.S. Pacific Region) have higher rates on the average than do cities in stagnant or declining regions (Quebec and New England).

Metropolitan Fiscal Disparities

While it was never our intention to undertake a detailed analysis of this complex matter, it is an important public sector issue. Put simply, our expectation was that fiscal disparities would be less pronounced in the case of urban Canada. Two ratio measures speak to this issue, one on the revenue side, the other on expenditures. For revenues per capita, we use a ratio of these data for the central city to the suburban ring — a value of 100 would indicate no difference between the metropolitan area's central city and its surrounding suburbs. The distribution of these ratio measures is highly variable, especially in the U.S., so we focus on the median value (Table 8-16). From a 1971 situation of no difference, there has developed a clear difference by 1976-77 pointing to greater fiscal disparities in the U.S.; disparities, as measured in this fashion, obviously exist in both countries to a substantial degree.

For expenditures, a different ratio measure was used: per capita total expenditures for the metropolitan area divided by those for the central city. In interpreting this ratio, the higher the value, the greater the metro expenditures are relative to the city, implying substantially greater per capita expenditures in the suburban ring. In 1976, the mean ratios were 1.8 and 1.5 for the U.S. and Canada respectively; the median values were 2.0 and 1.5. This evidence, albeit limited, is not contrary to expectation.

Controlling for Size, Region and Geopolitical Structure

Throughout the empirical analysis, consideration has been given to whether or not observable differences are related, first, to the difference in the urban size distribution between the two countries and, second, to the fact that in Canada the central city tends to represent a higher proportion of the metropolitan area population. We have, on occasion, also controlled by region. This will not be done for the public finance analysis for two reasons. One is that there is only a limited theory from which one might draw propositions about regional variations. Secondly, preliminary examination of these data confirm a belief that the key geographic context for urban public finance is the province or state. Geographic variation in these measures is not likely to occur, since the key intergovernmental relationships that hold in a state, province or region can meaningfully be assumed constant over the cities lying in the region. Since our regional groupings combine states and to a lesser extent provinces, we therefore forego this analysis.

City Size Effects Previously, it was shown that, overall, there was not much cross-national difference in the proportion of revenues arising from intergovernmental transfers. But some indication of a potentially important difference emerges under the size control. In general, there is a tendency for the larger Canadian cities to get less assistance than the smaller ones, whereas in the United States there is less of a tendency in this regard. This might reflect a view in various provincial administrations that the big cities are "doing fine, thank you." It is also possible that the largest central cities are politically underrepresented in the provincial legislatures. In the United States, on the other hand, the equalizing effects of federal contributions under entitlement programs need to be recognized. For 1971, the data indicate that, proportionately, federal assistance did decline as city size declined; it was more or less constant across city size by 1976. This should not be too surprising. The urban lobby which pushed for federal assistance has been preponderantly "big city" in nature—it would take some time before smaller cities with less sophisticated administrations learned how to tap into federal funds. At the same time, as with many federal programs, congressional representatives have worked diligently to broaden the geographic reach of federal urban programs so that communities in their district can become beneficiaries of what is perceived as their rightful share of the largesse.

The importance of the property tax as a source of revenue for Canadian cities persists at all levels of size and for both time periods. Furthermore, not only is this tax proportionately less important in the U.S., but also its importance has declined at all levels of city size. The Canadian situation in contrast remains essentially unchanged. In both countries, however, it is generally true that the larger the city, the more other forms of taxation are being utilized. Thus, when senior governments increase transfer payments, thereby reducing the tax burden, the major beneficiaries are property owners in smaller urban centers. Urban Canadians pay much higher property taxes on a per capita basis. This finding also clearly holds regardless of city size, and it does so for both time periods. Yet another resource-side finding that is unaffected by city size is that gross revenues per capita are substantially higher in Canadian cities; this too remains stable over time. Thus, the findings concerning a number of cross-national differences on urban revenues are strengthened by their being independent of city size differences between Canada and the U.S.

On the expenditure side, none of the cross-national differences previously established are removed by controlling for size. At all levels of size, American cities allocate a greater share of their expenditures to police and fire protection. There is relatively little variation in this proportion by size in both countries, which would seem to contradict the conventional wisdom that bigger American cities have to allocate more money to combat crime and arson. The conventional wisdom does receive support from the per capita data for the U.S.—the larger cities do spend more than smaller ones. Again, however, the per capita difference observed for 1976 persists regardless of size. This is equally true for differences in total expenditures—Canadian cities spend more.[11]

Geopolitical Structure It has been clearly established that in Canada proportionately more central cities represent a higher fraction of their respective metropolitan areas than in the U.S.[12] Does this difference underlie the overall cross-national public finance differences detected in our investigation and further shown to be largely independent of metropolitan size? Broadly speaking, the answer is no.

The greater reliance of American central cities on transfer payments holds true no matter what the central city/metropolitan population ratio is. Controlling for the geopolitical structure also does not weaken the finding that Canadian cities consistently rely on the property tax as the primary taxing mechanism—note that the per capita property tax payment is consistently higher. Finally, the substantially higher total gross revenues per capita available to Canadian financial administrators persist, regardless of the level of the control variable.

Turning to expenditure differences, they too are largely unaffected by this control. With respect to the expenditure share devoted to protection, only in the high ratio cities (0.7 to 1.0) for 1976 does the difference disappear. There was not a marked difference between the two countries in per capita protection expenditures on police and fire in 1971. Controlling for the geopolitical structure does not alter this finding, nor does it diminish in any way the consistently higher expenditures in Canadian cities in 1976. Finally, in relation to total expenditures (for 1976 only) the control again has no effect.

Attempts to measure fiscal disparities would of necessity be expected to be sensitive to this particular control variable. If the geographic territory of a central city is limited in relation to the total metropolitan area, that city is cut off from potentially expanding its taxable assessment base through urban growth compared to a city with an extensive boundary and much developable vacant land.

For the revenue measure, the control does have some effect. Disparities remain greater in the U.S. when comparing cities with lower values on the control variable (that is, the small central city situation), but they tend to disappear as the control value score rises and are in fact reversed in the 1976 data in the case where the central city is large. Another perspective on disparities was afforded by comparing total expenditures per capita for the metropolitan area as a whole with those in the central city. We had found evidence of markedly higher disparities in the U.S. metropolitan areas, and this difference is not removed by the control variable. On balance, then, we remain properly cautious but positive in asserting that fiscal disparities are significantly less acute in Canadian metropolitan areas than they are in the U.S.

Major Metropolitan Centers

It is well known that the urban "fiscal crisis" is characteristically most severe in large cities in the U.S. Paired comparisons should reveal whether or not our expectations that American cities are facing more severe fiscal problems than those in Canada can be confirmed.

Consider first the resource or revenue side. The U.S. data are for 1972 and 1977, while those for Canada are for 1971 and 1976 to allow linkage with Canadian census data for those years. Again, the fact that, within each country, the cities are in different states and provinces means that there will be considerable variation among them. City governments are very much affected by the rule-making and programs of their respective senior governments. Because of this senior government milieu, the three Canadian cities are more different from one another than on other variables examined in this fashion.

As with all cities, these largest ones have become increasingly reliant upon transfers from senior governments as a revenue source; Vancouver and Montreal, however, run counter to this trend (Table 8-17). Furthermore, in common with all Canadian cities, transfers from the federal level are insignificant, whereas no U.S. city had less than one-quarter of its intergovernmental transfers from the U.S. federal source—most were above half. In general, American cities receive proportionally more transfer funds than do Canadian cities of equivalent size.

Property taxes were expected to be significantly more important as a resource base in Canadian cities. While there is a tendency for the three Canadian cases to be located in the higher proportions (property tax as a percent of total gross revenues), the evidence is not conclusive (Table 8-18). In addition to proportional analysis, one can usefully consider the property tax burden as approximated by per capita data. For both periods, the Canadian cities are much higher on this measure, with the obvious exception of Baltimore which is atypical in certain respects among American cities for reasons too complex to broach here.

One of the key differences to emerge from these data is the amount of money available to municipalities to spend for public services (as measured by total gross revenues per capita) (Table 8-19). Vancouver is clearly in an advantageous position in comparison with its American pairs. Toronto is for the most part in a similarly advantageous position; it must be remembered that, as part of a two-level metropolitan system, Toronto is freed from providing a number of key services. Montreal occupies the middle ground between what appears to be an affluent Baltimore and a Houston which is probably spending more, to cope with rapid growth, and hence must raise more revenues.

Are the cross-national differences in expenditures on protection, which were apparent for all cities and which persisted under various controls, evident in these paired comparisons? They are very much so (Table 8-20). Again only Baltimore is exceptional. Canadian cities spend proportionately less and on per capita terms substantially more than their various American pairs.

For total gross expenditures the differences are somewhat more muted by the fact that Toronto, Cleveland and St. Louis are all rather similar in this regard (Table 8-21). Other than this, however, the overall pattern is similar to that for other variables.

Shifting to the metropolitan scale, an interesting reversal occurs on expenditures per capita. American metropolitan areas generally outspend the Canadian ones, indicating the high per capita expenditures in their suburbs, which must occur to reverse the central-city differences. This leads naturally to a consideration of fiscal disparities. Employing the same two measures as previously, the overall fiscal disparities are not substantially reduced through the paired comparisons. Rather they are thrown into sharp relief (Tables 8-22 and 8-23). Only two American metropolitan areas have ratios less than the highest Canadian score, and many of the U.S. cities examined had sizable ratio scores (greater than 1.75) when the metropolitan per capita expenditures are computed against those for the corresponding central city. Disparities on the revenue side are less clear cut. Although revenue disparities have been reduced in Montreal from 1971 to 1976, it compares poorly with Baltimore and is now only marginally better than San Francisco-Oakland. Washington, which as a national capital may be an unusual case, and St. Louis are both in a more favorable situation than Toronto (assuming again that 100, which means city per capita revenues equal those for the suburban ring, is a desirable score).

This brief excursion into the world of big-city finance serves to underscore the persistent differences uncovered in the analysis of the two sets of metropolitan centers. Controlling simultaneously for size, geopolitical structure and regional location does not eliminate the differences, though in a few cases there is some lessening of their magnitude. Hence, we can be even more confident than before that the analysis of urban public finance, limited as it is, supports the general notion of meaningful cross-national differences.

Fiscal Health

One of the consequences of the fiscal disparities that exist in many U.S. metropolitan areas is the increasingly perilous fiscal condition of American central cities. We developed two working hypotheses on the fiscal condition of American and Canadian central cities. These were as follows: firstly, for a point in time Canadian central cities will exhibit greater fiscal health than will American central cities, and, secondly, over time, Canadian cities will exhibit an improvement in fiscal health relative to their American counterparts, as measured by municipal bond ratings. The expectation is that American cities will tend to show an aggregate decline in bond ratings; the ratings for Canadian cities will tend to increase or remain stable. Essentially, municipal bond ratings are utilized as a guide for investors to assess the default risks related to owning bonds sold by municipalities to raise capital.[13] A considerable literature on municipal bond ratings exists that suggests that changes in bond ratings do appear to be closely related to the fiscal condition of rated cities. A major and appropriate source of data for the U.S. is the ratings of municipal bonds by Moody's Investors Service. These ratings are straightforward in interpretation, have been administered consistently, and provide a wide coverage for the U.S. over a series of years. For Canadian cities, it was necessary to collect data using mail surveys addressed to senior finance officials in thirty-four municipalities (all central cities).

In comparing the two sets of central cities, a difficulty arises because of the absence of ratings in many instances in Canada, especially among smaller urban centers (less than 100,000). To a greater extent than in the U.S., these cities place their bonds through more limited channels, almost always in Canada, obviating the need to access U.S. capital markets and, by extension, obviating the need for any formal ratings. No Canadian rating agency has developed to perform the function met by such firms as Moody's

Investors Services and Standard and Poor's Corporation. The smaller scale of borrowing and the fewer number of bond issuers would probably provide an insufficient market for such a firm.

Another factor is that in certain provinces, such as Alberta and British Columbia, capital financing for municipalities is undertaken by a provincially established agency; the net effect is that central cities need not be individually rated. Thus, for example, in British Columbia, only Vancouver, which operates under its own civic charter and is independent of the provincial finance authority, has a bond rating. Finally, in Canada, provinces closely monitor local government finances and vigorously enforce their own strictures against borrowing for operating purposes.

For the ten Canadian cities which had a Moody's credit rating, the notable feature is that they all had some type of "A" rating with 6 of 10 in the "gilt-edged" categories of "Aaa" and "Aa". While limited in extent, these data and comments from financial officers of non-rated cities comparing their cities to others of similar nature indicate the strong fiscal condition of Canadian central cities in the mid-1970s.

Comparing this distribution against that for the United States allows a test of the first hypothesis (Table 8-24). The vast majority, just over 90 per cent, of U.S. central cities were in some type of "A" category, attesting to their general fiscal well-being. This is, however, a *lesser proportion* than in Canada.

Again, a lesser proportion of central cities are in the gilt-edged categories (almost half as against 60 per cent in Canada). An important difference between the two countries lies in the existence of a "low" tail in the American distribution. With twenty-three central cities with ratings of Baa1 or lower for these cities, the investor is being cautioned about the city's repayment ability. It might be argued that the difference is more apparent than real as a result of the absence of ratings for smaller Canadian central cities. Inspection reveals that of the twenty-three American cities with low ratings, thirteen had fewer than 100,000 people. Canadian cities of this size could conceivably be rated in this range if done so by Moody's. But this group of twenty-three also contains the central cities of some of the principal metropolitan areas in the country — New York (Caa), Buffalo (Ba), Boston, Detroit, Philadelphia and Newark (all Baa). No major central cities in Canada had such low ratings. It is this situation together with the proportional differences in the 1977 distributions for the two countries that leads to a cautious acceptance of the hypothesis that Canadian central cities appear to enjoy better fiscal health at a point in time.

An examination of changes in bond ratings from 1970 to 1980 permits a test of the second hypothesis. Using the same set of cities, bond ratings for general obligation bonds were compared and the changes in rank recorded.

These changes were mapped, and a striking difference was immediately apparent. In no case in Canada has there been a decline in bond ratings over this period. In the U.S., however, there are declines in 16 per cent of the cases. The regional nature of bond-rating changes in the U.S. is also clear. The declines are concentrated in New England, the Middle Atlantic states, Michigan and to a lesser extent Ohio. The other regions of the country show increases in ratings, especially in the West and Southwest. There are some striking anomalies in this pattern—specifically St. Louis and New Orleans. One additional feature of the U.S. pattern merits comment. The much publicized decline of New York City's bond ratings has possibly had state-wide repercussions, since the fiscal ills of a city of such importance inevitably weaken the financial basis of the entire state of New York. It is notable that the major cities of New York state all experienced a decline in their ratings over this period. In contrast, urban areas in the immediate adjacent states of New Jersey and Connecticut appear to be benefitting from the redistribution of economic activity and taxable land uses away from New York City. Thus, Stamford, which has been the site of corporate headquarters relocating from New York City, is the only city in Connecticut to show a gain in this period. There is no evidence to suggest that city credit ratings in Canada have affected provincial credit ratings in any way.

One final observation on the pattern of change is that cities in Canada showing gains in the past decade are in that part of Canada, Southern Ontario, traditionally viewed as part of the industrial heartland along the Windsor-to-Quebec City axis. This contrasts sharply with the general condition of the industrial heartland in the U.S.[14] Yet, recent trends suggest that the economies of Southern Ontario's cities are suffering some of the same structural problems which beset those in the manufacturing core region in the U.S. What is different is that these Ontario cities do not contain a spatially concentrated "underclass," predominantly non-white in character, with unusually heavy demands for public services. Their local governments have in numerous instances been integrated and reorganized by the legislative fiat of the provincial government, thereby placing the local governments on a sounder financial footing.

The evidence on changes over time clearly leads to an acceptance of the second hypothesis. While the ratings for Canadian cities either remained constant or increased, there was a measurable decline in the ratings for a number of American central cities. As a specific case in point, there was an increase from 1977 to 1980 in the proportion of U.S. central cities with ratings of Baal or lower. This emphasizes the distributional difference noted in the discussion of the first hypothesis which showed that there was a greater proportion of low-rated cities in the U.S. group.

TABLE 8-1
DISTRIBUTION OF SCORES ON THE INDEX
OF MUNICIPAL FRAGMENTATION[1]

I.M.F. Score	Cumulative per cent of metropolitan areas with scores within the specified class	
	USA (1972)	CANADA (1971)
0.000 to 0.014	10.0	26.5
0.015 to 0.025	20.0	50.0
0.026 to 0.039	30.0	73.5
0.040 to 0.054	40.0	82.4
0.055 to 0.064	50.0	88.2
0.065 to 0.079	60.0	91.2
0.080 to 0.102	70.0	100.0
0.103 to 0.121	80.0	100.0
0.122 to 0.163	90.0	100.0
0.164 to 0.434	100.0	100.0
Mean	0.082*	0.031*
Std. Dev.	0.068	0.033
	(n=264)[2]	(n=34)

*Significant at .001 level.

[1]The index of municipal fragmentation is the ratio of the number of municipalities in a metropolitan area to the per thousand population resident in municipally governed areas. The higher the score the more fragmented an area is.

[2]There are 264 SMSAs in the U.S. in 1972.

Source: Calculated by authors from U.S. Bureau of the Census, 1972, Census of Governments, Volume 1, Governmental Organisation, Table 19, Local Governments and Public School Systems in Individual SMSAs: 1972; D.M. Ray *et al.*, *Canadian Urban Trends* (Toronto: Copp Clark, 1976) Vol. 1, National Perspective: Table A1.3.

TABLE 8-2
INDEX OF MUNICIPAL FRAGMENTATION
FOR SELECTED CITIES

Montreal	0.031
Baltimore	0.014
Minneapolis/St. Paul	0.064
San Francisco/Oakland	0.022
Toronto	0.009
Pittsburgh	0.124
St. Louis	0.102
Washington	0.050
Vancouver	0.018
Seattle	0.052
Portland	0.068
San Diego	0.012

Source: Calculated by the authors from data used in Table 8-1.

TABLE 8-3
THE NUMBER OF LOCAL GOVERNMENT UNITS IN SELECTED
SMSA'S RANKED BY POPULATION SIZE (1972)

	Population 1972 (millions)	Local Governments
New York	9.944	538
Chicago	7.085	1172
Los Angeles-Long Beach	7.000	232
Philadelphia	4.878	852
Detroit	4.489	241
Boston	3.417	147
San Francisco-Oakland	3.132	302
Washington, D.C.	2.999	90
Dallas-Fort Worth	2.446	288
St. Louis	2.400	483
Pittsburgh	2.396	698
Baltimore	2.125	29
Houston	2.124	304
TORONTO[1]	2.086	47
Newark	2.082	207
Cleveland	2.046	210
Minneapolis-St. Paul	1.996	218
Atlanta	1.684	86
Anaheim (etc.)	1.527	111
San Diego	1.443	151
Milwaukee	1.426	149
Seattle[3]	1.421	269
VANCOUVER[2]	1.082	60
Portland[3]	1.007	298

[1]Municipality of Metropolitan Toronto (1971, Population); count of local governments—1968 data.

[2]Vancouver Census Metropolitan Area (1971); local government count is an estimate.

[3]1970 Population.

Source: Advisory Commission on Intergovernmental Relations, *Trends in Metropolitan America* (Washington, D.C.: U.S. Government Printing Office, 1977), Table 16 and calculations by the authors.

TABLE 8-4
TRANSFER PAYMENTS: INTER-GOVERNMENTAL REVENUES
AS A PERCENTAGE OF TOTAL REVENUES

Metropolitan Area

| | CANADA | | USA | |
	1971	1976	1972	1977
mean	46.4*	42.8	37.2*	43.4
std.dev.	8.3	11.2	8.5	8.4
median	46.8	45.5	36.5	42.8
n	36	22	263	258

Central Cities

| | CANADA | | USA | |
	1971	1976	1972	1977
mean	20.4***	16.6*	24.6***	36.6*
std.dev.	10.4	9.3	13.1	12.0
median	18.8	15.0	24.5	35.7
n	39	35	258	274

  * significant at .001 level
*** significant at .1 level

Source: Authors' calculations

TABLE 8-5
GENERAL PURPOSE TRANSFERS (UNCONDITIONAL) AS
A PERCENTAGE OF ALL TRANSFERS

Moncton, New Brunswick	92.9
Toronto, Ontario	25.5
Winnipeg, Manitoba	34.9
Saskatoon, Saskatchewan	18.8
Edmonton, Alberta	35.1

Source: Report of the Tri-Level Task Force on Public Finance; Vol. 3; Appendix B—Analysis
of Local Government Finance in Selected Urban Regions, (Ottawa: Minister of Supply
and Services, 1976).

TABLE 8-6
ALL TAXES AS A PERCENTAGE OF TOTAL REVENUES,
METROPOLITAN AREAS, CENTRAL CITIES AND SUBURBS

| | CANADA | | | | USA | | | |
| | 1971 | | 1976 | | 1972 | | 1977 | |
	metro	city	metro	city	metro	city	metro	city
mean	42.8	63.4*	43.0	38.5	45.2	49.4*	39.4	41.0
std.dev.	7.5	17.5	11.0	15.1	10.2	12.6	10.7	12.2
median	41.0	68.0	39.0	33.0	44.6	49.4	38.0	39.4
n	37	40	22	35	264	259	258	274

Metropolitan Suburbs (or Balance of Metro Areas)

| | CANADA | | USA | |
	1971	1976	1972	1977
mean	30.5*	37.6	44.7*	39.2
std. dev.	16.3	20.2	12.3	14.7
median	25.8	42.0	44.3	38.7
n	37	17	259	256

* significant at .001 level

Source: Authors' calculations

TABLE 8-7
THE PROPERTY TAX AS A PERCENTAGE OF TAXATION REVENUES,
METROPOLITAN AREAS, CENTRAL CITIES AND SUBURBS

| | CANADA | | | | USA | | | |
| | 1971 | | 1976 | | 1972 | | 1977 | |
	metro	city	metro	city	metro	city	metro	city
mean	85.2	78.7*	84.5	80.0**	84.6	64.9*	81.4	62.6**
std. dev.	7.2	20.4	6.6	10.6	12.6	24.2	14.5	26.5
median	84.6	82.6	83.3	81.7	86.1	62.6	83.8	60.5
n	37	38	21	35	259	260	258	274

Metropolitan Suburbs

| | CANADA | | USA | |
	1971	1976	1972	1977
mean	92.7*	81.4	63.2*	87.4
std. dev.	23.6	20.6	24.3	15.1
median	88.8	82.5	61.1	92.2
n	35	16	256	256

* significant at .001 level
** significant at .01 level

Source Authors' calculations

TABLE 8-8
THE PROPERTY TAX AS A PERCENTAGE OF
TOTAL REVENUES, CENTRAL CITIES

| | CANADA | | USA | |
	1971	1976	1972	1977
mean	49.4*	29.7	32.1*	25.8
std.dev.	14.6	11.0	15.0	14.2
median	54.5	25.5	29.1	23.4
n	38	32	259	274

* significant at .001 level

Source: Authors' calculations

TABLE 8-9
PROPERTY TAX PER CAPITA, METROPOLITAN
AREAS AND CENTRAL CITIES

| | CANADA | | | | USA | | | |
| | 1971 | | 1976 | | 1972 | | 1977 | |
	metro	city	metro	city	metro	city	metro	city
mean	158.4**	132.1*	251.8	152.3*	177.8**	77.0*	241.2	103.7*
std. dev.	46.7	58.7	81.8	56.4	78.4	66.0	108.2	92.2
median	166.3	138.5	248.0	134.0	172.0	55.0	225.3	70.3
n	37	34	21	31	260	259	259	261

* significant at .001 level
** significant at .01 level

Source: Authors' calculations

TABLE 8-10
REVENUES PER CAPITA, METROPOLITAN
AREAS AND CENTRAL CITIES

| | CANADA | | | | USA | | | |
| | 1971 | | 1976 | | 1972 | | 1977 | |
	metro	city	metro	city	metro	city	metro	city
mean	440.2	250.6	713.9	531.0**	454.7	238.1	742.3	422.7**
std. dev.	119.4	87.2	224.0	181.3	138.0	156.0	225.8	267.2
median	449.0	255.0	723.5	504.5	420.5	186.5	697.0	343.5
n	37	36	22	32	264	258	258	260

** significant at .01 level

Source: Authors' calculations

TABLE 8-11
EXPENDITURES ON PROTECTION AS A PERCENTAGE
OF TOTAL EXPENDITURES, CENTRAL CITIES

| | CANADA | | USA | |
	1971	1976	1972	1977
mean	15.3*	14.3*	23.3*	20.8*
std. dev.	5.4	6.4	9.9	8.4
median	14.6	13.3	22.5	20.0
n	37	37	258	275

* significant at .001 level

Source: Authors' calculations

TABLE 8-12
PROTECTION EXPENDITURES PER CAPITA, CENTRAL CITIES

| | CANADA | | USA | |
	1971	1976	1972	1977
mean	39.3**	71.9*	45.8**	32.8*
std. dev.	13.9	29.5	18.2	14.4
median	40.0	77.8	41.4	31.0
n	33	35	259	262

 * significant at .001 level
** significant at .01 level

Source: Authors' calculations

TABLE 8-13
TOTAL EXPENDITURES PER CAPITA, METROPOLITAN AREAS

| | CANADA | | | | USA | | | |
	1971		1976		1972		1977	
	metro	city	metro	city	metro	city	metro	city
mean	468.7	n.a.	782.5	526.8**	463.8	236.9	728.1	414.8**
std.dev.	115.3	n.a.	257.9	202.9	147.5	170.2	208.5	264.0
median	478.0	n.a.	787.5	511.0	434.5	185.5	689.0	349.0
n	37	n.a.	22	33	264	258	259	261

** significant at .01 level

Source: Authors' calculations

TABLE 8-14
VIOLENT CRIME PER 100,000 POPULATION

	CANADA (1976)			USA (1975)		
	metro	city	balance	metro	city	balance
mean	93.3*	107.4*	58.8*	436.4*	656.0*	275.4*
std.dev.	51.7	94.4	35.5	232.0	455.3	193.8
n	31	26	17	219	243	212

(1) VIOLENT CRIME RATES BY CITY SIZE

size class	metro	city	balance	metro	city	balance
over 1 mil.	181	468	66	612	1165	328
0.5 to 1 mil.	139	205	91	454	756	252
0.1 to 0.49 mil.	68	94	36	401	571	274
under 0.1 mil.	76	64	61	202	278	137

(2) VIOLENT CRIME RATES BY REGION, METROPOLITAN AREAS

Atlantic	58	New England	228	South Atlantic	570
Quebec	104	Mid-Atlantic	335	East-South Central	406
Ontario	76	East-North Central	407	West-South Central	454
Prairies	147	West-North Central	319	Mountain	468
B.C.	105	Pacific	470		

(3) VIOLENT CRIME RATES BY CITY TO METROPOLITAN POPULATION RATIO

	CANADA			USA		
ratio	metro	city	balance	metro	city	balance
0.0—0.29	85	126	19	411	823	297
0.3—0.49	129	216	48	450	718	261
0.5—0.69	73	69	85	434	523	274
0.7—1.0	94	86	53	449	457	277

* significant at .001 level

Source: Authors' calculations

TABLE 8-15
PROPERTY CRIME PER 100,000 POPULATION

| | CANADA (1976) | | | USA (1975) | | |
	metro	city	balance	metro	city	balance
mean	5363.9	6301.2	3938.6	5249.0	6978.9	3816.5
std. dev.	1406.5	1781.0	1842.3	1556.3	2297.8	1623.0
n	31	26	17	221	243	214

(1) PROPERTY CRIME RATES BY CITY SIZE

size class	metro	city	balance	metro	city	balance
over 1 mil.	5345	8533	5760	5943	7863	4869
0.5 to 1 mil.	6000	7440	3809	5498	7596	4005
0.1 to 0.49 mil.	5183	6940	4416	5049	6819	3554
under 0.1 mil.	5277	5299	3465	4848	5665	3313

(2) PROPERTY CRIME RATES BY REGION

Atlantic	4585	New England	4659	South Atlantic	5749
Quebec	4020	Mid-Atlantic	3930	East-South Central	4475
Ontario	5500	East-North Central	5095	West-South Central	4977
Prairies	6354	West-North Central	5213	Mountain	6603
B.C.	6957	Pacific	6385		

(3) PROPERTY CRIME RATES BY CITY TO METROPOLITAN RATIO

| | CANADA | | | USA | | |
ratio	metro	city	balance	metro	city	balance
0.0−0.29	6483	9698	4883	4876	7530	4136
0.3−0.49	4603	5967	3710	5230	7163	3859
0.5−0.69	5171	6349	4408	5490	6726	3680
0.7−1.0	5428	6126	3580	5527	6069	3358

Source: Authors' calculations

TABLE 8-16
RATIO OF REVENUES PER CAPITA (CITY) TO REVENUES PER CAPITA (BALANCE)

| | CANADA | | USA | |
	1971	1976	1972	1977
median	29.7	54.5	28.6	33.3
mean	34.7	51.9	41.4	47.7
std. dev.	28.3	35.4	37.4	44.3
n	33	16	256	252

Note: The order of these statistics is somewhat different in order to focus attention on the median, given the large amount of variation in this variable (as shown in the standard deviations).

Source: Authors' calculations

TABLE 8-21
EXPENDITURES PER CAPITA, SELECTED CITIES
AND METROPOLITAN AREAS, 1976-77

Cities		Metropolitan Areas	
Montreal	541.60	Montreal	624.90
Baltimore	1293.90	Baltimore	976.30
Houston	294.20	Minneapolis-St. Paul	1033.90
		San Francisco-Oakland	1150.90
Toronto	507.40		
Pittsburgh	336.60	Toronto	706.80
Cleveland	500.20	Pittsburgh	641.80
Milwaukee	348.80	St. Louis	631.20
St. Louis	511.90	Washington	1168.20
Vancouver	622.40	Vancouver	822.50
Seattle	459.50	Seattle	832.10
Portland	361.70	Portland	833.30
San Diego	252.40	San Diego	912.60

Source: Authors' calculations

TABLE 8-22
RATIO OF METROPOLITAN EXPENDITURES PER CAPITA
TO CITY EXPENDITURES PER CAPITA, 1976/77

Montreal	1.19
Baltimore	0.75
Minneapolis-St. Paul	2.10
San Francisco-Oakland	1.34
Houston	2.54
Toronto	1.39
Pittsburgh	1.91
Cleveland	1.83
Milwaukee	2.85
St. Louis	1.23
Vancouver	1.32
Seattle	1.81
Portland	2.30
San Diego	3.62

Source: Authors' calculations

TABLE 8-23
RATIO OF REVENUES PER CAPITA (CITY) TO REVENUES PER
CAPITA (BALANCE), SELECTED METROPOLITAN AREAS

	1971/72	1976/77
Montreal	41.2	72.0
Baltimore	154.4	170.1
Minneapolis-St. Paul	26.5	35.0
San Francisco-Oakland	64.5	67.7
Toronto	64.6	67.0
Pittsburgh	52.4	43.6
St. Louis	64.8	79.9
Washington	221.5	196.8
Vancouver	80.0	80.0
Seattle	34.7	45.6
Portland	32.8	34.3
San Diego	17.3	18.0

Source: Authors' calculations

TABLE 8-24
MUNICIPAL BOND RATINGS FOR CANADIAN
AND AMERICAN CITIES

	Ratings	USA (1977)[1] Number	Per cent	CANADA Number	Date of Rating
1.	Aaa	29	11.1	3	1977 (2); not known (1)
2.	Aa	99	37.9	3	1976 (2); 1975 (1)
3.	A1	65	24.9	1[2]	1974
4.	A	45	17.2	3	1977 (1); 1976 (1); 1975 (1)
5.	Baa1	8	3.1		
6.	Baa	13	5.0		
7.	Ba	1	0.4		
8.	B	0	—		
9.	Caa	1	0.4		
10.	Ca	0	—		
11.	C	0	—		
	No ratings at present			20	
		261	100.00	30	

[1]These are the ratings as of 1977; the actual date of the rating is not known.

[2]This city expects that a new rating would be Aa.

[3]No city under 100,000 population has a rating; two of the larger non-rated places expect new ratings would be Aa, based on knowledge of comparable urban centers.

Source: Moody's Municipal and Government Manual (New York: Moody's Investors Service, 1977), and a mail survey of Canadian cities (February, 1978).

9

A MULTIVARIATE APPROACH
TO METROPOLITAN DIFFERENCES

This, the third and final empirical chapter, analyzes metropolitan areas using a series of more complex "multivariate" statistical techniques that deal with many dimensions of comparison simultaneously. Why resort to more sophisticated multivariate analyses? It has been clearly demonstrated in the two previous chapters that there are important cross-national differences between metropolitan Canada and metropolitan America. Two points need to be borne in mind, however. The first is that there are many characteristics and features of metropolitan areas that have not been analyzed systematically in a comparative fashion. The second is that each variable or dimension of comparison has been examined essentially in isolation from other variables. Yet, common sense alone suggests that there must be important interrelationships among many of these variables. In the United States, for example, the high levels of violent crime in inner cities, which are in turn related to poverty and race, have been a contributing factor in encouraging people to move out; this is readily evident from data on propensity to move in the *Annual Housing Surveys* of the U.S. Department of Housing and Urban Development. As the net population losses mount in the central cities, services, and related employment, are closed down in central districts, and new outlets are opened in the suburbs. The growing suburban population and its desire for quality services, especially for safe, sound schooling and for the protection of residential districts, leads to the incorporation of new units of local government and, eventually, fragmentation. These few examples are sufficient to demonstrate the point—these variables are interrelated and must ultimately be treated simultaneously in a multivariate fashion in which the set of interrelationships or intercorrelations is the foundation for analysis.

APPROACHING THE PROBLEM

The central working hypothesis examined here is that, within the metropolitan areas of North America, Canadian metropolitan areas are a distinct and recognizable group. This proposition is consistent with the fundamental argument—namely, that Canadian metropolitan centers, while having certain features and characteristics in common with American centers, are sufficiently distinctive to require a separate theoretical treatment, a different policy making framework and a contrasting experiential sensibility.

The research strategy used to attack this issue begins by treating all the metropolitan areas as a whole, as one data set—in essence, we threw away the border, albeit temporarily and only conceptually. Then, rather than attempting to reduce more than 150 variables to a smaller number of potentially interpretable and differentiable factors on the basis of the cross-national comparative analysis, we identified a number of dimensions of comparison across which there were clear and meaningful Canadian/American differences. If a distinctive grouping of Canadian centres could not be established on the basis of these, then it would be most unlikely that it would emerge using any other of the collected data.

Three multivariate methods were utilized in the analysis of the selected variables. They are factor analysis, cluster analysis and discriminant analysis. An extended discussion of these methods is not appropriate here,[1] but a few general comments are needed. Factor analysis is at root a data reduction and simplifying procedure, taking a number of variables and reducing them to a smaller number of clusters of highly interrelated variables, called factors. The interpretation of these factors can assist the researcher in understanding the nature of the complex interrelationships between selected variables which are themselves measures of the characteristics of the subject under study—in this instance, the metropolitan areas of the United States and Canada. Values for each observation, called scores, are generated for each factor. While Canadian and American cities were merged into one set of observations, the ability to identify the two sets separately later was retained. Thus, it was possible to compare the metropolitan centres in terms of their factor scores. This is most useful when investigating similarities or differences, since these scores are key indicators of the distinctiveness of the two city sets.

A central purpose in using cluster analysis (or grouping analysis) was to observe how the individual metropolitan centers behaved as they were each progressively joined together in a linking procedure, culminating in one grand linked group.[2] This would allow judgment on how distinctive Canadian cities were within a total North American city set. Both the factor scores for each metropolitan area and the values of the selected variables were used as data inputs for separate cluster analyses. This allowed some sense of the stability of the results from two methods. In addition, a second corroborating form of cluster analysis was used to validate the linkage results. In this procedure, the observations are treated as one group, which is then broken down into various clusters. These clusters could be compared with those formed through the additive linkage procedure.

The approach in the discriminant analysis is somewhat different, since the metropolitan centres are maintained as two separate groups. There are two fundamental questions posed. Can the two groups—U.S. and Canadian cities—be discriminated using a set of selected variables? If an effective or powerful discriminant function can be determined, then this indicates the distinctiveness of the two *a priori* groups. If not, then the groups are more similar than different on these chosen variables. The second question is whether or not cases can be properly classified using the discriminant function. In other words, would a Canadian urban area be grouped by the discriminant function with the Canadian or American classes? To which group would an American urban area be assigned? If there is considerable misclassification, then the efficacy of the discriminant function is called into question and by extension the distinctiveness of the classes.

FACTOR ANALYSIS

A list of thirty-four variables was developed as the basis for the first step in the multivariate investigation (Table 9-1). The selection of the variables was based on prior knowledge about their ability to demonstrate clear differences between American and Canadian urban areas. In this group, the emphasis on fiscal variables (fourteen out of thirty-four) reflected a conviction that public finance and local government structure were very important differentiators, as noted in Chapter 8.[3] The interrelationships between these variables were factor analyzed for the 317 metropolitan areas (277 in the U.S. and 40 in Canada) that constituted the combined metropolitan sets. Using a fairly conventional cut-off criterion, this first analysis yielded a ten-factor solution which accounted for 79 per cent of the total variance.[4] No factor accounted for more than one-quarter of the total variance, and at least five factors were little more than one- or two-variable factors. An examination of the inter-variable correlations showed that there was a high degree of correlation between many variables measuring different facets of the same phenomenon (for example, the metropolitan geography of economic activity as measured by the central-city share variables or public revenues against taxation). Accordingly, the set of variables was reduced in anticipation of achieving a more parsimonious and useful description through factor analysis. The results of the multivariate discriminant analysis were also used as a guide to which variables should be retained; this analysis is discussed later in the chapter. Fourteen variables were eliminated from the analysis using the foregoing procedure.

The second set, consisting of twenty variables (Table 9-2), was subjected to the same method of factor analysis described above. A much more satisfactory result was obtained, with a factor structure comprised of four factors and accounting for 86 per cent of the total variance being generated. The principal factor accounted for about 40 per cent of the variance, with each of the other factors contributing from 10 to 20 per cent. The factors were also reasonably interpretable (Table 9-3). The interpretation begins with the simplest factors and proceeds to the more complex ones. Factor 4 is a rather elemental factor, being made up of two variables each loading strongly and positively. These variables measure population and household change in the suburban periphery, and thus this factor could be termed "suburban demographic change." The third factor is a bipolar factor and comprises most of the fiscal variables in the analysis. The interpretation placed on Factor 3 is that it denotes a central city/suburban fiscal contrast, a contrast that is reinforced by non-fiscal variables. The proportion of foreign born among the central-city population is positively associated with other measures of central-city characteristics (higher levels of protection expenditures and the fiscal disparity measure). The suburban end of this dimension is picked out by the proportion of single-family units in the housing stock (a proportion that generally rises as one moves into suburbia and that is higher for American metropolitan areas overall) and the high levels of education expenditure, an important priority in suburban America given the perceptions of a disadvantaged city public school system. That this factor connotes a relatively disadvantaged central city is somewhat reinforced by further analysis. Various studies have attempted to develop and apply indices to show which cities in the United States are economically, socially and fiscally in the worst condition. Using a recently revised index for 1975, more than half of the cities in the highest quintile (one-fifth) of the "distressed" cities were also found to be in the highest quintile with respect to their scores on this third factor.[5] Cities like Cleveland, Detroit, St. Louis, Newark, Atlanta and other leading American cities were highly ranked on both lists, rankings that in this case will not be envied.

Given that American cities constitute the preponderance of the observations, we expected to find a factor associated with the presence of a non-white population; such a factor has consistently emerged in numerous other factorial analyses of the American city.[6] These expectations were borne out in Factor 2, which accounted for almost 20 per cent of the variance. The non-white variables are positively associated with measures of violent crime (without implying any causal link) and another facet of central-city distress, fiscal transfers from federal sources. Contrasting with this well-defined cluster of variables is a measure of family structure. The lack of association between the family structure variables and the others suggests a central-city environment that is not as conducive to family life as it might be, a point made in Chapter 7. Furthermore, as was noted in the discussion of demography in Chapter 3, the American non-white population is characterized by a high proportion of "broken" families. Such households are disproportionately living in the central cities. Finally, Factor 1 clearly represents the variables which measure the central-city share of economic activity—these variables are strongly and positively clustered together. That they connect with the measure of family structure and the measure of city-to-metropolitan income disparity leads to the conclusion that this factor will pick out cities which have a vital central city and have retained economic activity; deconcentration will have occurred but not to the detriment of the central city. Metropolitan areas with economically weaker central cities, relatively speaking, will score negatively on this factor. This factor might be labelled "metropolitan form," conveying some sense of economically stronger and weaker central cities.

Further analysis of the factor scores for each of the four factors revealed a considerable degree of difference between the Canadian and American metropolitan centers. This is shown by a comparison of the mean factor scores for the two sets of centers (Table 9-4). Factor scores are produced in a standardized form that eliminates scale differences in the variables (that is, they are normally distributed around a central measure—a mean of zero) and can therefore have both positive and negative values. In addition, almost all values (99+ per cent) lie between -3 and +3 as a result of the standardization procedure.

What is immediately apparent is that in every case the Canadian mean scores have a different sign from the American means. The magnitude of the differences in the mean values is particularly striking. In each instance, the American mean would have to be increased by about seven to nine times the original value to be equivalent to the Canadian mean.

The direction of the mean scores is also revealing. We interpreted the first factor broadly to convey central-city strength and economic vitality. On average, Canadian cases score positively while American ones are negative— less deconcentration for the former and noticeably more for the latter. For the second factor, metropoles containing central cities with high proportions of non-whites, with high crime rates and higher levels of fiscal dependency score positively. Overall, the American cases show positive scores on this factor while Canadian centres are strongly negative. With respect to the third factor, the Canadian cases (with one exception, Chicoutimi-Jonquière) are uniformly positive, whereas the American distribution of scores is much more variable, as the standard deviation suggests. Many large centres score positively on this factor, but the majority of American metropolitan areas score negatively. This suggests some commonality among larger places in North America with respect to fiscal capacity, higher expenditures on protection services and lower proportions of single-family units in the housing stock. What keeps the smaller Canadian cities in the positive score category is that they have a relatively high proportion of immigrants and a higher proportion of non-single-family structures in their housing stock. In this sense they can be viewed as smaller versions of the larger metropolitan centres, which is not the case for their U.S. counterparts. Finally, on the fourth factor, which indicates growth on the periphery of the city, a high positive score indicates rapidly burgeoning suburbs, such as is the case for Edmonton and Phoenix. Again, the Canadian average is clearly positive, though not dramatically so, and the American mean is negative, although only marginally so.

The analysis of the mean scores provides further evidence to corroborate the earlier findings that the components of the U.S. metropolitan settlement system exhibit more diversity compared to the Canadian components. For three of the four factors the standard deviations are higher for the U.S. cases than for the Canadian. The high standard deviation for the Canadian centers on the fourth factor is caused by a few strongly positive scores for cities which exhibited very high growth rates in the period under analysis—something they have in common with a few favored American centres.

Thus, even without undertaking grouping analyses, these findings are a confirmation of the argument that, on the whole, Canadian cities are distinctively different from those in America. However, the factor analysis does not address directly the issue of whether or not Canadian cities form a distinctive and coherent group within a North American framework. On any factor, there are particular American cities that score more positively (or negatively in the case of factor 2) than certain Canadian ones. Perhaps these cities will appear within one or more Canadian groupings? Thus, the cities must be grouped to determine if the Canadian centers fall into one or more distinctive groups that are separate from the groups in which American centers lie.

GROUPING ANALYSES

There are a variety of ways to use these factor scores for each metropolitan area; in this case, there were four scores for each of the 317 metropolitan areas. Since the primary interest was in the distinctiveness of the Canadian cities as a group, these scores were made to be the input data to a cluster analysis. For this particular cluster analysis, *each* metropolitan area is essentially treated as a *cluster of one*. The computer algorithm then links cities that on the basis of the input variables (the four factor scores in this instance) are most similar to one another. This linking procedure is followed until all the cases (or metropolitan centers) are linked together, thereby forming one massive group. What this type of cluster analysis, known as centroid analysis, can reveal is whether or not Canadian metropolitan centers are linked first to other Canadian centers or to American centers. Inevitably, Canadian centers will be connected to American ones as the algorithm proceeds to form the one final group containing all the 317 cases, but at what stage of the analysis does this linking of Canadian and American cities occur? From the standpoint of this research and given the rationale in the selection of the variables, the Canadian cities should form a major and separate cluster before connecting to any sizable American cluster. Secondly, this connection should come late in the whole linkage process.

The results of this cluster analysis are very satisfactory. There are 40 Canadian metropolitan areas in the North American metropolitan set of 317. Of these, 31 (or 77.5 per cent) formed a distinct Canadian cluster or group before being connected to the very large, principally American group. This latter group comprised 257 metropolitan areas (including 92 per cent of all American cases and only 3 Canadian cases) at the time of the linkage. This key linking occurred on step 309, which was very close to the final step (316) — this is almost 98 per cent of the way through the linkage process. A separate group of 6 Canadian cities, which was formed by step 293, remained apart until step 314, when it was finally linked to the main group.

These findings offer good support for the proposition of a distinctive and separate group of Canadian cities within a North American context. But the case cannot rest solely on this analysis, convincing though it may be. Some might argue that the factor scores are not "real," that they are statistical artifacts, and that they impose an unwarranted and arbitrary structure on the data. To address this objection, a cluster analysis using the basic twenty raw variables (rather than the four scores which were a transformation of these variables) is of value. The findings of this cluster analysis would either strengthen or qualify the conclusion that a distinctive Canadian city exists.

Therefore, the cluster analysis was repeated using the variables themselves directly as the data input; thus, instead of each metropolitan centre having the four factor scores as their attributes or values, they had twenty attributes. The logic of the linkage process was the same for this second analysis. The results were as convincing as the ones already obtained. Of the 40 Canadian cities, fully 34 (or 85 per cent) were joined together in a separate group before joining the dominant U.S. group at step 296. While this was earlier than the previous critical linkage, it was still very late in the linkage process (it represents 94 per cent of the way through). At the time of the Canada-U.S. linkage, the dominant American group contained almost exactly the same number of cases as in the first analysis—258 or 93 per cent of the American centers. There were six Canadian centers which did not join the principal Canadian group. A small distinctive cluster (comprising Thunder Bay, Sault Ste. Marie and St. Catharines-Niagara Falls) joined the North American group at step 310. Three other cities linked with an American city: Chicoutimi-Jonquière was linked to Albany-Schenectady-Troy and on the very next step joined a very large group of American cases (207 in total); Regina was linked to another Great Plains center—Lawton, Oklahoma—and then joined the North American group at step 310; and, finally, Toronto was linked to Miami, with its high percentage of foreign-born immigrants and similar functional role as a managerial or control center, at step 307, then almost immediately (step 309) joined the main North American group.

The analysis using the variables rather than the transformed scores provides further grounds for the conclusion that a distinctive Canadian city exists. But even more confirmation was possible using another form of cluster analysis. This method partitions or splits a set of cases into clusters (in some sense it is the reverse of the previous procedure). Upon completion of the partitioning process each case belongs to the cluster whose center is closest to that case.[7] In this instance, the 317 metropolitan centers represented the set. The expectation was that a predominantly Canadian cluster would be formed. An exploratory analysis using the thirty-four original variables generated 4 clusters. Two were single-city clusters, both American. The two dominant clusters contained 139 and 176 cases respectively. Of the 40 Canadian cities, 39 were in the smaller group, and only Toronto was in the larger American group. Although this was not overwhelming evidence, it pointed to some potential cohesiveness amongst the Canadian cities. Therefore, this analysis was repeated using the more refined data set of twenty variables and specifying the successive formation of up to ten clusters. The results are both interesting and confirmatory. At the first separation into two clusters, 38 of the 40 Canadian centres were in one cluster, together with 82 American ones. The second and larger cluster of 197 was thus overwhelmingly American. With the formation of four clusters, the Canadian metropoles constituted a clearly distinct and "Canadian" cluster of 40 cases (39 Canadian cases and Anchorage, Alaska). This remained intact through the formation of five clusters. At the next step, however, a small mixed group of 15 cases (9 Canadian and 6 American) was created, and this cluster retained its unique composition until the very last step. Among the Canadian cities in this group were the six that constituted the secondary Canadian group in the centroid linkage analysis. Their clustering here together with a number of rapidly growing American metropolitan centers suggests that population growth, especially in the outer city, is the functional basis for this small and unique mixed group.

The 30 remaining cities from the dominant Canadian group (at the five-cluster stage) comprised a persistent and stable group (along with Anchorage) which survived until the final, ten-cluster stage. At that point, only Toronto split away and joined an American group (of 43 cities, including Toronto). Again, a connection with Miami was evident. With the exception of one large group, which contained Chicoutimi-Jonquière and 67 American cases, all six other clusters contained only American centers.

The overall conclusion from these cluster analyses is that the Canadian cities emerge as places that have more in common with each other than they do with American cities. The variables chosen serve well to differentiate Canadian cities effectively from American ones, and thus the distinctiveness thesis is strongly supported.

The grouping analyses which were performed proved their worth since they did yield additional insights. Not only do Canadian cities exhibit a distinct geographic coherence within the initial framework of a "North American" set, but so also do subsets of American metropolitan areas. The specifically regional nature of certain of the American groups reinforces a point already made more than once in the univariate chapters and previously in this chapter. There is considerable variability within the U.S. metropolitan experience. On the whole, its diversity is greater than within the Canadian system. This, it could be argued, is a function of scale or, alternatively, the greater variety of the physical resource base and regional conditions of urban America. America's subtropical regions and desert areas have proven to be more readily settled, despite severe environmental constraints, than Canada's boreal forest and the cold deserts of the tundra. Whatever the reason, it is a documentable difference between the two systems. The fact that the regional character of the American system emerges from the grouping analyses gives an even greater confidence to the principal finding. The results, considering the U.S. cities alone, are consistent with a reality that geographers have skillfully described and interpreted.

The American regional groupings are not presented and discussed in detail, for this would be diversionary from the main theme of the chapter, which is to document the distinctiveness of Canadian and American urban centers. But having made the claim that these findings have a reality to them and are not the product of statistical sleight of hand, a couple of examples are needed.

About three-quarters of the way through the linkage process, a well-defined southern group had been formed, arcing down from the sprawling complex of cities on Chesapeake Bay to Waco in central Texas. A few steps later, this group was linked with two other smaller clusters to form a larger but still predominantly southern group. Just over 40 metropolitan areas in all comprise this group (Map 9-1). That "the South" itself is far from uniform is attested to by the absence of many of Florida's metropoles; these rapidly growing centers linked with others in the West to form a small, distinctive but not geographically contiguous group. Another noticeable feature is the exclusion of the metropolitan areas in western Texas—they connect, however, with cities in the Great Plains and the more agriculturally oriented regions of the Mid West to form another recognizable regional grouping, although there are small secondary outliers in the South and the West (Map 9-2). Not unexpectedly, larger metropolitan centers appear to have a different profile on the factor scores used as the basis for the groupings. In both instances, large metropolitan areas in these regions are conspicuously absent—the exceptions being Dallas, Houston and Indianapolis. These and other regionally recognizable constellations of cities fit tolerably well into a regional matrix of the United States as established by geographers. This consistency lends more support to the principal finding of Canadian distinctiveness than if the U.S. groupings had been much less geographically recognizable—less real, one might say.

DISCRIMINANT ANALYSIS

The analysis so far has shown the different character of Canadian cities when they are contrasted to cities in the U.S. (as revealed by the factor analysis), and it has been demonstrated that under various grouping procedures Canadian cities emerge as a distinctive group. In short, the selected variables serve to differentiate Canadian cities within a North American set. Precisely which variables are the most important in setting apart the cities can be revealed through another form of multivariate analysis—namely, discriminant analysis.

The initial goal in discriminant analysis is to distinguish statistically between two or more groups of cases. These sets or groups are defined by particular research contexts; in this case, there are two groups—American and Canadian cities. In using this technique, a set of discriminating variables are selected which measure attributes on which the groups are expected to differ. Having done precisely this as a result of the numerous univariate comparisons, it is clear that this method is particularly appropriate for the present analysis, enabling a focus upon the variables which differentiate Canadian from American metropolitan centers.

This statistical procedure is also extremely useful in classification or assignment problems. Assuming the existence of classes or groups, it allows the assignment of unclassified cases to one or another of known classes. This is done on the basis of the discriminant function (simply, a linear combination of the discriminating variables) determined in the first part of the statistical method. If, as was done in our analysis, a sample of cities from both groups is taken and treated as unassigned, as if it were not known whether the city was American or Canadian, how well does the discriminant function perform in correctly assigning such cities to the two groups?

This particular procedure was first used with the initial set of thirty-four variables. The primary purpose at this stage was to ascertain those variables which contributed little to the discriminant function. This was done in two ways—by examining the order of entry of the variables in a stepwise discriminant analysis together with an inspection of the standardized coefficients of the variables in the discriminant function.[8] Combining these results with those of the factor analyses of the original thirty-four variables enabled a reduction of the multivariate set to twenty variables (see again Tables 9-1 and 9-2).

The discriminant analysis was repeated for the same twenty variables employed in both the factor and cluster analyses. We considered first the matter of determining the most important of the discriminating variables. Next, we examined how well the discriminant function performed in differentiating between Canadian and American metropolitan areas and how well it performed in classifying unassigned cases. Since there are only two groups, there can only be one discriminant function in this instance (the number of functions generated by the algorithm is always one less than the number of groups). Using a sequential stepwise procedure and a criterion which eliminated variables which contribute little to the ability to discriminate between the two groups, a ten-variable discriminant function was obtained. The variables were included in the function according to their order of entry into the function and their standardized coefficients (Table 9-5); this table ranks the variables in order of their importance as discriminators according to the order of entry. The variables which contributed most to the function—as shown by the size of their coefficient—were the proportion of households which were families with children still at home (FAMKIDC) and the proportion of foreign born (FORBRN). All other variables were secondary in nature; of these, the most important differentiator was the variable measuring federal fiscal transfers to the central city (FEDTRANS) (the sign is ignored in the interpretation of these coefficients).

There are two measures which gauge the effectiveness of this discriminant function in differentiating between the Canadian and American centers. The canonical correlation is one. For this ten-variable function, the coefficient is 0.901. The higher the correlation (maximum possible value is 1.0), the more powerful is the function in terms of explaining group differences.

The second statistic of interest is the group means that are determined for the groups under analysis. In addition to the two groups, Canada and the U.S., through a split sample procedure two additional groups were created for use in the classification part of this analysis. There is a very clear separation of the Canadian and American groups as shown by these values (Table 9-6). This further attests to the effectiveness of the discriminant function. This is reinforced graphically by inspecting the histogram of the scores of individual cases in the discriminant function (Chart 9-1). The separation is clear and convincing. Therefore, in general terms, there was a clear discrimination between American and Canadian metropolitan centres on the basis of the selected variables. Secondly, these variables formed a function which discriminated very effectively between the groups. Thirdly, the most important discriminatory variables were those that are indicators of the relative livability and attractiveness of the central parts of Canadian metropolitan areas compared to the more disadvantaged and less livable facets of the inner sections of American metropolitan areas.

The results just described presage the success of the classification part of the analysis. With a large number of cases, it is possible to use what is called a split-sample validation. Intuitively, it is better to develop a discriminant function using only part of the total sample of cases, since that function can then be applied to the remaining cases to see how well it classifies them into the two groups of interest. This approach ensures a truer test of the power of the discriminant function, since the function is estimated on one set of cases and then applied to an independent set. Utilizing this procedure, the two groups were randomly split into subsets (the Canadian subset comprised 7 cases, the U.S. subset 54 cases). The residual cases not used in the original computation of the function were indeed properly assigned to their respective groups. There was no misclassification (Table 9-7). This result further confirms that the variables selected were effective in differentiating between American and Canadian metropolitan centres.

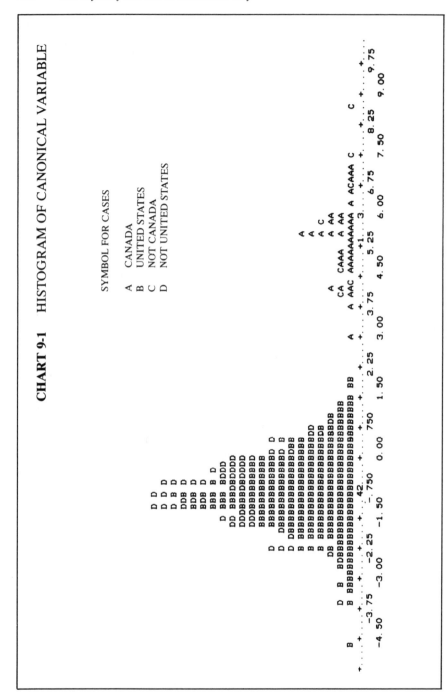

CHART 9-1   HISTOGRAM OF CANONICAL VARIABLE

SYMBOL FOR CASES

A   CANADA
B   UNITED STATES
C   NOT CANADA
D   NOT UNITED STATES

SUMMARY

The central purpose in undertaking the more complex multivariate analyses reported on in this chapter was to ascertain whether or not Canadian metropolitan areas were substantially different from their American counterparts when certain variables used in the univariate aspects of this study were allowed to interact simultaneously with one another. Such an approach is imperative to acknowledge and honor the multi-faceted and complex character of metropolitan areas. No single variable can capture that complexity, although certain simple indicators have proven to be very useful in specific kinds of urban analysis— for example, the population density gradient.

Overall, the results of the various multivariate analyses generally support the contention that Canadian cities are sufficiently different and distinctive within a North American context that they require separate consideration. While Canadian and American cities may be subject to similar causative processes, such as the transformation of employment structures, population deconcentration or immigration, there are other processes which are structured differently and perform differently, such as, intergovernmental relations. Furthermore, even where similar processes are at work, as in international migration and suburbanization, these processes are at work in metropolitan settings in the two countries that have vitally different characteristics, so that the outcomes are likely to be different, even for these common processes. The findings of the factor analyses, of the various grouping techniques, and of the effective performance of the discriminant function, when taken together and combined with the earlier univariate results, pose a significant challenge to continentalist thinking. They demonstrate that Canadian urban areas are very different places to those in the United States. Hence, the notion of the "North American City" can be of only limited value and may be potentially misleading.

TABLE 9-1
LIST OF 34 VARIABLES FOR MULTIVARIATE ANALYSIS

		Variable Acronym
R1	% Single Fam. Dwell Units in Metro Housing Stock, 1970.	SFDWEL
R2	Expressway Lane Miles Per Capita, 1979.	XLMLS
R3	Population Change 1970-75 in Balance.	POPCHNG
R4	Household Change 1970-75 in Balance.	HSECHNG
R5	% Households—Fam. w/Children at Home, Metro 1970.	FAMKIDM
R6	% Households—Fam. w/Children at Home, CC 1970.	FAMKIDC
R7	Ratio, CC Mean Income to Metro Mean Income 1970.	INCDISP
R8	% Non-White, Metro.	NONWHTM
R9	% Non-White, CC.	NONWHTC
R10	% Foreign Born, CC.	FORBRN
R11	% Manufacturing Establishments, City/Metro, 1972.	MANEST
R12	% Manufacturing Employees, City/Metro, 1972.	MANEMP
R13	% Wholesale Employees, City/Metro, 1972.	WHSLEMP
R14	% Retail Sales, City/Metro 1972.	RETSALE
R15	% Retail Establishments, City/Metro, 1972.	RETEST
R16	% Service Sales, City/Metro, 1972.	SERVSAL
R17	% Service Establishments, City/Metro, 1972.	SERVEST
R18	% Hospital Beds, City/Metro 1975.	HOSPBED
R19	Violent Crime, CC 1975.	VIOLCRIM
R20	Property Crime, CC 1975.	PROPCRIM
R21	Intergov Rev/Total Gen Rev. 1977.	TRANSFR
R22	Intergov Rev (Feds)/Intergov. Rev. 1977.	FEDTRANS
R23	Property Taxes/Total Taxes, CC 1977.	PT/TAX
R24	Property Taxes/Total Gen Rev., CC 1977.	PT/GREV
R25	Property Taxes Per Capita, CC 1977.	PT/CAP
R26	Total General Rev Per Capita, City/Bal. 1977.	REVCAP
R27	Education per Total Gen Expenditure, Metro 1977.	EDUCEXP
R28	Pub Health, Welfare/Total Gen Expenditure, CC 1977.	WELLEXP
R29	Police, Fire/Total Gen Expenditure, CC 1977.	PROTEXP
R30	Sanitation and Sewage/Total Gen Expenditure, CC 1977.	SSEXP
R31	Education per Capita, Metro 1977.	EDUCCAP
R32	Pub Welfare (Incl. Hosp and Health)/Capita, CC 1977.	WELLCAP
R33	Police and Fire Per Capita, CC 1977.	PROTCAP
R34	Total Gen Expenditure Per Capita, CC 1977.	EXPCAP

Notes: All dates are listed for U.S.A. data sources.
      CC = Central City
      R1 = Identification for a variable

Source: Authors

TABLE 9-2
LIST OF 20 VARIABLES FOR MULTIVARIATE ANALYSIS: SECOND STAGE

		Variable Acronym
R1	% Single Fam. Dwell Units in Metro Housing Stock, 1970.	SFDWEL
R2	Expressway Lane Miles Per Capita, 1979.	XLMLS
R3	Population Change 1970-75 in Balance.	POPCHNG
R4	Household Change 1970-75 in Balance.	HSECHNG
R5	% Households—Fam. w/Children at Home, Metro 1970.	FAMKIDM
R6	% Households—Fam. w/Children at Home, CC 1970.	FAMKIDC
R7	Ratio, CC Mean Income to Metro Mean Income 1970.	INCDISP
R8	% Non-White, Metro.	NONWHTM
R9	% Non-White, CC.	NONWHTC
R10	% Foreign Born, CC.	FORBRN
R13	% Wholesale Employees, City/Metro, 1972.	WHSLEMP
R15	% Retail Establishments, City/Metro, 1972.	RETEST
R17	% Service Establishments, City/Metro, 1972.	SERVEST
R19	Violent Crime, CC 1975.	VIOLCRIM
R20	Property Crime, CC 1975.	PROPCRIM
R22	Intergov Rev (Feds)/Intergov. Rev. 1977.	FEDTRANS
R23	Property Taxes/Total Taxes, CC 1977.	PT/TAX
R26	Total General Rev Per Capita, City/Bal. 1977.	REVCAP
R27	Education per Total Gen Expenditure, Metro 1977.	EDUCEXP
R33	Police and Fire Per Capita, CC 1977.	PROTCAP

Notes: All dates are listed for U.S.A. data sources.
CC = Central City
R1 = Identification for a variable

Source: Authors

TABLE 9-3
FACTOR LOADINGS

Variable	Factor 1	Factor 2	Factor 3	Factor 4
SERVEST	0.952			
RETEST	0.941			
WHSLEMP	0.868			
FAMKIDC	0.559	-0.482		
INCDISP	0.522			
NONWHTC		0.844		
NONWHTM		0.789		
FEDTRANS		0.642		
VIOLCRIM		0.543		
FAMKIDM		-0.552		
REVCAP			0.701	
PROTCAP			0.562	
FORBRN			0.541	
SFDWEL			-0.621	
EDUCEXP			-0.539	
POPCHNG			-0.539	0.820
HSECHNG				0.754

Source: Authors

MAP 9-1   SOUTHERN GROUP OF METROPOLITAN CENTERS

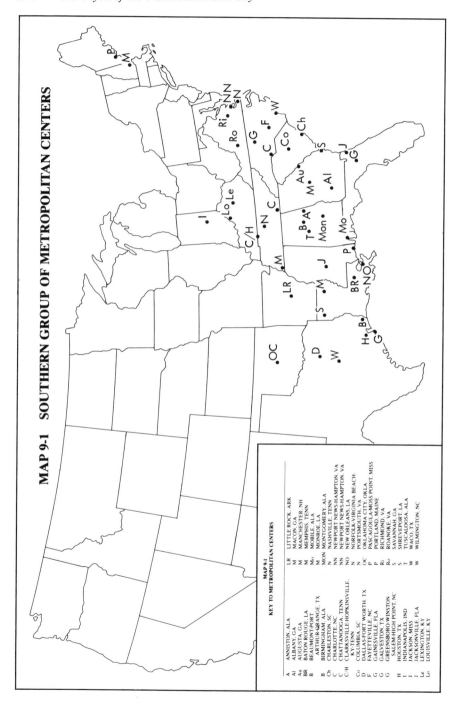

MAP 9-1
KEY TO METROPOLITAN CENTERS

A	ANNISTON, ALA	LR	LITTLE ROCK, ARK
Al	ALBANY, GA	M	MACON, GA
Au	AUGUSTA, GA	M	MANCHESTER, NH
BR	BATON ROUGE, LA	M	MEMPHIS, TENN
B	BEAUMONT-PORT	Mo	MOBILE, ALA
	ARTHUR-ORANGE, TX	M	MONROE, LA
B	BIRMINGHAM, ALA	MON	MONTGOMERY, ALA
Ch	CHARLESTON, SC	N	NASHVILLE, TENN
C	CHARLOTTE, NC	NN	NEWPORT NEWS-HAMPTON, VA
C	CHATTANOOGA, TENN	NN	NEWPORT NEWS-HAMPTON, VA
C/H	CLARKSVILLE-HOPKINSVILLE,	NO	NEW ORLEANS, LA
	KY-TENN	N	NORFOLK-VIRGINIA BEACH-
Co	COLUMBIA, SC		PORTSMOUTH, VA
D	DALLAS-FORT WORTH, TX	OC	OKLAHOMA CITY, OKLA
F	FAYETTEVILLE, NC	P	PASCAGOULA-MOSS POINT, MISS
G	GAINESVILLE, FLA	P	PORTLAND, MAINE
G	GALVESTON, TX	Ri	RICHMOND, VA
G	GREENSBORO-WINSTON-	Ro	ROANOKE, VA
	SALEM-HIGH POINT, NC	S	SAVANNAH, GA
H	HOUSTON, TX	S	SHREVEPORT, LA
I	INDIANAPOLIS, IND	T	TUSCALOOSA, ALA
J	JACKSON, MISS	W	WACO, TX
J	JACKSONVILLE, FLA	W	WILMINGTON, NC
Le	LEXINGTON, KY		
Lo	LOUISVILLE, KY		

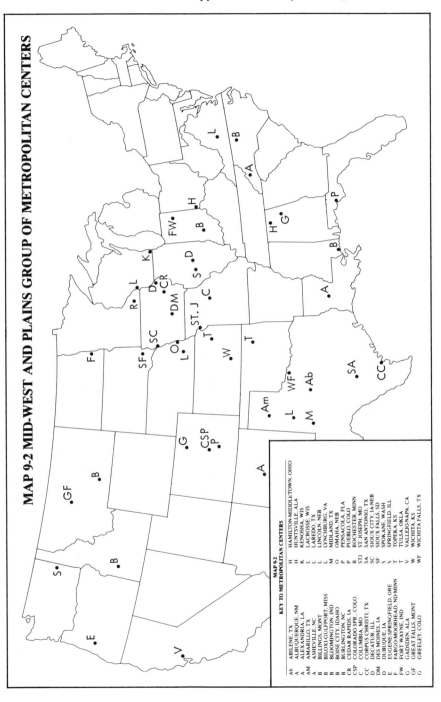

MAP 9-2 MID-WEST AND PLAINS GROUP OF METROPOLITAN CENTERS

MAP 9-2
KEY TO METROPOLITAN CENTERS

Ab	ABILENE, TX	H	HAMILTON-MIDDLETOWN, OHIO
A	ALBUQUERQUE, NM	H	HUNTSVILLE, ALA
A	ALEXANDRIA, LA	K	KENOSHA, WIS
AM	AMARILLO, TX	L	LACROSSE, WIS
A	ASHEVILLE, NC	L	LAREDO, TX
B	BILLINGS, MONT	L	LINCOLN, NEB
B	BILOXI-GULFPORT, MISS	M	LYNCHBURG, VA
B	BLOOMINGTON, IND	M	MIDLAND, TX
B	BOISE CITY, IDAHO	O	OMAHA, NEB
B	BURLINGTON, NC	P	PENSACOLA, FLA
CR	CEDAR RAPIDS, IA	P	PUEBLO, COLO
CSP	COLORADO SPR., COLO	R	ROCHESTER, MINN
C	COLUMBIA, MO	STJ	ST. JOSEPH, MO
CC	CORPUS CHRISTI, TX	SA	SAN ANTONIO, TX
D	DECATUR, ILL	SC	SIOUX CITY, IA-NEB
DM	DES MOINES, IA	S	SIOUX FALLS, SD
D	DUBUQUE, IA	S	SPOKANE, WASH
E	EUGENE-SPRINGFIELD, ORE	S	SPRINGFIELD, ILL
FW	FARGO-MOORHEAD, ND-MINN	T	TOPEKA, KS
F	FORT WAYNE, IND	T	TULSA, OKLA
G	GADSDEN, ALA	V	VALLEJO-NAPA, CA
GF	GREAT FALLS, MONT	W	WICHITA, KS
G	GREELEY, COLO	WF	WICHITA FALLS, TX

10

MAKING PLAIN THE DIFFERENCE

The Canadian is often a baffled man because he feels different from his British kindred and his American neighbours, sharply refuses to be lumped with either of them, yet cannot make plain this difference.

J.B. Priestley

Canada and the United States are distinct and distinguishable places and societies. Moreover, and in keeping with our thrust that cities are tightly integrated into the societies of which they form an important part, Canadian and American cities differ markedly and across well-defined dimensions. These are our principal conclusions. Here, we review briefly our primary findings to establish the basis for the discussion which follows in which the implications of our findings are addressed.

CONTEXTUAL DIFFERENCES

Values and Social Setting

Several striking differences became apparent from the discussion in Chapters 2 and 3:

National Character: While there are dangers in overdrawing national character traits, it is clear that Canadians and Americans exhibit quite distinct "characters," particularly in the ways in which they view themselves and the myths they hold. Again, keeping in mind that these are broad generalizations, Americans place great value on being American and see that as comprising great pride in their system of government (sometimes making American government and democratic institutions synonymous with democracy itself); valuing the individual and individual initiative and the competitiveness that goes with such values; decrying government involvement in their affairs and seeing the United States as the last bastion of free (meaning private) enterprise; and expressing and exhibiting great assuredness about the "American way" and its attendant values.

In contrast, Canadians are less doctrinaire, are seen by others and themselves as being deferential to authority, seem to value collective and government action more than individual effort, are less competitive, and generally much less sure about what exactly comprises being a Canadian. In fact, one of the few readily identifiable elements of the Canadian character was the great and ongoing search for the "Canadian identity," which has so preoccupied scholars, popular writers and indeed the "average" Canadian, whoever or whatever he or she might be.

Mosaics and Melting Pots: With such a strong sense of "Americanness," it is not surprising that the prevailing social "myth"[1] is that of the melting pot, wherein immigrant groups are expected to shed their ethnicity and adopt the ways of the dominant American culture. In Canada, with a less well-developed national identify, the prevailing social mythology is that of the mosaic, reinforced by government policy, through the Ministry of State for Multiculturalism. Given Canada's heritage with two founding nations, and in the absence of a strong sense of what constitutes "Canadianism," such a state of affairs is predictable. In some sense, the Canadian mosaic myth is also practical, since Canada has a relatively larger proportion of its population born outside Canada than does the United States. Thus, the mosaic is a pragmatic mythology to help make the demographic reality of Canada legitimate. The present absence of institutionalized racism in Canada is also in keeping with this mythology and again differentiates Canada from the United States.

Elites and Mobility: Canadians are much more tolerant of ruling elites and oligarchs than are Americans. This so-called "ascriptive" (as opposed to "merit-based") social system is a logical concomitant of the other facets of the Canadian character, for which deferential and collective behaviors were seen to be more widespread than in the United States. However, in spite of the myth of meritocracy in the United States and of ascription in Canada, both nations exhibit relatively similar degrees of geographic mobility and upward social mobility.[2] Our review of the relevant literature uncovered similarities where differences had been thought to exist, though ample evidence also supported the greater influence by, and acceptance of, bureaucratic and other elites in Canada.

Political Systems and Institutions

Despite apparent similarities deriving from the fact that both nations are English-speaking democracies, rooted in the English common law tradition (Quebec provides an essential Canadian exception to both of these statements) and federal in nature, important differences characterize the political systems and institutions in the two countries. Among the most vital discussed in Chapter 5 were:

The Revolution versus Evolution Debate: This debate points out that Canada and the United States launched their respective governments under very different circumstances: the United States through revolution; Canada through gradual evolution and devolution. Some have linked the greater deference in Canada to the more conservative "anti-revolutionaries" who helped to found English Canada, the United Empire Loyalists, an argument reviewed in Chapter 2. The debate, and its resolution, lie well beyond immediate concerns, but the fact that the debate has attracted so much attention, and the evidence garnered to support it, do support a conclusion that from the very beginnings, founding principles of government differed widely in Canada and the United States. From "life, liberty and the pursuit of happiness" in the United States to "peace, order and good government" in Canada, two very different political systems were to emerge.

The Parliamentary and Congressional Systems: American government is established on a careful system of checks and balances between the legislature (the Congress), the executive (the president and all of the departments of government that carry out legislated mandates) and the judiciary. Rising above all is the U.S. Constitution, the sole arbiter of the balance point. In Canada, even given the new Canadian Charter of Rights and Freedoms, it is still not clear that this charter has the ability to severely restrict parliamentary action, because, under the parliamentary system, parliament is supreme and its laws constitute "the supreme law" of the land. In any event, parliaments in Canada have much more power under this system than do Congress and the state legislatures.

This greater power is reinforced by another British tradition in Canada, that of party discipline, whereby members of a given political party, either at the federal or provincial level, are obligated to vote the way their party leaders and caucuses decide that they are to vote. This means that a party with a clear-cut majority can pass legislation with little difficulty if it merely follows established parliamentary procedures. The indecisiveness of Congress and state legislatures is well documented in contrast, stemming in part from the lack of strong party discipline. In short, the machinery for making and changing laws differs greatly between Canada and the United States at both the federal and state/provincial levels.

Federalism and Regionalism: On the surface, it is here, in the nature of the federal system, that there should be great similarities, since both countries have enormous land masses and are relatively less densely populated than other major regions. Both countries developed roughly from east to west, so there should be similar regional variations on a north-south axis across the U.S.-Canadian border. In the event, things worked out quite differently. Whereas, initially, the U.S. confederation was envisioned as comprising a weak central government and strong state governments with vital states' rights, over the past two centuries the U.S. federal system has come to be dominated by the central federal government with a more limited scope for independent action by the states. In Canada, the reverse has occurred. Initially conceived of as a federation with a very strong central government and clearly subservient provinces, a series of court decisions and the provincial control of education, resources and cities have put provinces collectively on essentially an equal footing with the government of Canada. Federal-provincial conferences abound to settle issues that could be solved almost by fiat in the United States by the federal government. This has brought a contentiousness and excitement to areas of federal-provincial overlap, cities being one of the more important issues. The sum and substance of the foregoing is quite simple: federalism in Canada is highly differentiated from that in the United States, and the role of cities is particularly different, with little in the way of direct Canadian federal presence in cities and urban affairs, a marked distinction from the American situation. In this regard it is worth remembering the observation by K.C. Wheare, a leading scholar on federalism, that U.S. federalism is unique and should not be seen in any sense as a general model.[3]

Economic Systems and Institutions

The themes of collectivism and acceptance of government involvement in economic matters, which are given differing emphasis in the two economies, result in distinctly different economic systems despite the overall similarities provided by being advanced capitalist societies. Both countries are typified by large service sectors and declining manufacturing activity in relative terms. The more prominent differences from Chapter 4 included:

Public versus Private Enterprise: Perhaps the one notion that captures best the distinctions in the two economies, and the notion that carries through our earlier explorations of values, is that of Canadian public enterprise. In contrast with the United States, the Canadian genius is not for private and individual enterprise, but rather for public enterprises such as the crown and mixed public/private entities that abound in Canada. These ventures are all expressions of the Canadian willingness to have government participate directly in the marketplace through the use of publicly owned companies and not just through regulation of the private sector. American-style free enterprise, based as it is on individual private action, is less highly prized in Canada than it is in the United States.

Structural Differences: The Canadian and American economies have very different industrial structures. Canada is really more like a developing nation than an advanced one, since it is so dependent upon the export of raw or semi-finished natural resources. This to a degree has grown out of the Canadian colonial heritage, in which it was seen by eighteenth-and nineteenth-century Britain as being a supplier of inputs to manufacturing, but not a competitor, either domestically within Canada or on world markets with the United Kingdom. Elements of the colonial economy and its class structure remain remarkably visible to this date in Canada, whereas the United States is much more the model of the technologically advanced manufacturing and service based economy considered typical of an advanced capitalist society. Another essential difference in economic structure stems from the extent to which Canada must engage in international trade for its livelihood. The Canadian economy engages in considerably more export and import activity and is called therefore an "open economy," since it is open to outside trade. Trade constitutes almost one-third of Canadian gross national product compared with less than one-tenth of gross national product in the United States.

Scale: The American economic system has more than ten times the output of the Canadian system. Such a scale difference also implies significant differences in product mix, markets and technological sophistication, some of which are evident in the enormous structural differences cited above. Scale also implies a necessary asymmetry in trade relations. For example, while it is common knowledge that Canadian trade with the United States dwarfs all other Canadian foreign trade links, it is not appreciated that U.S. purchases from and sales to Canada similarly constitute the largest trade ties that the United States maintains. This in part stems from the fact that these links represent major components of Canadian economic well-being, whereas they represent important but far less noticeable elements in American economic health.

Branch Plants and Foreign Ownership: As a result of historical forces and a number of ill-conceived Canadian policies, a disproportionate part of the Canadian economy is owned by foreigners, most notably by American firms. As we saw, major shares of manufacturing, energy and mining in Canada are owned by American multinational corporations. This greatly limits Canadian policy options, as recent dilemmas over keeping pace with U.S. interest rates so clearly demonstrate. An analogous situation in the United States would be intolerable; Americans have recently balked at major acquisitions in the United States by foreign firms, despite the fact that only 1 per cent of all assets in the United States are foreign owned compared with roughly 25 per cent in Canada. Branch plants also limit scope for Canadian manufacturing, since most research and development and advanced services such as marketing and finance are often carried on outside Canada, depriving Canada of expertise in these fields and of the future benefits that can flow from such indigenous knowledge.

Savings Behavior: Since the early 1970s, Canadians have been saving at a rate twice as great as Americans. This has had major consequences for urban development, since it has provided an enormous pool of mortgage funds. It has also provided needed capital for capital-intensive resource development and retooling of aging and outmoded manufacturing. The United States has not had the benefit of these domestic savings pools and has used foreign borrowings and encouraged direct foreign investment over the past decade, approaches that would have been difficult to fathom two decades ago. Very different financial institutions exist to provide savers with outlets for surplus funds. Canada has a national banking system with the five largest banks having thousands of branches in all provinces. The U.S. banking system is still largely state-based, comprised of some of the largest banks in the world, but also of thousands of small local and state banks. The Canadian financial system is consistent with earlier discussions on elitism and centralization, while U.S. banks are consistent with populist notions relating to fears about big city bankers and the power of centralized institutions.

URBAN DIFFERENCES

Our empirical examination of a broad range of urban variables in Canada and the United States turned up many significant differences. The comparisons began by looking at one variable at a time, comparing measures for these variables among Canadian and American cities, and then proceeded to the more complex, but equally revealing, simultaneous comparison of many factors at once. The major findings in Chapters 7, 8 and 9 were:

Single-Variable Comparisons

Urban form: Selected variables pointed in the direction of a Canadian urban form that is considerably denser and more compact than its American counterpart. Evidence from the analysis of population density gradients, and the proportion of single- and multiple-family units in the housing stock, led to this result.

Transportation and Travel: In keeping with a denser and more compact urban form, there is evidence of important differences in the supply of urban transportation and also a different mix of travel behaviors. First, it was shown that there are more than four times as many lanes of freeway available to the average American metropolitan resident compared with the analogous Canadian. Second, Americans own and operate 50 per cent more automobiles. Third, patronage of public transit facilities is, on a per capita base, two-and-a-half times higher in Canada's urban regions than it is in the United States. Consistent with these findings, Americans are much more likely to rely on the private automobile to commute to work than are urban Canadians, and Americans travel nearly 25 per cent farther to work as a result, reinforcing our prior judgment that American urban areas are more spread out. The physical accommodation of the extensive U.S. urban freeway system also is a contributory factor.

Urban Populations: It is necessary to avoid broad generalizations about the urban dwellers of the continent. Canadian cities have much higher proportions of foreign-born residents than do those in the United States, but on the other hand the American city has considerably higher proportions of non-whites. As well, Canadian central cities have income characteristics that differ in minor ways from those of their surrounding suburbs, but American central cities exhibit incomes that are considerably lower than those of their own suburban areas. Canadian cities also seem to be home to "traditional" families to a greater extent than is true in the United States. More generally, it seems that Canadian urban areas (both central cities and suburbs) have higher proportions of the traditional families with husband, wife and children living together. In short, it cannot be said that the Canadian central city has experienced the flight of middle-income families to the suburbs to the extent that American cities have.

Urban Growth and Decline: Evidence again points to much greater stability in the Canadian central city and metropolitan area. Unlike those in the United States, Canadian central cities have on average been growing over the past decade. There have been no massive population losses to parallel those documented for such U.S. cities as St. Louis and Detroit. While keeping their households, population and employment bases, Canadian cities have also continued to attract and maintain high-quality shopping and services for residents and workers alike.

Urban Safety: The general perception that cities are unsafe and that urban dwellers are prey for muggers and molesters is much more supportable in the United States than it is in Canada. However, even for American urban regions care must be taken not to overgeneralize because violent crime rates vary enormously, with many American central cities being as safe as those in Canada. However, when generalizing from one set of urban areas to the other, it is fair to note that violent crimes per capita are substantially higher in the United States (by almost six times in the case of central cities) and that on average the perception of the American city being markedly less safe than the Canadian city is a reliable one.

Urban Government: There are two sets of findings that serve to clearly differentiate Canadian local governments from those in the United States. First, despite American distrust of government, there are many more governments in the United States on a per capita base than in Canada. This fragmentation of local government function, in a paradoxical way, is an expression of the American value of individualism. Given the proliferation of special-purpose districts, it is not surprising that American urban regions are difficult to govern and to finance. In contrast, in Canada there has been a much greater tendency to regionalize urban functions and to centralize them in urban mini-federations, such as Metro Toronto. The relative health of Canadian and American central cities is related to this fragmentation and balkanization in the United States; Canadian cities are significantly healthier from a fiscal perspective. While neither Canadian nor American central cities at this time are financially self-sufficient, Canadian cities come closer to the mark. The deficiency is made up overwhelmingly by the provinces, in contrast to the U.S., where deficiencies are beihg made up by the states and, more importantly, the federal government together, leaving cities more dependent on federal funds and their vicissitudes than is the case in Canada where direct federal urban aid is essentially non-existent.

Multidimensional Simultaneous Comparisons

When taking and statistically combining a number of dimensions, Canadian cities are distinctly different from American cities. One approach successfully groups Canadian cities among themselves and American cities among themselves, with only a few misgrouped cities. This leads to a conclusion that Canadian cities form a distinctly different group from American cities. A second procedure allowed the development of a statistically based equation that could almost perfectly discriminate between Canadian and American cities by looking at numerous dimensions of comparison for each of more than three hundred cities.

As a whole, these multidimensional analyses provide the strongest evidence yet that Canadian cities and their suburbs are distinctly different from their American equivalents. They complement and extend the single-variable comparisons. Taking all this together leads to a confident conclusion about the distinctiveness of Canadian cities, and about the limits of the concept of the North American city.

Of course, the concept of the North American city has descriptive and explanatory value at the scale of broad and global comparisons. It rightly sets cities in North America apart from those in other broad world regions. But the great danger is that urban researchers too readily slide into continentalist thinking, which generally means that Canadian cities are taken for granted and their similarities with American cities assigned paramountcy. What we assert is that in attempting to understand cities within the North American continental setting, the national context matters a great deal. What we have shown is that important and persistent urban differences exist. They arise in the final analysis from the complex interactions between the geographically uneven resource bases, different social histories, contrasting developments of political institutions and intergovernmental relations and the particular configurations and the interrelationships of the respective economic orders. Above all, there exists a differing constellation of beliefs and values that clearly show that two peoples inhabit the continent, living in very different kinds of cities. Urban places that are made in the U.S. are different in numerous significant respects from those made in Canada. To that extent, there is an important qualitative cross-national difference in the daily lives of millions of people in North America.

IMPLICATIONS

Two major implications follow directly from these conclusions. In turn, from these flow a range of closely related subsidiary points that need to be kept in mind in future urban research and policymaking.

First, this work suggests that it is possible to generalize about the "North American City" only in a limited manner. The documented distinctions separating Canadian from American cities should provide the basis for skepticism about such loosely structured continentalist notions. They should also force considerably greater and more general skepticism and reappraisal about the continentalist approach to a host of other issues in Canada and the United States. The work implies, moreover, that it is not particularly useful to speak in broad terms either about "the American City" or "the Canadian City." There is such rich variation in both city sets to suggest that, while generalization might be possible with respect to certain dimensions, one must be extremely cautious about making sweeping statements concerning either city set, let alone both sets together. Overgeneralization is too common in urban studies and, more generally, the social sciences.

The second implication derives from the first. In essence, it is meaningless, and in the extreme dangerous and misleading, to talk about cities abstracted from their specific cultural contexts, since cities are both products and shapers of these contexts. Consequently, two major schools of urban scholarship need to rethink carefully their approaches, assumptions, methods and conclusions. It was noted at the outset of this study that both structural Marxists and, at the opposite pole, the neo-classical urban economists seek to explain cities almost entirely in economic or materialist terms. Quite obviously, these explanations differ in the extreme, yet paradoxically both are strongly united in their common view that economic forces hold the key to a proper understanding of urban dynamics, urban issues and by extension urban policy making. Neither group sees the city as being an integral element in a wider cultural reality, a place in which culture is transformed and yet itself is a dynamic product of culture. Somehow cities are seen as having an existence and *raison d'être* that is explainable without reference to the broader cultural context. Since many of the observed differences between Canadian and American cities have in this study been traced back to deeply rooted cultural differences between the two societies, the foundations upon which these divergent, but essentially economic-based, views of urban development processes rest are considerably weakened. Just as the practicing "continentalist" must go back to the drawing board to rethink that concept, so must the structural Marxist and neo-classical urban economist return to his or her own starting point to develop more appropriate conceptions that explicitly account for the importance of the cultural context for the city, and for urban change and continuities. Instead of assuming away institutional and cultural detail, as their reductionist methods have forced them to do through naive simplifications in the past, practitioners of these schools of urban scholarship will need in the future to place much greater stress on cultural matters.

Thus, we challenge those students of urban phenomena who in the past were all too prone to oversimplify and overgeneralize in their quest for powerful, universally applicable propositions about city form, its growth and its inhabitants. Our work implies that progress in the years to come is much more likely to derive from rather different research styles and strategies. This would compel the future urban researcher/analyst to:

i. be more sensitive to local specifics and contexts (micro details);

ii. be more sensitive to broader societal issues and contexts in order to be able to place the specific urban setting in its appropriate cultural milieu (macro details);

iii. spend as much effort on synthesizing these micro/macro views as has been spent in the past on rigorous analysis of either micro or macro phenomena; to be a good synthesizer implies further that the urban analyst have strong command of both the micro and macro processes and institutions that together shape the city and its context in turn;

iv. be more alert to differences and be less preoccupied with finding often superficial and illusory generalities;

v. take increasingly a comparative perspective where differences and similarities are accorded equal weight and where the recent obsession of social scientists with derivation of general rules, theories and empirical findings will of necessity be dampened by the reality imposed by the comparative approach, wherein assumed similarities often give way on closer analysis to deeper-seated and frequently fundamental differences in urban structure and urban function, differences that in the end obviate meaningful generalization and force the analyst to appreciate the specifics of the urban setting under study.

None of this is to suggest that the task is likely to be an easy one, or necessarily an achievable one, since we are essentially asking urban scholars to be both generalists with respect to broad cultural contexts within which cities develop yet also specialists about specific cities and about specific urban issues or phenomena. Having simultaneous working knowledge of the whole panoply of fields that relate to the cultural context of cities is not a readily accomplished feat. Yet, urban scholars should go well beyond this knowledge as they continue to study specific urban problems and questions. Only through a simultaneous command of the different levels of analysis and their interrelation will it be possible to develop the kind of synthetic, contextually based knowledge about cities that holds the key to opening up new perspectives concerning the origin, functioning and development of cities in Canada, the United States and elsewhere.

At the level of the urban, we hope this book will stimulate further comparative research on cities in North America. As the foregoing remarks imply, a variety of research designs will be needed, including cross-national attitude surveys specifically oriented to urban issues and the city-forming processes; comparative case studies of small sets of cities in both countries by locally based researchers following a common method; and continued research at the macro scale drawing on census and other secondary sources. The complex nature of cities and city systems will not be revealed by one or two researchers pursuing any one strategy but rather will require simultaneous efforts across a wide range of approaches. Also critically necessary is the connection of this urban level research with wider scale socio-economic and political processes that transcend the urban.

Just as we are urging considerably greater responsibility on urban scholars, we are also, and at the same time, urging them to be much more skeptical than they have been in the past about the utility and generality of findings that are based on implicit and often fanciful assumptions about the similarities of the systems they are studying. In our quest for powerful and "scientific" generalizations and theories, we have too frequently assumed away the important differences that in fact characterize the urban systems and urban phenomena that fall under our analytic gaze. The "North American City" was one such generalization that we have shown to be of limited operational utility, precisely because of its failure to comprehend the depth and the importance of differences, focusing instead as it did on similarities. The dangers of using superficial overgeneralizations have also been discussed previously with respect to careless borrowing of policies from one "North

American" urban environment, the United States, to another, Canada. It would be equally fruitless were American urban policymakers to come to Canada to borrow from some of its more successful urban achievements, such as rapid transit, the fruitlessness of the exercise deriving from the fundamental differences that exist with respect to urban form and travel behavior. By extension, policymakers in developing countries need to develop their own policies and research bases which reflect the local and differing contexts of Third World cities. Applying prescriptions grounded in essentially American urban theory and empirical knowledge is dangerous and inappropriate.

While simplifying the world has been, and continues to be, a valid goal for certain styles of inquiry, such simplification must be done in an appropriate manner. When and where a variety of specific circumstances and broad cultural contexts make such simplification unwise or untenable, research workers should not assume this annoying richness away. Rather they should become better acquainted with it so that more meaningful and powerful results can be derived, all be they less general than current fashion in the social sciences would have hoped for. These and related assertions are contrary to the thrust of a powerful intellectual tradition wherein regularities, generalizations and law-like statements are sought by social scientists. Our view and the results of our studies direct us towards a mode of research that is more culturally (and therefore historically) informed, with greater emphasis on interpretation and understanding than on the discovery of regularities and generalization.[4]

To theorize about the city in cultural context is to treat it as the product of both dominant and subordinate cultures and, simultaneously, to recognize cities as the loci for the production or remaking of these cultures. By situating cities in the context of their societies, we are able to observe how the cultural motifs of a society are embedded in the form of its cities and in the daily lives of their inhabitants. We can also think of the city as a socioeconomic and political element in the total organization of a society. It is worth recalling that, until this century, only a minority of the world's population knew city life. Not until the mid-nineteenth century did the urban residents of a region, England, first exceed the rural folk. Massive and unprecedented urbanization later in that century meant concomitant changes in the social organization of culture. The urban places produced under the new urbanization in turn represented and conveyed to their residents and migrants the new culture.

Thinking about and studying Canadian and American cities explicitly within their cultural context adds, we believe, to the understanding of the nature of these fascinating urban places. It is a challenging and exciting venture, which will require the command of a range of research methods and skills. The reward is not only increased knowledge of the cities of North America but a fresh perspective on the Canadian and American cultural contexts themselves. Never again should they be seen without a proper regard for the urban experience and the ways in which cities help shape and structure the national context. The linkages and interactions must be thought of and studied in their entirety, thereby closing a circle that has for too long remained open.

Notes

NOTES TO CHAPTER 1

1. Walter Stewart, *As They See Us* (Toronto: McClelland and Stewart, 1977).
2. For examples of the North American city viewed through an American lens in recent urban research see: Maurice Yeates and Barry Garner, *The North American City* (New York: Harper and Row, 1976); Brian J.L. Berry, "Urbanization and Counterurbanization," *Urban Affairs Annual Review*, Volume 11 (Beverly Hills: Sage Publications, 1976); Brian J.L. Berry, *Comparative Urbanization: Divergent Paths in the Twentieth Century* (New York: St. Martin's Press, 1981); and Maurice Yeates, *North American Urban Patterns* (New York: Wiley, 1980). For a review of a range of continentalist writing in urban geography, see John Mercer, "On Continentalism, Distinctiveness and Comparative Urban Geography," *Canadian Geographer* 23 (1979): 119-39.
3. Larry S. Bourne, ed., *Internal Structure of the City*, 2d ed. (New York: Oxford University Press, 1982), Introduction, 3-27; Ronald J. Johnston, *The American Urban System* (New York: St. Martin's Press, 1982).
4. Risa Palm, *The Geography of American Cities* (New York: Oxford University Press, 1981), 8-9.
5. Risa Palm, "Urban Geography: City Structures," *Progress in Human Geography* 6 (1982), 90.
6. A potent critique of this phase of Canadian urban renewal and housing policy is provided in Michael Dennis and Susan Fish, *Programs in Search of a Policy* (Toronto: Hakkert, 1972). An interesting contrast with the U.S. is provided by the extent to which private capital was involved in large-scale urban renewal in Canada in the absence of government policies and programs. For details, see Robert Collier, *Contemporary Cathedrals* (Montreal: Harvest House, 1975).
7. The details of the data and the methods used to analyze it are discussed in Chapter 7.

8. Michael A. Goldberg and John Mercer, "Canadian and U.S. Cities: Basic Differences, Possible Explanations, and the Meaning for Public Policy," *Papers of the Regional Science Association* 45(1980):159.
9. Jeffrey Simpson, *Discipline of Power: The Conservative Interlude and the Liberal Restoration* (Toronto: Macmillan, 1984), 61.
10. Population growth beyond metropolitan areas which forms the core of Berry's counterurbanization argument (see Berry, *Comparative Urbanization*) is less apparent in Canada and in fact there is evidence that there is not a major movement in Canada away from metropolitan areas on the scale of the phenomenon in the United States. See, for example, work by: Ira M. Robinson, *Canadian Urban Growth Trends* (Vancouver: University of British Columbia Press, 1981); Len Gertler, "The Changing Metropolis and the Blumenfeld Blues," in Larry S. Bourne and John Hitchcock, eds., *The Metropolis: Proceedings of a Conference in Honour of Hans Blumenfeld* (Toronto: University of Toronto Press, 1985); James Simmons and Larry S. Bourne, *Recent Trends and Patterns in Canadian Settlement, 1976-1981* (Major Report No. 23, Centre for Urban and Community Studies, University of Toronto, 1984); and Gerald D. Hodge and Mohammed A. Qadeer, *Towns and Villages in Canada* (Toronto: Butterworth, 1983).
11. M. Bloch, "Toward a Comparative History of European Societies," in Frederic C. Lane, ed., *Enterprise and Secular Change: Readings in Economic History* (Homewood, IL: R.D. Irwin, 1953), 507.
12. See Donald Kerr, "Review of George A. Nader, *Cities of Canada, Vols. I and II*," *Annals of Association of American Geographers* 61, no. 1 (1977), 165.
13. For a critical review of the modest literature prior to 1979, see Mercer, "On Continentalism." Among the more notable cross-national works are William Bunge and Ronald R. Bordessa, *The Canadian Alternative: Survival, Expeditions, and*

Urban Change, York Geographical Monographs, no. 2, (Toronto: York University, 1975); D. Michael Ray and Robert A Murdie, "Canadian and American Urban Differences," in Brian J.L. Berry, ed., *City Classification Handbook: Methods and Applications* (New York: Wiley, 1972), 181-210.

14. Our interest in establishing the distinctiveness of Canadian cities goes back into the mid-1970s and spans a number of academic and professional papers over the past decade including: Michael A. Goldberg and Michael Y. Seelig, "Canadian Cities: The Right Deed for the Wrong Reason," *Planning* 41, no. 3(1975):8-13; Mercer, "On Continentalism"; Michael A. Goldberg, "Housing and Land Prices in Canada and the U.S.," in Michael Walker and Lawrence B. Smith, eds., *Public Property?: The Habitat Debate Continued* (Vancouver: Fraser Institute, 1977), 207-54; Goldberg and Mercer, "Canadian and U.S. Cities"; John Mercer and Michael A. Goldberg, "The Fiscal Condition of Canadian and American Cities," *Urban Studies* 21(1984): 233-43; John Mercer and Michael A. Goldberg, "Value Differences and their Meaning for Urban Development in Canada and the United States," in Gilbert A. Stelter and Alan F.J. Artibise, eds., *Power and Place: Canadian Urban Development in the North American Context* (Vancouver: University of British Columbia Press, 1985); and Barry Edmonston, Michael A. Goldberg and John Mercer, "Urban Form in Canada and the United States: An Examination of Urban Density Gradients," *Urban Studies* 22(1985): 209-17.

15. For a structural Marxist interpretation, see Michael Dear and Allan J. Scott, eds., *Urbanization and Urban Planning in Capitalist Society* (New York: Methuen, 1981); and David Harvey, "The Political Economy of Urbanization in Advanced Capitalist Societies," in G. Gappert and H. Rose, eds., *The Social Economy of Cities* (Beverly Hills: Sage Publications, 1975).

16. G. Clark and M. Dear, *State Apparatus: Structures and Language of Legitimacy* (Winchester, MA: Allen and Unwin, 1984).

17. See Raymond Williams, "Base and Superstructure in Marxist Cultural Theory," *New Left Review*, 82(1973):3-16.

18. Reviewing the recent literature in urban economics, a non-economist reader would be struck by the absence of cultural and non-economic context, as demonstrated by a perusal of leading journals such as the *Journal of Urban Economics* and the *Journal of Regional Science* (to name but two), and such scholarly books as: E.S. Mills, *Studies in the Structure of the Urban Economy* (Baltimore: Johns Hopkins University Press, 1972), and two books by Harry Richardson, *The New Urban Economics and Alternatives* (London: Pion, 1977), and *Urban Economics* (Hinsdale, IL: Dryden Press, 1978).

19. Ian Masser, "Some Methodological Considerations," in Philip Booth, ed., "Design and Implementation of Cross-National Research Projects," TRP #44, (Sheffield, England: Department of Town and Regional Planning, University of Sheffield, 1983), 14.

20. Masser has provided a fuller discussion of issues in conducting cross-national research studies. See Ian Masser, "Comparative Planning Studies: A Critical Review," TRP #33, (Sheffield, England: Department of Town and Regional Planning, University of Sheffield, 1981).

21. Michael Harloe, "Notes on Comparative Urban Research," in Dear and Scott, *Urbanization and Urban Planning*, 179.

22. Ibid.

23. John Walton, "Comparative Urban Studies," *International Journal of Comparative Sociology* 22 (1981):34.

24. Brian T. Robson, *Urban Social Areas* (London: Oxford University Press, 1981).

25. See Mercer, "On Continentalism"; Goldberg and Mercer, "Canadian and U.S. Cities"; and Mercer and Goldberg, "Value Differences," 1985. A complete presentation of Berry's view is found in Berry, *Comparative Urbanization*, 167.

26. Berry, *Comparative Urbanization*, 166.

27. For extensive discussions of the distinctiveness of the Canadian economic system and its elite structure, see Wallace Clement, *Continental Corporate Power* (Toronto: McClelland and Stewart, 1977).

28. Harloe, "Notes".

29. For example, a recent study by Alperovich addresses a durable theme in urban studies: the distribution of cities in different countries according to urban population size. A relatively simple relationship has been imputed between the size of an urban center and its numerical rank (in terms of its

size) of all cities within its country. The relationship observed for the U.S. case has been sought in other national settings. Alperovich's findings, however, suggest that the U.S. is unique in its distribution of urban places according to their size. Additionally, Canada stands out not only as very different from the U.S., but also from all other countries treated by Alperovich. This new work strengthens our argument that cities must be treated in national context and generalization beyond this context is perilous. For details, see Gershon Alperovich, "A New Testing Procedure of the Rank Size Distribution" (Ramat-Gan, Israel: Department of Economics, Bar Ilan University, 1984), mimeographed.

NOTES TO CHAPTER 2

1. The nature and possible consequences of changing values are explored cross-nationally by Inglehart. Unfortunately, Canada was not included in the surveys although the U.S. was. Ronald Inglehart, *The Silent Revolution: Changing Values and Political Styles Among Western Publics* (Princeton: Princeton University Press, 1977).
2. One example would be the embodiment of the values of the "founding fathers" in the U.S. Constitution and the impact of that document on subsequent value systems and behavior. For keen insight into this relationship, see Geoffrey Vickers, *Value Systems and Social Process* (London: Tavistock, 1968).
3. Sociologists have written extensively on the relationships between collective ideas and values and the surface features of social reality. Gurvitch is one influential writer in this vein. Georges Gurvitch, *Essais de Sociologie* (Paris: Recueil Sirey, 1938); Phillip Bosserman, *Dialectical Sociology: An Analysis of the Sociology of Georges Gurvitch* (Boston: Porter Sargent, 1968).
4. These and other data in this paragraph are based on national surveys. For details, see Lawrence LeDuc and J. Alex Murray, "Public Opinion and North American Integration: Pragmatic Nationalism," in Jon Pammett and Brian Tomlin, eds., *The Integration Question: Political Economy and Public Policy in Canada and North America* (Toronto: Addison-Wesley, 1984).
5. Even for a small country like Canada there

is a large literature that bears on this continuity. For the U.S., the literature on the topic is vast. Scholars such as Hartz and Lipset are important figures for both countries. Some basic works are: Louis Hartz, *The Liberal Tradition in America* (New York: Harcourt Brace, 1953); Louis Hartz et al., *The Founding of New Societies* (New York: Harcourt Brace, 1964); Seymour M. Lipset, *The First New Nation* (New York: Basic Books, 1963) and Seymour M. Lipset, *Revolution and Counterrevolution* (New York: Anchor Books, 1970). Here we simply acknowledge two works of this genre that we found especially helpful: Michael Kammen, *People of Paradox: An Inquiry Concerning the Origins of American Civilization* (New York: Oxford University Press, 1980); David Bell and Lorne Tepperman, *The Roots of Disunity: A Look at Canadian Political Culture* (Toronto: McClelland and Stewart, 1979).
6. For examples see, Alex Inkeles, "Continuity and Change in the American National Character," in Seymour M. Lipset, ed., *The Third Century: America as a Post-Industrial Society* (Chicago: University of Chicago Press, 1979), 389-416; John Porter, "Canadian Character in the Twentieth Century," in W.E. Mann, ed., *Canada: A Sociological Profile* (Toronto: Copp Clark, 1971). Also see John Meisel, "Who are We? Perceptions in English Canada," *Proceedings of the Conference on the Future of the Canadian Confederation* (Toronto: University of Toronto, 1977). It is particularly interesting to observe how Canadian ambivalence about identity and the elements of national character spill over into self-images of ethnic groups. For two compelling examples, see Saul Hayes, "Some Differences between Canadian and U.S. Jewry," *Viewpoints* 1 (1966):3-10, and Ben Lappin, "Canadian Jewry and the Identity Crisis," *Viewpoints* 2 (1967):9-14.
7. Seymour M. Lipset, "The Value Patterns of Democracy: A Case Study in Comparative Analysis," *American Sociological Review* 28 (1963):515-31.
8. This has been a key theme in the influential writings of the Canadian historian William Morton. See, for example, William L. Morton, *The Canadian Identity* (Madison: University of Wisconsin Press, 1961); William L. Morton, *The Kingdom*

of Canada (Toronto: McClelland and Stewart, 1969).

9. Bell and Tepperman, *Roots of Disunity*, Chapter 3, 72-107, analyze the loyalist issue at some length and draw some conclusions that are at odds with much of the literature concerning the tradition of deference in Canadian society, and with Lipset's view in particular. Also see David V.J. Bell, "The Loyalist Tradition in Canada," *Journal of Canadian Studies* 5 (1970): 22-33.

10. Allan Smith, "National Images and National Maintenance: The Ascendancy of the Ethnic Idea in North America," *Canadian Journal of Political Science* 14 (1981):227-57.

11. Acadians, francophones living in the Maritime provinces, maintain a sense of separateness from the Quebecois.

12. Kenneth McRoberts and Dale Postgate, *Quebec: Social Change and Political Crisis* (Toronto: McClelland and Stewart, 1980); Susan Mann Trofimenkoff, *The Dream of Nation: A Social and Intellectual History of Quebec* (Toronto: Macmillan, 1983).

13. Edgar Z. Friedenberg, *Deference to Authority: The Case of Canada* (White Plains, NY: M.E. Sharpe, 1980); Edward Highbee, "Centre Cities in Canada and the United States," in J.W. Watson and T. O'Riordan, *The American Environment: Perceptions and Policies* (New York: Wiley, 1976), 145-60; Morton, *Canadian Identity*.

14. For an interesting cross-national comparison which emphasizes legal differences between Canada and the United States, see W.V. Monopoli, "Equality before the Law," in Robert Presthus, ed., *Cross-National Perspectives: United States and Canada* (Leiden: E.J. Brill, 1977).

15. Alan Gowans, "A Comparison of Authority Symbols in United States and Canadian Urban Architecture, 1800-1900," keynote address to Canadian-American Urban Development Conference, University of Guelph, Ontario, August 1982. For useful background on the American and Canadian built environment, see Alan Gowans, *Images of American Living: Four Centuries of Architecture and Furniture as Cultural Expression* (Philadelphia: Lippincott, 1964); Alan Gowans, *Building Canada: An Architectural History of Canadian Life* (Toronto: Oxford University Press, 1966).

16. Andrew Malcolm, "Squeaky-Clean Toronto Nails Every Scrap of Litter," *New York Times*, 28 October 1980. Even cleanliness is taken to be an indicator of "national character," according to media-styled experts.

17. The idea that there is a valued tradition of "toryism" in Canada has been explored in diverse ways. Bell and Tepperman, *Roots of Disunity*, Charles Taylor, *Radical Tories: The Conservative Tradition in Canada* (Toronto: Anansi, 1982); Tom Truman, "A Scale for Measuring a Tory Streak in Canada and the United States," *Canadian Journal of Political Science* 10 (1977), 597-614.

18. James S. and Nancy G. Duncan, "A Cultural Analysis of Urban Residential Landscapes in North America: The Case of the Anglophone Elite," in John A. Agnew, John Mercer and David E. Sopher, eds., *The City in Cultural Context* (Boston: Allen and Unwin, 1984), 255-76.

19. Samuel D. Clark, "Canada and Her Great Neighbour," in S.D. Clark, *The Developing Canadian Community*, 2d ed. (Toronto: University of Toronto Press, 1968), 227.

20. The past thinking of Canadians about government (or the state) is ably reviewed by Whitaker. Reg Whitaker, "Images of the state in Canada," in Leo Panitch, ed., *The Canadian State: Political Economy and Political Power* (Toronto: University of Toronto Press, 1977), 28-68.

21. A powerful statement of the survival thesis in Canadian letters is that of Margaret Atwood. Atwood also conveys her clear sense that Canada both culturally and as a place is different from America. Margaret Atwood, *Survival: A Thematic Guide to Canadian Literature* (Toronto: Anansi, 1972); see also August J. Fry, *On the Battle of Stoney Creek and other Allegories* (Amsterdam: Free University of Amsterdam, 1982) for other comments on differences in American and Canadian literature.

22. Leslie Armour, *The Idea of Canada and the Crisis of Community* (Ottawa: Steel Rail, 1981).

23. Ibid., xiii.

24. What is sometimes overlooked, however, is that the federal government played a positive role in fostering stronger provincial administrations.

25. The strength of regional identity in Can-

ada and its political consequences have been investigated by numerous scholars from different disciplines. David J. Elkins and Richard Simeon, *Small Worlds: Provinces and Parties in Canadian Political Life* (Toronto: Methuen, 1980); David B. Knight, "Canada in Crisis: The Power of Regionalisms," in D.G. Bennett, ed., *Tension Areas of the World* (Champaign, IL: Park Press, 1982); Mildred A. Schwartz, *Politics and Territory: The Sociology of Regional Persistence in Canada* (Montreal: McGill-Queen's University Press, 1974); Mason Wade, ed., *Regionalism and the Canadian Community, 1867-1967* (Toronto: University of Toronto Press, 1969).

26. George Woodcock has written on regionalism and identity in Canada in a perceptive and very readable manner. George Woodcock, *The Canadians* (Cambridge: Harvard University Press, 1979).

27. Pierre Elliott Trudeau, *Federalism and the French Canadians* (Toronto: University of Toronto Press, 1968).

28. Daniel J. Elazar and Joseph Zikmund, eds., *The Ecology of American Political Culture* (New York: T. Corwell, 1975).

29. For examples of generally approving positions, see Samuel D. Clark, "Canada and the American Value System," in S.D. Clark, *The Developing Canadian Community* (Toronto: University of Toronto Press, 1968); Frank G. Vallee and D.R. Whyte, "Canadian Society: Trends and Perspectives," in B. Blishen et al., *Canadian Society: Sociological Perspectives* (Toronto: Gage, 1968). Criticism from Canadian and to a lesser extent American scholars has been considerable; nevertheless Lipset's characterizations are widely recycled. Some trenchant examples are Bell and Tepperman, *Roots of Disunity*; Gad Horowitz, "Notes on Conservatism, Liberalism and Socialism in Canada," *Canadian Journal of Political Science* 11 (1978): 383-99; Irving Louis Horowitz, "The Hemisphere Connection," *Queen's Quarterly* 80 (1973): 327-59; Tom Truman, "A Critique of Seymour Lipset's Article, 'Value Differences, Absolute or Relative. The English-speaking Democracies,' " *Canadian Journal of Political Science* 4, no. 4 (1972), 497-525.

30. Lipset, *The First New Nation*, 521. It is much to Lipset's credit, that over the years he has consistently taken up his own challenge. His most ambitious, and in many ways most interesting work in this vein is a critical review of his own work and the body of research that followed over the next two decades. While largely adhering to initial positions, he brings considerably more evidence to bear. See Seymour M. Lipset, "Canada and the United States: The Cultural Dimension," in Charles F. Doran and John H. Sigler, eds., *Canada and the United States* (Englewood Cliffs, NJ: Prentice-Hall, 1985).

31. John Porter, *The Vertical Mosaic* (Toronto: University of Toronto Press, 1965); Libbie and Frank Park, *Anatomy of Big Business* (Toronto: James Lewis and Samuel, 1973); Wallace Clement, *The Canadian Corporate Elite: An Analysis of Economic Power*, Carleton Library No. 89 (Toronto: McClelland and Stewart, 1975); Peter C. Newman, *The Canadian Establishment*, Vols. 1 and 2 (Toronto: McClelland and Stewart, 1975).

32. For discussions of deference see Lipset, *The First New Nation*; Friedenberg, *Deference to Authority*; William Mishler, *Political Participation in Canada: Prospects for Democratic Citizenship* (Toronto: Macmillan, 1979); W.L. Morton, *The Canadian Identity*, 2d ed. (Toronto: University of Toronto Press, 1972), especially Chapter 3. On American individualism and lack of deference, see Richard Hofstadter, *The American Political Tradition* (New York: Vintage Books, 1973); Nathan Glazer, "Individualism and Equality in the United States," in Herbert Gans et al., eds., *On the Making of Americans: Essays in Honor of David Riesman* (Philadelphia: University of Pennsylvania Press, 1979), 121-42; Eugene J. McCarthy, "American Politics and American Character," in Roger L. Shinn, ed., *The Search for Identity* (New York: Harper and Row, 1964), 79-87; James O. Robertson, *American Myth, American Reality* (New York: Hill and Wang, 1980), especially 127-211.

33. Stephen J. Arnold and James G. Barnes, "Canadian and American National Character as a Basis for Market Segmentation," in Jagdish N. Sheth, ed., *Research in Marketing*, vol. 2 (Greenwich, CT: JAI Press, 1979), 1-35. This paper also provides a concise review of the comparative literature on national character.

34. Gordon F.N. Fearn, *Canadian Social Organization* (Toronto: Holt, Rinehart and Winston, 1973).

35. Armour, *Idea of Canada*.

36. Carl Berger, *The Sense of Power: Studies on the Ideas of Canadian Imperialism, 1867-1914* (Toronto: University of Toronto Press, 1970), 160-61.

37. Tom Atkinson and Michael A. Murray, *Values, Domains and the Perceived Quality of Life: Canada and the United States* (Toronto: Institute for Behavioural Research, York University, 1982).

38. Werner Stark, *The Social Bond: An Investigation into the Bases of Law-Abidingness* (New York: Fordham University Press, 1976).

39. Dallas Cullen, J.D. Jobson and Rodney Schneck, "Towards the Development of a Canadian-American Scale: A Research Note," *Canadian Journal of Political Science* 11 (1978):409-18. Too much should not be made of this, however, for the researchers used only a moderate-sized group of Alberta residents as respondents.

40. Atkinson and Murray, *Values, Domains*.

41. David C. McClelland, *The Achieving Society* (Princeton: Van Nostrand, 1961). See also Geert Hofstede, *Culture's Consequences: International Differences in Work-Related Values* (Beverly Hills, CA: Sage, 1980).

42. Alex C. Michalos, *North American Social Report*, Vol. 5, *Economics, Religion and Morality* (Boston: D. Reidel, 1982), 168-70. Michalos's monumental effort is a storehouse of comparative information on Canada and America. We make frequent use of his pioneering research. Not being able here to give his work a full review, we urge our readers to browse in Michalos's five volumes—it will be time well spent though, like us, you will disagree with particular interpretations.

43. Anthony H. Richmond, "Immigration and Racial Prejudice in Britain and Canada," in Jean Leonard Elliott, ed., *Two Nations, Many Cultures: Ethnic Groups in Canada* (Scarborough, Ont.: Prentice-Hall, 1979), 290-310.

44. Peter C. Pineo, "The Social Standing of Ethnic and Racial Groupings," *Canadian Review of Sociology and Anthropology* 14 (1977), 147-57.

45. Frances Henry, *The Dynamics of Racism in Toronto*, Research Report (Downsview,

Ont.: York University, 1978); Dorothy Quann, *Racial Discrimination in Housing*, Discussion Paper: Canadian Council on Social Development (Ottawa: C.C.S.D., 1979).

46. The work of Allan Smith has ben especially helpful on this topic. Allan Smith, "Metaphor and Nationality in North America," *Canadian Historical Review* 51 (1970), 247-75; Allan Smith, "National Images and National Maintenance"; and Allan Smith, "American Culture and the English Canadian Mind at the End of the Nineteenth Century," *Journal of Popular Culture* 4, no. 3 (1971):1045-51.

47. Again the literature on this topic is immense. To make a start one might usefully consult American works cited in note 32 of this chapter. For a critical (or neo-Marxist) perspective, see James O'Connor, *Accumulation Crisis* (New York: Basil Blackwell, 1984). And for how the concept has been treated in American letters, see Sam B. Girgus, *The Law of the Heart: Individualism and the Modern Self in American Literature* (Austin: University of Texas Press, 1979).

48. J.W. Berry and G.J.S. Wilde, eds., *Social Psychology: The Canadian Context* (Toronto: McClelland and Stewart, 1972), 43. See also Mason Wade, ed., *Canadian Dualism* (Toronto: University of Toronto Press, 1960).

49. It is important to maintain a sense of perspective on this for individual self-interest is an integral socio-psychological element of Canadian life. Smith provides a salutary reminder that this has been part of Canadian thinking about the nature of society. Allan Smith, "The Myth of the Self-made Man in English Canada, 1850-1914," *Canadian Historical Review* 59 (1978), 189-219; also Michael Bliss, *A Living Profit: Studies in Social History of Canadian Business, 1883-1911* (Toronto: McClelland and Stewart, 1974).

50. While the total of public works expenditures on infrastructure does not rival that on military expenditures (which have been of tremendous importance to the domestic economy and certain cities in the urban system), they are not insignificant. The latest and perhaps an extreme case is the 234-mile Tennessee-Tombigbee Waterway. Its proponents claim that it will be a major asset to regional economic development

and urban growth in the Gulf region; the impact on Mobile near the mouth of the Tombigbee is already considerable. By its 1985 opening the project is estimated to cost $1.9 billion in public expenditures.

51. "Sensible Handling of Issues Needed to Manage Canadian-American Relations," *Canada Weekly* 9 (2 December 1981); report of a speech made by Allan Gotlieb to the sixth biennial conference of the Association of Canadian Studies in the United States.

52. Americans are accustomed to thinking of Canada as a very peaceable place. Nevertheless, rebellions, insurrection, and mob violence are part of the historical record. They have tended to be glossed over, however, and are decidedly not part of the face that Canada presents to its neighbor.

53. See Berger, *Sense of Power.*

54. Gunnar Myrdal, *An American Dilemma: The Negro Problem and Modern Democracy* (New York: Harper and Row, 1944), 16-17, cited in Alex C. Michalos, *North American Social Report*, vol. 2 (Boston: D. Reidel, 1980), 4.

55. Michalos, *North American Social Report*, vol. 2, 147.

56. Ibid., vol. 2, 141.

57. Pierre deVise, *Misused and Misplaced Hospitals and Doctors: A Locational Analysis of the Urban Health Care Crisis* (Washington, DC: Association of American Geographers, Resource Paper No. 22, 1973); Mark Rosenberg, "Physician Location Behaviour in Metropolitan Toronto," *Canadian Geographer* 28 (1984):158-70.

NOTES TO CHAPTER 3

1. Christopher Leman, *The Collapse of Welfare Reform: Political Institutions, Policy and the Poor in Canada and the United States* (Cambridge, MA: MIT Press, 1980), xiii.

2. For a devastating account of how bureaucratic rule-making and implementation worked against one group, European Jews, seeking entrance to Canada and escape from the impending Holocaust, see Irving Abella and Harold Troper, *None is Too Many* (Toronto: Lester and Orpen Dennys, 1983).

3. Dennis H. Clairmont and F.C. Wien, "Race Relations in Canada," in Jay E. Goldstein and Rita M. Bienvenue, eds., *Ethnicity and Ethnic Relations in Canada* (Toronto: Butterworths, 1980), 309-24.

4. Jacqueline Desbarats, "Thai Migration to Los Angeles," *Geographical Review* 69 (1979):302-18.

5. Alex C. Michalos, *North American Social Report*, vol. 1, *Foundations, Population and Health* (Boston: D. Reidel, 1980), Chapter 2 and Table 20.

6. Carl Berger, *The Sense of Power: Studies on the Ideas of Canadian Imperialism, 1867-1914* (Toronto: University of Toronto Press, 1970), 148-49.

7. Warren E. Kalbach and Wayne W. McVey, *The Demographic Bases of Canadian Society*, 2d ed. (Toronto: McGraw-Hill Ryerson, 1979), Table 2:1, 46.

8. Italian home-purchases and rehabilitation in the Grandview-Woodlands area in inner-city Vancouver provide an excellent illustration of this. See John Mercer and Deborah A. Phillips, "Attitudes of Homeowners and the Decision to Rehabilitate Property," *Urban Geography* 2 (1981):216-36.

9. The U.S. Census cannot reveal, therefore, the numerical strength of ethnic populations for most are recorded as native-born Americans. Utilizing other methods of ethnic measurement, Smith provided estimates of the magnitude of the ethnic population. Data from national sample surveys show that an ethnic identification is possible for almost four-fifths of the American population. Depending on the survey, only about two-thirds could identify with a national origin (other than American). Trend data show a general decline in this ability in the 1970s. Tom W. Smith, "Ethnic Measurement and Identification," *Ethnicity* 7 (1980):78-95.

10. Each of the principal positions has a significant literature associated with it. Leading scholars associated with the three American views outlined here are Milton Gordon, *Assimilation in American Life* (New York: Oxford University Press, 1964); Milton Gordon, *Human Nature, Class and Ethnicity* (New York: Oxford University Press, 1978), Chapters 2 and 3; Nathan Glazer and Daniel Patrick Moynihan, eds., *Ethnicity: Theory and Experience* (Cambridge, MA: Harvard University Press, 1975); Herbert Gans "Symbolic Ethnicity: The Future of Ethnic Groups and Cultures in America," in Herbert Gans et al., *On the Making of*

Americans (Philadelphia: University of Pennsylvania Press, 1979).

11. Kogila Moodley, "Canadian Ethnicity in Comparative Perspective: Issues in the Literature," in Jorgen Dahlie and Tissa Fernando, eds., *Ethnicity, Power and Politics in Canada* (Toronto: Methuen, 1981), 6-21.

12. Allan Smith, "National Images and National Maintenance: The Ascendancy of the Ethnic Idea in North America," *Canadian Journal of Political Science* 14 (1981): 227-57.

13. Judith A. Nagata, "One Vine, Many Branches: Internal Differentiation in Canadian Ethnic Groups," in Jean Leonard Elliott, ed., *Two Nations, Many Cultures: Ethnic Groups in Canada* (Scarborough, Ont.: Prentice-Hall, 1979), 173-81. Also see Reginald W. Bibby, "The Delicate Mosaic: A National Examination of Intergroup Relations in Canada," *Social Indicators Research* 5 (1978):169-79.

14. Wsevolod W. Isajiw, "Definitions of Ethnicity," in Goldstein and Bienvenue, *Ethnicity and Ethnic Relations*, 23.

15. Peter C. Pineo, "The Social Standing of Ethnic and Racial Groupings," *Canadian Review of Social Anthropology* 14 (1977): 147-57.

16. Wsevolod W. Isajiw, ed., *Ukrainians in American and Canadian Society* (Jersey City: M.P. Kots, 1976), 337.

17. While multiculturalism has political benefits it also has political costs. For more on this issue, see Howard Brotz, "Multiculturalism in Canada: A Muddle," *Canadian Public Policy* 6 (1980):41-46; Lance W. Roberts and R.A. Clifton, "Exploring the Ideology of Canadian Multiculturalism," *Canadian Public Policy* 8 (1982): 88-94.

18. Kogila Moodley, "Canadian Ethnicity," 13.

19. William Alonso, "The Demographic Factor In Housing for the Balance of this Century" in Michael A. Goldberg and George Gau, eds., *North American Housing Markets into the Twenty-First Century* (Cambridge, MA: Ballinger, 1983), 33-50.

20. Carol Agocs, "Ethnic Settlement in a Metropolitan Area: A Typology of Communities," *Ethnicity* 8 (1981):127-48; Leo Driedger and G. Church, "Residential Segrega-tion and Institutional Completeness: A Comparison of Ethnic Minorities," *Canadian Review of Sociology and Anthropology* 2 (1974): 30-52; Leo Driedger, "Ethnic Boundaries: A Comparison of Two Urban Neighborhoods," *Sociology and Social Research* 62 (1978):193-211. For a useful review, see Carol Agocs, "Ethnic Groups in the Ecology of North American Cities," *Canadian Ethnic Studies* 11 (1979):1-18.

21. Fernando Penalosa, *Review of Language Diversity and Language Contact: Essays by Stanley Lieberson,* in *Language Problems and Language Planning* 8 (1984), 240. Lieberson has been a prominent researcher on language relations in Canada, with particular attention to Montreal.

22. Don Cartwright, *Official Language Populations in Canada: Patterns and Contacts* (Montreal: Institute for Research on Public Policy, 1980); Don Cartwright, "Language Policy and the Organization of Territory: A Canadian Dilemma," *Canadian Geographer* 25 (1981):205-24.

23. Sheila McLeod Arnopolous and Dominique Clift, *The English Fact in Quebec* (Montreal: McGill-Queen's University Press, 1980).

24. Alfred A. Hunter, *Class Tells: On Social Inequality in Canada* (Toronto: Butterworths, 1981).

25. Jean A. Laponce, "The City Centre as Conflictual Space in the Bilingual City: The Case of Montreal," in Jean Gottman, ed., *Centre and Periphery: Spatial Variation in Politics* (Beverly Hills: Sage, 1980).

26. R.C. Hutchinson, "Religion, Morality and Law in Modern Society," in P. Slater, ed., *Religion and Culture in Canada* (Ottawa: Canadian Corporation for Studies in Religion, 1977), cited in Michalos, *North American Social Report*, vol. 5, 139.

27. Henry Milner, *Politics in the New Quebec* (Toronto: McClelland and Stewart, 1978). See Chapter 8 for some background on the Confederation of Catholic Trade Unions, which deconfessionalized only in 1960, becoming the Confederation of National Trade Unions (CNTU). Labor remains organizationally divided in Quebec.

28. Michalos, *North American Social Report*, vol. 5, Tables 1 and 2, 150-51.

29. It is worth noting that separate schools in Ontario predate Confederation.

30. Michalos, *North American Social Report*,

vol. 5, 144. This has caused American religious sociologist Will Herberg to note that the "religion of America is religion." See Will Herberg, *Protestant-Catholic-Jew* (Garden City, N.Y.: Anchor Books, 1960), especially Chapter 5, 72-98.

31. Michalos, *North American Social Report*, vol. 5, 145. This opinion tends to contradict Lipset's view that Canadians are more "conservative." See Seymour M. Lipset, "The Value Patterns of Democracy: A Case Study in Comparative Analysis," *American Sociological Review* 28, 515-31.

32. D.G. Taylor, P.B. Sheatsley and A.M. Greeley, "Attitudes Towards Racial Integration," *Scientific American* 238, no. 6 (1978):42-49.

33. The current need to remove racial barriers and eliminate dual housing markets echoes a situation described and a policy goal advocated by one of us ten years ago. John Mercer and John Hultquist, "National Progress Toward Housing and Urban Renewal Goals," in John S. Adams, ed., *Urban Policymaking and Metropolitan Dynamics* (Cambridge, MA: Ballinger, 1976), 101-62. Evidence of progress in this regard during the 1970-80 decade can be found in John F. Kain, "Black Suburbanization in the Eighties: A New Beginning or a False Hope," in J. Quigley and D. Rubinfeld, eds., *An Agenda for Metropolitan America* (Berkeley and Los Angeles: University of California Press, forthcoming).

34. Office of Policy Development and Research, *A Survey of Citizen Views and Concerns About Urban Life* (Washington, DC: U.S. Department of Housing and Urban Development, HUD-PDR-306, 1978).

35. In a privatized society, solutions to problems are sought in a highly personalized fashion— withdrawal is a prominent one. G. Turkel, "Privatism and Orientations Towards Political Action," *Urban Life* 9 (1980), 217-35.

36. Warren E. Kalbach, *Ethnic Residential Segregation and its Significance for the Individual in an Urban Setting* (Toronto: Centre for Urban and Community Studies, University of Toronto, Research Paper No. 124, 1981).

37. The Edmonton and Winnipeg experiences are not totally similar. In Edmonton, it is the middle and lower-middle class suburb of Mill Woods that has been the focus of racial tension while in Winnipeg it is the lower-income central-city area just to the north of the Portage and Main core intersection.

38. Racial categories such as "non-white" are not used nor directly reported in the Canadian Census.

39. In saying this we do not mean to belittle earlier important urban and historical studies, such as those on Africville in the Halifax metropolitan area and on blacks in Canada. D.H. Clairmont and Dennis W. Magill, *Africville: The Life and Death of a Canadian Black Community* (Toronto: McClelland and Stewart, 1974); Robin W. Winks, *The Blacks in Canada: A History* (Montreal: McGill-Queen's University Press, 1971).

40. Leman, *Collapse of Welfare Reform*, 11.

41. Michalos, *North American Social Report*, vol. 5, 27.

42. Ibid., 27.

43. Ibid., 28.

44. Hunter, *Class Tells*, 66-67.

45. Allan Moscovitch, "The Canadian Economy and Inequality," in Allan Moscovitch and Glenn Drover, eds., *Inequality: Essays on the Political Economy of Social Welfare* (Toronto: University of Toronto Press, 1981), 58-98.

46. Leman, *Collapse of Welfare Reform*.

47. Raymond Morris and C. Michael Lanphier, *Three Scales of Inequality* (Don Mills, Ont.: Longman Canada, 1977).

48. A. Gordon Darroch, "Another Look at Ethnicity, Stratification and Social Mobility in Canada," *Canadian Journal of Sociology* 4 (1979), 1-25.

49. Leading proponents of this position would include Robert A. Dahl, *A Preface to Democratic Theory* (Chicago: University of Chicago Press, 1956); Anthony Downs, *An Economic Theory of Democracy* (New York: Harper, 1957); David B. Truman, *The Government Process* (New York: Knopf, 1953); Nelson W. Polsby, *Community Power and Political Theory: A Further Look at Problems of Evidence and Inference* (New Haven: Yale University Press, 1980).

50. C. Wright Mills is very much identified with this conception. C. Wright Mills, *The Power Elite* (New York: Oxford University Press, 1956). The writing of Grant McConnell is in a similar vein. Grant

McConnell, *Private Power and American Democracy* (New York: Knopf, 1966). The notion that the federal government is subservient to special interests remains a minority position amongst liberal scholars. See, for example, J. David Greenstone, ed., *Public Values and Private Power in American Politics* (Chicago: University of Chicago Press, 1982). That the state is the instrument of the ruling class is a central tenet of many Marxist writers on the state and on class relations. A more general discussion of ties between economic interests and political power can be found in Charles E. Lindblom, *Politics and Markets* (New York: Basic Books, 1977).

51. Peter C. Pineo and John C. Goyder (1973), "Social Class Identification of National Sub-groups," in James E. Curtis and William G. Scott, eds., *Social Stratification in Canada* (Scarborough, Ont.: Prentice-Hall, 1973), 187-96. Hunter, *Class Tells*, Chapter 12, covers some of the evidence on class consciousness but was perhaps unaware of other surveys such as the 1979 national survey on social change and reported by Tom Atkinson et al. *Social Change in Canada* (Downsview, Ont.: Institute for Behavioural Research, York University, 1982).

52. Richard Harris, *Class and Housing Tenure in Modern Canada*, Research Paper No. 153 (Toronto: Centre for Urban and Community Studies, University of Toronto, 1984).

53. The work of Kalbach and McVey, *Demographic Bases*, should be acknowledged as being of particular value in improving our understanding of Canadian society.

54. Michalos, *North American Social Report*, vol. 1, 34.

55. Ibid., 34-35.

56. Cary Davis, Carl Haub and Joanne Willette, "U.S. Hispanics: Changing the Face of America," *Population Bulletin* 38, no. 3 (1983):15.

57. John Reid, "Black America in the 1980's," *Population Bulletin* 37, no. 4 (1982):Table 3, 11.

58. Kalbach and McVey, *Demographic Bases*, Chapter 4.

59. Arlavel Thornton and Deborah Freedman, "The Changing American Family," *Population Bulletin* 38, no. 4 (1983), 8.

60. Ibid., 19-20.

61. Michalos, *North American Social Report*, vol. 1, Table 19, 81.

62. Ibid., 46.

63. Wayne Grady, "The Abortionist," *Saturday Night* 99, no. 7 (1984):38.

64. Thornton and Freedman, "Changing American Family," 24.

65. Kalbach and McVey, *Demographic Bases*, Table 11.5, 274.

66. John Mercer, "Locational Consequences of Housing Policies for the Low-Income Elderly: A Case Study," in Stephen M. Golant, ed., *Location and Environment of Elderly Population* (Washington, DC: V.H. Winston, 1979).

67. Michalos, *North American Social Report*, vol. 5, p. 171.

68. Office of Policy Development and Research, *Survey of Citizen Views*; Tom Atkinson, *A Study of Urban Concerns* (Toronto: Institute for Behavioural Research, York University, 1982).

NOTES TO CHAPTER 4

1. For further discussion see the classic work by W.T. Easterbrook and Hugh G.J. Aitken, *Canadian Economic History* (Toronto: Macmillan, 1963). A recent interpretation is by William L. Marr and Donald G. Paterson, *Canada: An Economic History* (Toronto: Macmillan, 1980).

2. This theory is associated with the important and original work of Harold Innis. A convenient entry to his ideas is his *Essays in Canadian Economic History*, ed. Mary Q. Innis (Toronto: University of Toronto Press, 1956).

3. Both Marr and Paterson, *Canada*, in Chapter 10, and Easterbrook and Aitken, *Canadian Economic History*, in Chapters 12, 14 and 18, stress the roles of transportation in opening up and developing the Canadian economy.

4. Albert W. Niemi, Jr., *U.S. Economic History*, 2d ed. (Chicago: Rand McNally 1980), 17.

5. The historical data in this chapter can be traced to three sources. For the United States, data come from U.S. Department of Commerce, Bureau of the Census, *Historical Statistics of the United States: Colonial Times to 1970*, Pts. 1&2 (Washington, D.C.: U.S. Government Printing Office, 1975). For Canada, two sources were used: M.C. Urquhart and K.A.H. Buckley, eds., *Historical Statistics of Canada* (Toronto: Macmillan, 1965), and its recently revised and updated successor,

F.H. Leacy, ed., *Historical Statistics of Canada*, 2d ed. (Ottawa: Statistics Canada, 1983).

6. The more recent data used to extend historical trends from the volumes of historical statistics come from several different volumes. The most complete resource for current U.S. information is U.S. Department of Commerce, Bureau of the Census, *Statistical Abstract of the United States, 1984*, 104th ed. (Washington, DC: U.S. Government Printing Office, 1984). This 10th Edition provided the bulk of the information used here although sometimes it was necessary to refer to earlier editions to obtain data for some intervening years not shown in the most recent edition. Where not explicitly noted in the text, U.S. data have come from the 104th Edition. For Canada, a great deal of current information came from Statistics Canada, *Canada Yearbook 1980-81* (Ottawa: Ministry of Supply and Services, 1981). Regrettably, this useful book has not been updated in almost four years, and we had to rely on other primary sources from Statistics Canada and elsewhere as shown on the tables in this Chapter. However, for a wide range of economic information for the most recent years we used Canada Department of Finance, *Economic Review, April, 1984* (Ottawa: Minister of Supply and Services, 1984). As with the U.S. data, where not cited explicitly, current data overwhelmingly have been drawn from these two sources.

7. Lukin Robinson, "The American Sponge," *The Canadian Forum*, November 1984, 9-13.

8. This point is discussed at length and effectively, by Wallace Clement, *Continental Corporate Power: Economic Elite Linkages between Canada and the United States* (Toronto: McClelland and Stewart, 1977), especially Chapters 1 through 4.

9. The key role of transportation in both Canada and the U.S. has been stressed by numerous writers who tie transportation improvements to the growth of both economies. In addition to the chapters cited in Niemi, *U.S. Economic History*, and Marr and Paterson, *Canada*, see for the U.S., Harold Barger, *The Transportation Industries, 1889-1956* (New York: National Bureau of Economic Research, 1957), and George R. Taylor, *The Transportation Revolution, 1815-1860* (New York: Holt,

Rinehart and Winston, 1951). For Canada, see G.P. de T. Glazebrook, *A History of Transportation in Canada*, Vols. I and II (Toronto: University of Toronto Press, 1964); and Harry L. Purdy, *Transportation Competition and Public Policy in Canada* (Vancouver: University of British Columbia Press, 1972).

10. The term "defensive expansionism" was coined to described the Canadian westward movement and the key role of the railroads in that expansion. See Marr and Paterson, *Canada*, 452.

11. See Marr and Paterson, *Canada*, Chapter 10 for Canada, and Niemi, *U.S. Economic History*, Chapters 4 and 5, for an excellent summary of government transportation roles in the U.S.

12. These and other historical transportation data on roads and railroad come from *Historical Statistics of the United States*, 2d ed., tables T1 through T246.

13. These data come from the *Statistical Abstract of the U.S.*, 104th ed., and from *Canada Yearbook, 1980/81*.

14. A detailed analysis of these changes in savings behavior concludes that they can in fact be explained by changes in incomes (appropriately defined) in Canada and the United States. For details, see, Ronald G. Wirick, "Paradoxes in Recent Canadian-American Personal Savings Behavior: Toward a 'Permanent' Resolution" (London, Ont.: Department of Economics, University of Western Ontario, May 1982), mimeographed.

15. Both Marr and Paterson, *Canada*, and Clement, *Continental Corporate Power*, stress the importance of the Canadian comprador role and tradition in understanding the nature of the Canadian economic system. The compradors are that fraction of the capitalist class whose principal allegiance is to a foreign-controlled base of power; typically, they are the senior executives and directors of branch plants under the control of a foreign parent, now largely American.

16. The relatively greater efficiency here should not be confused with later discussions on Canadian domination by foreign capital. The former refers to the domestic financial system while the latter to ownership of non-financial assets.

17. This point is made at some length, supported by empirical analysis, in Jonathan Mark and Michael A. Goldberg, "Neigh-

bourhood Change: A Canadian Perspective," *The Annals of Regional Science* (forthcoming, 1986).

18. For two complementary but different viewpoints on the federal role in urban affairs see, Michael A. Goldberg, "The BNA Act, NHA, CMHC, MSUA, etc.: 'Nymophobia' and the On-Going Search for an Appropriate Canadian Housing and Urban Development Policy," in Michael Walker, ed., *Canadian Confederation at the Crossroads* (Vancouver: The Fraser Institute, 1978), 320-61; and Richard S. Morris, *Bum Rap on America's Cities: The Real Causes of Urban Decay* (Englewood Cliffs, NJ: Prentice-Hall, 1978), especially Chapters 7 through 12, 109-184.

19. Herschel Hardin, *A National Unaware: The Canadian Economic Culture* (Vancouver: J.J. Douglas, 1974). An analysis of the efficiency of public and private enterprises in five countries (Canada and the United States included) provides some interesting evidence to extend Hardin's argument. See Thomas E. Borcherding, Werner W. Pommerehne, and Friedrich Schneider, "Comparing the Efficiency of Private and Public Production: The Evidence from Five Countries" (Burnaby, B.C.: Department of Economics, Simon Fraser University, 1982), mimeographed. A uniquely Canadian public enterprise should also be noted here and that is local government land banking. See J. Piper, "Saskatoon Robs the Bank," *Ekistics* 233 (1975):265-67.

20. See Clement, *Continental Corporate Power*, and more passionately, Kari Levitt, *Silent Surrender* (Toronto: Macmillan of Canada, 1970).

21. See Robert L. Parry, *Galt, U.S.A.* (Toronto: MacLean-Hunter, 1971), and more recently Fred Harrison, "U.S. has own set of investment controls, Ottawa points out," *Financial Post*, 3 July 1982, S3.

22. This point is made quite strongly in John Hutcheson, *Dominance and Dependency: Liberalism and National Policies in the North Atlantic Triangle* (Toronto: McClelland and Stewart, 1978). Clement, *Continental Corporate Power*, and Marr and Paterson, *Canada*, also note the counterproductive results of the national policy.

23. Marr and Paterson, *Canada*, 379.

24. Clement, *Continental Corporate Power*, stresses the roles of elites particularly in his analyses. In a somewhat different context, that of senior bureaucrats, Colin Campbell supports Clement's ideas. See Colin Campbell, *Governments Under Stress* (Toronto: University of Toronto Press, 1983).

25. Parry, *Galt, U.S.A.* Interestingly, Parry revisited the former Galt area (now known as Cambridge, Ontario) in 1979, eight years after his initial book. He found great change and that much of the local industry was being bought back by local enterpreneurs. His updated observations were published in a series of six articles in *The Financial Post*, beginning on 18 August 1979. He also published a revised book *Galt, U.S.A.* (Toronto: MacLean-Hunter, 1979). Some very interesting observations on the impacts of foreign ownership on Canadian cities and on the Canadian urban system more generally can be found in Len Gertler and Ronald Crowley, *Changing Canadian Cities: The Next 25 Years* (Toronto: McClelland and Stewart, 1977), especially 154-59.

26. Goldberg, "BNA Act," makes this point at some length. The argument is also supported by the greater power of the provinces in Canada whose creatures cities are. See Roger Gibbins, *Regionalism* (Toronto: Butterworths, 1982) for a discussion of the roles of provinces and states with regard to the respective federal governments in the two nations.

27. An interesting example of how the private sector became engaged in Canadian central-city renewal projects on a scale then unknown in the U.S., in contrast to prevailing myths as discussed in the text, can be found in Robert Collier, *Contemporary Cathedrals* (Montreal: Harvest House, 1975). For two cases of local government enterpreneurship in Toronto and Vancouver see D. Hulchanski, *St. Lawrence and False Creek* (Vancouver: UBC Planning Papers, 1984).

28. For an extensive review of such land use controls in Canada and the United States, see Michael A. Goldberg and Peter Chinloy, *Urban Land Economics* (New York: Wiley, 1984), Chapter 11, 302-47.

29. Ibid., Chapter 8, 221-46.

30. Constitutional protection of real property rights is discussed in Edward Conrad Smith, ed., *The Constitution of the United States*, 11th ed. (New York: Barnes and Noble, 1979).

31. An interesting analysis of the difficulties faced by the Canadian federal authorities when they sought to become involved in urban affairs can be found in Elliot J. Feldman and Jerome Milch, "Coordination or Control? The Life and Death of the Ministry of State for Urban Affairs," in Lionel D. Feldman, ed., *Politics and Government of Urban Canada*, 4th ed. (Toronto: Methuen, 1981), 246-64.

32. A long overdue and important research effort is currently underway at the University of Toronto's Centre for Urban and Community Studies. See for example, S.E. Corke, *Land Use Controls in British Columbia: A Comparative Analysis of Provincial Planning Legislation*, Land Policy Paper no. 3 (Toronto: Centre for Urban and Community Studies, University of Toronto, 1982).

33. We discuss this issue in more detail in Chapter 7 where we present a range of data that supports the assertion made here, namely that Canadians rely much less on private automobiles and make almost 2 1/2 times as much use of public transit facilities.

34. See for details, John R. Meyer and Jose A. Gomez-Ibanez, *Autos, Traffic and Cities* (Cambridge, MA: Twentieth Century Fund, 1981).

35. Urbanics Consultants, *A Study of the Market Development Opportunities in the LRT South Corridor* (Calgary, Alberta: Planning Department, City of Calgary, 1978). For a comparison of Edmonton and Calgary see Eliane Guillot, "LRT Design Choices: Edmonton and Calgary," *Traffic Quarterly* 37, no. 3 (1983), 337-54.

36. San Diego's new "Trolley" is the sole recent exception. See Paul van Slambrouck, "San Diego's Do-It-Yourself Trolley," *Mass Transit*, June 1981, 64. Also see an entire issue of *Mass Transit* in July 1983 devoted to LRT with major articles on San Diego, Canada and a summary of North American LRT systems.

NOTES TO CHAPTER 5

1. For details about constitutional history and about the respective constitutions of Canada and the United States, see for Canada: W.L. Morton, *The Critical Years* (Toronto: McClelland and Stewart, 1964);

Elmer A. Driedger, *The British North America Acts 1867 to 1975* (Ottawa: Ministry of Supply and Services, 1976); Peter H. Russell, *Leading Constitutional Decisions* (Toronto: Macmillan of Canada, 1978); and *The Constitution Act, 1982* (Ottawa: Ministry of Supply and Services, 1982). For the United States, see: Richard Hofstadter, *The American Political Tradition* (New York: Knopf, 1948); Henry Steele Commager, *Freedom and Order* (Cleveland, OH: World Publishing, 1966); and Edward Conrad Smith, ed., *The Constitution of the United States*, 11th ed. (New York: Harper and Row, 1979).

2. Lipset's arguments are detailed in a number of places. The following set out well and document his argument. Seymour M. Lipset, "The Value Patterns of Democracy: A Case Study in Comparative Analysis," *American Sociological Review* 28, no. 4 (1963), 515-31; Seymour M. Lipset, "Revolution and Counterrevolution—Some Comments at a Conference Analyzing the Bicentennial of a Celebrated North American Divorce" in Richard A. Preston, ed., *Perspectives on Revolution and Evolution* (Durham, NC: Duke University Press, 1979), 22-45; and Seymour M. Lipset, *The First New Nation* (New York: Norton, 1979).

3. A number of authors have elaborated upon Lipset's ideas in several areas. Elites have been subjected to particularly close scrutiny. See Robert Presthus, *Elites in the Policy Process* (London: Cambridge University Press, 1974); Robert Presthus, ed., *Cross-National Perspectives: United States and Canada* (Leiden, Netherlands: E.J. Brill, 1977); Robert Presthus, "Evolution and Canadian Political Culture: The Politics of Accommodation," in Richard A. Preston, ed., *Perspectives on Revolution and Evolution*, 103-32. This edited volume also deals with the issue at some considerable length.

4. Several scholars have been very critical of Lipset for what they see as the incompleteness of his analysis and his misinterpretation of the data. The most compelling of these are to be found in Tom Truman, " A Critique of Seymour M. Lipset's Article, 'Value Differences, Absolute or Relative: The English Speaking Democracies,' " *Canadian Journal of Political Science* 4, no. 1 (1971):497-525; and Gad Horowitz, "Conservatism, Liberalism, and Socialism

in Canada: An Interpretation," *Canadian Journal of Economics and Political Science* 32, no. 2 (1966):141-71.

5. Lipset, "Value Patterns of Democracy," 521.

6. Michael Kammen, *People of Paradox: An Inquiry Concerning the Origins of American Civilization* (New York: Oxford University Press, 1980), 243.

7. Commager, *Freedom and Order*, 119.

8. Hofstadter, *American Political Tradition*, 10.

9. Ibid., 16.

10. Roger Gibbins, *Regionalism: Territorial Politics in Canada and the United States* (Toronto: Butterworths, 1982), 110.

11. Several scathing criticisms have come out about the passage and royal assent of *The Constitution Act, 1982*. For particularly trenchant commentaries before the fact, see Donald V. Smiley, *Canada in Question: Federalism in the Eighties*, 3d ed. (Toronto: McGraw-Hill Ryerson, 1980), and Donald V. Smiley, "The Challenge of Canadian Ambivalence," *Queen's Quarterly* 88, no. 1 (1981), 1-12, and shortly after the fact by Keith Banting and Richard Simeon, ed., *And No One Cheered* (Toronto: Methuen, 1983).

12. As Gibbins, *Regionalism*, 25, observes, the B.N.A. Act was to be a "Constitution similar in principle to that of the United Kingdom".

13. For details of the Canadian constitutional "debate" see Morton, *Critical Years*, and Kenneth McNaught, *The Pelican History of Canada* (Harmondsworth, England: Penguin Books, 1982), especially Chapters 6 through 9, inclusive.

14. In addition to Gibbins, *Regionalism*, an excellent source of information on the tensions and balance in the Canadian confederation, particularly as it relates to resource revenues, can be found in Garth Stevenson, *Unfulfilled Union* (Toronto: Gage, 1982).

15. Driedger, *British North America Acts*, 29.

16. Smith, *Constitution of United States*, 50.

17. Gibbins, *Regionalism*, 22-23, makes a similar observation. For a more far-reaching and general discussion of the concept and implementation of federalism see Herman Bakvis, *Federalism and the Organization of Political Life: Canada in Comparative Perspective* (Kingston, Ont.: Institute of Intergovernmental Relations, Queen's

University, 1981); and Preston King, *Federalism and Federation* (Baltimore: Johns Hopkins University Press, 1982).

18. Smith, *Constitution of United States*, 53.

19. Gibbins, *Regionalism*, 22.

20. Stevenson, *Unfulfilled Union*, 56.

21. Gibbins, *Regionalism*, 26-27.

22. Driedger, *British North America Acts*, 24-29.

23. The resource issue, as noted earlier, has been addressed by both Gibbins, *Regionalism*, and Stevenson, *Unfulfilled Union*. A particularly interesting treatment of the issue can be found in John Richards and Larry Pratt, *Prairie Capitalism: Power and Influence in the New West* (Toronto: McClelland and Stewart, 1980).

24. Gibbins, *Regionalism*, 42-43.

25. Stevenson, *Unfulfilled Union*, 61.

26. For a discussion of the problems facing the Canadian federal government in its attempts to become a major player in the urban policy sector in Canada see: Michael A. Goldberg, "The BNA Act, NHA, CMHC, MSUA, etc.: 'Nymophobia' and the On-Going Search for an Appropriate Canadian Housing and Urban Development Policy," in Michael Walker, ed., *Canadian Confederation at the Crossroads* (Vancouver: The Fraser Institute, 1978), 320-61; and Elliot J. Feldman and Jerome Milch, "Coordination and Control: The Life and Death of the Ministry of State for Urban Affairs," in Lionel D. Feldman, ed., *Politics and Government of Urban Canada*, 4th ed. (Toronto: Methuen, 1981), 246-64. It is interesting to contrast this with the U.S. federal role, for example with respect to highway and urban transportation planning. See for an interesting example, Transportation Research Board, Research Results Digest #136, "State Highway Programs Versus the Spending Powers of Congress" (Washington, DC: Transportation Research Board, 1982).

27. Feldman and Milch, "Coordination and Control," 261. Additional useful insight on the founding and foundering of the Ministry of State for Urban Affairs can be found in the following studies: Len Gertler, "The Challenge of Public Policy Research," *Canadian Journal of Regional Science* 2, no. 1 (1979):77-89; and two papers in a Special Issue of the *Canadian Journal of Regional Science* edited by Gertler in the spring of 1982 (5, no. 1), Allan O'Brien,

"The Ministry of State for Urban Affairs: A Municipal Perspective," 83-94; Audrey D. Doerr, "Organizing for Urban Policy: Some Comments on the Ministry of State for Urban Affairs," 95-101.

28. Gabriel Almond and Sydney Verba, *The Civic Culture* (Princeton, NJ: Princeton University Press, 1963). For Canada and U.S. comparison see Robert Presthus, "Aspects of Political Culture and Legislative Behavior: United States and Canada", in Robert Presthus, ed., *Cross-National Perspectives: United States and Canada* (Leiden: E.J. Brill, 1977), 7-22.

29. Presthus, *Cross National Perspectives*, 7.

30. For supporting evidence see: Nathaniel Beck and John Pierce, "Political Involvement and Party Allegiances in Canada and the United States", in Presthus, *Cross National Perspectives*, 23-43; David J. Elkins and Richard Simeon, *Small Worlds: Provinces and Parties on Canadian Political Life* (Toronto: Methuen, 1980), Chapter 2, 31-76; and Stephen J. Arnold and Douglas J. Tigert, "Canadians and Americans: A Comparative Analysis", in K. Ishwaran, ed., *International Journal of Comparative Sociology* 15 (1974): 68-83.

31. The issue of deference to authority and government in Canada has attracted much comment by scholars over the past several decades. Most critical commentators it should be noted have been Americans who have tended to perceive the phenomenon in American terms as standing in contradiction to American values of individualism. For the deference discussions see: Seymour Lipset, *First New Nation*, especially 248-73 and contrast with U.S. attitudes on 110-112; Edgar Z. Friedenberg, *Deference to Authority: The Case of Canada* (White Plains, NY: M.E. Sharpe, 1980); William Mishler, *Political Participation in Canada: Prospects for Democratic Citizenship* (Toronto: Macmillan of Canada, 1979); W.L. Morton, *The Canadian Identity*, 2d ed. (Toronto: University of Toronto Press, 1972), especially Chapter 3. For the corresponding view of American individualism and lack of deference see: Richard Hofstadter, *The American Political Tradition* (New York: Vintage Books, 1973); Nathan Glazer, "Individualism and Equality in the United States", in Herbert Gans et al., eds., *On the Making of Americans: Essays in Honor of David Riesman* (Philadelphia: University of Pennsylvania Press, 1979), 121-42; Eugene J. McCarthy, "American Politics and American Character," in Roger L. Shinn, ed., *The Search for Identity* (New York: Harper and Row, 1964), 79-87; James O. Robertson, *American Myth, American Reality* (New York: Hill and Wang, 1980), especially Chapter 2, 127-211; and most interestingly Alex Inkeles, "Continuity and Change in the American National Character," in Seymour Lipset, ed., *The Third Century: America as a Post-Industrial Society* (Chicago: University of Chicago Press, 1979), 389-416. For a fascinating and historical perspective see David W. Brogan, *The American Character* (New York: Alfred A. Knopf, 1944).

32. This point is stressed by Gibbins, *Regionalism*, in his analysis of federalism and regionalism in Canada and the United States. Also see Inkeles, "Continuity and Change." The recently completed bargaining over oil pricing and resource taxation is an excellent example of the dynamic nature of Canadian federalism as the federal government has had to do battle first with the West (Alberta, British Columbia, and Saskatchewan) and now with Atlantic Canada (the traditional "have-not" region), particularly with Nova Scotia and Newfoundland. An excellent analysis of the basis for such resource-based battles can be found in Richards and Pratt, *Prairie Capitalism*.

33. One view of American federal administrations suggests that they have been, in essence, captured by special interests. This contrasts with the popular view in U.S. political culture that government serves all the people but not "big interests". J. David Greenstone, ed., *Public Values and Private Power in American Politics* (Chicago: University of Chicago Press, 1982).

34. Elkins and Simeon, *Small Worlds*, 21-26.

35. Gibbins, *Regionalism*, comments (169-73) that even asking such a question is unthinkable to an American and stands distinctly at odds with the Canadian approach noted by him (173-89).

36. For details of Canadian metropolitan government see C.R. Tindal, *Structural Changes in Local Government: Government for Urban Regions* (Toronto: Institute of Public Administration of Canada, 1977). For a comparative analysis of the

reform of local governments in Canada and the United States, see John Mercer, *Comparing the Reform of Metropolitan Fragmentation, Fiscal Dependency and Political Culture in Canada and the United States*, Occasional Paper no. 61 (Syracuse, NY: Metropolitan Studies Program, Maxwell School, Syracuse University, 1982).

37. The B.N.A. Act is, in essence, incorporated into the new Canadian constitution, brought into existence in 1982 (*The Constitution Act, 1982*).

38. This point is raised and discussed in a critique of Lipset's writing. David Bell and Lorne Tepperman, *The Roots of Disunity: A Look at Canadian Political Culture* (Toronto: McClelland and Stewart, 1979), 24-31.

39. Bell and Tepperman, *Roots of Disunity*, Chapter 3, 72-107, spend considerable time analyzing the loyalist issue and drawing some conclusions that are at odds with much of the traditional literature and with Lipset's view in particular.

40. Robert Presthus and William V. Monopoli, "Bureaucracy in the United States and Canada: Social, Attitudinal, and Behavioral Variables," in Presthus, *Cross National Perspectives*, 176-90.

41. Colin Campbell, *Governments under Stress: Political Executives and Key Bureaucrats in Washington, London and Ottawa* (Toronto: University of Toronto Press, 1983).

42. Colin Campbell and George Szablowski, *The Superbureaucrats: Structure and Behaviour in Central Agencies* (Toronto: Macmillan of Canada, 1979).

43. For details see *The Constitution Act, 1982* (Ottawa: Minister of Supply and Services, 1982). For a discussion of the relatively greater role of provinces and their designates, municipalities, in regulating urban development in Canada as compared with the United States, see Goldberg, "BNA Act."

44. Smith, *Constitution of United States*, 132.

45. Herschel Hardin, *A Nation Unaware: The Canadian Economic Culture* (Vancouver: J. J. Douglas, 1974), especially Part II, 54-140.

46. Annmarie H. Walsh, *The Public's Business: The Politics and Practices of Government Corporations* (Cambridge, MA: MIT Press, 1978); and Albert Lepawsky, "Style and Substance in Contemporary Planning: The

American New Deal's National Resources Planning Board as a Model," *Plan Canada* 18, no. 3 (1978):153-87. Hardin, *Nation Unaware*, also looks at American models and concludes much greater Canadian public activity exists.

47. Richards and Pratt, *Prairie Capitalism*, devote considerable effort to exploring this kind of "public enterprise" culture in two quite different political environments: the politically conservative province of Alberta and the socially advanced province of Saskatchewan. In this vein it is worth noting that it was the Social Credit party in British Columbia that exploited the crown corporation as enterpriser most vigorously after initially launching B.C. Hydro and the B.C. Railway as crown ventures in the 1960s, well before the democratic-socialist New Democratic Party controlled B.C. politics from 1972-1975. Similarly, it was the Progressive Conservative government in Ontario that aggressively marketed rapid transit technology across Canada, the United States and elsewhere in the world through a crown corporation.

48. This interest in private as opposed to public action has been documented and analyzed in two classic studies by Sam Bass Warner dealing with Boston and with Philadelphia respectively. See *Streetcar Suburbs* (Cambridge, MA: Harvard University Press, 1962); and *The Private City* (Philadelphia: University of Pennsylvania Press, 1968).

NOTES TO CHAPTER 6

1. See Jane Jacobs, *Cities and the Wealth of Nations* (New York: Knopf, 1984).

2. Initial results of this survey are in Canada Mortgage and Housing Corporation, *Public Priorities in Urban Canada: A Survey of Community Concerns* (Ottawa: Canada Mortgage and Housing Corporation, 1979). A full report is Tom Atkinson, *A Study of Urban Concerns* (Toronto: Institute for Behavioural Research, York University, 1982).

3. T.R. Balakrishnan and G.K. Jarvis, "Changing Patters of Spatial Differentiation in Urban Canada, 1961-71," *Canadian Review of Sociology and Anthropology* 16, no. 2 (1979):218-27.

4. The anti-urban sentiment in the United

States is well documented in Morton and Lucia White, *The Intellectual Versus the City* (Cambridge, MA: Harvard University Press, 1962).

5. Empirical evidence to support anti-urban public views in the United States can be found in Stephen J. Arnold and James G. Barnes, "Canadian and American National Character as a Basis for Market Segmentation," in Jagdish N. Sheth, ed., *Research in Marketing*, vol. 2 (Greenwich, CT: JAI Press, 1979), 1-35. Gallup polls over the years have revealed similar discontent in America with urban living.

6. R.M. Yearwood, "Land Speculation and Development: American Attitudes," *Plan Canada* 9, no. 1 (1968):15-23; and Peter J. Smith, "Public Goals and the Canadian Environment," *Plan Canada* 11, no. 1 (1970):4-11. One study indicates that although people move to a suburban area, they would prefer more central locations if they were affordable. Norman Shulman and R.E. Drass, "Motives and Modes of Internal Migration: Relocation in a Canadian City," *Canadian Review of Sociology and Anthropology* 16, no. 3 (1979):333-42.

7. We have already noted this interest in private as opposed to public action in the classic studies by Sam Bass Warner dealing with Boston and Philadelphia respectively (see Chapter 5, note 48). For a broader view of the complex relationship between the structure of cities and a cultural analysis of American society, see Warner's *The Urban Wilderness: A History of the American City* (New York: Harper and Row, 1972).

8. For an extension of this argument see Michael A. Goldberg, "Municipal Arrogance or Economic Rationality: The Case of High Servicing Standards," *Canadian Public Policy* 6, no. 1 (1980):78-88. An interesting comparative analysis of servicing and development costs for Calgary, Edmonton, Houston and Phoenix can be found in Gary Sands, *Land-Office Business* (Lexington, MA: Lexington Books, 1982). Builders and developers in the Canadian cities viewed the more stringent servicing standards and other government regulations as contributing more to higher housing prices than did the American respondents.

9. Beginning in the 1960s a serious look was taken at the impacts of federal urban poli-

cies in the U.S. The result was a broad range of criticisms from all across the political spectrum. From the right came a blistering critique of urban renewal programs in Martin Anderson, *The Federal Bulldozer* (Cambridge, MA: MIT Press, 1964). From the left came Herbert Gans, *The Urban Villagers* (Glencoe, IL: The Free Press, 1962). Analogous criticisms levelled at the short-lived and U.S.-based urban renewal folly in Canada came from 1964-69 by Michael Dennis and Susan Fish, *Programs in Search of a Policy* (Toronto: Hakkert, 1972). Finally, the negative impacts of freeways on central city growth were documented in P. deLeon and J. Enns, *The Impact of Highways on Metropolitan Dispersion: St. Louis*, Rand Report P-5061 (Santa Monica, CA: The Rand Corporation, 1973).

10. A portion of the population movement has been in response to economic opportunities the expansion of which is related to federal subsidies and investments in the American South and West. Despite the absence of widespread urban blight or middle-income flight, the late 1960s and early 1970s saw a spate of "Canadian urban crisis" writing. Leading works of the period which reflect this message include: N.H. Lithwick, *Urban Canada: Problems and Prospects* (Ottawa: Central Mortgage and Housing Corporation, 1970); Paul Hellyer, *Report of the Task Force on Housing and Urban Development* (Ottawa: Queen's Printer, 1969); Dennis and Fish, *Programs in Search*, and Robert Collier, *Contemporary Cathedrals* (Montreal: Harvest House, 1975).

11. For a discussion of federal efforts to take on more responsibility in urban affairs see: Elliot J. Feldman and Jerome Milch, "Coordination or Control? The Life and Death of the Ministry of State for Urban Affairs," in Lionel D. Feldman, ed., *Politics and Government of Urban Canada*, 4th ed. (Toronto: Methuen, 1981), 246-64. A study in the mid-1970s by David Bettison suggests that the federal role in urban policy may be greater than we argue here. Bettison's findings are based on his review of the impacts of federal policy on urban development in Alberta. See David Bettison, *The Politics of Canadian Urban Development* (Edmonton, Alta.: The University of Alberta Press, 1975), especially

294-325, which summarize his argument and findings.

12. Some of the literature dealing with the fiscal crisis in American cities which derives in part from inappropriate regional governmental structures includes: Roger E. Alcaly and David E. Mermelstein, *The Fiscal Crisis of American Cities* (New York: Vintage Books, 1977) and Roy E. Bahl, ed., *The Fiscal Outlook for Cities* (Syracuse: Syracuse University Press, 1978). For discussion of the more general issue of reforming local and regional government as a response to fragmentation see: Annmarie H. Walsh, *The Urban Challenge to Government* (New York: Praeger, 1969); and Robert L. Bish and Vincent Ostrom, *Understanding Urban Government: Metropolitan Reform Reconsidered* (Washington: American Enterprise Institute for Public Policy Research, 1973).

13. Arnold and Barnes, "National Character."

14. For a detailed discussion of the difficulty encountered in the U.S. by metropolitan governmental reformers and the contrast with the Canadian situation, see John Mercer, *Comparing the Reform of Metropolitan Fragmentation, Fiscal Dependency, and Political Culture in Canada and the United States*, Occasional Paper No. 61 (Syracuse, NY: Metropolitan Studies Program, Maxwell School, Syracuse University, 1982). A complementary discussion can be found in Andrew Sancton, "Conclusion: Canadian City Politics in Comparative Perspective," in Warren Magnusson and Andrew Sancton, eds., *City Politics in Canada* (Toronto: University of Toronto Press, 1983), 291-317.

15. These latest figures are from the *1981 Census of Canada* and from the *1983 Survey of Consumer Finances* in the United States. These figures are noteworthy for several reasons. First, the Canadian homeownership rate has jumped ahead of the American rate for the first time. Second, the U.S. rate is down from the 65 per cent level recorded in the *1977 Survey of Consumer Finances*. Third, these rates in the two countries have always been very close to each other, which is the principal point to be made indicating that greater Canadian concern for public action notwithstanding, the institution of private property is alive and well and firmly entrenched in Canada. The data for Canada can be found in Canada Mortgage and Housing Corporation, *1983 Canadian Housing Statistics* (Ottawa: Canada Mortgage and Housing Corporation, 1984). The recent U.S. survey is reported on and analyzed in Robert B. Avery, Gregory E. Elliehausen, Glenn B. Canner, and Thomas A. Gustafson, "Survey of Consumer Finances, 1983," *Federal Reserve Bulletin* 70, no. 9 (September 1984):679-92.

16. Arnold and Barnes, "National Character."

17. G. Turkel, "Privatism and Orientations Towards Political Action," *Urban Life* 9, no. 2 (1980):217-35.

18. Samuel D. Clark, *The Developing Canadian Community* (Toronto: University of Toronto Press, 1968), and Carl Berger, *The Sense of Power: Studies on the Ideas of Canadian Imperialism, 1867-1914* (Toronto: University of Toronto Press, 1970), treat in some considerable depth the historical and social forces that have led to the emergence of such different societies on the same continent despite so many commonalities.

NOTES TO CHAPTER 7

1. Our choice of data is guided by the major themes explored in the book. Data selection was constrained nevertheless by data availability and comparability because we needed variables or measurements that are readily compared. While there have been some difficulties with data sources, we do not believe they are sufficiently serious to invalidate our conclusions nor deter future investigations. One difficulty, for example, is the limited geographic availability of certain data items. This has resulted in variations in the number of cities for which particular data items were required. Thus, for example, in our comparison of crime rates, 1976 data were available for only 31 of the 40 Canadian and 219 of the 277 U.S. metropolitan areas used in the analysis. We would have preferred to have a more complete data base but this was not possible. Again, data were sometimes available for the metropolitan areas but not for the central city, limiting comparison in these instances. For the crime measures, data were available for only 26 central cities in Canada.

A deficiency in Canadian public finance

data was encountered. Canada has no equivalent to the U.S. *Census of Governments*, published every five years. Data was culled with considerable effort from provincial statistics on municipal affairs. To the best of our ability, these data are comparable with U.S. data items reported in the *City and County Data Book, 1977*. Another problem area is the lack of a national data base in Canada on the Central Business Districts (CBD) for the metropolitan centers. Such a data base exists in the U.S. and is employed, for example, in the *Census of Retailing*. There are, however, problems in defining the Central Business District across the country and this may affect the quality of the data. Nevertheless, one can investigate (cautiously) retail trends in the CBDs, both absolutely and in relation to the metropolitan area. We are convinced *a priori* that a cross-national comparison would show Canadian metropolitan CBDs to be more important retail centers than their American counterparts in equivalent sized metropolitan areas. This would be another important piece of evidence buttressing the argument of a more livable and preferred central city in Canada with considerable purchasing power potential still in place. Without undertaking a national survey such data are not publicly available in Canada, and so this potentially important cross-national comparison could not be carried out.

2. It is appropriate here to convey a sense of the scale of our data base; analysis for our tabled results is not to be readily found on the pages of some census volume or in a microfiche drawer. Rather, they required data collection, coding, data file construction, computation, rechecking and final computation. After completing the first stages of collection, coding, and checking, our data files contained 248 items for the 40 Canadian urban areas, for both the entire metropolitan area and its central city. For the U.S., there were 265 items for the 277 Standard Metropolitan Statistical Areas (SMSAs), again for both the metropolitan area and its central city. From this very large and comprehensive data base, we computed 222 variables for every metropolitan center in our study (317 in total), yielding a variable data matrix with 70,734 cells.

The variables included measures for the metropolitan area, the central city and a third geographic unit, the balance (or suburban ring, the data being obtained by subtracting the value of the central city from the metropolitan total). Typically, the variables were simple percentage and ratio measures, some being standardized on a per capita basis. To illustrate, we computed a variable which expresses that proportion of an urban area's housing stock which is in single detached units. This percentage figure is available for every metropolitan area, every central city and every balance. Also, we computed various descriptive statistics, such as means, standard deviations and medians. These summary values are for each country so that we can see how American metropolitan areas as a group (or cities or suburban rings) compare with their Canadian counterparts, again as a group. Typically, it is these summary values which are tabled in this and the subsequent chapter and form the basis for our interpretation. We also made use of scores (or values) for selected metropolitan areas or central cities. The procedures followed in Chapter 9 are outlined there in more detail. To assist the flow and readability of this and the next two empirical chapters, the detailed evidence upon which our findings rest is to be found tabled at the end of the chapters. Space constraints dictate against displaying more than thirty variables in our tables. Other detailed results are available upon request from the authors.

3. This increasing complexity has given rise to a new terminology—suburbia has now been termed the "outer city." Peter Muller, *The Outer City: The Geographical Consequences of the Urbanization of the Suburbs* (Washington, D.C.: Association of American Geographers, Resource Paper no. 75-2, 1976).

4. William Bunge and Ronald Bordessa, *The Canadian Alternative: Survival, Expeditions and Urban Change*, York Geographical Monographs no. 2 (Toronto: York University, 1975); William Coffey, "Income Relationships in Boston and Toronto: A Tale of Two Countries," *Canadian Geographer* 22 (1978), 112-29; Michael A. Goldberg, "Housing and Land Prices in Canada and the U.S.," in L.B. Smith and M. Walker, eds., *Public Property: The Habitat Debate Continued* (Vancouver:

Fraser Institute, 1977).

5. In 1970, the 243 SMSAs in the United States represented 93.4 per cent of the urban population, while the 22 CMAs in Canada accounted for 80.6 per cent (1971 data).

6. James W. Simmons and Larry S. Bourne, "Defining Urban Places: Differing Concepts of the Urban System," in L.S. Bourne and J.W. Simmons, eds., *Systems of Cities* (New York: Oxford University Press, 1978).

7. The most recent census data in Canada available to us when we collected our data base are for 1976 when Statistics Canada conducted a mid-decade national census, though substantially less detailed than the decennial census of 1971. No such equivalent census is carried out in the United States, but where possible 1975 data are employed as the corresponding year. The use of data for a noncensus year in the United States does create some problems. In the primary data source, *The City and County Data Book, 1977*, 1975 data for New England urban areas are reported for a new spatial unit—the New England County Metropolitan Area—and not for SMSAs. Thus without a large-scale reconstruction of this new unit for 1970 data, we must exclude 20 New England SMSAs from the analysis. The U.S. cases are therefore 257 rather than 277 for many variables; for certain other variables from different sources the number of cases may vary, sometimes greater, sometimes fewer. One effect is to deflate the amount of population decline in the United States, since many of the excluded areas were already in a loss situation in 1960-70.

8. One alternative would have been to use a different U.S. census geographic unit—the Urbanized Area. This is less likely to be overbounded than the SMSA. However, the range of data items which are available for Urbanized Areas is far less compared to that for the SMSAs. For this research, we accepted some degree of overbounding in the comparisons to permit access to the desired range of data items. A cross-national comparison on certain variables using Urbanized Areas and the CMAs and CAs would be worthwhile, however.

9. Barry Edmonston, Michael A. Goldberg and John Mercer, "Urban Form in Canada and the United States: An Examination of Urban Density Gradients," *Urban Studies* 22 (1985): 209-17.

10. See ibid. for a further discussion of recent trends.

11. Since we have no data for revenue-miles on privately owned and operated heavy rail transit, our conclusion is somewhat qualified.

12. With respect to the measurement of ethnicity, the discussion in Chapter 3 reminds us that this is far from simple and apparently "hard" data must be treated cautiously. Nativity, or more precisely, the proportion of the population which is foreign born, is used in our analysis since for the 1970 and earlier censuses the U.S. Census recorded ethnic status *only* for those who are foreign born or have one or more parents foreign born. In contrast, *all* Canadians were at that time "required" by the Census to identify themselves with an ethnic group (based on the male lineage). As was noted in Chapter 3, there have been important changes in both American and Canadian census procedures in 1980 and 1981.

13. For more detail, see John Mercer, "On Continentalism, Distinctiveness and Comparative Urban Geography: Canadian American Cities," *Canadian Geographer* 23 (1979), 119-39. Stelter has also noted striking differences in the population growth experience of Canadian and American cities in the first half of the nineteenth century. Even earlier, in the eighteenth century, he identifies an imperial presence (British colonial authority) as important in the siting and development of urban settlements; this centralized direction was largely absent in the neighboring republic. Gilbert Stelter, "The City-Building Process in Canada," in Gilbert A. Stelter and Alan F.J. Artibise, eds., *Shaping the Urban Landscape: Aspects of the Canadian City-Building Process* (Ottawa: Carleton University Press, 1982), 1-29, especially 12-13.

14. Brian J.L. Berry, "The Counterurbanization Process: How General," in Niles M. Hansen, ed., *Human Settlement Systems: International Perspectives on Structure, Change and Public Policy* (Cambridge, MA.: Ballinger, 1977), 37.

15. For a concise and clear review of the application of these concepts by factorial ecology and some related problems, see David F. Ley, *A Social Geography of the City*

(New York: Harper and Row, 1983), 75-92. An important critique is by Ronald J. Johnston, "Residential Area Characteristics: Research Methods for Identifying Sub-Areas," in David Herbert and Ronald J. Johnston, eds., *Social Areas in Cities*, vol. 1 (London: Wiley, 1976), 193-235.

16. What needs to be recognized, however, is that numerous immigrants are skilled, educated, and employable. This class of immigrant, favored by recent immigration policies, has no initial need of cheap housing in the inner city accessible to unskilled work in the city core, the traditional destination of the stereotypical immigrant and one from which he or she was expected to struggle up and out, both socially and geographically. Rather they head directly to the housing and employment opportunities afforded by the outer city. The Canadian Census data permit this point to be illustrated. In 1981 for example, in three big-city suburbs (Scarborough-Toronto, Surrey-Vancouver and Burlington-Hamilton) the percentage of the foreign born population that had entered Canada in the last two years was 6.0, 7.8 and 4.5 per cent respectively. It is not unreasonable to infer that a substantial number moved immediately into these suburban municipalities, though this cannot be proven without survey evidence.

17. A leading urban scholar tends to err in this direction in a recent comparative essay. Berry states: "Where there are differences between what is happening to cities in the United States on the one hand, and Canada and Australia on the other, they are to be found in the deep-seated white racism that exists as an additional feature of American culture, rather than in any differential pattern of rewards flowing from the commitment to competitive private lives." Brian J.L. Berry, *Comparative Urbanization* (New York: St. Martin's Press, 1981), 167.

18. Jan Morris, "Flat City," *Saturday Night* 99, no. 6 (1984):44.

NOTES TO CHAPTER 8

1. Fortunately, that situation is beginning to change with recent publications. Report of the Resource Task Force on Constitutional Reform *Municipal Government in a New Canadian Federal System* (Ottawa: Federation of Canadian Municipalities,

1980); Richard M. Bird and Enid Slack, *Urban Public Finance in Canada* (Toronto: Butterworths, 1983). A growing number of articles on urban public finance can be found in the *Canadian Tax Journal*.

2. This study is described in Dominic Del-Guidice and Stephan M. Zacks, "The 101 Governments of Metro Toronto," in Lionel D. Feldman and Michael Goldrick, eds., *Politics and Government of Urban Canada*, 2d ed. (Toronto: Methuen, 1968), 237-47. While this case study suggests there are 101 special district or purpose governments in Metropolitan Toronto, a statement accepted at face value by Yeates and Garner (1980), examination of the criteria employed by the U.S. Bureau of the Census indicated that many Toronto area "governments" would not be considered to meet these criteria. To ensure a more accurate comparison, such units are eliminated, yielding a Toronto total of forty-seven.

3. An account of the process leading to the formation of the first metropolitan government in Canada (Toronto) is to be found in a first-rate study of Frederick G. Gardiner, Metro's initial Chairman. Timothy J. Colton, *Big Daddy* (Toronto: University of Toronto Press, 1980).

4. William E. Hudson, "The New Federalism Paradox," *Policy Studies Journal* 8, no. 6 (1980):900-906. Hudson concludes that "instead of promoting local autonomy, the new Federalism grants . . . have helped to reduce city government autonomy," 901.

5. Although our study does not reach into the 1980s, it is worth noting that the Reagan administration, through its budget cuts, is shifting more of the urban fiscal aid burden to the states. Given the traditional composition and outlook of state legislatures, this has worked against the interests of central cities and their residents. According to one commentator, Reagan sees this as a realignment of administrative structure with a traditional American political culture. Donald Devine, "American Culture and Public Administration," *Policy Studies Journal* 11, no. 2 (1982): 255-60.

6. See Bird and Slack (1983), and Dale Richmond (1980), "Provincial-Municipal Tax and Revenue Sharing: Reforms Accomplished, 1978 Compared with 1971," in Lionel Feldman, ed., *Politics and Govern-*

ment of Urban Canada, 4th ed. (Toronto: Methuen, 1980), 162-201.

7. More can be learned about the evolution of Washington's role in intergovernmental relations from a multi-volume study published by ACIR. U.S. Advisory Commission on Intergovernmental Relations, *The Federal Role in the Federal System: The Dynamics of Growth* (Washington, DC: U.S. Government Printing Office, 1980 and 1981). See also Paul Dommel, *The Politics of Revenue Sharing* (Bloomington: Indiana University Press, 1974).

8. D.R. Bean, "Forecasting the Future of Federalism," in Advisory Commission on Intergovernmental Relations, *The Future of Federalism* (Washington, D.C.: U.S. Government Printing Office, 1981), 9.

9. George F. Break, "Fiscal Federalism in the United States," in Advisory Commission on Intergovernmental Relations, *Future of Federalism*, 62.

10. Advisory Commission on Intergovernmental Relations, *Future of Federalism*.

11. For central cities in metropolitan areas of greater than 1 million, the mean total gross expenditure per capita is higher for the U.S. than that for Canada while the U.S. median is substantially less (almost $100.00) than the Canadian. This indicates that there is considerable variation in this category within the United States—while some large cities spend a great deal, others spend relatively little. Generally, the Canadian means and medians are less different.

12. John Mercer, "On Continentalism, Distinctiveness and Comparative Urban Geography," *Canadian Geographer* 23 (1979): 119-39; see Table 6.

13. For more detail on the nature of municipal bonds and other aspects of this analysis, see John Mercer and Michael A. Goldberg, "The Fiscal Condition of American and Canadian Cities," *Urban Studies* 21 (1984): 233-43.

14. The work of Maurice Yeates on Canada's heartland is considered to be definitive. A revision to his important work, *Main Street*, is now available. M. Yeates, *Main Street: Windsor-Quebec City* (Toronto: Macmillan of Canada, 1975); M. Yeates, *Main Street: Concentration and Deconcentration in the Windsor-Quebec City Axis* (Ottawa: Lands Directorate, Environment Canada, 1985).

NOTES TO CHAPTER 9

1. Introductory statements on these techniques are available for the interested reader. For factor analysis, see Jae-On Kim and Charles W. Mueller, *Introduction to Factor Analysis*, Sage University Paper series on Quantitative Applications in the Social Sciences, 07-013 (Beverly Hills: Sage Publications, 1978); for discriminant analysis, see William R. Klecka *Discriminant Analysis*, Sage University Paper series on Quantitative Applications in the Social Sciences, 07-019 (Beverly Hills: Sage Publications, 1980); for cluster analysis, see Maurice Lorr, *Cluster Analysis for Social Scientists* (San Francisco: Jossey-Bass, 1983).

2. Our selection of particular types of cluster analysis was guided by the findings of a careful comparison of a range of such procedures. See Juan E. Mezzich and Herbert Solomon, *Taxonomy and Behavioral Science: Comparative Performance of Grouping Methods* (New York: Academic Press, 1980).

3. This conviction rested in part on the empirical results reported in Chapter 8.

4. The cut-off criterion was that the eigenvalue for a factor should exceed 1.0 for it to be considered worth interpreting. The particular factor analysis used here was the BMP P4M algorithm, with principal factor analysis specified as the method of extraction. Orthogonal rotation was performed. For an introductory discussion of extraction and rotation issues, see Jae-On Kim and Charles W. Mueller, *Factor Analysis*, Sage University Paper series on Quantitative Applications in the Social Sciences, 07-014 (Beverly Hills: Sage Publications, 1978).

5. Katherine L. Bradbury, "Urban Decline and Distress: An Update," *New England Economic Review* (July-August 1984), 39-55.

6. See B.J.L. Berry, ed., *City Classification Handbook, Methods and Applications* (New York: Wiley, 1972).

7. This analysis utilized the BMD PKM algorithm and is known as K-means clustering, where K represents the number of clusters. The other cluster procedure (the centroid linkage method) utilized the BMD P2M algorithm.

8. It is hard to improve on Klecka's straight-

forward summary of the *stepwise* procedure: "A forward stepwise procedure begins by selecting the individual variable which provides the greatest univariate discrimination. The procedure then pairs this first variable with each of the remaining variables, one at a time, to locate the combination which produces the greatest discrimination. The variable which contributed to the best pair is selected. The procedure goes on to combine the first two with each of the remaining variables to form triplets. The best triplet determines the third variable to be entered. This procedure of selecting variables on the basis of the one which adds the most discrimination to those already selected continues until all possible variables have been selected or the remaining variables do not contribute a sufficient increment," Klecka, *Discriminant Analysis*, 53.

NOTES TO CHAPTER 10

1. Myth is used here as Joseph Campbell does to mean deep-seated societal truths. For details on the role of myths in society, see Joseph Campbell, *Myths to Live By* (New York: Bantam Books, 1972).
2. In his analysis of ruling elites in Canada, the United Kingdom and the United States, Colin Campbell suggests a good deal of social mobility in Canada and the U.S., but not in the U.K. See Colin Campbell, *Governments Under Stress* (Toronto: University of Toronto Press, 1983), especially Chapter 12.
3. K.C. Wheare, *Federal Government* (London, England: Oxford University Press, 1953). When looking at cities the differences between U.S. and Canadian federalism come into very clear focus. In September 1984 one of us (Goldberg) attended a conference in Berkeley, California at the University of California entitled, "An Agenda for Metropolitan America." In two days and nearly a dozen academic papers, the focus of the conference never waivered fom the federal government's varied role in setting and carrying out such an agenda. It stood in stark contrast to the course of similar conferences in Canada in which the federal government may participate but is never seen as holding the key to either defining the problems or finding the solutions. For details, see John Quigley and Daniel Rubinfeld, eds., *An Agenda for Metropolitan America* (Berkeley and Los Angeles: University of California Press, 1985).
4. Compared to recent decades, there exist sharply divergent views over the conduct of social science research. Pointing in a new direction is hardly original, therefore. Many of the major issues engaging philosophy, theory, methods and the practice of empirical research are ably discussed by Andrew Sayer, himself a specialist in urban and regional studies. Andrew Sayer, *Method in Social Science* (London: Hutchinson, 1984).

Bibliography

Abella, Irving, and Harold Troper. *None Is Too Many*. Toronto: Lester, Orpen Dennys, 1983.

Adachi, Ken. *The Enemy that Never Was*. Toronto: McClelland and Stewart, 1976.

Agnew, John, John Mercer and David Sopher, eds. *The City in Cultural Context*. Boston: Allen and Unwin, 1984.

Agocs, Carol, "Ethnic Settlement in a Metropolitan Area: A Typology of Communities," *Ethnicity* 8 (1981):127-48.

————, "Ethnic Groups in the Ecology of North American Cities," *Canadian Ethnic Studies* 11 (1979):1-18.

Alcaly, Roger E., and David E. Mermelstein. *The Fiscal Crisis of American Cities*. New York: Vintage, 1977.

Almond, Gabriel, and Sydney Verba. *The Civic Culture*. Princeton, NJ: Princeton University Press, 1963.

Alonso, William. "The Demographic Factor in Housing for the Balance of This Century." In *North American Housing Markets into the Twenty-First Century*, eds. Michael A. Goldberg and George Gau, 33-50. Cambridge, MA: Ballinger, 1983.

Alperovich, Gershon. "A New Testing Procedure of the Rank Size Distribution." Ramat-Gan, Israel: Department of Economics, Bar Ilan University, 1984, mimeograph.

Anderson, Martin. *The Federal Bulldozer*. Cambridge, MA: MIT Press, 1964.

Armour, Leslie. *The Idea of Canada and the Crisis of Community*, Ottawa: Steel Rail, 1981.

Arnold, Stephen J., and Douglas J. Tigert. "Canadians and Americans: A Comparative Analysis." *International Journal of Comparative Sociology* 15(1974):68-83.

————, and James G. Barnes. "Canadian and American National Character as a Basis for Market Segmentation." In *Research in Marketing: Volume 2*, ed. Jagdish N. Sheth, 1-35. Greenwich, CN: JAI Press, 1979.

Arnopolous, Sheila McLeod, and Dominique Clift. *The English Fact in Quebec*. Montreal: McGill-Queen's University Press, 1980.

Atkinson, Tom. *A Study of Urban Concerns*. Toronto: Institute for Behavioral Research, York University, 1982.

————, et al. *Social Change in Canada*. Toronto: Institute for Behavioral Research, York University, 1982.

————, and Michael A. Murray. *Values, Domains and the Perceived Quality of Life: Canada and the United States*. Toronto: Institute for Behavioural Research, York University, 1982.

Atwood, Margaret. *Survival: A Thematic Guide to Canadian Literature*. Toronto: Anansi, 1972.

Avery, Robert B., Gregory E. Elliehausen, Glenn B. Canner, and Thomas A. Gustafson. "Survey of Consumer Finances, 1983." *Federal Reserve Bulletin* 70, no. 9 (1984):679-92.

Bahl, Roy E., ed. *The Fiscal Outlook for Cities*. Syracuse: Syracuse University Press, 1978.

Bakvis, Herman. *Federalism and the Organization of Political Life: Canada in Comparative Perspective*. Kingston, ON: Institute of Intergovernmental Relations, Queen's University, 1981.

Balakrishnan, T.R., and G.K. Jarvis. "Changing Patters of Spatial Differentiation in Urban Canada, 1961-71." *Canadian Review of Sociology and Anthropology* 16, no.2 (1979), 218-27.

Banting, Keith, and Richard Simeon, eds. *And No One Cheered*. Toronto: Methuen, 1983.

Barger, Harold. *The Transportation Industries, 1889-1956*. New York: National Bureau of Economic Research, 1951.

Bean, D.R. "Forecasting the Future of Federalism." In Advisory Commission on Intergovernmental Relations, *The Future of Federalism*. Washington, DC: U.S. Government Printing Office, 1981.

Beck, Nathaniel, and John Pierce. "Political Involvement and Party Allegiances in Canada and the United States." In *Cross-National Perspectives: United States and Canada*, ed. Robert Presthus, 23-43. Leiden, Netherlands: E.J. Brill, 1977.

Bell, David V.J. "The Loyalist Tradition in Canada." *Journal of Canadian Studies* 5, no. 2 (1970):22-33.

_____, and Lorne Tepperman. *The Roots of Disunity: A Look at Canadian Political Culture*. Toronto: McClelland and Stewart, 1979.

Berger, Carl. *The Sense of Power: Studies on the Ideas of Canadian Imperialism, 1867-1914*. Toronto: University of Toronto Press, 1970.

Berry, Brian J.L. ed. *City Classification Handbook, Methods and Applications*. New York: J. Wiley and Sons, 1972.

_____. "Urbanization and Counterurbanization." *Urban Affairs Annual Review*, Vol. 11, Beverly Hills: Sage, 1976.

_____. "The Counterurbanization Process: How General." In *Human Settlement Systems*, ed. Niles M. Hansen, Cambridge, MA: Ballinger, 1978.

_____. *Comparative Urbanization: Divergent Paths in the Twentieth Century*. New York: St. Martin's Press, 1981.

Berry, J.W., and G.J.S. Wilde, eds. *Social Psychology: The Canadian Context*. Toronto: McClelland and Stewart, 1972.

Bettison, David. *The Politics of Canadian Urban Development*. Edmonton: University of Alberta Press, 1975.

Bibby, Reginald W. "The Delicate Mosaic: A National Examination of Intergroup Relations in Canada." *Social Indicators Research* 5(1978):169-79.

Bird, Richard M., and Enid Slack. *Urban Public Finance in Canada*. Toronto: Butterworths, 1983.

Bish, Robert L., and Vincent Ostrom. *Understanding Urban Government: Metropolitan Reform Reconsidered.* Washington: American Enterprise Institute for Public Policy Research, 1973.

Bliss, Michael. *A Living Profit: Studies in Social History of Canadian Business, 1883-1911.* Toronto: McClelland and Stewart, 1974.

Bloch, M. "Toward a Comparative History of European Societies." In *Enterprise and Secular Change: Readings in Economic History*, ed. Frederic C. Lane, Homewood, IL: R.D. Irwin, 1953.

Borcherding, Thomas E., Werner W. Pommerehne, and Friedrich Schneider. "Comparing the Efficiency of Private and Public Production: The Evidence from Five Countries." Burnaby, B.C.: Department of Economics, Simon Fraser University, 1982, mimeograph.

Brogan, David W. *The American Character.* New York: Alfred A. Knopf, 1944.

Bosserman, Phillip. *Dialectical Sociology: An Analysis of the Sociology of Georges Gurvitch.* Boston: Porter Sargent, 1968.

Bourne, Larry S., ed. *Internal Structure of the City.* 2nd ed. New York: Oxford University Press, 1982.

Bradbury, Katherine L. "Urban Decline and Distress: An Update." *New England Economic Review* (July-August 1984): 39-55.

Break, George F. "Fiscal Federation in the United States." in Advisory Commission on Intergovernmental Relations, *The Future of Federalism.* Washington, D.C.: U.S. Government Printing Office, 1981.

Brotz, Howard. "Multiculturalism in Canada: A Muddle." *Canadian Public Policy* 6 (1980): 41-46.

Bunge, William, and Ronald Bordessa. *The Canadian Alternative: Survival, Expeditions and Urban Change.* York Geographical Monographs, No. 2. Toronto: York University, 1975.

Campbell, Colin. *Governments under Stress.* Toronto: University of Toronto Press, 1983.

————, and George Szablowski. *The Superbureaucrats: Structure and Behavior in Central Agencies.* Toronto: Macmillan of Canada, 1979.

Campbell, Joseph. *Myths to Live By.* New York: Bantam Books, 1972.

Canada. Ministry of Finance. *Economic Review.* Ottawa: Minister of Supply and Services, April 1984.

Canada Mortgage and Housing Corporation. *Public Priorities in Urban Canada: A Survey of Community Concerns.* Ottawa: Canada Mortgage and Housing Corporation, 1979.

————. *1983 Canadian Housing Statistics.* Ottawa: Canada Mortgage and Housing Corporation, 1984.

Cartwright, Don. *Official Language Populations in Canada: Patterns and Contacts.* Montreal: Institute for Research on Public Policy, 1980.

————. "Language Policy and the Organization of Territory: A Canadian Dilemma." *Canadian Geographer* 25 (1981):205-24.

Clairmont, D.H., and Dennis W. Magill. *Africville: The Life and Death of a Canadian Black Community*. Toronto: McClelland and Stewart, 1974.

————, and F.C. Wien. "Race Relations in Canada." In *Ethnicity and Ethnic Relations in Canada*, eds. Jay E. Goldstein and Rita M. Bienvenue, 309-24. Toronto: Butterworths, 1980.

Clark, Gordon, and Michael Dear. *State Apparatus: Structures and Language of Legitimacy*. Winchester, MA: Allen and Unwin, 1984.

Clark, Samuel D., ed. *The Developing Canadian Community*. Toronto: University of Toronto Press, 1968.

Clement, Wallace. *The Canadian Corporate Elite: An Analysis of Economic Power*. Carleton Library No. 89. Toronto: McClelland and Stewart, 1975.

————. *Continental Corporate Power: Economic Linkages between Canada and the United States*. Toronto, Ont.: McClelland and Stewart, 1977.

Coffey, William. "Income Relationships in Boston and Toronto: A Tale of Two Countries." *Canadian Geographer* 22 (1978):112-29.

Collier, Robert. *Contemporary Cathedrals*. Montreal: Harvest House, 1975.

Colton, Timothy J. *Big Daddy*. Toronto: University of Toronto Press, 1980.

Commager, Henry Steele. *Freedom and Order*. Cleveland, OH: World Publishing Company, 1966.

Corke, S.E. *Land Use Controls in British Columbia: A Comparative Analysis of Provincial Planning Legislation*. Land Policy Paper No. 3, Toronto: Centre for Urban and Community Studies, University of Toronto, 1982.

Cullen, Dallas, J.D. Jobson, and Rodney Schneck. "Towards the Development of a Canadian-American Scale: A Research Note." *Canadian Journal of Political Science* 11 (1978): 409-18.

Dahl, Robert A. *A Preface to Democratic Theory*. Chicago: University of Chicago Press, 1956.

Darroch, A. Gordon. "Another Look at Ethnicity, Stratification and Social Mobility in Canada." *Canadian Journal of Sociology* 4 (1979): 1-25.

Davis, Cary, Carl Haub, and Joanne Willette. "U.S. Hispanics: Changing the Face of America." *Population Bulletin* 38, no. 3 (1983).

Dear, Michael, and Allan J. Scott, eds. *Urbanization and Urban Planning in Capitalist Society*. New York: Methuen, 1981.

DelGuidice, Dominic and Stephan M. Zacks. "The 101 Governments of Metro Toronto." In *Politics and Government of Urban Canada*. 2nd ed., eds. Lionel D. Feldman and Michael Goldrick, 237-247. Toronto: Methuen, 1968.

deLeon, P., and J. Enns. *The Impact of Highways on Metropolitan Dispersion: St. Louis*. RAND Report P-5061, Santa Monica, CA: RAND Corporation, 1973.

Dennis, Michael, and Susan Fish. *Programs in Search of a Policy*. Toronto: Hakkert, 1972.

Desbarats, Jacqueline. "Thai Migration to Los Angeles." *Geographical Review* 69 (1979):302-18.

Devine, Donald. "American Culture and Public Administration." *Policy Studies Journal* 11, no. 2 (1982):255-60.

deVise, Pierre. *Misused and Misplaced Hospitals and Doctors: A Locational Analysis of the Urban Health Care Crisis.* Resource Paper No. 22. Washington, D.C.: Association of American Geographers, 1973.

Doerr, Audrey. "Organizing for Urban Policy: Some Comments on the Ministry of State for Urban Affairs." *Canadian Journal of Regional Science* 5, no. 1 (1982):95-101.

Dommel, Paul. *The Politics of Revenue Sharing.* Bloomington, IN: Indiana University Press, 1974.

Downs, Anthony. *An Economic Theory of Democracy.* New York: Harper, 1957.

Driedger, Elmer A. *The British North America Acts 1867 to 1975.* Ottawa: Minister of Supply and Services, 1976.

Driedger, Leo. "Ethnic Boundaries: A Comparison of Two Urban Neighborhoods," *Sociology and Social Research* 62 (1978):193-211.

————, and G. Church. "Residential Segregation and Institutional Completeness: A Comparison of Ethnic Minorities," *Canadian Review of Sociology and Anthropology* 2 (1974):30-52.

Duncan, James S., and Nancy G. Duncan. "A Cultural Analysis of Urban Residential Landscapes in North America: The Case of the Anglophone Elite." In *The City in Cultural Context*, eds. John A. Agnew, John Mercer and David E. Sopher, 255-76. Boston: Allen and Unwin, 1984.

Easterbrook, W.T., and Hugh G.J. Aitken. *Canadian Economic History.* Toronto: Macmillan, 1963.

Edmonston, Barry, Michael A. Goldberg, and John Mercer. "Urban Form in Canada and the United States: An Examination of Urban Density Gradients." *Urban Studies* 22 (1985):209-17.

Elazar, Daniel J., and Joseph Zikmund, eds. *The Ecology of American Political Culture.* New York: T. Corwell, 1975.

Elkins, David J., and Richard Simeon. *Small Worlds: Provinces and Parties in Canadian Political Life.* Toronto: Methuen, 1980.

Fearn, Gordon F.N. *Canadian Social Organization.* Toronto: Holt Rinehart and Winston, 1973.

Feldman, Elliot J., and Jerome Milch. "Coordination or Control? The Life and Death of the Ministry of State for Urban Affairs." In *Politics and Government of Urban Canada.* 4th ed., ed. Lionel D. Feldman, 246-64. Toronto: Methuen, 1981.

Friedenberg, Edgar Z. *Deference to Authority: The Case of Canada.* White Plains, NY: M.E. Sharpe, 1980.

Fry, August J. *On the Battle of Stoney Creek and Other Allegories.* Amsterdam: Free University of Amsterdam, 1982.

Gans, Herbert. *The Urban Villagers.* Glencoe, IL: Free Press, 1962.

————. "Symbolic Ethnicity: The Future of Ethnic Groups and Cultures in America." In *On the Making of Americans*, eds. Herbert Gans et al. Philadelphia: University of Pennsylvania Press, 1979.

Gertler, Len. "The Challenge of Public Policy Research." *Canadian Journal of Regional Science* 2, no. 1 (1979):77-89.

————. "The Changing Metropolis and the Blumenfeld Blues." *The Metropolis:*

Proceedings of a Conference in Honour of Hans Blumenfeld, eds. Larry S. Bourne and John Hitchcock. Toronto: University of Toronto Press, 1985.

————, and Ronald Crowley. *Changing Canadian Cities: The Next 25 Years.* Toronto: McClelland and Stewart, 1977.

Gibbins, Roger. *Regionalism: Territorial Politics in Canada and the United States.* Toronto: Butterworths, 1982.

Girgus, Sam B. *The Law of the Heart: Individualism and the Modern Self in American Literature.* Austin: University of Texas Press, 1979.

Glazebrook, G.P. de T. *A History of Transportation in Canada.* Vols. 1-2, Toronto: University of Toronto Press, 1964.

Glazer, Nathan. "Individualism and Equality in the United States." In *On the Making of Americans: Essays in Honor of David Riesman,* eds. Herbert Gans, et al., 121-42. Philadelphia: University of Pennsylvania Press, 1979.

————, and Daniel Patrick Moynihan, eds. *Ethnicity: Theory and Experience.* Cambridge: Harvard University Press, 1975.

Goldberg, Michael A. "Housing and Land Prices in Canada and the U.S.." In *Public Property: The Habitat Debate Continued,* eds. L.B. Smith and M. Walker, 207-54. Vancouver: Fraser Institute, 1977.

————. "The BNA Act, NHA, CMHC, MSUA, etc.: 'Nymophobia' and the On-Going Search for an Appropriate Canadian Housing and Urban Development Policy." In *Canadian Confederation at the Crossroads,* ed. Michael Walker, 320-61. Vancouver: Fraser Institute, 1978.

————. "Municipal Arrogance or Economic Rationality: The Case of High Servicing Standards." *Canadian Public Policy* 6 no. 1 (1980): 78-88.

————, and Peter Chinloy. *Urban Land Economics.* New York: John Wiley and Sons, 1984.

————, and John Mercer. "Canadian and U.S. Cities: Basic Differences, Possible Explanations, and the Meaning for Public Policy." *Papers of the Regional Science Association* 45, (1980):159-83.

————, and Michael Y. Seelig. "Canadian Cities: The Right Deed for the Wrong Reason." *Planning* 41, no. 3 (1975): 8-13.

Gordon, Milton. *Assimilation in American Life.* New York: Oxford University Press, 1964.

————. *Human Nature, Class and Ethnicity.* New York: Oxford University Press, 1978.

Gowans, Alan. *Images of American Living: Four Centuries of Architecture and Furniture as Cultural Expression.* Philadelphia: Lippincott, 1964.

————. *Building Canada: An Architectural History of Canadian Life.* Toronto: Oxford University Press, 1966.

Grady, Wayne. "The Abortionist." *Saturday Night* 99, no. 7 (1984): 38.

Greenstone, J. David, ed. *Public Values and Private Power in American Politics.* Chicago: University of Chicago Press, 1982.

Guillot, Eliane. "LRT Design Choices: Edmonton and Calgary." *Traffic Quarterly* 37, no. 3 (1983):337-54.

Gurvitch, Georges. *Essais de Sociologie*. Paris: Recueil Sirey, 1938.

Hardin, Herschel. *A Nation Unaware: The Canadian Economic Culture*. Vancouver: J.J. Douglas, 1974.

Harloe, Michael. "Notes on Comparative Urban Research." In *Urbanization and Urban Planning in Capitalist Society*, eds. Michael Dear and Allan J. Scott, New York: Methuen, 1981.

Harris, Richard. *Class and Housing Tenure in Modern Canada*. Research Paper No. 153, Toronto: Centre for Urban and Community Studies, University of Toronto, May 1984.

Harrison, Fred. "U.S. Has Own Set of Investment Controls, Ottawa Points Out." *Financial Post* (July 3, 1982):S3.

Hartz, Louis. *The Liberal Tradition in America*. New York: Harcourt Brace, 1953.
———— et al. *The Founding of New Societies*. New York: Harcourt Brace, 1964.

Harvey, David. "The Political Economy of Urbanization in Advanced Capitalist Societies." In *The Social Economy of Cities*, eds. G. Gappert and H. Rose. Beverly Hills: Sage, 1975.

Hayes, Saul. "Some Differences between Canadian and U.S. Jewry." *Viewpoints* 1 (March 1966): 3-10.

Hellyer, Paul. *Report of the Task Force on Housing and Urban Development*. Ottawa: Queen's Printer, 1969.

Henry, Frances. *The Dynamics of Racism in Toronto*. Research Report. Toronto: York University, 1978.

Herberg, Will. *Protestant-Catholic-Jew*. Garden City, NY: Anchor, 1960.

Highbee, Edward. "Centre Cities in Canada and the United States." In *The American Environment: Perceptions and Policies*, eds. J.W. Watson and T. O'Riordan, 145-60. New York: John Wiley and Sons, 1976.

Hodge, Gerald D., and Mohammed A. Qadeer. *Towns and Villages in Canada*. Toronto: Butterworth, 1983.

Hofstadter, Richard. *The American Political Tradition*. New York: Vintage, 1973.

Hofstede, Geert. *Culture's Consequences: International Differences in Work-Related Values*. Beverly Hills, CA: Sage, 1980.

Horowitz, Gad. "Conservatism, Liberalism, and Socialism in Canada: An Interpretation." *Canadian Journal of Economics and Political Science* 32, no. 2 (1966): 141-71.

————. "Notes on Conservatism, Liberalism and Socialism in Canada." *Canadian Journal of Political Science* 11 (1978):383-99.

Horowitz, Irving Louis. "The Hemisphere Connection." *Queen's Quarterly* 80 (1973):327-59.

Hudson, William E. "The New Federalism Paradox." *Policy Studies Journal* 8, no. 6 (1980):900-906.

Hulchanski, D. "St. Lawrence and False Creek." Vancouver: U.B.C. Planning Papers, Canadian Planning Issues, No. 10, 1984.

Hunter, Alfred A. *Class Tells: On Social Inequality in Canada.* Toronto: Butterworths, 1981.

Hutcheson, John. *Dominance and Dependency.* Toronto: McClelland and Stewart, 1978.

Hutchinson, R.C. "Religion, Morality and Law in Modern Society." In *Religion and Culture in Canada*, ed. P. Slater. Ottawa: Canadian Corporation for Studies in Religion, 1977.

Inglehart, Ronald. *The Silent Revolution: Changing Values and Political Styles Among Western Publics.* Princeton: Princeton University Press, 1977.

Inkeles, Alex. "Continuity and Change in the American National Character." In *The Third Century: America as a Post-Industrial Society*, ed. Seymour Lipset, 389-416. Chicago: University of Chicago Press, 1979.

Innis, Mary Q. *Essays in Canadian Economic History.* Toronto: University of Toronto Press, 1956.

Isajiw, Wsevolod W., ed. *Ukrainians in American and Canadian Society.* Jersey City: M.P. Kots, 1976.

———. "Definitions of Ethnicity." In *Ethnicity and Ethnic Relations in Canada,* eds. Jay E. Goldstein and Rita M. Bienvenue. Toronto: Butterworth, 1980.

Jacobs, Jane. *Cities and the Wealth of Nations.* New York: Alfred A. Knopf, 1984.

Johnson, Ronald J. *The American Urban System.* New York: St. Martin's Press, 1982.

———. "Residential Area Characteristics: Research Methods for Identifying Sub-Areas." In *Social Areas in Cities*, Vol. 1, eds. David Herbert and Ronald J. Johnston, 193-235. London: Wiley, 1976.

Kain, John F. "Black Suburbanization in the Eighties: A New Beginning or a False Hope?" In *An Agenda for Metropolitan America*, eds. J. Quigley and D. Rubinfeld. Berkeley and Los Angeles: University of California Press, 1985.

Kalbach, Warren E. *Ethnic Residential Segregation and its Significance for the Individual in an Urban Setting* (Toronto: Centre for Urban and Community Studies, University of Toronto, Research Paper No. 124, 1981).

———, and Wayne W. McVey. *The Demographic Bases of Canadian Society.* 2d ed. Toronto: McGraw-Hill Ryerson, 1979.

Kammen, Michael. *People of Paradox: An Inquiry Concerning the Origins of American Civilization.* New York: Oxford University Press, 1980.

Kerr, Donald. "Review of George A. Nader, *Cities of Canada, Vols. I and II, Annals of Association of American Geographers* 61, no.1 (1977):163-65.

Kim, Jae-On and Charles W. Mueller. *Introduction to Factor Analysis* and *Factor Analysis.* Sage University Paper series on Quantitative Applications in the Social Sciences, 07-013 and 07-014. Beverly Hills: Sage, 1978.

King, Preston. *Federalism and Federation.* Baltimore: Johns Hopkins University Press, 1982.

Klecka, William R. *Discriminant Analysis.* Sage University Paper series on Quantitative Applications in the Social Sciences, 07-019. Beverly Hills: Sage, 1980.

Knight, David B. "Canada in Crisis: The Power of Regionalisms." In *Tension Areas of the World*, ed. D.G. Bennett. Champaign, IL: Park Press, 1982.

Laponce, Jean A. "The City Centre as Conflictual Space in the Bilingual City: The Case of Montreal." In *Centre and Periphery: Spatial Variation in Politics*, ed. Jean Gottman. Beverly Hills: Sage, 1980.

Lappin, Ben. "Canadian Jewry and the Identity Crisis." *Viewpoints* 2 (1967):9-14.

Leacy, F.H., ed. *Historical Statistics of Canada*. 2d ed. Ottawa: Statistics Canada, 1983.

LeDuc, Lawrence, and J. Alex Murray. "Public Opinion and North American Integration: Pragmatic Nationalism." In *The Integration Question: Political Economy and Public Policy in Canada and North America*, eds. Jon Pammett and Brian Tomlin. Toronto: Addison-Wesley, 1984.

Leman, Christopher. *The Collapse of Welfare Reform: Political Institutions, Policy and the Poor in Canada and the United States*. Cambridge, MA: MIT Press, 1980.

Lepawsky, Albert. "Style and Substance in Contemporary Planning: The American New Deal's National Resources Planning Board as a Model." *Plan Canada* 18, no. 3 (1978):153-87.

Levitt, Kari. *Silent Surrender*. Toronto: Macmillan, 1970.

Ley, David F. *A Social Geography of the City*. New York: Harper and Row, 1983.

Lindblom, Charles E. *Politics and Markets*. New York: Basic Books, 1977.

Lipset, Seymour M. "The Value Patterns of Democracy: A Case Study in Comparative Analysis." *American Sociological Review* 28, no. 4 (1963): 515-31.

_____. *Revolution and Counterrevolution*. New York: Anchor, 1970.

_____. "Revolution and Counterrevolution—Some Comments at a Conference Analyzing the Bicentennial of a Celebrated North American Divorce." In *Perspectives on Revolution and Evolution*, ed. Richard A. Preston, 22-45. Durham, NC: Duke University Press, 1979.

_____. *The First New Nation*. New York: Norton, 1979.

_____. "Canada and the United States: The Cultural Dimension." In *Canada and the United States*, eds. Charles F. Doran and John H. Sigler. Englewood Cliffs, NJ: Prentice-Hall, 1985.

Lithwick, N.H. *Urban Canada: Problems and Prospects*. Ottawa: Central Mortgage and Housing Corporation, 1970.

Lorr, Maurice. *Cluster Analysis for Social Scientists*. San Francisco: Jossey-Bass, 1983.

Mark, Jonathan, and Michael A. Goldberg. "Neighbourhood Change: A Canadian Perspective." In *The Annals of Regional Science*, (forthcoming, 1986).

Marr, William L., and Donald G. Paterson. *Canada: An Economic History*. Toronto: Macmillan, 1980.

Mass Transit. July, 1983.

Masser, Ian. "Comparative Planning Studies: A Critical Review." *TRP#33*. Sheffield, England: Department of Town and Regional Planning, University of Sheffield, 1981.

_____. "Some Methodological Considerations." In *Design and Implementation of Cross-National Research Projects*, ed. Philip Booth, TRP #44. Sheffield, England: Department of Town and Regional Planning, University of Sheffield, 1983.

McCarthy, Eugene J. "American Politics and American Character." In *The Search for Identity*, ed. Roger L. Shinn, 79-87. New York: Harper and Row, 1964.

McClelland, David C. *The Achieving Society*. Princeton: Van Nostrand, 1961.

McConnell, Grant. *Private Power and American Democracy*. New York: Knopf, 1966.

McNaught, Kenneth. *The Pelican History of Canada*. Harmondsworth, England: Penguin, 1982.

McRoberts, Kenneth, and Dale Postgate. *Quebec: Social Change and Political Crisis*. Toronto: McClelland and Stewart, 1980.

Meekison, J. Peter. *Canadian Federalism: Myth or Reality*. 3d ed. Toronto: Methuen, 1977.

Meisel, John. "Who are We? Perceptions in English Canada." *Proceedings of the Conference on the Future of the Canadian Confederation*. Toronto: University of Toronto, 1977.

John Mercer. "On Continentalism, Distinctiveness and Comparative Urban Geography: Canadian and American Cities." *Canadian Geographer* 23 (1979): 119-39.

_____. "Locational Consequences of Housing Policies for the Low-Income Elderly: A Case Study," in Stephen M. Golant, ed., *Location and Environment of Elderly Population* (Washington, DC: V.H. Winston, 1979).

_____. "Comparing the Reform of Metropolitan Fragmentation, Fiscal Dependency, and Political Culture in Canada and the United States." Syracuse, NY: Occasional Paper no. 61, Metropolitan Studies Program, Maxwell School, Syracuse University, 1982.

_____, and Michael A. Goldberg. "The Fiscal Condition of American and Canadian Cities." *Urban Studies* 21 (1984):233-43.

_____. "Value Differences and their Meaning for Urban Development in Canada and the United States." In *Power and Place: Canadian Urban Development in the North American Context,* eds. Gilbert Stelter and Alan Artibise. Vancouver: University of British Columbia Press, 1985.

_____, and John Hultquist. "National Progress Toward Housing and Urban Renewal Goals." In *Urban Policymaking and Metropolitan Dynamics*, ed. John S. Adams, 101-62. Cambridge, MA: Ballinger, 1976.

_____, and Deborah A. Phillips. "Attitudes of Homeowners and the Decisions to Rehabilitate Property." *Urban Geography* 2 (1981):216-36.

Meyer, John R., and Jose A. Gomez-Ibanez. *Autos, Traffic and Cities*. Cambridge, MA: Twentieth Century Fund, 1981.

Mezzich, Juan E., and Herbert Solomon. *Taxonomy and Behavioral Science: Comparative Performance of Grouping Methods*. New York: Academic Press, 1980.

Michalos, Alex C. "Foundations, Population and Health." *North American Social Report: Volume 1.* Boston: D. Reidel, 1980.

_____. "Crime, Justice and Politics." *North American Social Report:* Volume 2. Boston: D. Reidel, 1980.

_____. "Economics, Religion and Morality." *North American Social Report: Volume 5.* Boston: D. Reidel, 1982.

Mills, C. Wright. *The Power Elite*. New York: Oxford University Press, 1956.

Mills, Edward S. *Studies in the Structure of the Urban Economy*. Baltimore: Johns Hopkins University Press, 1972.

Milner, Henry. *Politics in the New Quebec*. Toronto: McClelland and Stewart, 1978.

Mishler, William. *Political Participation in Canada: Prospects for Democratic Citizenship*. Toronto: Macmillan, 1979.

Monopoli, W.V. "Equality before the Law." In *Cross-National Perspectives: United States and Canada*, ed. Robert Presthus. Leiden: E.J. Brill, 1977.

Moodley, Kogila. "Canadian Ethnicity in Comparative Perspective: Issues in the Literature." In *Ethnicity, Power and Politics in Canada*, eds. Jorgen Dahlie and Tissa Fernando, 6-21. Toronto: Methuen, 1981.

Morris, Jan. "Flat City." *Saturday Night* 99, no. 6 (1984):44.

Morris, Raymond, and C. Michael Lanphier. *Three Scales of Inequality*. Don Mills, ON: Longman Canada, 1977.

Morris, Richard S. *Bum Rap on America's Cities: The Real Causes of Urban Decay*. Englewood Cliffs, NJ: Prentice-Hall, 1978.

Morton, William L. *The Critical Years*. Toronto: McClelland and Stewart, 1964.
————. *The Kingdom of Canada*. Toronto: McClelland and Stewart, 1969.
————. *The Canadian Identity*. 2d ed. Toronto: University of Toronto Press, 1972.

Moscovitch, Allan. "The Canadian Economy and Inequality." In *Inequality: Essays on the Political Economy of Social Welfare*, eds. Allan Moscovitch and Glenn Drover, 58-98. Toronto: University of Toronto Press, 1981.

Muller, Peter. *The Outer City: The Geographical Consequences of the Urbanization of the Suburbs*. Washington, DC: Association of American Geographers, Resource Paper No. 75-2, 1976.

Myrdal, Gunnar. *An American Dilemma: The Negro Problem and Modern Democracy*. New York: Harper and Row, 1944.

Nagata, Judith A. "One Vine, Many Branches: Internal Differentiation in Canadian Ethnic Groups." In *Two Nations, Many Cultures: Ethnic Groups in Canada*, ed. Jean Leonard Elliott, 173-81. Scarborough, ON: Prentice-Hall, 1979.

Newman, Peter C. *The Canadian Establishment, Vols 1 and 2*. Toronto: McClelland and Stewart, 1975.

Niemi, Albert W., Jr. *U.S. Economic History*. 2d ed. Chicago, IL: Rand McNally, 1980.

O'Brien, Allan. "The Ministry of State for Urban Affairs: A Municipal Perspective." *Canadian Journal of Regional Science* 5, no. 1 (1982):83-94.

O'Connor, James. *Accumulation Crisis*. New York: Basil Blackwell, 1984.

Office of Policy Development and Research. *A Survey of Citizen Views and Concerns About Urban Life*. Washington, DC: U.S. Department of Housing and Urban Development, HUD-PDR-306, May, 1978.

Palm, Risa. *The Geography of American Cities*. New York: Oxford University Press, 1981.

————. "Urban Geography: City Structures." *Progress in Human Geography* 6 (1982):89-95.

Park, Libbie, and Frank Park. *Anatomy of Big Business.* Toronto: James Lewis and Samuel, 1973.

Parry, Robert L. *Galt, U.S.A.* Toronto: MacLean-Hunter, 1971; revised, 1979.

Penalosa, Fernando. "Review of *Language Diversity and Language Contact: Essays by Stanley Lieberson*" in *Language Problems and Language Planning* 8 (1984): 240.

Pineo, Peter C. "The Social Standing of Ethnic and Racial Groupings." *Canadian Review of Social Anthropology* 14 (1977):147-57.

_____, and John C. Goyder. "Social Class Identification of National Sub-groups." In *Social Stratification in Canada*, eds. James E. Curtis and William G. Scott, 187-96. Scarborough, ON: Prentice-Hall, 1973.

Piper, J. "Saskatoon Robs the Bank." *Ekistics* 233 (1975):265-67.

Polsby, Nelson W. *Community Power and Political Theory: A Further Look at Problems of Evidence and Inference.* New Haven: Yale University Press, 1980.

Porter, John. *The Vertical Mosaic.* Toronto: University of Toronto Press, 1965.

_____. "Canadian Character in the Twentieth Century." In *Canada: A Sociological Profile*, ed. W.E. Mann. Toronto: Copp Clark, 1971.

Presthus, Robert. *Elites in the Policy Process.* London, England: Cambridge University Press, 1974.

_____, ed. *Cross-National Perspectives: United States and Canada.* Leiden: E.J. Brill, 1977.

_____. "Evolution and Canadian Political Culture: The Politics of Accommodation." In *Perpectives on Revolution and Evolution,* ed. Richard A. Preston. Durham, NC: Duke University Press, 1979.

Purdy, Harry L. *Transportation Competition and Public Policy in Canada.* Vancouver: University of British Columbia Press, 1972.

Quann, Dorothy. *Racial Discrimination in Housing.* Discussion Paper: Canadian Council on Social Development. Ottawa: C.C.S.D., 1979.

Quigley, John, and Daniel Rubinfeld, eds. *An Agenda for Metropolitan America.* Berkeley and Los Angeles: University of California Press, 1985.

Ray, D. Michael. *Canadian Urban Trends: Volume 1, National Perspective.* Toronto: Copp-Clark, 1976.

_____, and Robert A. Murdie. "Canadian and American Urban Differences." *City Classification Handbook: Methods and Applications*, ed. Brian J.L. Berry, 181-210. New York: Wiley, 1972.

Reid, John. "Black America in the 1980's." *Population Bulletin* 37, no. 4, (1982).

Report of the Resource Task Force on Constitutional Reform. *Municipal Government in a New Canadian Federal System.* Ottawa: Federation of Canadian Municipalities, 1980.

Richards, John, and Larry Pratt. *Prairie Capitalism: Power and Influence in the New West.* Toronto: McClelland and Stewart, 1980.

Richardson, Harry. *The New Urban Economics and Alternatives.* London, England: Pion, 1977.

_____. *Urban Economics.* Hinsdale, IL: Dryden, 1978.

Richmond, Anthony H. "Immigration and Racial Prejudice in Britain and Canada."

In *Two Nations, Many Cultures: Ethnic Groups in Canada*, ed. Jean Leonard Elliott, 290-310. Scarborough, ON: Prentice-Hall, 1979.

Richmond, Dale. "Provincial-Municipal Tax and Revenue Sharing: Reforms Accomplished, 1978 Compared with 1971." In *Politics and Government of Urban Canada*. 4th ed., ed. Lionel Feldman, 162-201. Toronto: Methuen, 1980.

Roberts, Lance W., and R.A. Clifton. "Exploring the Ideology of Canadian Multiculturalism." *Canadian Public Policy* 8 (1982):88-94.

Robertson, James O. *American Myth, American Reality*. New York: Hill and Wang, 1980.

Robinson, Ira M. *Canadian Urban Growth Trends*. Vancouver: University of British Columbia Press, 1981.

Robinson, Lukin. "The American Sponge." *The Canadian Forum* 64, no. 743 (November 1984):9-13.

Robson, Brian T. *Urban Social Areas*. London: Oxford University Press, 1981.

Rosenberg, Mark. "Physician Location Behaviour in Metropolitan Toronto." *Canadian Geographer* 28 (1984):158-70.

Russell, Peter H. *Leading Constitutional Decisions*. Toronto: MacMillan, 1978.

Sancton, Andrew. "Conclusion: Canadian City Politics in Comparative Perspective." In *City Politics in Canada*, eds. Warren Magnusson and Andrew Sancton, 291-317. Toronto: University of Toronto Press, 1983.

Sands, Gary. *Land-Office Business*. Lexington, MA: Lexington, 1982.

Sayer, Andrew. *Method in Social Science,* London: Hutchinson, 1984.

Schwartz, Mildred A. *Politics and Territory: The Sociology of Regional Persistence in Canada*. Montreal: McGill-Queen's University Press, 1974.

Shulman, Norman, and R.E. Drass. "Motives and Modes of Internal Migration: Relocation in a Canadian City." *Canadian Review of Sociology and Anthropology* 16, no. 3 (1979):333-42.

Simmons, James W., and Larry S. Bourne. "Defining Urban Places: Differing Concepts of the Urban System," in *Systems of Cities*, eds. L.S. Bourne and J.W. Simmons. New York: Oxford University Press, 1978.

————. *Recent Trends and Patterns in Canadian Settlement, 1976-1981*. Major Report No. 23, Centre for Urban and Community Studies, University of Toronto, 1984.

Simpson, Jeffrey. *Discipline of Power: The Conservative Interlude and the Liberal Restoration*. Toronto: Macmillan, 1984.

Smiley, Donald V. *Canada in Question: Federalism in the Eighties*. 3d ed. Toronto: McGraw-Hill Ryerson, 1980.

————. "The Challenge of Canadian Ambivalence." *Queen's Quarterly* 88, no. 1 (1981):1-12.

Smith, Allan. "Metaphor and Nationality in North America." *Canadian Historical Review* 51 (1970):247-75.

————. "American Culture and the English Canadian Mind at the End of the Nineteenth Century." *Journal of Popular Culture* 4, no. 3 (1971):1045-51.

————. "The Myth of the Self-made Man in English Canada, 1850-1914." *Canadian Historical Review* 59 (1978):189-219.

_____. "National Images and National Maintenance: The Ascendancy of the Ethnic Idea in North America." *Canadian Journal of Political Science* 14 (1981):227-57.

Smith, Edward Conrad, ed. *The Constitution of the United States*. 11th ed. New York: Harper and Row, 1979.

Smith, Peter J. "Public Goals and the Canadian Environment." *Plan Canada* 11, no.1 (1970):4-11.

Smith Tom W. "Ethnic Measurement and Identification." *Ethnicity* 7 (1980):78-95.

Stark, Werner. *The Social Bond: An Investigation into the Bases of Law-Abidingness*. New York: Fordham University Press, 1976.

Statistics Canada. *Canada Yearbook 1980-81*. Ottawa: Ministry of Supply and Services, 1981.

Stelter, Gilbert. "The City-Building Process in Canada." In *Shaping the Urban Landscape: Aspects of the Canadian City-Building Process*, eds. Gilbert A. Stelter and Alan F.J. Artibise, 1-29. Ottawa: Carleton University Press, 1982.

Stevenson, Garth. *Unfulfilled Union*. Toronto: Gage, 1982.

Stewart, Walter. *As They See Us*. Toronto: McClelland and Stewart, 1977.

Taylor, Charles. *Radical Tories: The Conservative Tradition in Canada*. Toronto: Anansi, 1982.

Taylor, D.G., P.B. Sheatsley, and A.M. Greeley. "Attitudes Towards Racial Integration." *Scientific American* 238, no. 6 (1978):42-49.

Taylor, George R. *The Transportation Revolution, 1815-1860*. New York: Holt, Rhinehart and Winston, 1951.

The Constitution Act, 1982. Ottawa: Minister of Supply and Services, 1982.

Thornton, Arlavel, and Deborah Freedman. "The Changing American Family." *Population Bulletin* 38, no. 4 (1983).

Tindal, C.R. *Structural Changes in Local Government: Government for Urban Regions*. Toronto: Institute of Public Administration of Canada, 1977.

Transportation Research Board. "State Highway Programs Versus the Spending Powers of Congress." *Research Results Digest*, #136, Washington, DC: Transportation Research Board, 1982.

Trofimenkoff, Susan Mann. *The Dream of Nation: A Social and Intellectual History of Quebec*. Toronto: MacMillan, 1983.

Trudeau, Pierre Elliott. *Federalism and the French Canadians*. Toronto: University of Toronto Press, 1968.

Truman, David B. *The Government Process*. New York: Knopf, 1953.

Truman, Tom. "A Critique of Seymour M. Lipset's Article, 'Value Differences, Absolute or Relative: The English Speaking Democracies.' " *Canadian Journal of Political Science* 4, no. 1 (1971):497-525.

_____. "A Scale for Measuring a Tory Streak in Canada and the United States." *Canadian Journal of Political Science* 10 (1977):597-614.

Turkel, G. "Privatism and Orientations Towards Political Action." *Urban Life* 9, no. 2 (1980):217-35.

Urbanics Consultants. "A Study of the Market Development Opportunities in the LRT South Corridor." Calgary, AB: Planning Department, City of Calgary, 1978.

Urquhart, M.C., and K.A.H. Buckley, eds. *Historical Statistics of Canada.* Toronto: MacMillan, 1965.

U.S. Advisory Commission on Intergovernmental Relations. *The Federal Role in the Federal System: The Dynamics of Growth.* Washington, DC: U.S. Government Printing Office, 1980 and 1981.

U.S. Department of Commerce, Bureau of the Census. *Historical Statistics of the United States: Colonial Times to 1970, Pts. 1&2.* Washington, DC: U.S. Government Printing Office, 1975.

_____. *Statistical Abstract of the United States.* 104th ed. Washington, D.C.: US Government Printing Office, 1984.

Vallee, Frank G., and D.R. Whyte. "Canadian Society: Trends and Perspectives." In *Canadian Society: Sociological Perspectives,* eds. B. Blishen et al. Toronto: Gage, 1968.

van Slambrouck, Paul. "San Diego's Do-It-Yourself Trolley." *Mass Transit,* (June, 1981):64.

Vickers, Geoffrey. *Value Systems and Social Process.* London: Tavistock 1968.

Wade, Mason, ed. *Canadian Dualism.* Toronto: University of Toronto Press, 1960.

_____. *Regionalism and the Canadian Community, 1867-1967.* Toronto: University of Toronto Press, 1969.

Walsh, Annmarie H. *The Urban Challenge to Government.* New York: Praeger, 1969.

_____. *The Public's Business: The Politics and Practices of Government Corporations.* Cambridge, MA: MIT Press, 1978.

Walton, John. "Comparative Urban Studies." *International Journal of Comparative Sociology* 22 (1981):22-39.

Ward, Peter. *White Canada Forever.* Montreal: McGill-Queen's University Press, 1978.

Warner, Sam Bass. *Streetcar Suburbs.* Cambridge: Harvard University Press, 1962.

_____. *The Private City.* Philadelphia: University of Pennsylvania Press, 1968.

_____. *The Urban Wilderness: A History of the American City.* New York: Harper and Row, 1972.

Wheare, K.C. *Federal Government.* London: Oxford University Press, 1953.

Whitaker, Reg. "Images of the State in Canada." In *The Canadian State: Political Economy and Political Power,* ed. Leo Panitch, 28-68. Toronto: University of Toronto Press, 1977.

White, Morton, and Lucia White. *The Intellectual Versus the City.* Cambridge: Harvard University Press, 1962.

Williams, Raymond. "Base and Superstructure in Marxist Cultural Theory." *New Left Review* 82 (1973):3-16.

Winks, Robin W. *The Blacks in Canada: A History.* Montreal: McGill-Queen's University Press, 1971.

Wirick, Ronald G. "Paradoxes in Recent Canadian-American Personal Savings Behavior: Toward a 'Permanent' Resolution." London, ON: Department of Economics, University of Western Ontario, May 1982, mimeograph.

Woodcock, George. *The Canadians*. Cambridge: Harvard University Press, 1979.

Yearwood, R.M. "Land Speculation and Development: American Attitudes." *Plan Canada* 9, no.1 (1968):15-23.

Yeates, Maurice. *Main Street: Windsor-Quebec City*. Toronto: MacMillan, 1975.

_____. *North American Urban Patterns*. New York: Wiley, 1980.

_____. *Main Street: Concentration and Deconcentration in the Windsor-Quebec City Axis*. Ottawa: Lands Directorate, Environment Canada, 1985.

_____, and Barry Garner. *The North American City*. New York: Harper and Row, 1976 and 1980.

Subject and Place Index

Name Index